The Legacy of Richard E. Wagner

Advanced Studies in Political Economy

Series Editors: Virgil Henry Storr
and Stefanie Haeffele

The Advanced Studies in Political Economy series consists of republished as well as newly commissioned work that seeks to understand the underpinnings of a free society through the foundations of the Austrian, Virginia, and Bloomington schools of political economy. Through this series, the Mercatus Center at George Mason University aims to further the exploration of and discussion on the dynamics of social change by making this research available to students and scholars.

Nona Martin Storr, Emily Chamlee-Wright, and Virgil Henry Storr,
How We Came Back: Voices from Post-Katrina New Orleans
Don Lavoie, *Rivalry and Central Planning: The Socialist Calculation
Debate Reconsidered*
Don Lavoie, *National Economic Planning: What Is Left?*
Peter J. Boettke, Stefanie Haeffele, and Virgil Henry Storr, eds.,
Mainline Economics: Six Nobel Lectures in the Tradition of Adam Smith
Matthew D. Mitchell and Peter J. Boettke, *Applied Mainline Economics:
Bridging the Gap between Theory and Public Policy*
Jack High, ed., *Humane Economics: Essays in Honor of Don Lavoie*
Edward Stringham, ed., *Anarchy, State and Public Choice*
Peter J. Boettke and David L. Prychitko, eds., *The Market Process: Essays in
Contemporary Austrian Economics*
Richard E. Wagner, *To Promote the General Welfare: Market Processes vs.
Political Transfers*
Donald J. Boudreaux and Roger Meiners, eds., *The Legacy of Bruce Yandle*
Ludwig M. Lachmann, *The Market as an Economic Process*
Peter J. Boettke and Alain Marciano, eds., *The Soul of Classical Political
Economy: James M. Buchanan from the Archives*
Peter J. Boettke, *The Struggle for a Better World*
Karen I. Vaughn, *Essays on Austrian Economics and Political Economy*
Peter J. Boettke and Christopher J. Coyne, eds., *The Legacy of Richard E. Wagner*

The Legacy of Richard E. Wagner

Edited by
Peter J. Boettke and Christopher J. Coyne

MERCATUS CENTER
George Mason University
Arlington, Virginia

About the Mercatus Center

The Mercatus Center at George Mason University is the world's premier university source for market-oriented ideas—bridging the gap between academic ideas and real-world problems.

A university-based research center, the Mercatus Center advances knowledge about how markets work to improve people's lives by training graduate students, conducting research, and applying economics to offer solutions to society's most pressing problems.

Our mission is to generate knowledge and understanding of the institutions that affect the freedom to prosper, and to find sustainable solutions that overcome the barriers preventing individuals from living free, prosperous, and peaceful lives.

Founded in 1980, the Mercatus Center is located on George Mason University's Arlington and Fairfax campuses.

978-1-942951-68-1 (case)
978-1-942951-69-8 (paper)
978-1-942951-70-4 (e-book)

Mercatus Center at George Mason University
3434 Washington Blvd., 4th Floor
Arlington, VA 22201
www.mercatus.org
703-993-4930

Cover design by Jessica Hogenson
Cover illustration by Travis Pietsch
Editorial and composition by Westchester Publishing Services

Contents

Figures

About Richard E. Wagner

Richard E. Wagner is an emeritus professor of economics at George Mason University as well as a distinguished senior fellow with the F. A. Hayek Program for Advanced Study in Philosophy, Politics, and Economics at the Mercatus Center at George Mason University. Previously, he was the Hobart R. Harris Professor of Economics at George Mason University. He received his PhD in economics from the University of Virginia in 1966. He joined the faculty of George Mason University in 1988, after holding positions at the University of California Irvine, Tulane University, Virginia Polytechnic Institute and State University, Auburn University, and Florida State University. During his tenure at George Mason University, he served as chair of the department of economics (1989–1995) and as director of graduate studies (1998–2004, 2006–2012).

Wagner's fields of interest include public finance, macroeconomics, and political economy. He is the author of more than 200 articles in professional journals and the author or editor of some 30 books and monographs, including *Inheritance and the State*, *Democracy in Deficit*, *The Fiscal Organization of American Federalism*, *To Promote the General Welfare*, *Public Finance in a Democratic Society*, and *Public Choice and Constitutional Economics*. He has also served as the chair on more than 30 dissertation committees at George Mason University. He was the coeditor of the scholarly journal *Constitutional Political Economy* from 1989 to 1997 and is currently a member of the editorial boards of *Constitutional Political Economy*, the *Journal of Public Finance and Public Choice*, *Public Finance and Management*, *Journal of Infrastructure, Policy, and Development*, and the *Review of Austrian Economics*. He also serves in an advisory relationship to such organizations as the Independent Institute, the Institute for Research on the Economics of Taxation, the James Madison Institute for Public Policy Studies, the Public Interest Institute, and the Virginia Institute for Public Policy.

Richard E. Wagner—A Scholar and Teacher of the Honorable Tradition of Political Economy

Peter J. Boettke and Christopher J. Coyne

When James M. Buchanan (1958, 5) introduced the Thomas Jefferson Center for Studies in Political Economy to his colleagues at the University of Virginia, he wrote, "The Thomas Jefferson Center strives to carry on the honorable tradition of 'political economy'—the study of what makes for a 'good society.'" He would add that this approach deploys the technical tools of economic theory to assess how alternative institutional environments affect the ability of individuals to pursue productive specialization and realize mutually beneficial exchange. Buchanan also suggests that the political economist must go further and bring into open and frank conversation the philosophical issues associated with the scope of governmental activities as well as the practical concerns with the scale of governmental activities. Buchanan's vision was, in short, a research and educational venture to take the tools of modern economic science and render them useful for the classical political economy project from Adam Smith to J. S. Mill. It was a revolutionary endeavor, and Buchanan was joined in that endeavor by Rutledge Vining, G. Warren Nutter, Ronald Coase, Leland Yeager, and Gordon Tullock. Their work, both jointly and individually, would change the way economists thought about microeconomics, macroeconomics, comparative institutional analysis, and, most significantly, the entire field of public economics and welfare economics.

It is this venture that Richard E. Wagner joined in the mid-1960s as a graduate student, and to which he has so prodigiously contributed in the subsequent decades. Wagner has been a voice of clarity in expressing insights developed by his teachers, as well as an original and creative thinker who has taken these ideas in new and novel directions. That is just one of his unique and valued skills as a scholar and teacher. His book on James Buchanan, for example, is subtitled "A Rational Reconstruction" (Wagner 2017). That it is, but in the process of reconstructing, Wagner also provides the best and clearest understanding of what Buchanan was pursuing in the project outlined earlier. Wagner has always been true to his own self in his research—or as he often puts it, "a no hyphen economist." In being himself, Wagner has made major contributions to Austrian economics, to public choice economics, to law and economics, to monetary economics and macroeconomics, and to political economy and social philosophy. Before we discuss these contributions, some background is in order.

Wagner was born in Jamestown, North Dakota, in 1941 but soon moved to Southern California and lived in the Los Angeles area for the rest of his childhood. He graduated from the University of Southern California in 1963, married his wife Barbara, and moved to Charlottesville, Virginia, where he received his PhD in economics in 1966. Wagner worked closely with all the faculty at the Thomas Jefferson Center and developed an ongoing research program in public finance and political economy. Over the next few decades, he held faculty positions at the University of California, Irvine, Tulane University, Virginia Polytechnic Institute and State University, Auburn University, and Florida State University. In 1988, Wagner accepted the position of Holbert L. Harris Professor of Economics at George Mason University, a position he held until his retirement at the end of the 2021–2022 academic year. During his time at Mason, he served as department chair from 1989 to 1995 and director of graduate studies on two occasions—1998–2004 and 2006–2012.

As mentioned, his scholarly writings have covered numerous topics in economic theory, political economy, and public affairs. According to Google Scholar, as of September 1, 2022, he has garnered 16,895 citations with an H-index of 55. Impressive as these scholarly metrics are, they do not capture the full extent of Wagner's contributions to public choice and political economy or his extensive contribution to intellectual life at George Mason University. The remainder of this introduction will discuss those attributes.

Let us begin with Wagner's intellectual contribution. He is one of the few students of Buchanan who fully committed to the "exchange paradigm" (Buchanan 1964). Economics in Wagner's hands is about exchange and the institutions within which exchange takes place. As a result, much of his scholarship explores how politics, law, and society shape economic relationships. In his comparison of market processes and political processes, Wagner has the ingenious observation that the magic number in markets is two, and the magic number in politics is three (Wagner 2016a, 2016b). In markets, both parties walk away better off through exchange. In politics, however, coalitions are formed so that two can join to defeat one in the allocation of resources.

To two wolves, a lamb appears but as dinner. That is a different sort of relationship than what takes place in market exchange.

Elsewhere, Wagner's (2010) discussion of the foreground and background of the rational choice and equilibrium mechanics, as well as his study of processes of creativity, discovery, and exchange, provides theorists with an exemplar of how to reconcile classical political economy, neoclassical economics, and market process economics into a coherent research program. Wagner reverses the conventional wisdom and wants to place the study of processes of exchange in the foreground while the conventional apparatus of basic economic reasoning, which provides the necessary coherence and intellectual discipline, remains in the background.

In addition to this foreground and background perspective, Wagner took seriously his point about the magic number being three in politics and, as Vilfredo Pareto, from whom Wagner takes much inspiration, did before him, explored the more complicated social relations that are formed in a complex political economy. From Pareto to Schumpeter to Wagner, in the field of public finance, the recognition of the entanglement of markets, states, and community was dubbed *fiscal sociology*, a topic that Wagner (2007) explores in depth in his book *Fiscal Sociology and the Theory of Public Finance*.

In subsequent work, Wagner stressed the conceptual weaknesses of any approach that worked with strict dichotomization of markets and states. In contrast, he emphasized the notion of entanglement, an idea he had been exploring ever since his review essay (Wagner 1966) on Mancur Olson's (1965) *The Logic of Collective Action*, where Wagner discusses pressure groups and political entrepreneurs. Wagner offers a fully developed framework of "entangled political economy" in his 2016 book, *Politics as a Peculiar Business*. As reflected in subsequent work, Wagner's framework has inspired a new generation of scholars to pursue the scientific research program of entangled political economy (see Hebert and Thomas 2021).

To further appreciate Wagner's impact, we should stress some of his main qualities as a colleague, teacher, and mentor. The first word that comes to mind is *generosity*. Wagner, the lifelong learner, used his classroom to give students a front-row seat to his production process and freely gave away ideas in the process. Think of some of his major conceptual ideas, such as the political manipulation of money and credit, or romance, realism, and the politics of reform. These are brilliant ideas, and Wagner invited his students and colleagues to explore them with him. He shared with his classes drafts of his book manuscripts as they were in development and used the feedback from students to improve his arguments. At the same time, Wagner guided students in their learning process, providing them with space to develop their own voices and ideas to which he would provide feedback. His generosity was a gift to generations of students, especially at George Mason University.

Wagner also always shared his *wisdom* of a half century of scholarship and teaching. As director of graduate studies, he would tell incoming PhD students that their goal was simple and achievable—16 courses, four exams, and 120 pages for a dissertation. If they did their job, they would know him not in his capacity as director but as a mutual learner in the discipline of political economy. To emphasize the scholarly quest, Wagner would stress that thinking without writing was merely daydreaming. He urged those around him to write. He also warned against perfectionism by stressing that all research is work in progress because we are constantly learning, absorbing new ideas, wrestling with new data, and struggling to find the most effective mode of communication.

While his generosity and wisdom are vital to an accurate overall accounting of Wagner's legacy, perhaps the most enduring impact for those who had the good fortune to work closely with him for many years is simply his shining *example* as an academic. Richard Wagner is a happy lifelong learner. During his time at GMU, he was never bitter and not prone to departmental squabbles. He was instead always a gracious and encouraging teacher and colleague. In short, he was an exemplary academic. The power of this trait in creating a culture of excellence in research and graduate education should not be forgotten or underestimated. He provided a necessary steady hand at times when the turbulence of academic activism and petty office politics could have created significant barriers to scholarship. Through his example, Wagner continues to teach us all how to prioritize the sheer joy of learning and how to maintain a sense of urgency in our teaching rather than getting caught up in negative-sum interactions.

Richard Wagner has been an intellectual hero to many of us in the scholarly communities within which he worked—for example, Public Choice Society and the Society for the Development of Austrian Economics—and with his retirement he will be greatly missed. However, as he stressed to both of us, he is retiring from teaching and *not* from thinking, and thus *not* from writing. As we celebrate his career, we also want to congratulate Richard Wagner and wish him the very best in the next chapter of his storied career.

OVERVIEW OF THE VOLUME

To celebrate Richard Wagner's career, we invited scholars to reflect on his academic contributions and legacy. The 13 chapters that follow discuss various aspects of his research program. In addition to illustrating the breadth of Wagner's legacy, the contributing authors demonstrate the ongoing relevance of his scholarly oeuvre as a living research program.

The first four chapters explore the foundations and nuances of Wagner's work in the area of political economy. Meg Tuszynski discusses the two foundational ideas in Wagner's scholarship that offer nuance to our understanding of institutions in human life. The first is that Wagner views economics as a theory of society rather than a narrow theory of rational action. The second is that Wagner focuses on the interplay between politics and economics rather than viewing them as distinct and separate arenas.

Randall G. Holcombe discusses the contributions of Wagner's theory of entangled political economy while emphasizing the importance of incorporating transaction costs into the framework. Transaction costs matter, he notes, because they influence which entities can interact with other entities in the entangled world. High transaction costs can prevent some entities from interacting with others. To highlight this point, he uses the example of a large private firm that has the resources and connections to hire effective lobbyists and make political contributions to lower the transaction costs of interaction with public-sector entities. Most private customers of the firm lack those resources and connections, which means they are prevented, via high transaction costs, from interacting with the same political entities in the same way as the firm. By noting the role that transaction costs play in entangled relationships, Holcombe offers one path for the further development of Wagner's framework.

Marta Podemska-Mikluch revisits Wagner's contributions in the 1970s and connects them to his more recent work in the area of entangled political economy. The first paper, coauthored with Warren Weber in 1975, analyzes the challenges in forming accurate perceptions of the price and quality of government outputs. The authors attribute these challenges to the bundling of government provision associated with reductions of governmental overlapping. The second paper, published in 1976, examines fiscal illusion resulting from a complex tax revenue structure. Finally, the third paper, also published in 1976, analyzes public advertising and argues that it is nothing more than an effort to foster citizens' acquiescence. Podemska-Mikluch notes that these papers reject the competitive model of democracy while appreciating the epistemic aspects of political interactions. She also notes that these papers served as the foundation for the study of the tension between liberalism and monopolistic democracy, which became a recurring theme throughout Wagner's scholarship. Among other things, Podemska-Mikluch's chapter shows the thematic continuity across Wagner's research program.

Next, Diana W. Thomas and Michael D. Thomas review three influences on Wagner's scholarship on entangled political economy. The first is the Austrian influence, which is apparent in Wagner's emphasis on the emergent nature of the market process and skepticism of interventions in those processes. The second is the Swedish influence, which is evident in Wagner's focus on the polity as a process of interaction and exchange. Finally, they discuss the Italian influence, which appears in Wagner's appreciation that certain groups have outsize influence on the outcomes of collective action. This chapter offers important historical context to Wagner's research program while demonstrating the contemporary relevance of these ideas for understanding the world.

The next two chapters explore issues associated with citizenship and constitutional systems. Viktor J. Vanberg explores the nuances of behavior and choice in two related settings—in the context of given institutional constraints and in the context of constitutional choice. He argues that the idea of the pursuit of self-interest takes on a different meaning in these different contexts. He makes the important distinction between situational rationality (case-by-case maximizing choice) and dispositional rationality (the recognition by individuals that by adopting a certain moral attitude they can realize a pattern of payoffs that is relatively more beneficial than pursuing situational logic). In addition to clarifying foundational analytical concepts in public choice and constitutional political economy, Vanberg's chapter highlights another theme central to Wagner's scholarship: the relationship between the mental orientations and habits of self-governance exercised by the citizenry and the characteristics of the political system under which citizens live.

Paul Dragos Aligica continues the exploration of the connection of Wagner's research in entangled political economy to our understanding of constitutionalism. Aligica contends that Wagner has made contributions to both public choice and constitutional political economy. In doing so, his work offers a bridge between two basic underlying visions of constitutionalism. The first vision emphasizes the importance of checks and balances operating at the systematic level with the aim of securing the rule of law. The second, what Aligica calls political or republican constitutionalism, contends that rights and the rule of law are part of the broader constitutional challenge that must also focus on the broader political process that reflects both good laws and the good disposition of the political body. Wagner's theory of entangled political economy offers a bridge, Aligica argues, because his framework combines a transactional, economic perspective with a social-based perspective. Aligica closes with a list of open research questions, which demonstrates the continuous relevance of Wagner's work for wrestling with some of the most pressing issues in constitutional political economy.

The next several chapters explore issues associated with cognition, society, relationships, and networks. James Caton delves into the social foundations of entanglement. He begins with the premise that society is naturally entangled. From here, he presents the microfoundations for a theory of entanglement that appreciates the importance of institutions grounded in shared mental models. He argues that a theory of entanglement requires a notion of agency integrating cognition across domains of activity. While Caton recognizes that we are all subject to existing culture on certain margins, he emphasizes that people have the power to adapt their mental models. As Caton's chapter shows, a theory of entanglement requires a theory of the human mind and the role that mental models play both in institutional choice and in choice within institutions.

Mikayla Novak examines Wagner's work in entangled political economy as contributing to relational scholarship. Relationships, which refer to connections between people and their collectives, are central to the theory of entanglement and Wagner's conception of political economy. This stands in contrast to orthodox treatments of political economy focused on equilibrium and the separation of economic and political categories. Novak discusses how focusing on relationships opens the door to the study of a wide range of social, economic, and political phenomena.

Next, Santiago J. Gangotena explores the connection between entangled political economy and network effects. He notes that people choose political and economic modes of interaction on the basis of the costs of employing a given mode. Network effects can arise when the cost of employing a mode declines in proportion to its relative prevalence in society. He discusses three factors—imitation, investments specific to the use of each mode, and entanglement between these investments—that can contribute to network effects. He then explores how network effects contribute to the emergence and evolution of the social configuration of economic and political interactions. He concludes by discussing opportunities for future research building off his insights.

The next three chapters explore broader theoretical contributions based on Wagner's scholarship. Abigail N. Devereaux offers a recasting of economic theory as systems theory and describes the seven "stepping stones" as a pathway to the systems-based alternative. Among other things, her approach appreciates that economic theory must be capable of incorporating salient socio-evolutionary dynamics including self-organized complexity, treating relationships between economic entities seriously, treating complex causality seriously, understanding the relationship between intervening agents and agents being intervened upon, and appreciating the limitations on interventionary actions. Devereaux's chapter offers an opportunity for subsequent developments, both theoretical and applied, based on the systems theory she develops.

Next, Jason Potts, Chris Berg, and Sinclair Davidson offer a Wagnerian-based vision of macroeconomics that draws on several schools of thought, including public choice economics, constitutional political economy, complexity economics, and evolutionary economics. They then use this framework to explore emerging cryptoeconomic systems and offer a new research field that they label "crypto-macroeconomics." To demonstrate the relevance of this new field, Potts, Berg, and Davidson discuss four subfields of crypto-macroeconomics: technology, constitutions, money, and policy.

Cameron Harwick's chapter contributes to monetary theory. Specifically, he generalizes monetary theory by considering the plans of economic agents to hold and dispose of liquidity in a much wider variety of forms than is usually taken account of in standard models. Harwick considers the importance of the network structure of economic actors in formulating monetary aggregates. He argues (1) that a Divisia index is closer to the subjectivist theoretical meaning of the money supply relative to traditional monetary aggregates, (2) that a broader perspective on liquidity services suggests a coordinationist perspective on both financial development and business cycles, and (3) that the supply of liquidity is best understood in terms of networks. Harwick's chapter demonstrates the relevance of Wagner's work in macroeconomics, which takes an ecological and coordinationist perspective for monetary theory.

In the final chapter, Adam Martin and Vincent Miozzi begin with a puzzle. Scholars articulate ways of seeing the world that they hope others will find convincing. At the same time, most scholarly works are read by only a small number of people at most. To begin to resolve this puzzle, they provide a theory of "expressive entrepreneurship," which holds that scholarly attempts to persuade can be understood as a form of entrepreneurship. The motivation to engage in the act of scholarship is, like voting in political elections, often expressive. In Martin and Miozzi's theory, scholars express their commitments to certain analytic and normative principles by communicating their way through their uneasiness. They illustrate their theory through the scholarly work of James Buchanan and Richard Wagner. Martin and Miozzi's chapter captures the entrepreneurial spirit of both Buchanan and Wagner, which is grounded in Buchanan's notion of the "honorable tradition of 'political economy'" that we discussed in the opening lines of this introduction.

We have included an appendix containing Richard Wagner's published works as of July 2022. This document contains a comprehensive listing of Wagner's career and scholarship. Wagner has had a storied career, but as the chapters in this volume make clear, his legacy is still being written.

REFERENCES

Buchanan, J. M. 1958. "The Thomas Jefferson Center for Studies in Political Economy." *University of Virginia Newsletter* 35, no. 2: 5–8.

———. 1964. "What Should Economists Do?" *Southern Economic Journal* 30, no. 3: 213–22.

Hebert, D. J., and D. W. Thomas, eds. 2021. *Emergence, Entanglement, and Political Economy.* Cham, Switzerland: Springer.

Olson, M., Jr. 1965. *The Logic of Collective Action: Public Goods and the Theory of Groups.* Cambridge, MA: Harvard University Press.

Wagner, R. E. 1966. "Pressure Groups and Political Entrepreneurs: A Review Essay." *Public Choice* 1: 161–70.

———. 2007. *Fiscal Sociology and the Theory of Public Finance: An Exploratory Essay.* Cheltenham, UK: Edward Elgar.

———. 2010. *Mind, Society, and Human Action: Time and Knowledge in a Theory of Social Economy.* New York: Routledge.

———. 2016a. "The Peculiar Business of Politics." *Cato Journal* 36, no. 3: 535–56.

———. 2016b. *Politics as a Peculiar Business: Insights from a Theory of Entangled Political Economy.* Cheltenham, UK: Edward Elgar.

———. 2017. *James M. Buchanan and Liberal Political Economy: A Rational Reconstruction.* Lanham, MD: Lexington Books.

Chapter 1

Thinking Differently about Institutions

The Entangled Political Economy of Richard E. Wagner

Meg Tuszynski

I n recent years, the various branches of economics that analyze the functions and evolution of institutions have undergone a radical reorientation. No longer do we live in a world dominated by one type of institutional economics, but instead we have scholars examining questions of institutions from a variety of different angles. Despite the relative saturation of the field, the work of Richard E. Wagner still provides insights that are at best relegated to the background of other theories. Though his work is rich with insights pertinent to the examination of institutions, two themes in Wagner's work are particularly important in this context. One, in contrast to the rational-actor framework that pervades much of the economic discipline, Wagner considers society to be the relevant object of scholarly inquiry. Two, he maintains that thinking about political and economic action as operating within two logically separable realms is not only categorically wrong but also leads to misleading conclusions. If instead we think of political and economic institutions as being indelibly *entangled*, this will allow us to gain new sorts of insights into the analysis of both current institutional structures and how these structures change over time.

As a student of James Buchanan, Wagner has long been associated with the public-choice tradition. Yet at the same time, he has pushed the boundaries of public choice far beyond their established margins. While public choice holds that individuals maintain their self-interested motivations when they move from the market to the political arena, Wagner forces us to think about whether the boundaries of these different arenas are really as clear-cut as we conventionally assume. If the world is not characterized by unique realms for markets and politics, but rather entangled, this makes our understanding of institutions somewhat more difficult. At least, it is no longer quite so simple to classify institutions as being purely political or purely economic. Instead, Wagner prefers to talk about ecologies of institutions, with varying degrees of fragility and robustness. Some ecologies can be decimated with the smallest changes to one of the parts. Some are quite robust to even large-scale shocks to the system. These systems are also continuously being generated and regenerated by the individuals participating within them.

Within this framework, understanding institutions and institutional change is not a matter of grappling just with formal rules or even with the relationship between formal and informal rules. Instead, we are faced with the difficult task of understanding the networks of individuals and their relationships that underlie these formal and informal rules. Wagner's work on entanglement can, in this sense, be complementary to existing analyses of institutions while at the same time allowing us to understand the processes behind the evolution of these institutions more fully, as I will explore later in the chapter.

Not only does Wagner himself think differently about institutions, but he has also encouraged others to think differently as well. In my own work with the Bridwell Institute for Economic Freedom at Southern Methodist University, I work regularly with the cross-national and cross-state indices of economic freedom. These indices help us understand the extent to which the institutions and policies of various places are consistent with the ideals of a market economy. And we know from decades of research that more economically free places tend to fare better on a variety of important indicators. While I do conduct empirical research in that tradition, my work with Wagner has allowed me to appreciate more fully the processes that alternatively lead to or hinder the development of these institutions in different countries, states, and metro areas. I know that my experience in this regard is not unique, as evidenced by the broad array of scholars who have beneficially incorporated Wagner's framework into their own research.[1]

In what follows, I will explain in detail exactly what Wagner's entanglement framework is. I will then give a brief explanation of the particular branch of institutional analysis into which Wagner's work fits. I am, to be sure, leaving out a great deal of important institutional work in this part, but my aim here is modest. I simply want to provide an examination of where I see Wagner's work as providing the most natural tangencies. I then turn to an explanation of what Wagner's work lends to institutional theory and why the alternative framework he provides is important. That is, I explain what sorts of questions benefit from taking entangled political economy as a starting point, rather than working with more conventional analytical tools. The final section concludes.

WHAT IS ENTANGLEMENT?

One thing that clearly distinguishes the work of Richard Wagner from that of other economists is his orientation toward his subject of inquiry. When examining problems that other economists are also examining, he has the unique ability to view them through a different analytical lens, allowing him to probe more deeply into dynamics that are missed by others. At the very least, he is able to bring to the foreground things that exist only in the background for other theorists and empiricists. His entanglement framework is just one example among many of how Wagner's tendency to see problems in a radically different way leads to conclusions that differ from those of the mainstream. Many of the best ideas are those that, once discovered, seem so obvious it is a wonder no one thought of them before. The entanglement framework is one such set of ideas. Like all innovative ideas, this framework is not entirely new. It simultaneously borrows ideas from the social and physical sciences and pushes ideas of the public-choice framework past its traditional boundaries. Yet this particular combination of ideas is truly radical.

Entanglement is, in essence, the idea that the actions of political and commercial entities are so intimately intertwined that it becomes difficult to understand either political or commercial activity in its pure form. Market actors have various sorts of relationships with political actors, which changes the character of both market and political activity. "Being entangled," according to Wagner (2016, vii), "means that a business typically cannot determine prudent conduct independently of the desires of relevant political entities." Further, "political entities can't determine prudent practice independent of the desires of commercial entities" (vii). Political activity is essentially a *peculiar* form of market activity. The Public Choice framework allows us to think about political activity by using many of the same tools we use to make sense of market activities. Legislators, for example, can in some ways be thought of as sellers of political programs and public goods projects. Yet the correspondence between political activity and market activity is not perfectly analogous. Although legislators must "sell" their constituents on the value of particular programs and projects, they are not the residual claimants on these programs and projects, which makes the character of these undertakings markedly different from that of similar market undertakings. We can, consequently, think of politics as being a somewhat peculiar sort of business.

Where the entanglement framework deviates from the logic of public choice is in the nature of the relationships of the participants. Within the public-choice framework, political and commercial activity are viewed as being additive. That is to say, political actors and market actors operate in unique realms. Both types of actors are driven by self-interest, but the sphere of the economic and the sphere of the political are logically separate. People are people, but their opportunities and constraints change depending on whether they are acting in a political or market capacity. The main sources of problematic outcomes within this framework are driven by (1) the fact that political actors retain their self-interest when moving from the marketplace to the voting booth or to political office and (2) political solutions impinging on the otherwise somewhat orderly workings of the marketplace. Within the entanglement framework, however, the boundaries between market and political activity are not so clear. Indeed, it is even difficult to point to a particular sort of market and claim that the participants are entirely directed by market forces in their activities. Likewise, it is difficult to point to any particular political arrangement and claim that it is insulated from market forces.

In many ways, the entanglement framework is pushing the public-choice framework to its logical conclusion. Not only are the interests of individuals in the political and commercial marketplaces more similar than the public-interest framework presupposes, but the institutions themselves lack the clear-cut distinctions we generally ascribe to them in textbook economics. It is practicing political economy in a way that takes both parts of the phrase seriously. There is not one realm called politics and another called the economy; rather, particular ecologies contain various sorts of institutions, some of which are predominantly driven by the forces of negotiation and contract, and some of which are predominantly driven by command and force.

It is tempting at first to think that this is merely the logic of interventionism (Mises [1940] 1998; Ikeda 1997, 2005) repackaged in new terms. Or perhaps this is just another way of describing cronyism (Lindsey and Teles 2017). Yet both the interventionist and the cronyism frameworks are additive formulations. In both schemes of thought, political forces are seen as intervening into the economy; that is to say, political forces disrupt the otherwise orderly workings of the marketplace. This suggests, then, that overcoming the problems of intervention is merely a matter of repealing the laws or revising the policies that are creating the problems in the first place. Certainly, this in itself is a difficult undertaking; but at least in theory we should be able to move back to a preintervention stage and alleviate some of the problems created by the intervention. The entanglement framework, however, forces us to more fully confront the fact that repealing any particular law or changing any particular policy is often unlikely to result in the intended outcomes—not because the repeal is incomplete but because repealing a specific policy does nothing to change the interactions among various political and market participants. To be sure, as Patrick and Wagner (2015, 104) explore, "these alternative analytical frameworks are not antagonistic, but rather they pertain to different domains of inquiry and bring different topics into the analytical foreground." In understanding the process of institutional change over time, the entanglement framework helps illuminate some insights that occupy the background of the interventionist framework. It is also this foreground-background distinction that sets Wagner's work apart from other frameworks for thinking about institutional change more generally.

TOOLS FOR ANALYZING INSTITUTIONS

As mentioned earlier, institutional analysis is no longer one monolithic theory but rather includes a variety of different analytical tools. While there are still scholars who believe that we can simply impose a more desirable set of institutions on populations who are stuck in suboptimal arrangements (Coyne 2008 explores this in detail), an influential strand of literature explores the nuances involved in creating institutional arrangements that best fit the underlying populations subject to those institutions. Within the broadly defined, small "L" libertarian types of institutional analysis, there are three key types of institutional analyses: (1) studies that examine the importance of institutions consistent with economic freedom, (2) studies that explore how even the best formal institutions will not be able to take hold unless the correlative informal institutions are also present, and (3) studies that encourage us to more fully understand the complexity of human arrangements. Taken together, these studies allow us to make sense of what sorts of institutions tend to lead to human flourishing, but also force us to seriously consider problems of complexity when contemplating institutional change.

The first set of analyses is largely empirical in nature and involves an examination of those institutions thought to be conducive to economic growth and development. The large (and growing) economic freedom literature occupies this space. We have a general idea, based on decades of observation, of which specific institutions are conducive to economic progress. These include limited governments, a strong legal system that protects property and arbitrates disputes impartially, sound money, freedom to trade internationally, and a circumscribed set of regulations on market activity. Not only has the economic freedom literature helped us understand the benefits of free markets and limited government, but more recent work in this area has helped uncover the factors that lead these specific institutions to exist more fully in some places but not others. Hundreds of papers have been written that use the cross-country, cross-state, or metropolitan area indices of economic freedom. Meta-analysis of this literature has found that economic freedom is overwhelmingly correlated with normatively "good" outcomes—like faster economic growth, lower levels of poverty, and faster employment growth—with very few observed drawbacks (Hall and Lawson 2014; Stansel and Tuszynski 2018).

The economic freedom literature, and the organizations that work to promote the movement toward more economically free societies, has created meaningful change for the better.[2] Throughout the 1980s and 1990s, the average country-level score on the Economic Freedom of the World Index increased at a relatively rapid pace, meaning a great many countries around the world became freer. This trend continued, albeit at a slightly slower pace, into the new millennium (Gwartney et al. 2021). However, while the economic freedom literature is fantastic at elucidating the benefits of the institutions consistent with economic freedom, it does not tell us much about how to go about getting these institutions in places where they do not already exist. Years of attempts by the development community to impose institutions on unreceptive populations have shown the folly of naively trying to export institutions (Coyne 2008). Even though places with more economically free institutions tend to fare better on a variety of metrics, the problem of how to achieve beneficial institutional change is not easily solved within the economic freedom literature.

In response to this problem, a related literature evaluates the importance of achieving institutional match between the informal institutions (norms, customs, etc.) of a society and the formal institutions (constitutional rules, statutes, etc.). Boettke, Coyne, and Leeson (2008) term this "institutional stickiness." As Williamson (2009) evaluates empirically, the presence or absence of a specific set of formal institutions is not the most important determinant of economic development, *even if* it is the case that most developed nations share a similar set of formal institutions, as explored in the economic freedom literature. Rather, a robust set of informal institutions may be more important. Further, these formal rules are most successful in those places where the underlying informal constraints are congruent with the formal constraints. Therefore, in order to achieve lasting institutional change, any modifications to existing institutions must be done in a way that is consistent with the underlying informal institutions already in place.

One thing the literature on informal institutions allows us to explain is institutional failure in areas that outwardly possess a set of institutions that have led to prosperity in other countries. Whereas early studies in institutional change focused on "getting the institutions right" (Scully 1988; de Soto 2000; Rodrik, Subramanian, and Trebbi 2004), the literature evaluating the importance of informal institutions makes clear that changes in the formal rules, if they are to have any success, cannot simply be imposed exogenously. Indeed, one surprising finding from this literature is that even the codification of existing informal institutions can lead to problematic development outcomes in some cases, since codification invites political interference into the otherwise orderly workings of a specific institutional ecology (Williamson 2009). Still, mismatch between the formal and informal institutions does not tell us everything about why institutional changes are successful in some areas but not in others. Certainly, institutional stickiness is a significant part of the story, but it is not the whole story.

The work of the Ostroms and their Bloomington School colleagues provides an even fuller picture of what it takes for institutional change to be effective. Elinor and Vincent Ostrom and others working in their Institutional Analysis and Development framework take seriously the idea that societies are complex human systems. Elinor Ostrom (2010, 652) admits that early in her career, she thought her task as a researcher "would be to undertake careful statistical analysis to identify which specific rules were associated with successful systems." In her attempt to catalog these rules, she "struggled to find rules that worked across ecological, social, and economic environments" (652). Rather, "the specific rules associated with success or failure varied extensively across sites" (652).

Instead, understanding institutional diversity became a hallmark of the Bloomington School. They sought to challenge the idea that governance necessarily requires a formal government. According to Vincent Ostrom, "One of the most important aspects of this work is the emphasis on the range of choices available for constituting ordered social relationships" (quoted in Aligica and Boettke 2009, 149). Even structures that look chaotic to outside observers might be well suited to the needs of a particular population. Institutions do not exist in a vacuum; they exist within particular social, cultural, and historical settings. Their work goes much further than the work on the importance of informal institutions in urging epistemological humility when attempting to modify existing sets of institutions.

Importantly for this discussion, the Ostroms and their Bloomington School colleagues understand that effective constraints can take a variety of forms. The boundaries between private constraints and public constraints, or market constraints and government constraints, are not always clear. We often make these distinctions in the social sciences in order to allow greater tractability to our theories, but this tractability might sometimes come at the expense of better understanding the real world. The Ostroms and their colleagues' arguments are not merely theoretical but also backed by years of experience in the field. It is not particularly useful within their framework to talk about market failures or even government failures. Instead, they encourage researchers to think deeply about the governance characteristics of the system and whether these sets of institutions are effectively solving the problems they have set out to solve.

Though Wagner is a direct intellectual descendant of James Buchanan, the former's work on entanglement very closely mirrors that of Vincent Ostrom. For Ostrom, the word "government" is largely an analytic fiction, which in fact refers to various different structures we have created that allow us to live together in greater harmony. In a piece describing recurring themes in Ostrom's body of work, Wagner (2005, 180) says "Ostrom treats government as a nexus of relationships within which people participate in their governance, not as a choosing entity that intervenes into a society to alter equilibrium outcomes." As is the case with Wagner, conflict and contestation—not placidity— take center stage for Ostrom.

Scholars working in all the different traditions just discussed have lent different perspectives to the discussion of institutional change. At various points throughout his work, Wagner has described what he is doing as looking at a particular problem through a different window. When it comes to institutional evolution, all the various sorts of studies discussed earlier are essentially looking at the same set of problems through different windows, and each is able to provide different and important perspectives on how we get on a path that encourages human flourishing. Wagner's entanglement theory provides yet another window through which to examine the problems associated with institutional change and provides insight into how we might overcome some of these problems.

To be sure, I am missing a great deal of the literature on institutional analysis here by focusing on just this particular strand. The work of Esther Duflo and Abjhit Banerjee, for example, is currently very much in vogue in the development community. This work aims to draw broader development implications from randomized control trials but suffers from the problem of assuming that we can export institutions relatively seamlessly from one context to another. Wagner's work forces us to think not only about the particular ways in which context matters but also about more complicated questions of how interactions among individuals, in both their political and economic capacities, can change the character of particular institutional ecologies.

ENTANGLEMENT AND INSTITUTIONS

What Does Entanglement Lend to Institutional Theory?

Wagner's approach to understanding institutions differs markedly from much of the prevailing work on institutions and thus leads to a different set of implications. The most important implication of Wagner's entanglement framework for economic analysis and understanding the process of economic change is that the institutional landscape is more complicated and interconnected than most existing theories acknowledge. Therefore, changes to any part of the system are likely to have effects that could not easily be anticipated before the change. Though Wagner's entanglement framework is clearly an outgrowth of public choice theory, the implications for institutional analysis are markedly different. In the public-choice framework, the primary reason institutional changes might fail to take hold is that political problems are standing in the way of such changes. For most scholars operating in the public-choice tradition, there is very clearly a realm denoted "political" and a separate realm denoted "economic," even if it is clear that the same agents operate in both realms. Yet if politics is seen as something that intervenes on the economy, then the solution is not exactly simple, but it is at least understandable. One would need to figure out how to break down the political barriers standing in the way of such changes. Once we shift our orientation and recognize that governments and markets are themselves somewhat fluid concepts, the problem of institutional change over time becomes much more difficult. Disentangling the pain point in the system that must be overcome in order to effect change is not such a simple matter within entangled systems. Instead, one must work through complicated sets of relationships within networked ecologies of enterprises.

Within the entanglement framework, we can still talk about political and economic organizations, as long as we recognize that these are in many cases logical fictions, at least if we are to assume they exist in some pure form. If we drill down to the micro level and analyze the actions and interactions of individuals, we can see that the same individual will at different times operate in a political and an economic capacity. Once we focus on this individual level, we can more clearly understand that even when operating in a political capacity, individuals cannot easily shed the self-interest that animates their private lives. While the self-interest portion of the entanglement framework also exists within public choice theory, Wagner's thoroughgoing emphasis on the idea that public and private enterprises do not have clear-cut boundaries is what differentiates it. As Wagner (2016, 33) explains, "The citizen plane is the only plane that exists within a democratic system. To theorize about political economy within a society that possesses a democratically organized polity requires recognition that both the political and the economic actions that are covered by the notion of political economy arise within a common analytical framework." Further, "while political personages can still influence societal configurations, they do so as participants inside societal processes and not as outside and impartial social mechanics" (39).

In recent work with Paul Dragos Aligica, Wagner challenges us to think about institutions not as external rules that structure human behavior but rather as the rules that we create for ourselves. "Societies and their rules," they say, "are inseparable: you cannot have a society without having rules that govern relationships and interactions" (Aligica and Wagner 2021, 72). Yet if societies *are* their institutions, this makes the process of institutional evolution more akin to gardening than to policy design, to borrow a metaphor that both F. A. Hayek and Vincent Ostrom have used. Modifying a particular constellation of institutions that has proved to be problematic (from the point of view of those participating in them) is not just a matter of changing some set of exogenously imposed rules and trusting that individuals will rationally respond to the change. It is important to keep in mind that in a world characterized by substantial entanglement, modifications to any particular institution are likely to have far-reaching effects beyond what either policymakers or private citizens might anticipate. Consequently, even internally generated changes require substantial ex post reflection in order to determine whether they are moving society in a more or less desirable direction. This is reminiscent of the important question laid out in Federalist No. 1: "whether societies of men are really capable or not of establishing good government from reflection and choice, or whether they are forever destined to depend for their political constitutions on accident and force" (Hamilton 1787).

In many ways, entanglement is an uncomfortable framework for those interested in understanding the process of institutional change because it forces us to seriously grapple with the complications of generating effective changes. We know from the economic freedom literature what types of institutions tend to promote prosperity, but we also recognize that we cannot just impose those institutions exogenously and expect them to stick. Moving toward an effective set of institutions is more complicated than even ensuring coherence between the formal and informal institutions (as

Williamson 2009 and others explore) or removing the political barriers standing in the way (as explored in the public choice literature). It requires us to contend with the networked nature of individuals and the institutions that structure their interactions. As Aligica and Wagner (2021, 80) explain, "Yes, institutions structure and channel action. And, yes, people respond in a rational manner to the relevant institutional arrangements they confront. Yet any particular institutional arrangement exists inside a societal plethora of such arrangements." Cultivating an effective institutional order requires substantial reflection not just on how a particular change affects a single set of outcomes but also on how it influences the entire set of related institutional arrangements.

The networked nature of individuals and their institutions additionally creates a strong argument for preserving substantial space for individual liberty. Certainly, many decisions, by their very nature, require collective decision-making. Yet it is important that these decisions be made by the proper collective. As Elinor Ostrom and her Bloomington School colleagues explore at length, decisions that are made by those individuals who directly benefit from creating the right set of constraints tend to be most effective. The relevant collective responsible for making decisions for local water basin management (Ostrom 1964) will be different from the relevant collective making decisions on the effective arrangements for police protection (Ostrom and Whitaker 1973). By delegating decision-making responsibility to the proper collective, not only can solutions be discovered that better fit the needs of the affected group, but also institutional modifications can be more easily pursued by those who understand the institutional ecology within which they are operating.

As Wagner (2014) explores, thinking about appropriate arrangements for collective decision-making goes far beyond discussions of federalism, since federal systems themselves can be either monopolistic or competitive in form. The devil, as they say, is truly in the details. In this case, both the constitutional and the institutional details matter. A system that encourages competition among various governmental units, and even some functional overlap, is preferred over one that encourages cartelization. Despite what representative-agent-type thinking might lead us to believe, all institutions exist within a particular social and institutional ecology, and concerns about other people and other existing institutions are relevant when determining how to make decisions that affect groups of people. This is where Wagner's ideas about entanglement come into play in a major way. If we take an entangled social-political-economic system as our starting point, we are likely to make different decisions than we would if we saw ourselves as making decisions for rational actors in a social and institutional vacuum.

Why Does It Matter? What Are the Important Implications?

The implications of this framework are just beginning to be understood, and many scholars are finding unique ways to apply these ideas. Not only is Wagner himself thinking differently about institutions, but his framework is allowing other scholars to think differently as well. Very recently, Marta Podemska-Mikluch and Mikayla Novak founded the Entangled Political Economy Research Network, which is dedicated to pushing the boundaries of this sort of research. Network scholars have presented papers exploring how entanglement can help us think differently about everything from militarization (Nathan Goodman) to innovation (Marta Podemska-Mikluch) to third-sector organizations (me).

Though Wagner's voluminous body of work covers a great variety of topics, one consistent subject he explores from a variety of angles is how fiscal institutions work and how they evolve over time. Unsurprisingly, many of Wagner's own entangled political economy papers, and many papers of his students and contemporaries, have examined fiscal issues as well. Recently, for example, Wagner (2019a) has explored how we can use his framework to understand fiscal deficits in a way that is radically different from most public-finance theorists. Within an additive framework of political economy, deficits are simply a technical problem that can be solved with a technical solution. Certainly, the presence and magnitude of deficits have changed over time with changes in formal rules, but Wagner's framework allows us to see that the real forces that lead to deficits are not at the level of the fiscal system but rather emerge through the actions of individuals operating in both their political and economic capacities within the system. This, naturally, complicates our analysis of deficits. It is clear that formal rule changes often do not result in the intended outcomes, as David Primo (2008) explores with respect to both federal and state governments. Wagner helps us understand exactly *why* those rule changes are often ineffective and illuminates how difficult the process of institutional change really is in an entangled world. Charles Blahous (2013, 2021) maps out the complicated history that has led to budget deficits at the US federal level, and lucidly explains how erroneous it is to attribute existing budgets to any single set of policies or political players. Rather, current deficits are the result of a complicated constellation of decisions that occurred in prior administrations. Wagner would take this a step further and highlight how the intertwined interests of individuals, both in their political and in their economic capacities, have over time led to our current state of deficits.

Arguably one of the leading public debates of our time is how to deal with income inequality, with Piketty's (2014) book reigniting these discussions among both academic scribblers and various sorts of public intellectuals. Mikayla Novak (2018a) explicitly uses Wagner's framework to gain insight into the complex issues surrounding wealth and income inequality. Most policymakers tend to treat problems of inequality as if they were objects of choice, and therefore can be remedied through political action. If, however, we treat inequality as an emergent phenomenon, one that has its origins not just in political or individual actions but in some complicated intermixing of the two, then we can see more clearly how difficult it is to use the tools of politics to alleviate these sorts of issues. Indeed, political action within this framework might be more likely to exacerbate than remedy problems of inequality. Novak highlights how the inequalities we so often attribute to the market are often caused by forces of entanglement. This alternative framework forces us to grapple with the idea that expanding the scope for individual liberty, rather than continuing to layer interventions on top of one another, might be a better mechanism for remedying problems of inequality. Policies and institutions that aim to raise wealth and income are infinitely preferable to those that seek to level wealth and income (Wagner 2010).

My own work has been highly influenced by Wagner. I have explored how his framework can help us better understand the nature and evolution of spontaneous orders—particularly, how orders that have characteristics that are undesirable as determined by those living within them can evolve over time (Tuszynski 2021). I term these "perverse spontaneous orders." Elsewhere, I have examined how precisely entangled political economy differs from other analyses of interventionism (Patrick and Wagner 2015). And I am currently working through how we can use the entanglement architecture to make sense of third-sector and philanthropic organizations (Tuszynski 2022), something that Novak (2018a) has also examined. We often think of these organizations as providing alternatives to either market or state action, but in reality the participants in these types of organizations have connections of various types to both market and state actors. Understanding how these sorts of interconnections influence this sector more broadly can help us gain insight that other analyses of third-sector organizations might miss.

Other areas that have benefited from Wagner's unique lens include our understanding of property rights (Salter 2016; Novak 2018b), blockchain (Allen, Berg, and Novak 2018; Berg, Berg, and Novak 2020), governance

(Salter and Callais 2019; Salter 2016; Wagner 2002, 2003, 2019b), and entre-preneurship (Podemska-Mikluch 2019; Salter 2017, 2020; Salter and Wagner 2018; Rajagopalan and Wagner 2013), just to name a few. While past stud-ies have yielded substantial new insights into a variety of areas, the future of this research is even more exciting. One hallmark of a useful framework is that it helps illuminate areas that the original creator could not have fore-seen. Wagner's work requires a radical reorientation for most economists. He is simultaneously pulling economics back toward its roots and pushing the boundaries of the discipline.

CONCLUSION

Armed with an understanding of entangled political economy, we could eas-ily become deeply skeptical about the ability of problematic institutions to change. Students of public choice at least can pinpoint the coalitions respon-sible for blocking beneficial changes and understand on some level the sorts of political problems that need to be overcome if we want changes to take hold. If, however, we are working within an entangled system, figuring out how to achieve beneficial institutional change is much more complicated. It is tempt-ing to conclude that change is so complicated as to leave us doomed to suffer in undesirable institutional ecologies.

Yet change *does* happen. Look at the country of Georgia, for example. After Georgia seceded from the Soviet Union in 1991, the country suffered a variety of political and economic problems. But after the Rose Revolution in 2003, which included no bloodshed, individuals in the country helped usher in an era of beneficial political and economic reforms and pursued a pointed pro-Western foreign policy. The year 2000 marked the first time the country had reliable enough data to appear on the Economic Freedom of the World (EFW) index, and at that time it entered with a ranking of 57 out of 125 ranked coun-tries. By the mid 2010s, the country was already ranked in the mid-teens, and according to the most recent version of the EFW index, the country currently enjoys the number five spot for economic freedom. What Wagner's frame-work helps us understand more fully is the process of economic change. The movement toward greater economic freedom in Georgia required gradual but consistent modifications in the behaviors and interactions of both political and market actors. While much of the economic analysis of institutional change provides us with useful snapshots at different points in time, Wagner's frame-work allows us to better see the full moving picture of what made that change occur the way it did.

Another way to see Wagner's framework as optimistic instead of nihilistic is by returning to the gardening metaphor used earlier. When I explain to my three-year-old son what it takes to grow a garden, I often mention the factors that are necessary but not sufficient for plants to thrive: adequate sunlight, ample water, proper temperatures, and fresh air. We can think of these elements similarly to the way we think about formal institutions. Yet we know that two gardeners can be presented with the exact same formal environment and experience very different outcomes. A thriving garden depends less on the formal factors and more on the smaller actions, as well as constant tending by the gardener. It is all these small actions, compounded over time, that lead to a thriving garden. Wagner's work helps us understand how we can alternatively cultivate or fail to cultivate a thriving institutional landscape.

NOTES

1. The Entangled Political Economy Research Network, which was started last year by Marta Podemska-Mikluch and Mikayla Novak, cites at least 10 books, 22 book chapters, and more than 100 journal articles that have used this framework to date.

2. The Fraser Institute in Canada is the premier organization promoting economic freedom around the world.

REFERENCES

Aligica, P. D., and P. J. Boettke. 2009. *Challenging Institutional Analysis and Development: The Bloomington School*. New York: Routledge.

Aligica, P. D., and R. E. Wagner. 2021. "Different Paths for Institutional Theory: Foundational Dichotomies and Theoretical Framing." *Journal of Public Finance and Public Choice* 36, no. 1: 69–85.

Allen, D., C. Berg, and M. Novak. 2018. "Blockchain: An Entangled Political Economy Approach." *Journal of Public Finance and Public Choice* 33, no. 2: 105–25.

Berg, A., C. Berg, and M. Novak. 2020. "Blockchains and Constitutional Catallaxy." *Constitutional Political Economy* 31, no. 2: 188–204.

Blahous, C. 2013. "Why We Have Federal Deficits: The Policy Decisions That Created Them." Mercatus Research, Mercatus Center at George Mason University, Arlington, VA.

———. 2021. "Why We Have Federal Deficits: An Updated Analysis." Mercatus Research, Mercatus Center at George Mason University, Arlington, VA.

Boettke, P. J., C.J. Coyne, and P. T. Leeson. 2008. "Institutional Stickiness and the New Development Economics." *American Journal of Economics and Sociology* 67, no. 2: 331–58.

Coyne, C. J. 2008. *After War: The Political Economy of Exporting Democracy*. Stanford, CA: Stanford University Press.

de Soto, H. 2000. *The Mystery of Capital: Why Capitalism Triumphs in The West and Fails Everywhere Else*. New York: Basic Books.

Gwartney, J., R. Lawson, J. Hall, and R. Murphy. 2021. *Economic Freedom of the World Annual Report*. Vancouver, Canada: Fraser Institute.

Hall, J. C., and R. A. Lawson. 2014. "Economic Freedom of the World: An Accounting of the Literature." *Contemporary Economic Policy* 32, no. 1: 1–19.

Hamilton, A. 1787. Federalist No. 1: General Introduction. In *The Federalist Papers*.

Ikeda, S. 1997. *Dynamics of the Mixed Economy: Toward a Theory of Interventionism*. New York: Routledge.

———. 2005. "The Dynamics of Interventionism." In *Advances in Austrian Economics*, Vol. 8, *The Dynamics of Intervention: Regulation and Redistribution in the Mixed Economy*, edited by P. Kurrild-Klitgaard, 21–58. New York: Elsevier.

Lindsey, B., and S. M. Teles. 2017. *The Captured Economy: How the Powerful Enrich Themselves, Slow Down Growth, and Increase Inequality*. New York: Oxford University Press.

Mises, L. (1940) 1998. *Interventionism: An Economic Analysis*. Irvington-on-Hudson, NY: Foundation for Economic Education.

Novak, M. 2018a. *Inequality: An Entangled Political Economy Perspective*. London: Palgrave Macmillan.

———. 2018b. "Property Rights in an Entangled Political Economy." *Journal des Economistes et etudes Humaines* 24, no. 1: 1–10.

Ostrom, E. 1964. "Public Entrepreneurship: A Case Study in Ground Water Basin Management." PhD diss., University of California, Los Angeles.

———. 2010. "Beyond Markets and States: Polycentric Governance of Complex Economic Systems." *American Economic Review* 100, no. 3: 641–72.

Ostrom, E., and G. Whitaker. 1973. "Does Local Community Control of Police Make a Difference? Some Preliminary Findings." *American Journal of Political Science* 17, no. 1: 48–76.

Patrick, M., and R. E. Wagner. 2015. "From Mixed Economy to Entangled Political Economy: A Paretian Social-Theoretic Orientation." *Public Choice* 164, no. 1–2: 103–16.

Piketty, T. 2014. *Capital in the Twenty-First Century*. Cambridge, MA: Belknap Press of Harvard University Press.

Podemska-Mikluch, M. 2019. "Inequality, Entanglement, and Entrepreneurship: The Role of Voluntary and Forced Investors." *Cosmos+Taxis* 6, no. 5: 26–30.

Primo, D. M. 2008. *Rules and Restraint: Government Spending and the Design of Institutions*. Chicago: University of Chicago Press.

Rajagopalan, S., and R. E. Wagner. 2013. "Legal Entrepreneurship within a System of Entangled Political Economy." *American Journal of Entrepreneurship* 6, no. 1: 24–36.

Rodrik, D., A. Subramanian, and F. Trebbi. 2004. "Institutions Rule: The Primacy of Institutions over Geography and Integration in Economic Development." *Journal of Economic Growth* 9: 131–65.

Salter, A. W. 2016. "Political Property Rights and Governance Options: A Theory of the Corporate Polity." *Journal of Private Enterprise* 31, no. 4: 1–20.

———. 2017. "The Personal and the Political: Implications of Constitutional Entrepreneurship." *New York University Journal of Law and Liberty* 10, no. 2: 587–607.

———. 2020. "Constitutionalism, Liberalism, and Political Entrepreneurship." *Advances in Austrian Economics* 25: 173–89.

Salter, A. W., and J. Callais. 2019. "A Theory of Self-Governance: De Facto Constitutions as Filters." *Journal of Public Finance and Public Choice* 34, no. 2: 127–47.

Salter, A. W., and R. E. Wagner. 2018. "Political Entrepreneurship, Emergent Dynamics, and Constitutional Politics." *Review of Social Economy* 76, no. 1: 281–301.

Scully, G. 1988. "The Institutional Framework and Economic Development." *Journal of Political Economy* 96, no. 3: 652–62.

Stansel, D., and M. Tuszynski. 2018. "Sub-national Economic Freedom: A Review and Analysis of the Literature." *Journal of Regional Analysis and Policy* 48, no. 1: 61–71.

Tuszynski, M. P. 2021. "Entanglement and Perverse Spontaneous Orders." In *Emergence, Entanglement, and Political Economy*, edited by D. Hebert and D. W. Thomas, 87–101. Cham, Switzerland: Springer.

———. 2022. "Beyond Markets and Governments: Fitting the Third Sector into the Entangled Political Economy Framework." Working paper.

Wagner, R. E. 2002. "Complexity, Governance, and Constitutional Craftsmanship." *American Journal of Economics and Sociology* 61, no. 1: 105–22.

———. 2003. "Polycentric Public Finance and the Organization of Governance." *European Journal of Management and Public Policy* 2: 3–15.

———. 2005. "Self-Governance, Polycentrism, and Federalism: Recurring Themes in Vincent Ostrom's Scholarly Oeuvre." *Journal of Economic Behavior & Organization* 57, no. 2: 173–88.

———. 2010. "Raising vs. Leveling in the Social Organization of Welfare." *Review of Law & Economics* 6, no. 3: 421–39.

———. 2014. *American Federalism: How Well Does It Support Liberty?* Arlington, VA: Mercatus Center at George Mason University.

———. 2016. *Politics as a Peculiar Business: Insights from a Theory of Entangled Political Economy.* Cheltenham, UK: Edward Elgar.

———. 2019a. "American Democracy and the Problem of Fiscal Deficits." *Public Policy Review* 15: 199–216.

———. 2019b. "Governance within a System of Entangled Political Economy." *Forest Policy and Economics* 107: 1–7.

Williamson, C. R. 2009. "Informal Institutions Rule: Institutional Arrangements and Economic Performance." *Public Choice* 139, no. 3: 371–87.

Chapter 2
Untangling Political Economy

Randall G. Holcombe

R ichard E. Wagner (2016) observes that the social sciences tend to analyze economic processes and political processes separately, in two different ways. First, the frameworks that social scientists use to analyze economic processes are different from the ones they use to analyze political processes. Second, they analyze economic and political processes as if they work independently. Economists have their models of market activity, and political scientists use different models to analyze political activity. The development of public choice as a subdiscipline goes some way toward eliminating this separation by using economic reasoning to analyze political decision-making, but even here, political processes are analyzed independently of market activity. Wagner notes that government faces many of the same challenges that businesses face, and that there are many interfaces in which market entities interact with government organizations. The interrelationships are complex, creating what Wagner calls an entangled political economy.

Before the 20th century, economics and politics were studied together under the heading of political economy. Political science separated from economics, and economic analysis ceased incorporating politics, at least partly as a result of Alfred Marshall's *Principles of Economics* (1890), which focuses on economic processes independent of political processes. By the mid-20th century, economics and political science were completely separate disciplines, and the influential books by Hicks (1939) and Samuelson (1947) defined the foundations of the discipline.[1] Economists derived conditions for optimal resource allocation, leaving to political science the challenge of implementing policies to satisfy those conditions.

The same was true of macroeconomics, building on Keynes (1936). Economists developed models showing how, in theory, aggregate demand could be managed to produce full employment with low inflation, leaving to political science the question of how government might organize its decision-making process to arrive at the outcome described in economic models.[2] The subdiscipline of public choice, developed in the second half of the 20th century, addressed one of these issues of separation, creating a framework for analysis that, as Buchanan (1975) describes, used economic methods to analyze political decision-making. Still, political processes were analyzed separately from economic processes. These models treated economic decision-making and political decision-making as separate spheres. Political decisions, once made, do influence economic decisions, and in democratic nations, the private sector of the economy does influence government decisions, but Wagner has emphasized that relationships between private organizations and government organizations are more entangled than is depicted in the way they are described by economic and political analysis.

THE ISSUE OF AGGREGATION

The interface between government and the private sector of the economy is almost always depicted in aggregate terms. Government designs policies and imposes them on the private sector. Meanwhile, voters and interest groups express preferences that determine who holds political power and influence the policies that government implements. Wagner (2007) describes this as additive political economy, represented in figure 2.1. The circles in figure 2.1 represent private-sector entities that interact with each other as buyers and sellers, and in other ways. They join organizations and interact through those organizations and within other social institutions. The lines connecting them show patterns of interaction. The rectangles in the figure represent

Figure 2.1. Additive political economy

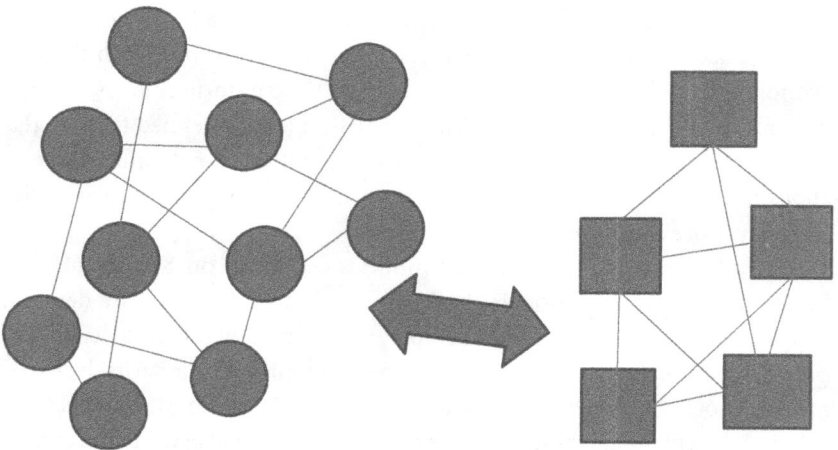

government entities, such as regulatory agencies, city councils, legislatures, tax authorities, and so forth. Similarly, the lines show patterns of interaction as agencies get instruction from legislatures and as those same agencies provide information to policymakers. Wagner (2016) refers to this way of thinking as additive political economy.

The arrow in figure 2.1 represents the aggregated nature of the analysis that relates the private sector with the public sector. Wagner discusses the bargaining process that occurs in determining the federal budget. Agencies negotiate with Congress to try to enlarge their budgets and compete with each other for a larger budgetary share. This is a competitive process, albeit under different institutions than exist in competitive markets, in which entities interact with each other, each responding to the incentives they face based on the necessarily limited information they possess.

The complex relationships that exist among private-sector entities and among government entities tend not to overlap as analyzed within additive political economy. Government imposes its policies on the private sector, and the private sector influences government through democratic political institutions, represented by the bidirectional arrow in figure 2.1. The private sector and the public sector are treated as aggregates, so one government interacts with one private sector. This is very obvious in macroeconomics, Wagner (2020) notes. Government, as a single unit, devises macro policy, and in the Keynesian framework that policy affects aggregate demand through its effects on aggregate consumption, investment, and its own aggregate spending. Representative agent models attempt to depict microfoundations for macroeconomics, but again the private sector is aggregated into a single representative agent.

The actual interactions between government and the private sector are more complex and more entangled and are better illustrated in figure 2.2, which is similar to what Wagner (2007) calls disjunctive political economy. This figure has the same number of circles and squares as in figure 2.1, but rather than depicting a bilateral relationship between the public and private sectors, the lines show that connections are more entangled. Government organizations and private firms interact with each other as people in each type of organization try to use the information available to them to make the best choices they can, given the incentives they face.

Macroeconomics tends to deal in aggregates more than other areas of the discipline, Wagner (2020) explains. Keynesian models deal with concepts like consumption demand and investment demand rather than with individual

Figure 2.2. Entangled political economy

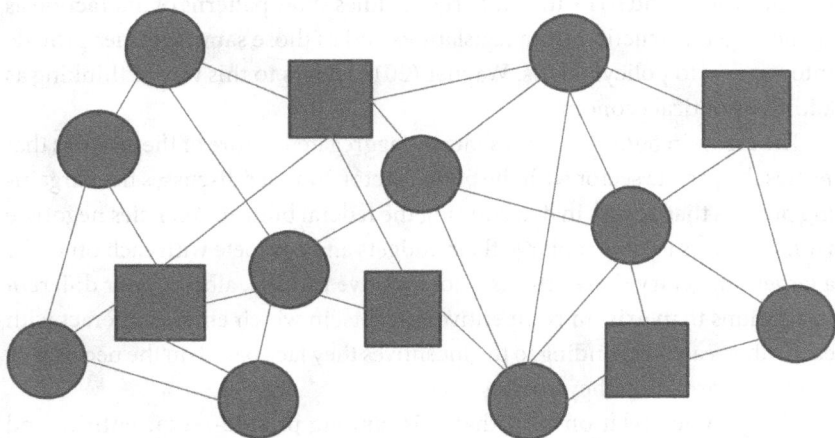

consumers and investors. Attempts to develop microfoundations for macro models have led to representative agent models, which depict the private sector as if it were a single individual. As Wagner (2020) emphasizes, macroeconomic problems arise because the plans of the many individuals in the economy are not consistent with each other and cannot be analyzed in models that aggregate individuals. Figure 2.2 depicts the many connections between private- and public-sector entities that exist in the real world.

One of the achievements of economic analysis has been to show how markets and prices can coordinate the activities of individuals to arrive at an orderly outcome, an idea discussed by Hayek (1945). Hayek emphasized that knowledge is often incomplete and often "tacit," meaning it can only be used by the people who have it. Markets enable people to coordinate their activities so that individuals can make use of the knowledge of others without having that knowledge themselves. Wagner notes that this idea applies to public-sector entities as well. They are not monolithic entities that impose their policies on the private sector. People within the public sector interact with each other to design public policy, and also interact with people in the private sector. Public policies, like markets, evolve in ways that are not planned, and could not be planned, by some central decision maker.

The economy consists of both private and public sectors, and there is a closer relationship between them than economists and political scientists typically depict in their models. Individual decision makers in both sectors make plans based on the information they have and the incentives they face, and individuals in both sectors interact with each other as the economy evolves and as public policy evolves. Public policy is not imposed by a centralized government but rather is developed through the interaction of individuals in both public and private sectors. The conjunctive political economy illustrated in figure 2.2 illustrates those connections, in contrast to figure 2.1, in which an aggregate government is depicted as interacting with an aggregate private sector. This is the entangled political economy, as Wagner depicts it.

Wagner works outside the equilibrium framework that characterizes mainstream economic analysis. People are not machines that mechanically choose an optimum, given the conditions they face. Individuals are creative, they can change their minds, and they can learn, in the face of incomplete information, prompting them to different actions even when facing the same conditions. There is an ongoing turbulence in both public and private sectors as creative individuals look for more effective ways of achieving their ends.

In equilibrium models, forces balance out, resulting in a stable and predictable equilibrium outcome. An entangled political economy generates a spontaneous order, but that order is neither predictable nor stable. Individuals interact with each other in an orderly fashion, but their decentralized decisions produce an outcome that cannot be foreseen, and the continuing reactions of individuals produce a social system that is continually evolving.

TRANSACTION COSTS AND ENTANGLEMENT

A transaction cost, following Coase (1960), is anything that stands in the way of a mutually advantageous exchange. One way to state the Coase theorem is that in the absence of transaction costs, resources are allocated to their highest-valued uses.[3] This is the case because if nothing stands in the way of a mutually advantageous exchange, those who can make the exchange will do it because both will be better off. In a hypothetical world of zero transaction costs, the entangled political economy will allocate all resources to their highest-valued uses and eliminate any economic inefficiency. But, transaction costs are real, and this section incorporates them into a model of an entangled political economy.

Note that in figure 2.2 the public- and private-sector entities are connected to other nearby entities, but that the farther away the entities are from each other, the less likely it is that there will be a connection. This could be because there are no mutually advantageous exchanges that distant entities could make with one another, but it also could be that transaction costs are higher for more distant entities, so transaction costs stand in the way of their making connections.

If someone in Pennsylvania wants to sell a used car and someone in Oregon would place a higher value on it than anyone else, there is a good chance the transaction will not take place. One reason is that the buyer in Oregon may not know about the seller in Pennsylvania. Second, even if the Oregon buyer sees the car in Pennsylvania advertised for sale, it would be difficult for the potential buyer to get firsthand information to verify the car's condition. Third, the cost of transporting the car from Pennsylvania to Oregon may be too great to make the transaction worthwhile. Transaction costs are real costs.

Transaction costs keep every entity in an entangled political economy from connecting to every other entity. So, to understand the nature of the connections in figure 2.2, and to understand when they will be made versus when they will not, transaction costs must be taken into account.

MARKETS AND GOVERNMENT

A major difference between market organization and government organization is that market organization is more decentralized. One of the insights offered by Wagner's vision of entangled political economy is that relationships between public and private entities in the economy are more complex than is commonly depicted in the public economics literature. A regulatory agency may be created by, and get its mission from, a legislature (a top-down relationship) and then impose regulations on firms covered by the legislation. However, the legislature will get information from the regulatory agency and legislation may be modified by that information, so interactions between legislators and regulators are not entirely top-down. Similarly, regulated firms may have input into the regulatory process, perhaps by influencing the design of the regulation or by negotiating with the regulators.

Stigler's (1971) capture theory of regulation offers an example of the influence that regulated firms can have on the regulatory process. The initial design of regulations and the regulatory activities of regulatory agencies will be determined by a negotiating process in which legislators and regulators will have their own goals and the outcome will be the result of a bargaining process that works favorably for all parties. As Stigler suggests, those who are being regulated will also participate in the negotiating process, through formal hearings and informal channels. Once regulations are in place, Stigler explains why, over time, those who are regulated can be expected to have an increasing influence over the regulatory process. Transaction costs between regulators and those they regulate are lower than those between regulators and the general public, whose interests they are supposed to be advancing. The regulatory process is more entangled than the top-down view of regulation suggests.

At the same time, those on the government side of the bargaining process have an advantage in that government action is based on the threat of force to be used against those who do not comply with its mandates. Figure 2.2 makes it appear as if interactions between government entities and market entities, or between government entities, are no different than those between market entities. The big difference, however, is that market entities deal with each other only through voluntary transactions, so both sides must agree that they are better off for a transaction to occur. The threat of force stands behind transactions with government entities.

Wagner (2016, 136–37) recognizes this, noting that government enterprises must generate a return to someone to retain political support, and they do so by imposing costs on others: "The political enterprise generates profits from its activities or else there would be no support for the enterprise. That profit, however, must be removed from the enterprise in indirect fashion as a cousin to money laundering. . . . Where will the political enterprise get the means to do this? The answer lies with [those] who contribute to support the political enterprise without receiving anything in return."

In negotiations between a legislature and a regulatory agency, for example, the legislature ultimately dictates to the regulatory agency, which must abide by what the legislature decides. While it is true that much must be left unspecified in regulations, leaving the agency some discretion, much is often intentionally left unspecified to purposely give the agency discretion. A legislature has the power to rein in regulatory activity it disapproves of, and ultimately can disband the agency. Legislators often want regulatory agencies to exercise discretion in ways that they do not want to spell out explicitly themselves.

The same holds true in negotiations between regulators and regulated firms. The capture theory notwithstanding, the regulatory agency holds the trump cards. Regulatory agencies can, and often do, impose costs on those they regulate. The connections are more complicated, and often more one-sided, than what is suggested by the lines in figure 2.2 connecting different public and private entities.

Wagner (2016) emphasizes the triadic nature of government actions. Government, the first element of the triad, produces benefits for some group of individuals, the second element. Costs are imposed on another group, the third element. The factor that separates those in the second element from those in the third is transaction costs. Those in the second element face low transaction costs and can bargain with those in government for their mutual advantage. Those in the third element face high transaction costs, and so they are left out of the bargaining process and bear costs as a by-product of the political bargaining process. They are analogous to those who bear the external costs of a smoke-polluting factory. The external costs are a by-product of the transactions between the factory and its customers, who can trade with each other because they face low transaction costs.

SIZE MATTERS

Figure 2.2 makes it appear as though all entities are about the same size. This might be interpreted as all entities having the same bargaining power, but the reality is that larger entities have more bargaining power than smaller ones. This introduces the question of how to define size. Among many possible dimensions, size in the private sector can be defined by the value of resources entities control. Firms that generate more revenue are in a better position to lower transaction costs so that they can bargain with others. They can use those resources to make it easier for others in the private sector to bargain with them, and equally significantly, they can use those resources to buy political influence (Holcombe 2018). Firms that can spend more on lobbying, that can make larger campaign contributions, and that can promise the support of more constituents can have more influence. Essentially, they use their resources to lower transaction costs so they can bargain with public-sector entities.

Smaller firms and most citizens do not have sufficient resources to be able to negotiate with legislators and regulators. Think about this from your own vantage point. If you wanted to influence pending legislation or capture a regulatory agency, how would you do it? For most readers of this chapter, the answer is that it would not be possible. As Downs (1957) notes, most individuals have no influence over political outcomes, which is why they tend to be rationally ignorant. Caplan (2007) goes a step further to argue that because most people have no political influence, they are rationally irrational. The reason most people have no influence is that they face high transaction costs, which prevent them from participating in the political bargaining process.

Larger economic entities have sufficient resources that allow them to buy their way into the bargaining process. They have something to offer political decision makers. Thus, connections will be stronger between large economic entities, which devote resources to lobbying and making campaign contributions, and which are able to buy connections by hiring people who have relationships with those in power. The revolving door between regulators and those they regulate reduces transaction costs by maintaining connections, so they have a conduit for channeling resources toward political influence. Larger entities, both public and private, can bargain with each other, but most people cannot engage in this bargaining because transaction costs are too high.

Wagner offers relationships like those in figure 2.2 as representative of an entangled political economy, but when transaction costs are figured in, they create a barrier between most people and government entities. This is somewhat true of smaller entities (how much of a two-way bargaining process is there between those who want a driver's license and the Division of Motor Vehicles?), and truer of larger government entities like legislatures. Most people can interact with the Division of Motor Vehicles if they choose. Most people cannot interact with the legislature. Thus there is an element of reality in figure 2.1, which shows a separation between public- and private-sector entities.

As Wagner (2016, 192) observes, "Might not tax-financed political enterprises tend to favor corporations over proprietorships, and perhaps large corporations over small corporations, because large corporations provide more nourishment for political parasitism?" Wagner goes on to note the advantages, in what amounts to lower transaction costs, of political dealing with one large firm rather than many small firms of the same aggregate size.

MARKET INSTITUTIONS

Markets are decentralized organizations, which facilitates bilateral interaction. While most people cannot interact directly with larger public-sector entities like legislatures, they can interact with the largest private-sector entities because market activities are decentralized and firms want to lower transaction costs so they can interact with potential customers. Market exchanges are bilateral, facilitating lower transaction costs. A legislature passes laws as an entire body, and those laws apply to everyone in the legislature's jurisdiction. Large numbers increase transaction costs. So, like the transaction costs for those who breathe the polluted air from nearby factories, transaction costs in the design of public policy are high because of large numbers and because bargaining is prevented. The decentralized nature of markets facilitates low transaction costs so people can bargain with each other.

Some of the largest economic entities in the world, such as Walmart, Amazon, and Apple, have created interfaces, such as retail stores and websites, that enable anyone who sees the opportunity for a mutually advantageous exchange to deal with them at low cost. Thus the lines connecting the circles (private-sector entities) in figures 2.1 and 2.2 are bidirectional relationships in which those entities interact as equals. Both must believe the interactions they undertake are to their advantage, or they will not deal with the other party.

Few readers will be unaware of how easy it is to deal with Amazon, Walmart, McDonald's, and numerous other private-sector entities. The decentralized organization of the market makes transaction costs low and facilitates these interactions so that even the smallest economic entity—say, a low-income household—can transact with the largest global corporations. It is easy for a consumer in the United States to buy a Samsung television or a Volkswagen automobile because the decentralized nature of market activity lowers transaction costs to facilitate exchange. Market institutions lower transaction costs to create an entangled economy.

POLITICAL INSTITUTIONS

In contrast to the bottom-up decentralized organization of markets, political institutions are centralized and have a top-down organization. Wagner's emphasis on the complexity of the political order is certainly correct, and his observation that relationships between private and public entities are entangled sheds light on the interrelationships between the public economy and the private. But Wagner also notes the triadic nature of government action. Government action benefits some, and others bear the cost as a result. Those who bear the costs do so because they face high transaction costs and are unable to enter the political bargaining process. So, there is something to the additive political economy model depicted in figure 2.1, in that transaction costs stand in the way of most people being able to negotiate in the design of public policy.[4]

For most people, interaction with government is a one-way street, in regard to both the costs imposed on them and the benefits they receive. They are required to pay their taxes and abide by government regulations and are threatened with penalties if they do not comply. The benefits, too, are for the most part produced with no negotiation. Government provides people with roads, parks, and police protection whether they want them or not, and most citizens are not in a position to bargain to alter the mix of goods. Transaction costs are too high for them to be able to negotiate.

This does not imply that citizens are getting a bad deal from government, although they may be. There is no assurance that the benefit received by those in the triadic relationship is greater than the cost imposed on others. The point here is not to weigh the costs and benefits but to note the limits to entanglement that are the result of high transaction costs. For most people, government dictates what benefits they will receive as well as the costs that will be imposed on them.

Political relationships are centralized, and by necessity, to the extent to which what government produces are public goods. Public goods in this sense means that the production applies to everyone. This may be laws and regulations, which everyone must follow, or it may be the more traditional vision of public goods like roads and parks that are made available to everyone. Unlike a supermarket, where shoppers can buy some items and avoid others, government production (in this sense) applies to everyone, and the large numbers that are covered preclude most individuals from negotiating about what they get and what costs they have to bear in return.

UNTANGLING POLITICAL ECONOMY

Bringing transaction costs into entangled political economy untangles it somewhat. Because of high transaction costs, not every entity can interact with every other entity, and transaction costs determine which entities can interact with each other. The size of an entity has a large influence over its ability to lower transaction costs and bargain with other entities. Size is multidimensional and includes the number of individuals represented by an entity as well as its economic size. Dealing with government entities, larger private entities can offer more political support in terms of both numbers of people and "contributions" to campaigns and parties. This enables them to buy their way into the low transaction cost group.

Decentralized relationships in the private sector entail lower transaction costs, facilitating interaction between large and small entities, regardless of their size. Even here, it is the large entities that act to lower transaction costs. Walmart opens retail locations to make it easy for people to buy from the retailer, and Amazon operates a website and delivers goods directly to make it easy for people to transact. Walmart and Amazon incur large costs to do so, but they are facilitating exchange with thousands of individuals, so the cost per transaction is relatively low. In the centralized arena of government, transaction costs are high for most people, but large organizations can use their size to buy membership into the low transaction cost group.

In most cases, the large entities lower transaction costs, because they have the resources to do so, and reap the benefits. Walmart opens stores so it can

Figure 2.3. Untangled political economy

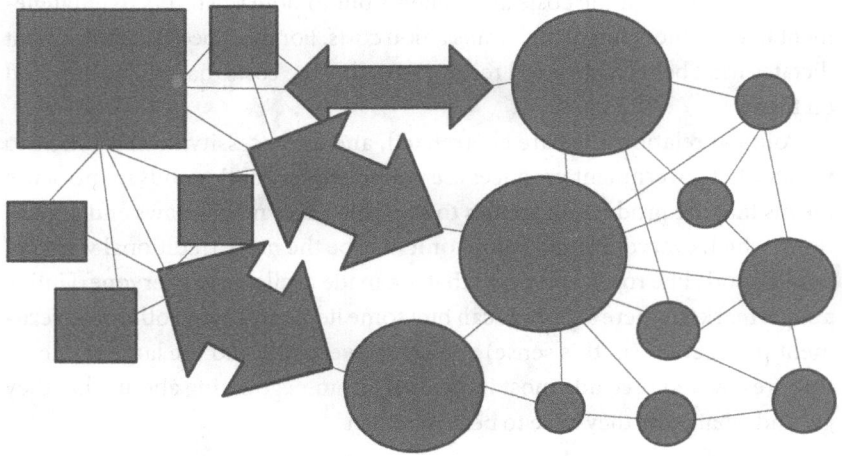

lower transaction costs with private-sector buyers, and it also hires lobbyists and makes political contributions to lower transaction costs with public-sector entities. Thus, high transaction costs prevent most Walmart customers from interacting with the legislature, but Walmart has the resources to reduce transaction costs so it can engage in political negotiation.

Figure 2.3 represents relationships in this partially untangled view of political economy. One difference between figure 2.3 and figures 2.1 and 2.2 is that the entities represented by circles and rectangles are different sizes, and the larger entities have a greater ability to lower transaction costs and negotiate with others. Figure 2.3 shows that private-sector entities (the circles) are interconnected with each other as in figure 2.1, owing to the low transaction costs that come with a decentralized economic organization. Similarly, government organizations interact with each other, but in a top-down manner. The large box is the legislature, which is connected to the agencies even though the agencies are not connected to each other. As with the additive model in figure 2.1, transaction costs prevent most private-sector entities from directly interacting with public-sector entities.

The exceptions are the economic elite, who have the resources to buy their way into the low-transaction-cost group. Figure 2.3 shows three of these, and the arrows show their interaction with both the legislature and other government agencies. Those who face low transaction costs in the political arena are the economic and political elite. They represent the entangled political economy—the entities who are able to interact with each other to create public policy.

Any model is an oversimplification, and the relationships in figure 2.3 might be made more realistic by drawing arrows pointing in one direction from the public-sector entities to the private-sector entities. The elite have a bidirectional relationship, but the relationship goes one way for the masses. They are subject to whatever public policies the elite produce.

Public policy making is indeed an entangled political economy, with the policies of public entities influencing private entities, and private entities influencing the policies created by those public entities. However, high transaction costs prevent most people from being a part of that entanglement. This is an area that deserves further attention in the entangled political economy framework.

CONCLUSION

Any model is a simplified depiction of reality that assumes some things away and makes some unrealistic assumptions. The purpose of those assumptions is to eliminate factors that are irrelevant or of minor importance to the issue being analyzed, and to emphasize the most important causal factors. The advantage is that stripping away the distractions of less relevant factors makes it easier to understand the phenomena represented in the model. The purpose of a model is to focus on the really important factors by eliminating those that are not important. There would be no need for the model if phenomena in the real world could be understood without it. The danger, however, is that the model builder will assume away factors that are important to the phenomena being analyzed, producing a model that is misleading and conclusions that imperfectly apply to the real world.[5]

Faulty models can be applied to produce counterproductive public policies. The entangled political economy framework emphasizes the complexity within social systems that often is relevant for policy purposes. It provides a greater appreciation for the nature of the spontaneous order that social systems provide, both in markets and in government, and suggests the perils of policies that develop top-down plans based on the assumption that the real world resembles standard economic models.

Wagner's entangled political economy focuses on the many interrelationships in an economy that often are assumed away. By not taking account of those relationships, and by not recognizing the ways in which individuals choose to act when faced with incomplete and changing information, economic models tend to depict a world that is more predictable and more stable than the entangled political economy of the real world. As a young research program, many details remain to be developed to understand all of the implications that accompany an entangled political economy. One factor that will determine the nature of these entangled relationships, and whether relationships exist at all, is transaction costs. This suggests a possible profitable direction for advancing the concepts in entangled political economy.

NOTES

1. For an insightful critique of the Hicks-Samuelson paradigm, see Kohn (2004).

2. Nordhaus (1975) initiated a literature on political business cycles that focuses on the challenge of using political institutions to implement macroeconomic policy.

3. Medema (2020) notes that there are many different interpretations of the Coase theorem, and much disagreement as to its relevance and even whether it is correct. For present purposes, the Coase theorem will be interpreted as stated in this sentence.

4. Wagner (2016, 215) says, "The polycentric orientation this book pursues does not eliminate the position of policy maker in society, but rather recognizes that that position is potentially open to everyone." This is true only in the most abstract sense, because most people, members of the masses, face high transaction costs and can have no influence on public policy—and it is difficult for those outside the elite to overcome the high transaction costs they face to join that elite group. That statement is true in the same sense that it is true that in the United States anyone can grow up to be president.

5. Much more could be said about the use of models in economics. See Musgrave (1981) and Holcombe (1989) for a more detailed discussion.

REFERENCES

Buchanan, J. M. 1975. "Public Finance and Public Choice." *National Tax Journal* 28, no. 4: 383–94.

Caplan, B. 2007. *The Myth of the Rational Voter: Why Democracies Choose Bad Policies.* Princeton, NJ: Princeton University Press.

Coase, R. H. 1960. "The Problem of Social Cost." *Journal of Law & Economics* 3: 1–44.

Downs, A. 1957. *An Economic Theory of Democracy.* New York: Harper & Row.

Hayek, F. A. 1945. "The Use of Knowledge in Society." *American Economic Review* 35: 519–30.

Hicks, J. R. 1939. *Value and Capital: An Inquiry into Some Fundamental Principles of Economic Theory.* Oxford: Clarendon Press, 1939.

Holcombe, R. G. 1989. *Economic Models and Methodology.* New York: Greenwood.

———. 2018. *Political Capitalism: How Economic and Political Power Is Made and Maintained.* Cambridge: Cambridge University Press.

Keynes, J. M. 1936. *The General Theory of Employment, Interest and Money.* London: Palgrave Macmillan.

Kohn, M. 2004. "Value and Exchange." *Cato Journal* 24, no. 3: 303–39.

Marshall, A. 1890. *Principles of Economics.* New York: Macmillan.

Medema, S. G. 2020. "The Coase Theorem at Sixty." *Journal of Economic Literature* 58, no. 4: 1045–128.

Musgrave, A. 1981. "Unreal Assumptions in Economic Theory: The F-Twist Untwisted." *Kyklos* 34, fasc. 3: 377–87.

Nordhaus, W. D. 1975. "The Political Business Cycle." *Review of Economic Studies* 42, no. 2: 169–90.

Samuelson, P. A. 1947. *Foundations of Economic Analysis.* Cambridge, MA: Harvard University Press.

Stigler, G. J. 1971. "The Theory of Economic Regulation." *Bell Journal of Economics and Management Science* 2, no. 1: 3–21.

Wagner, R. E. 2007. *Fiscal Sociology and the Theory of Public Finance.* Cheltenham, UK: Edward Elgar.

———. 2016. *Politics as a Peculiar Business: Public Choice in a System of Entangled Political Economy.* Cheltenham, UK: Edward Elgar.

———. 2020. *Macroeconomics as Systems Theory: Transcending the Micro-Macro Dichotomy.* Cham, Switzerland: Palgrave-Macmillan.

Chapter 3

The Epistemic Origins of Richard E. Wagner's Realist Defense of Liberalism

Marta Podemska-Mikluch

R ichard E. Wagner is not one for reminiscing about where he has been and seems far more interested in what lies ahead (Wagner 2020). This is probably why, in referencing his past works, Wagner rarely cites publications that are more than 10 years old. Those only familiar with Wagner's recent works, and unaware of his future orientation, might interpret this absence of older references as a sign of discontinuation, as a suggestion that the Richard Wagner of the 1970s worked on questions and topics different from those that have occupied the Richard Wagner of the 2010s and 2020s. But while Wagner's scholarship has certainly grown and evolved in the 56 years since his first publication (Wagner 1966), the key elements of his research program can already be found in his early contributions. Over the course of his career, Wagner has deepened and advanced his early ideas, revealed their interrelation, and culminated the effort by developing the holistic framework now known as entangled political economy (Wagner 2009, 2016). To elucidate the cohesion of Wagner's contribution, this chapter revisits three of Wagner's early papers and relates them to his more recent work.

There are at least three reasons scholars might want to engage with Wagner's early works. First, they are bound to find inspiration. The Wagner of the 1970s was already a radical thinker, pursuing an understanding of the "workings of real-world institutions" (Wagner 1976b, 46) and concerned about "the conquest of the free enterprise system of social organization by the bureaucratic, monopolistic state" (Wagner 1976a, 99). As Wagner's scholarship developed over the subsequent decades, these notions remained at the core of his realist defense of classical liberalism.[1] Second, these early essays are valuable in their own right, independent of subsequent developments. The Wagner of the 1970s wrote mostly for economists, clearly elucidating how his works departed from the mainstream. For some readers, especially those accustomed to the canons of neoclassical economics, these early works might offer a more familiar starting point. And third, readers will find a unique pathway for applying the tools of economics to the study of politics. Wagner applies the economic toolset to politics without turning politics into economics. For instance, where other economists view political competition as a prerequisite for the economic analysis of politics, Wagner accepts politics as inherently monopolistic and applies economic thinking nonetheless.

Scholars interested in adopting the approach of entangled political economy in their intellectual adventures should feel encouraged by its growing popularity. It has been used to analyze the adoption of the Troubled Assets Relief Program (Smith, Wagner, and Yandle 2011), income and wealth inequality (Novak 2018), public policy as an emergent phenomenon (Podemska-Mikluch 2014), municipal bankruptcy (Moberg and Wagner 2014), bailouts and bankruptcies (Dellisanti and Wagner 2018), the emergence of blockchains and their impact on social interactions (Allen, Berg, and Novak 2018), contraceptive insurance mandates (Podemska-Mikluch 2018), coordinating processes that align political and market activities (Podemska-Mikluch and Wagner 2015), the effectiveness of cultural policy in Brazil (Dekker and Rodrigues 2019), the role of talk and rhetoric (Martin 2021), and the emergence of social movements (Novak 2021), among other topics.

Given the richness of Wagner's work—with more than 30 books and 200 journal articles published in almost six decades of an awe-inspiring career—any attempt to make sense of this abundance is sure to be incomplete. So no claims to completeness are made here. I simply focus on three of Wagner's early contributions and connect them to entangled political economy, an analytical approach Wagner formed in the 2010s. I chose to focus on the papers that analyze the budgetary consequences of changes in governmental overlapping (Wagner and Weber 1975), fiscal illusion (Wagner 1976b), and public advertising (Wagner 1976a). While the selection might seem idiosyncratic at first, these papers have much in common. They explore epistemic qualities of political processes and lay the foundation for the study of the tension between liberalism and democracy, characteristic of Wagner's scholarship. The subsequent sections offer short summaries of the three papers. The final section concludes with a brief discussion of what these three papers have in common, how they relate to entangled political economy, and why Wagner's scholarship can be characterized as the realist defense of classical liberalism.

EXPLOITING MONOPOLY POSITION THROUGH BUNDLED PROVISION

One of the core elements of Wagner's entangled political economy is the critique of the standard competitive theories of democracy. While competition is a universal quality of human affairs, there is little to suggest that political competition should operate akin to market competition. For one, residual claimancy—a key feature of market competition—is absent from political interactions (Wagner and Yazigi 2013; Wagner 2016). The seeds of Wagner's distinction between the different substantive institutional environments within which competition occurs can be found in his 1975 paper with Warren E. Weber (Wagner and Weber 1975). Wagner and Weber open their paper with the question of whether governments are better understood as competitive or monopolistic suppliers of public output. The paper examines these two models of government in the context of the budgetary consequences of the changes in the organization of government in metropolitan areas. First, the authors note that organization of government in metropolitan areas has two key structural features: fragmentation and overlapping. When organization of metropolitan governments is characterized by fragmentation, the same service is provided by multiple governments, allowing the individual a choice among mutually exclusive providers. When organization of metropolitan governments is characterized by overlapping, individual components of public output are provided by separate units of government. As the authors recognize, there is little agreement among scholars on the role fragmentation and overlapping play in the supply of public output. Those concerned with the natural propensity of governments toward monopoly see fragmentation and overlapping as necessary to curtail this tendency. In contrast, those who believe democratic governments act as competitive suppliers of public output regardless of their organizational structure view fragmentation and overlapping as unnecessary burdens, respectively responsible for raising the costs of coordination and magnifying the administrative burden.

In their comparison of the competitive and monopolistic models of governments, Wagner and Weber focus on the reduction of governmental overlapping, contrasting the provision of a particular bundle of services by a multitude of single-service governments with the provision of the same bundle of services by a single multiservice government. The authors model competitive suppliers of public output as output maximizers and monopolistic suppliers as budget maximizers, both subject to zero-profit, zero-loss constraints. When the reduction of governmental overlapping occurs, the zero-profit constraint no longer applies to each service; instead, there is a single constraint on the provision of bundled services. If the overlapping governments were perfectly competitive suppliers, the reduction in governmental overlapping should have no impact on output—single-service and multiservice governments would provide services up to the point where marginal revenue equals average cost.

In contrast, if the government were a budget-maximizing entity, the increase in the line of provided services would lead to an increase in total public expenditure. As the authors conclude, "By expanding the line of services offered by a single unit of government, a constraint on government behavior is removed, which provides an additional degree of freedom for a budget maximizing government" (Wagner and Weber 1975, 672). The authors go on to explain that the reduction of governmental overlapping allows for the practice of "full-line forcing," which entails "requiring a buyer to purchase all of services jointly, rather than being able to select among components of that line" (672). The authors' subsequent empirical analysis suggests that the size and composition of public budgets change with changes in the organization of government, leading them to conclude that metropolitan governments are more usefully analyzed as monopolistic suppliers.

Wagner and Weber do not directly speak to the epistemic consequences of reductions in governmental overlapping. Such possibility is only suggested in a footnote (Wagner and Weber 1975, 675). That said, the paper lays the foundation under the exploration of the challenges to the formation of accurate price-output perceptions that are so prominent in Wagner's subsequent scholarship. No doubt, full-line forcing contributes to the complexity of publicly provided services—the greater the number of services financed by taxation, the smaller the share of each individual service within the provided bundle of goods, making it more difficult for buyers to form accurate price-output perceptions. The impact of these difficulties on the overvaluation of publicly funded services is explored in depth in Wagner's examination of public advertising (Wagner 1976a), summarized below.

CREATING FISCAL ILLUSION THROUGH COMPLEX REVENUE STRUCTURES

In his 1976 paper "Revenue Structure, Fiscal Illusion, and Budgetary Choice," Wagner (1976b) sets out to examine the impact of fiscal institutions on the stock of knowledge possessed by voters, focusing on fiscal illusion. This might appear to be an examination of rational ignorance in the context of fiscal policy. But as many have argued, fiscal illusion cannot be explained by rational ignorance alone (Oates 1988)—in order to consider the passive income tax withholding as different from the active income tax payments made at the end of each month, voters need to be systematically biased, or irrational, not (just) rationally ignorant. Despite the long interest in fiscal illusion among social scientists, many economists have given up on the concept altogether, as it appears to violate the assumption of rationality and the unbiased expectations that rationality entails.

Wagner (1976b, 46) argues that there is nothing irrational about fiscal illusion and that the misunderstanding comes from viewing individuals "as responding to matters of form rather than of substance." Form is a matter of praxeology; it simply describes the universal quality of economizing on means in the pursuit of ends. The substance of action is a product of catallaxy. Rational choice theory focuses on form and ignores substance—choice is at the focus of analysis while the substance of choice is left in the background. This primacy of form over substance is consistent with the neoclassical assumption of objective information: reality and the perception of reality are one and the same in standard economic models. In contrast, Wagner follows Immanuel Kant in differentiating between noumena, or the unchanging structures of the universe, and phenomena, or perceptions of reality. This distinction creates a need for some process of reconciliation between the two: "To form a hypothesis as to the price of public output, a citizen must take the primary sense data and create a pattern or interpretation" (Wagner 1976b, 50). In markets, there is little difference between noumena and phenomena: perceived prices are the same as real prices. However, when output is publicly funded, the issue is more complex. Hypotheses about the unit price of government are likely to differ depending on the method used to finance public output. There is the actual tax burden, and then there are the associated sense data, which might differ if the payment comes in the form of a monthly bill (akin to a utility bill) or if it is automatically withheld from every paycheck. Sense data might also differ if the taxes are raised through a single-base revenue structure as opposed to a multibase revenue structure. The complexity of a multibase revenue structure makes it more difficult to form an accurate perception of the price of public output. Complexity encourages abstraction—only a small selection of the different types of fiscal extractions would be included in the formation of a perception (Wagner 1976b, 53).

The primacy of epistemics in Wagner's (1976b) treatment of fiscal illusion becomes apparent when we contrast it with popular rational-ignorance theories of politics. For Wagner (2016), rationality is contextual because, as previously mentioned, the substance of human action is a product of catallaxy.

Different institutional environments foster different social interactions, which in turn means that generated sense data will be different in different institutional environments. Humans are rational, and praxeology is universal, but rationality is dynamic and contextual because the substance of human action is dynamic and contextual. In contrast, the concepts of rational ignorance (Downs 1957; Wittman 1995) and rational irrationality (Caplan 2008) are focused on the incentives embedded in collective choice: when the cost of gathering information is greater than the benefit, voters make uninformed or indulgent choices. Wagner (1976b) agrees that when choice is collective, accurate perceptions are of lesser consequence to citizens than when choice is individual. But in Wagner's exploration, rational ignorance plays only a compounding role in the creation of fiscal illusion. The primary role is played by the institutional environment and by the type of feedback it provides (Martin 2010). It is easy to conclude from Wagner's paper that there would be little rational ignorance if sense data closely reflected reality; low stakes would not get in the way of accurate perceptions. If sense data regarding the price of government output reflected reality as market prices do, citizens would need to invest effort in becoming uninformed or biased. But when sense data do not closely reflect reality, it might be impossible to form accurate perceptions, regardless of incentives.

By treating information as objective—by failing to distinguish between information and knowledge where it matters (Yeager 2005)—formulations such as rational ignorance and rational irrationality focus explicitly on poor incentives to become informed. In Caplan's (2008) portrayal, politicians' desire to be effective moderates voters' indulgence and prevents even worse policies from being adopted. Wagner's grounding of fiscal illusion in the distinction between reality and perceptions of reality suggests that these incentives play only a secondary role. Far more important are the epistemic consequences of institutional structures, as they might foster the ability to actively influence citizens' perceptions of the cost of government. As Wagner (1976b, 46) writes, "The ability of fiscal institutions to create fiscal illusion depends on the ability of such institutions to influence the hypothesis a person forms about the cost of government."

Observing the connection between available sense data and perceptions of reality, in the context of fiscal illusion, allowed Wagner to consider the active role public agents play in the creation of that illusion. As will become clearer in the subsequent discussions of public advertising, for Wagner, political entrepreneurs play an important role in the erosion of knowledge-generating processes and contribute to the absence of relevant counterfactuals that such erosion brings about. In comparing the difference between the search for prices in markets and the same search in politics, Wagner (1976b, 58) explains that in politics "the cost of information is more like that of finding eggs at an Easter egg hunt, only some of the eggs are well hidden because the person who placed the eggs does not want them all discovered, and moreover, the locator does not have strong incentive to search diligently because he cannot keep, at least directly, the fruits of his search."

SECURING ACQUIESCENCE THROUGH PUBLIC ADVERTISING

On the surface, Wagner's "Advertising and the Public Economy" explores the purpose and impact of public advertising. Why do government agencies advertise their programs and intentions? What is the influence of public advertising on the consumption of publicly provided services? Wagner starts the analysis of public advertising by noting that advertising by private sellers is subject to a debate between critics and supporters and that critics can be divided into two groups. The first group accepts the standard economic assumption of given preferences and believes that advertising is wasteful because it creates barriers to entry, unnecessarily raises costs, and is an inefficient method of providing information. The second group, inspired by the work of J. K. Galbraith, believes that preferences are endogenous to the market process and that advertising creates the desire for products and services that one would not want otherwise—the dependence effect. Owing to the dependence effect, advertising is responsible for an oversupply of goods and services in the private sector and for the relative neglect of the public sector.

On the other side of the debate, the defenders of private advertising point to its informational role in educating consumers about available products and services, its role in signaling trustworthiness, and its pro-competitive effects resulting in lower prices. As Wagner carefully explains, these common pro-advertising arguments fail to address the "dependence effect" critique of advertising. By assuming that preferences are given, they leave Galbraith's argument unanswered, suggesting that the viability of advertising is contingent on the existence of given wants. Yet, as Wagner proceeds to argue, it is possible to believe that wants are altered by economic activity and defend advertising, nonetheless. Galbraith and Wagner agree that market activity increases desires, but they differ in their perceptions of whether that makes for a better or worse life. Galbraith views men as easily manipulated and sabotaged, with proliferation of wants a sign of a dependence. In contrast, for Wagner (1976a, 87), proliferation of wants is an expression of an ongoing pursuit of a better life, "one facet of the continuing quest for new forms of life." In accepting advertising as a feature of a free society, Wagner adopts a view of human nature as engaged in an ongoing pursuit of improvement, where the goal is not to satisfy wants but to replace them with new and better wants. This view, quite distinct from the assumption of given and stable preferences (Stigler and Becker 1977), can also be found in, among others, Frank Knight ([1921] 2012), Ralph Harris and Arthur Seldon ([1959] 2014), and James Buchanan ([1979] 1999, 259), who notably proclaimed that "man wants liberty to become the man he wants to become."

Wagner transitions into the debate of public advertising by noting that critics of private advertising tend to view market economy as mostly monopolistic, while the defenders of private advertising view it as inherently competitive. Given this tight connection between the view of a market economy and the stance on private advertising, Wagner sets to analyze public advertising from two perspectives: that of a competitive democracy (with competition among political parties akin to competition among market firms) and that of a monopolistic democracy (with bureaucrats and politicians playing a far more active role than would be possible in a competitive setting).

In a competitive view of democracy, electoral competition is thought to generate an outcome similar to that of market competition: market competition is won by those who best serve customers; electoral competition is won by those who best serve voters. This view assumes that preferences of voters are given and that elections transform voter preferences into public policies. While the particularities of how voter preferences end up being reflected in public policies depend on the specific institutions within which voting takes place, elections are nonetheless an instrument of democracy because they give the people influence over policy making. In contrast, in a monopolistic model of democracy, politicians and bureaucrats "have their own rules of action" (Wagner 1976a, 93), so public policy cannot be reduced to an expression of voters' preferences.

Outside political campaigns and recruiting, what is the point of government advertising in a competitive democracy? Whether the government produces public or private goods, consumer choice is absent. For public goods, consumption is necessitated by production, with national defense or mosquito control serving as prime examples in this regard. Whether these services are advertised or not, total consumption is the same. Similarly, there is no consumer choice when it comes to government production of private goods financed through taxation. As Wagner (1976a, 92–93) explains, "The individual is not in a position to choose between social security and some private insurance alternative. He must 'buy' social security regardless of what he decides to do about private insurance; that is, he must continue to pay taxes to support social security regardless of what option he might prefer." When government provision is sponsored through taxation, as opposed to user charges, there can be no meaningful consumer choice, no matter if the goods are private or public in nature. There seems to be no room for advertising within the competitive theory of democracy.

Where the competitive view of democracy highlights the similarities between markets and politics, the monopoly model focuses on the differences. Wagner employs a comparative analogy to illustrate these differences, focusing on what the supply of groceries would look like in a two-party democracy. While there would be competition for the right to operate the store, the store itself would be a monopoly. In deciding who gets the right to operate the store, the voters would choose between two baskets of groceries. After the elections, when voters received their groceries, they would often learn that the contents and price of the basket were quite different from what was promised. Unable to resell the provisions, and with no other grocery store in sight, they would have little recourse but to accept the provided basket.

False advertising is not a sustainable business practice in a competitive market. In contrast, the institutional complexity characteristic of public provision makes it difficult to verify the claims made by public agencies. As Wagner explains, the goods and services provided by the government tend to share the characteristics of credence goods—goods for which the consumer cannot determine the extent of services that were required even ex post (e.g., car maintenance and repairs) (Darby and Karni 1973). Credence goods create prime conditions for demand inducement—unable to determine and verify the actual desired quantity, buyers can do little but follow the seller's suggestions. This is equivalent to the outward shift of the demand curve: consumed quantity increases, and buyers pay higher prices per unit of service than they would if they could assess quality accurately. While Wagner agrees that credence services exist in the private sector, he notes that the tendency toward overvaluation is far stronger in the public sector. The inability to assess the quality of public services is exacerbated by the dearth of alternatives—public provision tends to crowd out private provision—and by the inability of voters to exercise choice even when alternatives exist, as they must pay for the public option even when they choose to consume the private alternative.

As discussed above, Wagner agrees with Galbraith on the ability of advertising to shape desires and preferences. However, Wagner's careful comparison of information provided by competitive private sellers with that provided by public agencies led him to conclude that the dependence effect is more likely to be produced by public advertising, resulting in social imbalance in favor of public over private provision—opposite of that predicted by Galbraith. Since claims made by public advertising are not easily verified, it is the publicly provided services that tend to be overvalued. In the absence of verifiable information, public advertising helps voters feel good about received services and secures their acquiescence. The primary function of public advertising is to "promote acquiescence in and to provide assurance about the prevailing public policies" (Wagner 1976a, 98).

Advertising does not play a significant role in Wagner's subsequent work. What we see instead is a shift to a broader discussion of the role language plays in politics. Political narratives, and associated sentiments and ideology, are usually connected to Vilfredo Pareto's distinction between logical and nonlogical action (Wagner 2016). Pareto argued that when there is no clear connection between action and consequences—between means and ends—logical action is impossible, with nonlogical action taking its place. Nonlogical action is often based on emotions, which are quite susceptible to rhetoric in the absence of other relevant sense data. In any case, there is plenty of talk in entangled political economy, as Martin (2021) shows with great clarity.

CONCLUSION

The three 1970s papers discussed here share a number of common themes: they provide a strong argument against the adoption of the standard competitive model of democracy, they examine the reasons that information generated in political processes is qualitatively different from the information produced in voluntary exchange, and they highlight the inherent tension between electoral, monopolistic democracy and liberalism. Bundled provision, fiscal complexity, and public advertising all contribute to the growth of government and to the erosion of voluntary interactions. As Wagner's subsequent work illustrates, such changes transform relationships of mutuality and equality into relationships based on status and standing, which in turn alter morality, aspirations, habits, and rationality (Wagner 2016).

As we learn from the discussion published alongside the 1976 paper on public advertising, Wagner's (1976a, 103) scholarship is motivated by a pursuit of understanding of political processes: "We all have a stake in the revitalization of our free enterprise system and a return to what in former language would be called a liberal democratic order," and "academic work that alters our understanding of government is a type of capital creation that can modify our political-economic environment in much the same manner that Crusoe's construction of a fishing net altered his environment." For Wagner, it is the understanding of government, and of political processes in general, that is the first step to the restoration of a liberal order.

As these quotes and the discussed papers suggest, Wagner's scholarly pursuit is positive in nature, its goal not to alter but to understand—it is an effort to understand political action without much attention to what ought to be. This realist approach makes Wagner's pursuit akin to that of Nicollò Machiavelli. And like Machiavelli, Wagner is also at risk of being misunderstood—the processes he describes are often vile, and the message he delivers is not an easy one to accept. Besides the risk of being misunderstood, there are other obstacles to following Wagner's path. It requires abandoning most of what mainstream economists hold dear; there is no room for equilibrium, utility, or efficiency as these concepts are incompatible with open-ended theorizing, which is at the core of entangled political economy. Moreover, Wagner's work is characterized by the commitment to seek understanding from within and to treat knowledge as invariably incomplete. Without an outside perspective, without a vantage point from which one could observe a society, there is no point to such intellectual exercises as the rule of law, optimal constitutional rules and a veil of ignorance, or any type of intervention. Despite these numerous challenges, the choice should be clear for those who, like Wagner, accept that an understanding of politics is foundational to the defense of liberalism.

NOTE

1. See Wagner (2018) for a discussion of muscular liberalism, which he contrasts with the sentimental liberalism of John Stuart Mill and John Rawls.

REFERENCES

Allen, D. W. E., C. Berg, and M. Novak. 2018. "Blockchain: An Entangled Political Economy Approach." *Journal of Public Finance and Public Choice* 33, no. 2: 105–25.

Buchanan, J. M. (1979) 1999. "Natural and Artifactual Man?" In *The Collected Works of James M. Buchanan*, Vol. 1, *The Logical Foundations of Constitutional Liberty*, edited by J. M. Buchanan, 246–59. Indianapolis: Liberty Fund.

Caplan, B. 2008. *The Myth of the Rational Voter: Why Democracies Choose Bad Policies*. Princeton, NJ: Princeton University Press.

Darby, M. R., and E. Karni. 1973. "Free Competition and the Optimal Amount of Fraud." *Journal of Law and Economics* 16, no. 1: 67–88.

Dekker, E., and C. A. Rodrigues. 2019. "The Political Economy of Brazilian Cultural Policy: A Case Study of the Rouanet Law." *Journal of Public Finance and Public Choice* 34, no. 2: 149–71.

Dellisanti, D., and R. E. Wagner. 2018. "Bankruptcies, Bailouts, and Some Political Economy of Corporate Reorganization." *Journal of Institutional Economics* 14, no. 5: 833–51.

Downs, A. 1957. *An Economic Theory of Democracy.* New York: Harper.

Harris, R., and A. Seldon. (1959) 2014. *Advertising in a Free Society.* London, UK: Institute of Economic Affairs.

Knight, F. H. (1921) 2012. *Risk, Uncertainty and Profit.* Mineola, NY: Dover Publications.

Martin, A. 2010. "Emergent Politics and the Power of Ideas." *Studies in Emergent Order* 3: 212–45.

———. 2021. "From Taciturn to Talkative Political Economy." In *Emergence, Entanglement, and Political Economy,* edited by D. J. Hebert and D. W. Thomas, 73–86. Cham, Switzerland: Springer International Publishing.

Moberg, L., and R. E. Wagner. 2014. "Default without Capital Account: The Economics of Municipal Bankruptcy." *Public Finance and Management* 14, no. 1: 30–47.

Novak, M. 2018. *Inequality: An Entangled Political Economy Perspective.* Palgrave Studies in Classical Liberalism. Cham, Switzerland: Palgrave Macmillan.

———. 2021. *Freedom in Contention: Social Movements and Liberal Political Economy.* Lanham, MD: Lexington Books.

Oates, W. E. 1988. "On the Nature and Measurement of Fiscal Illusion: A Survey." In *Taxation and Fiscal Federalism: Essays in Honour of Russell Mathews,* edited by G. Brennan, B. Singh Grewal, and P. D. Groenewegen, 65–82. Canberra, Australia: Australian National University Press.

Podemska-Mikluch, M. 2014. "Public Policy: Object of Choice or Emergent Phenomena? Lessons from the Polish Medical Reimbursement Act." In *Entangled Political Economy,* edited by S. Horwitz and R. Koppl, 93–110. Advances in Austrian Economics. Bingley, West Yorkshire, England: Emerald Group Publishing Limited.

———. 2018. "Contraception without Romance: The Entangled Political Economy of State and Federal Contraceptive Insurance Mandates." In *James M. Buchanan: A Theorist of Political Economy and Social Philosophy,* edited by R. E. Wagner, 263–90. Remaking Economics: Eminent Post-War Economists. Cham, Switzerland: Springer International Publishing.

Podemska-Mikluch, M., and R. E. Wagner. 2017. "Economic Coordination across Divergent Institutional Frameworks: Dissolving a Theoretical Antinomy." *Review of Political Economy* 29, no. 2: 249–66.

Smith, A., R. E. Wagner, and B. Yandle. 2011. "A Theory of Entangled Political Economy, with Application to TARP and NRA." *Public Choice* 148, no. 1–2: 45–66.

Stigler, G. J., and G. S. Becker. 1977. "De Gustibus Non Est Disputandum." *American Economic Review* 67, no. 2: 76–90.

Wagner, R. E. 1966. "Pressure Groups and Political Entrepreneurs: A Review Article." *Papers on Non-Market Decision Making* 1, no. 1: 161–70.

———. 1976a. "Advertising and the Public Economy: Some Preliminary Ruminations." In *The Political Economy of Advertising,* edited by D. Tuerck, 81–100. Washington, DC: American Enterprise Institute.

———. 1976b. "Revenue Structure, Fiscal Illusion, and Budgetary Choice." *Public Choice* 25, no. 1: 45–61.

———. 2009. "Property, State, and Entangled Political Economy." In *Markets and Politics: Insights from a Political Economy Perspective,* edited by W. Schafer, A. Schneider, and T. Thomas, 37–49. Marburg: Metropolis.

———. 2016. *Politics as a Peculiar Business: Public Choice in a System of Entangled Political Economy*. Cheltenham, UK: Edward Elgar.

———. 2018. "James Buchanan's Liberal Theory of Political Economy: A Valiant but Failed Effort to Square the Circle." In *Buchanan's Tensions: Reexamining the Political Economy and Philosophy of James M. Buchanan*, edited by P. J. Boettke and S. Stein, 15–41. Tensions in Political Economy. Arlington, VA: Mercatus Center at George Mason University.

———. 2020. "Entangled Political Economy: Mixing Something Old with Something New." Working paper.

Wagner, R. E., and W. E. Weber. 1975. "Competition, Monopoly, and the Organization of Government in Metropolitan Areas." *Journal of Law and Economics* 18, no. 3: 661–84.

Wagner, R. E., and D. Yazigi. 2013. "Form vs. Substance in Selection through Competition: Elections, Markets, and Political Economy." *Public Choice* 159, no. 3: 503–14.

Wittman, D. A. 1995. *The Myth of Democratic Failure: Why Political Institutions Are Efficient*. Chicago: University of Chicago Press.

Yeager, L. B. 2005. "Why Distinguish between Information and Knowledge?" *Econ Journal Watch* 2, no. 1: 82.

Chapter 4

Emergence, Process, and the Asymmetries of Regulation

Wagnerian Political Economy

Diana W. Thomas and Michael D. Thomas

> The primacy of process over structure is conveyed nicely by considering a galloping horse. Some people looking at snapshots will see all four of the horse's hoofs to be off the ground. Taken as an equilibrium observation, it would have to be concluded that a horse can fly, or at least, levitate. The snapshot of the flying horse ignores the underlying causal process through which that observation emerged.
>
> —Richard E. Wagner, "Value and Exchange:
> Two Windows for Economic Theorizing"

Flying horses are rarely the topic of conversation among economists who aspire to offer explanations of the social world based on the assumption of rationality. Yet, to Richard E. Wagner and his students, flying horses have been an important part of classroom discussions. The point of this allegory is to illustrate to his students the limitations of the toolkit of the overly deterministic models favored by many economists, and to provide a starting point for a conversation about the dynamic interplay of forces propelling economic systems. Like the snapshot of the galloping horse, static models of market exchange obscure the dynamic aspects of human action, as well as the responsiveness of human agents to environmental and institutional factors that provide the background for economic activity.

The example of the snapshot of a horse in midair is not just a teaching tool, however. It also offers a handy representation of some of the core characteristics of Wagner's contributions to scholarship in economics and is indicative of his most important intellectual influences. In contrast to the more static approaches of macroeconomics and public economics, which are often employed to justify public policy intended to fix market failure problems, Wagner's work emphasizes the process approach to political economy. Standard economic models may give the illusion that economic systems can settle into a static equilibrium or that they can, with the help of policy intervention, perform at target growth rates. But, like a snapshot that captures only one moment in time, standard economic models are unable to capture the intricacies of the dispersed economic processes that lead up to the moment in time they depict.

In contrast to such static perspectives, Wagner offers more dynamic descriptions of economic activity, and his approach emphasizes a process perspective on economic activity that acknowledges the emergent characteristics of economic outcomes. The emphasis on the emergent properties of economics systems is an acknowledgment of the complexity of the market process for which no single actor has complete knowledge of the relevant social/political/economic landscape. As a result of having this process perspective, Wagner does not share the optimism many economists have for what intervention can do to help coordinate collective action, that is, action taken by a group of people rather than an individual.

Throughout his career, Wagner's scholarship has embraced the insights of his mentor and professor, James Buchanan. These insights, which form the basis of public choice theory, suggest that individuals are self-interested in both markets and politics (behavioral symmetry) and that, as a result, private interests have systematic and predictable effects on the institutions that govern the public sphere such that a few individuals can have an outsize impact on the economy through political intervention.

Beyond these behavioral concerns and predictions, Wagner's contribution to political economy conceives of the economic and political spheres of human action as overlapping and containing predictable nodes of influence. Humans form patterns of organization and collective action that are based on the problems they are trying to solve. As opposed to a hierarchical view of social order, where institutions are planned with superordinate and subordinate goals, Wagner's conception emphasizes overlapping and contested institutions of collective action. Wagner (2021) calls this polycentric way of thinking about social theorizing "entangled political economy." His idea of "fiscal sociology," to provide an example, presents something akin to a flowchart demonstrating the complexity of jurisdictional contestability, where the competition over influence is not only a matter of local versus national governance but also of jurisdictional competition and overlap between different bureaucratic agencies (regulation of agricultural water use is an obvious and illustrative example in which fertilizer use and production of runoff is governed by the US Department of Agriculture, Environmental Protection Agency, and state government rules).

The goal of this chapter is to review three important influences on Wagner's scholarship and to offer some thoughts on what aspects of those influences have shaped his work and form the core of his own theory of entangled political economy. Our reading of Wagner focuses on three distinct sets of ideas that have shaped his work. First, the Austrian influence. The Wagnerian view emphasizes the emergent nature of market processes and mistrusts benevolent interventions in the name of crisis that are difficult to remove once established (Tollison and Wagner 1991). We offer Carl Menger's work (Streissler and Streissler 1994) as particularly influential on this strand of his thought. Second, the Swedish influence. Wagner's scholarship centers on viewing the polity as governed by a process of preference aggregation, where the rules of the game determine the relative efficiency of collective choices. This institutional process approach in Wagner's work is importantly influenced by Knut Wicksell (1958) through James Buchanan (with Gordon Tullock 1999), which is why we label it the Swedish influence. Third, the Italian influence. Wagner seeks to identify nodes of outsize importance where interest groups have influence on the outcomes of collective action. Wagner's work shows how such influential groups create asymmetries in intervention and regulation. We argue that this aspect of his work is influenced importantly by the Italian public-finance tradition, and we focus on Amilcare Puviani (1903) as a specific influence.

We proceed as follows. The second section reviews the aspects of Carl Menger's (Streissler and Streissler 1994) and Knut Wicksell's (1958) work that we believe have had particular importance for Wagner's work. The third section describes how Puviani's (1903) work in public finance was influential in bringing about a synthesis in Wagner's thinking on asymmetries in an entangled and emergent process of intervention. In the fourth section, we offer some examples from Wagner's work to illustrate the importance of these influences.

BROAD INTELLECTUAL INFLUENCES

Menger—Market Process and Emergence

Carl Menger was unique among the contributors to the marginalist revolution because of his emphasis on individual decisions that are based on the comparison of individual purchases with known alternatives. Unlike William Stanley Jevons and Léon Walras, who are associated with the shift in economic thinking toward calculus, Menger was less concerned with revealing prices that set fixed ratios between various production and consumption decisions, and instead focused on the process of discovery and the emergence of knowledge. While marginal thinking allowed for a better understanding of the reconciliation of individual plans through markets, Menger emphasized that the reconciliation of idiosyncratic and sometimes erroneous plans would also lead to the discovery of new knowledge. His process-oriented description of individual choice allows for the emergence of diverse outcomes rather than predicting a deterministic response to stimulus. The other marginalists thought that the addition of calculus would help us find objective values for resources that were used in dispersed and diverse ways, like the marginal value of a piece of land, unit of labor, or marginal unit of capital (emphasizing homogeneity among inputs). Wagner suggests that the central difference between Menger and the other marginalists was his focus on the development of an analytical framework that could account for discovery rather than just the reconciliation of individual plans:

> It is clear that Menger shared with his neoclassical brethren this focus on explaining variations in prices by variations in consumer valuation of the marginal unit. Yet it is also clear that he used his analytical apparatus differently than did the other neoclassicals. . . .
>
> In the Walrasian orientation that came to dominate neoclassicism, the central analytical problem is to explain the structure of relative prices and the allocation of resources among competing uses in a setting where knowledge is frozen, and time is suspended. In this analytical schema, changes in knowledge are sources of exogenous shocks when time is allowed to elapse. In sharp contrast, Menger sought to develop an analytical framework where the passing of time and the development of knowledge, institutions, and organizations that accompanied the passing of time occupied the analytical foreground and were not injected as exogenous shocks. (Wagner 1999, 5)

Menger's approach focused on endogeneity because he attempted to explain how knowledge emerged between various actors. Wagner makes this emergence perspective central to his own approach and seeks to treat all social phenomena as endogenous and the result of competition between groups and individuals to realize plans. In contrast to an equilibrium-based model that treats all change as exogenous and "is incapable of generating what it purports to explain, and so is confined to describing conditions for consistency" (Wagner 2007, 138), Wagner's explanations place the context of decision-making at the center. In one example, he likens crowds of pedestrians to a parade, illustrating that the same topography and even the same people can be ordered in different ways depending on the specific purpose individuals are pursuing on different days (Wagner 2010).

This Mengerian insight that the process of preference reconciliation results in the discovery of new knowledge that continually feeds back into the institutional structure and reshapes the process into the future pervades Wagner's work. He offers another application of it in his paper titled "Design vs. Emergence in a Theory of Federalism: Toward Institutional Reconciliation" (Wagner 2014). In this paper, Wagner explains why he believes that a description of federalism as a competitive system is problematic. His major objection to this description is that for a system to be competitive, the structure of the system must be emergent and continually changing as the competitive process operates. He suggests that federalism cannot be characterized as competitive, because of its clearly defined institutional spheres of influence, which do not overlap or change over time.

An emergent system requires a description unlike the snapshot of the horse. The outcome of a social process is ultimately dependent on the subjective purposes of the individuals and groups that make up the polity as well as the features of the environment influencing those choices.

Wicksell—Institutional Structure and Process View

Menger's focus on the market as a process of preference reconciliation and information discovery forms the background of Wagner's thought on markets. As his aforementioned treatment of the theory of federalism (Wagner 2014) suggests, his perspective on collective action in politics similarly focuses on dynamic preference reconciliation processes and the institutional structure underlying such processes. His theory of entangled political economy offers a picture of private and public actors jointly shaping the public sphere through various interconnections and institutional nodes. This theory of mutual interdependence between the public and private spheres of collective action is importantly influenced by the work of the Swedish economist Knut Wicksell, who, in his *Finanztheoretische Untersuchungen*, describes public decision-making processes from the perspective of preference reconciliation akin to the market process.

In Wicksell's rendering, an application of conceptual unanimity moves the process of collective action closer to the ideal of economic efficiency with an assessment of taxes according to individual benefit. Deviations from unanimity can be justified when the goal is to maximize collective benefit, but they also have the potential to result in ever-greater levels of redistribution favoring the preferences of smaller groups. In Wicksell's rendering, the application of a unanimity principle could allow for collective action to play a much larger role in public decision-making because it would make the results more efficient and more just.

Wagner is influenced by Wicksell in the sense that he thinks about how the institutional structure of government affects the relative importance of different groups in collective action. Supermajority rules, for example, represent a movement in the direction of unanimity in public decision-making and ultimately greater efficiency in the sense of being representative of constituent preferences. Under a supermajority, however, fewer policies are enacted. Wagner looks to Wicksell to think about how policy desired by an interest group could be made into law while imposing costs on others who did not favor the policy. In this way of thinking, unanimity becomes a yardstick for an assessment of the type of error public policy will create. A reduction in the level of consent required for collective action reduces "the error of failing to undertake beneficial activities. At the same time, however, it necessarily increases the error of undertaking activities that were not worthwhile to taxpayers, as against being worthwhile only to subsets of taxpayers because the costs were placed on others" (Wagner 2012, 524).

Wicksell thought so poorly of the imposition of private will by some on others that he advocated unanimity as a constraint on passing laws. Wicksell's particular historical period was one of more limited suffrage, so unanimity was less costly in the context of Sweden in the early 20th century, yet even in that context Wicksell understood that unanimity could be overly restrictive in some circumstances.

Wagner takes from Wicksell insight into two specific features of institutional design: first, that the design of the rules will change the outcome of the process, and second, that interest groups will advocate for their own partial interests, which do not necessarily reflect the aggregate interests of the group. Unanimity minimizes error through representation but also constrains the ability to solve collective action problems. This very practical problem of tradeoffs gives us a way to understand Wagner's presentation of entangled political economy as a messy set of institutions that gropes toward solutions with many errors. What emerges is less about what is right for a particular political and economic order and more about what is likely to occur given different kinds of rules.

There is a tradeoff between limiting collective action and encouraging the formation of minimum winning coalitions that impose costs on others. As the size of the group increases, so, too, does the cost of implementing a unanimity rule. This suggests that for very large social orders, smaller subgroups will necessarily make choices that have disproportionate effects on the rest of society.

Puviani—The Asymmetries of Intervention

Menger's process perspective paired with Wicksell's idea of tradeoffs in collective action provides a picture of the political process that is very much in line with the standard public-choice approach Wagner was trained in at the University of Virginia. It is through the influence of the Italianate school of public finance, and specifically Amilcare Puviani (1903), that Wagner's thought ultimately synthesized the Austrian process perspective and public-choice perspective into his theory of entanglement.

Puviani's specific contribution that is important for Wagner is the idea of fiscal illusion (Puviani 1903). Fiscal illusion is the failure on the part of taxpayers to accurately perceive the cost of public policy. It occurs when government revenue generation is so complex that taxpayers cannot correctly assess their share of the tax burden. Because revenue collection is separated from spending decisions, voters are led to believe that any given level of public expenditure costs them less than what it actually does. Puviani observes that interest groups discover complicated fiscal revenue procedures, not intentionally, but because these work to obscure the costs imposed on others by their preferred policies. This discovery of institutional mechanisms is emergent, and it facilitates coalition building by muting opposition to increased revenue collection. Groups learn ways to get the policy outcomes they desire without necessarily planning some conspiracy against the public. By creating novel institutional structures (e.g., making the tax code more and more complex), some groups will gain relative power in the social order and will have an outsize effect on collective action as a result.

It was important to Puviani's thesis that fiscal illusion—"government acting to hide the burden of taxes from the public"—did not work as a "deliberate plan" on the part of the political actors (Buchanan 1960, 60). Rather, these entrepreneurs discovered how to finance a given level of government in a way that minimized the "perceived burden" of what Wagner (1976, 49) would later call the "Fiscal Extraction Device."

For Wagner, Puviani crystallized why a perspective focusing on emergence and discovery helped explain asymmetries in regulation (or institutional change). Policy innovations are asymmetric to the extent that they are harder to undo than they are to discover in the first place. Since Puviani explained how this can be done emergently, there is no undoing that can be done without both explaining the unintended process in the status quo and planning a correction. It therefore involves more cognitive and resource costs to undo a policy than it does to implement it in the first place.

EXAMPLES

Democracy in Deficit

Coauthored with James Buchanan, Wagner's book *Democracy in Deficit* (1977) offers an early entangled political economy perspective that combines the three intellectual influences highlighted earlier. Buchanan and Wagner (1977) argue that Keynes's (1936) theory of aggregate demand and supply shocks was rhetorically useful for fiscal entrepreneurs in rejecting the old-school fiscal religion and obtaining favored policy. In keeping with Puviani's approach, it was not necessary to suggest that Keynes planned an approach that would maximize deficits, but merely that his theoretical innovation would allow for the maximization of the partial plans of interest groups. To accurately apply Keynes's theory, there must be a measure not only of an economic bust requiring fiscal stimulus but also of an economic boom, which would recommend austerity and public savings.

Deficit spending is much more attractive for policymakers as fiscal entrepreneurs in times of economic bust. By contrast, few policymakers declare an economic boom and propose savings and austerity; instead, booms are associated with a new normal of higher growth rates. There is no incentive for a consistent application of Keynes's theory within the public space, no reward for the entrepreneur who pushes for public savings. As a result, Buchanan and Wagner argue, Keynes's theory is reduced to the level of convenient rhetoric and contributes to the long-run accumulation of public debt.

By emphasizing the importance of the rhetorical impact of Keynes's argument, Buchanan and Wagner (1977) combine emergence and a process perspective on politics. Mengerian emergence explains how Keynes's theory was applied in practice. A Wicksellian understanding helps explain how institutional rules determine fiscal patterns and interest group dynamics. Puviani helps explain why recovering the "old time fiscal religion" of balanced budgets is more difficult than the move to the Keynesian paradigm. *Democracy in Deficit* is therefore a great example of the synthesis of these different intellectual influences represented in Wagner's (and of course also Buchanan's) body of scholarship.

Transitional Gains Trap

In his 1991 article "Romance, Realism, and Economic Reform," Wagner extends the idea of the transitional gains trap (Tullock 1975). In Tullock's original formulation of the concept, political rents create gains that are only transitional because they are quickly capitalized and ultimately increase the cost of production such that a removal of the political rent would hurt the recipient. As a result, beneficiaries of political rents will be willing to expend resources in order to maintain their privileged positions, which exceed the cost of the policy to society as a whole. Tullock identifies this situation as a trap because a scenario in which the socially inefficient policy would be removed is, at least theoretically, unimaginable. Tollison and Wagner (1991) extend Tullock's original insight by showing that even from a long-run, dynamic perspective, transitional gains to a regulated industry will exceed the losses to society from keeping an inefficient policy in place. Their insight suggests that policy reform should focus on preventing the creation of new rents rather than the removal of existing inefficient policies.

We believe this article is ultimately an application of the idea of Puviani's fiscal entrepreneur, who "discovers" arguments for the creation and redistribution of rents in his favor. These arguments, even if they are ultimately found to be flawed or unfavorable, will persist because no coalition can capture the benefits of regulatory change after this regulation has been put into place. Wagner and Tollison's dynamic version of the transitional gains trap is also a precursor to Wagner's entanglement perspective; it offers a perspective on policy that is based on a nonhierarchical structure of political economy as a network, a flowchart, or a functional, overlapping competing jurisdiction model (Frey and Eichenberger 1995), which means that the key institutional insight is that there is balance between different nodes. If any one group escapes contestability, they introduce sclerosis into the system, which is hard to undo and affects all the other nodes in the system.

Entangled Political Economy

In his work on the idea of entanglement, Wagner (2021, 10) uses ecological and topological analogies to describe the context of emergent collective action in the public market square. This emphasis on context harks back to Menger's incorporation of knowledge of place and time as well as discovery, an emphasis shared with Hayek (1945). Menger's concept of emergence focuses us on the importance of dialogue when we approach collective action in the social space (Martin 2021). This dialogue can either be epistemically open, which allows for greater unanimity of purpose, or be relatively closed, which means that a few interest groups dominate the space while imposing costs on others. This recognition of dialogue and interaction allows Wagner to see that emergence applies not only to the development of institutional rules but also to the evolution of these rules over time as institutions adapt.

Some of this adaptation of entangled systems of political economy occurs in the way that Puviani (1903) described, without explicit design, but with consequences that are hard to disentangle once they have been put in place. Fiscal illusion, as discussed earlier, describes a case where institutions evolve to obscure the costs of public expenditure from those who are bearing the costs. Buchanan and Wagner (1977) describe the legacy of Lord Keynes as having a similar type of path dependence that is hard to undo once the rhetoric is discovered. We discuss the erosion of state and local control on expenditures over time as central government borrowing plays a larger role in financing expenditures (Thomas and Thomas 2021). All these examples of entangled systems ultimately suggest a kind of path dependence toward sclerosis as governments become less able to take advantage of local knowledge in the design and implementation of programs over time. In Wagner's theory of entangled political economy, Puviani's concept of unplanned but path-dependent evolution looms large: despite the fact that intervention is usually the result of an unplanned and emergent process, it is always difficult to reverse.

CONCLUSION

Richard Wagner's work throughout his career has, with different intensity at various times, embraced three distinct ideas that ultimately coalesce into his theory of entangled political economy. These three ideas are the Austrian concept of emergence and market process (importantly exemplified by Carl Menger's work), Knut Wicksell's Swedish perspective on the importance of institutional structure and process in collective action, and the Italianate discovery of asymmetries in the development of institutional evolution toward sclerotic systems that allow smaller groups to maintain outsize influence through emergent processes that lead to phenomena like fiscal illusion, as discussed by Amilcare Puviani (1903).

We have highlighted these different influences here because they shape our perspective on Wagner's work and reveal the most important facets of his theory of entanglement, which ultimately describes a process of institutional evolution that gravitates toward emergent outcomes that can have outsize influence on certain groups. Rather than offering a static snapshot of social institutions frozen in time, Wagner's theory allows us to see the nodes and connections that shape the process of institutional evolution over time toward an emergent outcome that is difficult to predict.

REFERENCES

Buchanan, J. M. 1960. "The Italian Tradition in Fiscal Theory." In *Fiscal Theory and Political Economy*, edited by J. M. Buchanan, 24–74. Chapel Hill: University of North Carolina Press.

Buchanan, J. M., and G. Tullock. (1962) 1999. *The Calculus of Consent: Logical Foundations of Constitutional Democracy*. Indianapolis: Liberty Fund.

Buchanan, J. M., and R. E. Wagner. (1977) 2000. *Democracy in Deficit: The Political Legacy of Lord Keynes*. Indianapolis: Liberty Fund.

Frey, B. S., and R. Eichenberger. 1995. "Competition among Jurisdictions. The Idea of FOCJ." In *Competition among Institutions*, edited by L. Gerken, 209–29. London: Palgrave Macmillan.

Hayek, F. A. 1945. "The Use of Knowledge in Society." *American Economic Review* 35, no. 4: 519–30.

Keynes, J. M. 1936. *The General Theory of Employment, Interest and Money*. London: Macmillan.

Martin, A. 2021. "From Taciturn to Talkative Political Economy." In *Emergence, Entanglement, and Political Economy*, edited by D. J. Hebert and D. W. Thomas, 73–86. New York: Springer.

Puviani, A. 1903. *Teoria della Illusione Finanziaria*. Reprint. Milan: Isedi.

Streissler, E. W., and M. Streissler. 1994. *Carl Menger's Lectures to Crown Prince Rudolph of Austria*. Cheltenham, UK: Edward Elgar.

Thomas, D. W., and M. D. Thomas. 2021. "The Fiscal Squeeze: Budgets between Fiscal Illusion, Fiscal Commons, and the Tyranny of Experts." In *Emergence, Entanglement, and Political Economy*, edited by D. J. Hebert and D. W. Thomas, 125–39. New York: Springer.

Tollison, R., and R. E. Wagner. 1991. "Romance, Realism, and Economic Reform." *Kyklos* 44, no. 1: 57–70.

Tullock, G. 1975. "The Transitional Gains Trap." *Bell Journal of Economics* 6, no. 2: 671–78.

Wagner, R. E. 1988. "The Calculus of Consent: A Wicksellian Retrospective." *Public Choice* 56, no. 2: 153–66.

———. 1999. "Carl Menger (1840–1921)." In *The Elgar Companion to Law and Economics*, edited by J. G. Backhaus, 412–19. Northampton, MA: Edward Elgar.

———. 2007. *Fiscal Sociology and the Theory of Public Finance: An Exploratory Essay*. Northampton, MA: Edward Elgar.

———. 2010. "A Macro Economy as an Emergent Ecology of Plans." Unpublished manuscript. Available at: http://mason.gmu.edu/~rwagner/Emergence%20&%20Macro.pdf (accessed August 30, 2022).

———. 2012. "Knut Wicksell and Contemporary Political Economy." In *Handbook of the History of Economic Thought: Insights on the Founders of Modern Economics*, edited by J. G. Backhouse, 513–25. New York: Springer.

———. 2014. "Design vs. Emergence in a Theory of Federalism: Toward Institutional Reconciliation." *Journal of Public Finance and Public Choice* 32, no. 1–3: 197–213.

————. 2021. "Emergence and Entanglement in a Theory of Political Economy." In *Emergence, Entanglement, and Political Economy*, edited by D. J. Hebert and D. W. Thomas, 7–26. New York: Springer.

Wicksell, K. 1958. "A New Principle of Just Taxation." In *Classics in the Theory of Public Finance*, edited by R. A. Musgrave and A. T. Peacock, 72–118. International Economic Association Series. London: Palgrave Macmillan.

Chapter 5

Public Choice, Behavioral Symmetry, and the Ethics of Citizenship
Viktor J. Vanberg

> It is only when the Homo economicus postulate of human behavior is combined with the politics-as-exchange paradigm that an "economic theory of politics" emerges from despair.
>
> —James M. Buchanan, "The Public Choice Perspective."

PUBLIC CHOICE AS ECONOMIC THEORY OF POLITICS

The public-choice research program sprang from a dissatisfaction with an economics that approached markets and politics from asymmetric theoretical perspectives. The asymmetry has two interrelated aspects. First, there was the asymmetry of a welfare economics that based its policy recommendations on the diagnosis of "market failures" by measuring the working properties of real-world markets against the standard of a theoretically "perfect market," yet tacitly presumed the political apparatus—from which it expected the remedy for the diagnosed market deficiencies to come—to work "perfectly," without ever asking whether real-world politics can be presumed to meet this standard. The second, interrelated asymmetry concerned the behavioral assumptions economists applied in their respective outlooks at markets and at politics. While markets were assumed to be populated by self-interested actors, equipped only with imperfect knowledge, the realm of politics was tacitly presumed to be governed by an "omniscient despot," exclusively concerned with maximizing social welfare.

The public-choice project was launched as an effort to rectify these asymmetries. Before any policy conclusions can responsibly be drawn, its advocates argued, realistic comparisons have to be made between the working properties of real-world markets and real-world politics. And such comparisons, they insisted, have to be based on a *behavioral symmetry* between the two realms, presuming that in politics "persons act not differently from other persons that the economist studies" (Buchanan [1983b] 2000, 24), that human beings do not change their nature when they move from one realm to the other. In other words, just as standard economic theory models persons interacting in market settings as pursuing their own interests, behavioral symmetry demands to apply the same assumption of self-interest motivation to persons populating the political arena.

The purpose of this chapter is to take a closer look at the "behavioral symmetry" postulate[1] in light of the distinction James M. Buchanan ([1983b] 2000, 24) has drawn between "two central elements in the inclusive public choice perspective," two elements that he describes in these terms: "One is the extension of the economists' utility-maximizing framework to the behavior of persons in various public-choosing roles. The second is the idealized conceptualization of politics as complex exchange" (Buchanan [1986] 2001, 71).[2] As Buchanan ([1983b] 2000, 24) suggests, traditional public choice theory can be said to "have been weighted toward the *Homo economicus* element," while his own favored constitutional political economy research program has "been more derivative from the politics-as-exchange paradigm."

The principal claim this chapter seeks to support is that with their different concerns—one focusing on behavior within *existing institutional constraints*, the other on issues of *constitutional choice*—the "two wings of modern public choice theory" (Buchanan [1983b] 2000, 24) direct attention to the fact that the assumption of rational, self-interested behavior must be understood somewhat differently when applied to individuals who take care of their own business as players in market settings as opposed to individuals as citizens of self-governing polities who are called on to jointly take care of their common concerns. More specifically, I will argue that the notion of rational pursuit of one's self-interest takes on a characteristically different meaning when the explanatory focus is on behavioral choices within given institutional constraints in contrast to inquiries that explore how individuals come to choose the institutional constraints to which they jointly submit.

BEHAVIORAL SYMMETRY AND CONSTITUTIONAL CHOICE

In a sense, the public-choice outlook at politics was meant to mirror the way welfare economists looked at markets. Just as the latter diagnosed real-world markets to be plagued by "failures" when compared with the ideal of perfectly working markets, public-choice economists insisted that real-world politics likewise "failed" when measured against its ideal image.[3] Yet, unlike welfare economists, who considered such diagnosis of "market failures" a sufficient basis for recommending government intervention, public choice scholars did not draw symmetric conclusions. Rather, the point they sought to make was that measuring either real-world markets or real-world politics against unrealizable ideal standards is of no help whatsoever for answering the question of how problems a society faces ought to be dealt with. The only meaningful way to seek answers to such questions is, from a public choice perspective, to compare and evaluate feasible institutional arrangements, both in markets and in politics.[4]

From such a comparative-institutions perspective, the appropriate strategy for correcting diagnosed shortcomings or "failures" in markets as well as in politics is reforms in the existing institutional framework rather than attempts at directly securing "better" outcomes.[5] And the task of institutional reform is to identify, and seek to implement, the institutional arrangements that promise to perform relatively best in dealing with the problems at hand. Stated in more general terms, the task of institutional reform is, as Buchanan ([1982] 2001, 46) puts it, to construct a "bridge between homo economicus on the one hand and 'social welfare' or 'group interest' on the other"—that is, to implement rules of the market game as well as of the game of politics that guide the agents' conduct in the respective realm in such manner that "the self-interested motivation on the part of the individuals might promote the welfare of the whole community of persons" (46).[6]

POLITICS AS EXCHANGE, DEMOCRACY, AND "PUBLIC INTEREST"

As a purely positive-explanatory exercise, public-choice analysis examines and compares the working properties of alternative institutional-organizational arrangements, remaining per se neutral as to how their respective merits ought to be assessed. In contrast, the politics-as-exchange paradigm clearly implies or presupposes a normative criterion in terms of which alternative arrangements are to be evaluated. It is based on the premise that, in general, social transactions or arrangements are to be positively valued to the extent that they result from voluntary agreement among the participants, in the same sense in which economists traditionally assign positive value to exchange transactions in markets, presuming that they were concluded within a legal-institutional framework that ensures their voluntariness.[7]

The politics-as-exchange paradigm is explicitly meant to characterize the normative foundation of a democratic society as, in John Rawls's (1971, 84) term, "a cooperative venture for mutual advantage."[8] The paradigm advances what Buchanan ([1985] 2001, 270) calls an "individualist-contractarian model of politics." As he elaborates, "The first and most critical presupposition that provides a foundation for any genuine democratic theory is that which locates sources of value exclusively in individuals. . . . That which is sought for in politics is not, and cannot be, that which exists independent of the values of the individuals who make up the political community. The object or aim of politics is the furtherance or achievement of the separate and several objects of the individuals who participate variously in the collective enterprise" (267, 269).

Because of its individualist normative premise, the politics-as-exchange paradigm focuses its evaluative attention on the processes from which policy outcomes result, in contrast to outlooks at politics that aim at evaluating outcomes as such, irrespective of the mode of their origin.[9] By locating the source for evaluation exclusively in individuals, the exchange paradigm becomes a natural part of the contractarian philosophical tradition.[10] Just as ordinary market exchange qualifies as legitimized and mutually beneficial because (or to the extent that) the participants voluntarily agree to it, in matters of politics it is, likewise, only from voluntary agreement among all persons involved that legitimacy and the promise of common benefit can be concluded. The bilateral exchange contracts between traders in markets find their political counterpart in the multilateral social contracts among citizens—that is, their agreement on the terms under which they are willing to participate in their "cooperative venture."[11]

For obvious reasons, such agreements are scarcely feasible at the level of day-to-day politics. The question of how "the complex political exchanges (may) be organized so as to ensure that all beneficiaries secure net gains in the process" (Buchanan [1979] 1999, 52) can be expected to find a positive answer only at the constitutional level, defining the rules of operation according to which day-to-day politics is to be carried out. Since rules prescribe standard procedures for how to deal with certain classes of issues, the contracting parties are unavoidably uncertain about how they will be personally affected in unknown future instances of their application, the more so as the generality of rules increases. To the extent that they are uncertain about their own potential affectedness, the contractors are induced to judge the working properties of rules from an impartial perspective, thereby increasing the scope for agreement.[12]

The multilateral exchange that persons engage in when agreeing to adopt rules for a "cooperative venture" they intend to join is an *exchange of commitments*, of mutual promises to honor the constraints the rules impose on them.[13] In agreeing to be so bound they may well be aware that occasionally these constraints may work to their disadvantage, yet will consider such joint commitment nevertheless beneficial as long as it promises to work overall to their net advantage.[14] It is in this sense that, notwithstanding the obviously conflictual nature of in-period politics, at the most general constitutional level of the "game of politics," individuals' separate interests can be reconciled with the "public interest," which in a democratic polity can have no other meaning than the *common interest* all citizens share in the institutional framework that allows them to pursue their respective interests in mutually compatible ways.[15]

BEHAVIORAL SYMMETRY AND SELF-GOVERNMENT

By calling for a behavioral symmetry in the study of markets and politics, the public-choice research program presupposes that what distinguishes these two realms is not the nature of the persons acting in them but the nature of the constraints that each provides for its internal operation. Individuals are equally presumed to pursue their own interests in both realms, but rationally adapt to the institutional and other constraints they confront in each case, resulting in different behavior patterns in response to differences in these constraints.

When behavior in markets—or, more generally, in the private-law society—is so contrasted with behavior in politics, the latter may be understood in a systems-neutral sense, applying equally to democratic, autocratic, totalitarian, or any other type of political regime. Whatever kind of system may be concerned, the explanatory task remains the same: inquiring into how self-interested individuals can be expected to rationally adapt their own conduct to the constraints the respective environment imposes on them. From the perspective of such inquiry, the "rules of the game"—be it of the private-law society or the polity—are treated as "exogenous data," as predefined constraints to which individuals can only adapt, not as variables they may choose to change. However, what distinguishes democratic polities from other types of political regimes is that they are systems of *self-government*, that the individuals who are subject to the "rules of the game" are at the same time the ultimate sovereigns in matters of constitutional choice. It is because of this very fact that in the case of democratic polities the postulate of "behavioral symmetry" needs to be qualified.

For a democratic polity to properly function as a system of self-government, individuals must in their capacity as citizens meet behavioral requirements that are characteristically different from those that a properly functioning market or private-law society asks of them. In their *private capacity* as market participants and as players in the private-law society, individuals *choose for themselves*, evaluating the predicted outcomes of alternative choice options in terms of how they will be personally affected by them. They are expected to consider the interests of others only insofar as the formal and informal rules of the game require them to do so. As citizen-members of a democratic polity, they act in their *public capacity* as participants in a political–collective choice process, the outcomes of which they *codetermine* together with their fellow citizens. Buchanan describes the difference between the two settings in these terms:

> The "theory of public choice" . . . involves the explicit introduction of a "democratic" model, one in which the rulers are also the ruled. The theory examines the behavior of persons as they participate variously in the formation of public or collective choices, by which is meant choices from among mutually exclusive alternative constraints which, once selected, must apply to all members of the community. In acting or behaving as a "public choice" participant, the individual is presumed to be aware that he is, in part, selecting results which affect others than himself. He is making decisions for a public, of which he forms a part.
>
> This characteristic feature of "public choice" distinguishes it sharply from "private choice." (Buchanan [1972] 2000, 29)

To be a "good member of the private-law society," it suffices to be a fair, law-abiding player and to honor the informal rules of decent conduct. To be a "good citizen" in an autocratic polity, it suffices to do the same, to honor the formal and informal rules of the regime. To be a "good citizen" in a democratic system of self-government involves more than compliance with whatever rules are in existence. It requires, in Buchanan's terms, an awareness of one's role as participant in public choices and a willingness to live up to the responsibility that such a role implies.[16] In his analysis of the state of democracy in America, Michael Sandel alludes to this difference in behavioral attitudes, contrasting "liberal" and "republican" conceptions of government:

> The liberal begins by asking how government should treat its citizens, and seeks principles of justice that treat persons fairly as they pursue their various interests and ends. The republican begins by asking how citizens can be capable of self-government, and seeks the political form and social conditions that promote its meaningful exercise. (Sandel 1996b, 27)
>
> According to republican political theory . . . sharing in self-rule . . . means deliberating with fellow citizens about the common good and helping to shape the destiny of the political community. (5)[17]

What Sandel describes as "deliberating about the common good," Buchanan refers to when, following Frank H. Knight,[18] he speaks of democracy as "government by discussion,"[19] identifying the "constitutional level of choice" as offering the best prospects for reaching a consensus on "the common good." As he puts it,

> The members of the group may, of course, disagree on the rules, as they discuss these at the constitutional level of decision. . . . But it is precisely at this constitutional stage that discussion in some meaningful sense can take place. It is this stage where analysis and argument can be helpful in resolving differences of opinion. . . . The reconciliation that is possible here is achieved through the fact that self-interest, as the individual himself perceives this, becomes less and less identifiable in any objectively measurable sense, for the individual is removed from the moment of pure conflict. (Buchanan [1966] 2001, 256)

In a similar sense, John Rawls ([1997] 1999, 579) speaks of "a well-ordered constitutional democracy . . . as a deliberative democracy," noting, "When citizens deliberate, they exchange views and debate their supporting reasons concerning public political questions. They suppose that their political opinions may be revised by discussion with other citizens; and therefore, these opinions are not simply a fixed outcome of their existing private or nonpolitical interests" (580).[20]

The *likelihood* of citizens agreeing on rules that they expect to work to their mutual benefit increases, as Buchanan notes, the more uncertain they are about the differential effects alternative rules may have on them personally in unknown future instances of their application. Yet, the *actual prospect* of reaching such an agreement depends on citizens' willingness to engage in a joint effort with their fellow citizens to search for rules that promise to be *mutually agreeable*. It depends, in other words, on their willingness, first, to actively participate in such discourse and, second, to expend mental effort on coming up with rule proposals that they expect to appeal to their fellow citizens as well, instead of focusing their attention on rules that they expect to favor themselves.

SELF-GOVERNMENT, GROUP SIZE, AND CITIZENSHIP

The behavioral attitudes a properly functioning system of self-government requires from its citizens are obviously more demanding than what a properly functioning market—or, more generally, a properly functioning private-law society—asks from its participants. Provided the relevant "rules of the market game" are adequately defined and sufficiently enforced, self-interested individuals can be trusted to adopt the required behavioral attitudes without demanding any further "public" engagement. It is, however, a much more challenging task to provide for an institutional-organizational environment that cultivates and encourages in citizens the behavioral attitudes required for effective self-government.

In his comparison of the liberal and republican theory of the state, Sandel emphasizes the difference between their respective principal concerns. While the former is primarily concerned with the question of what institutional arrangements are most hospitable to individual liberty, the latter asks the question of what institutional arrangements are most hospitable to self-government.[21] The difficulties in providing for arrangements as the republican theory requires are caused by the very publicness of the shared outcomes that citizens coproduce with their active participation in political processes, difficulties that increase with group size. As groups grow larger, the likelihood of an individual participant's contribution having a noticeable effect on the collective outcome decreases, as does the incentive to pay whatever cost one's own engagement involves. Furthermore, with growing group size, the need to delegate decision-making authority to representatives increases, further diluting the connection between an individual citizen's contribution and the shared final outcome.

As Vincent Ostrom details in his *Political Theory of a Compound Republic* (1971), the issue of how to balance the potential advantages of a larger group size with the challenges it poses for the prospect of effective self-government has been a central subject of discussion in *The Federalist Papers*. The general federalist principle of the "dispersion of authority among diverse legislative, executive, and judicial structures" (Ostrom 1986, 123), suggested there as a workable compromise,[22] is subsumed by Ostrom under the label "compound republic." In "a highly federalized (or compounded) system of government" (120), he argues, the "reiteration of patterns of self-government implies that people participate in diverse publics that have critical awareness of what it means to be self-governing" (123).[23]

Such a federalist principle of organization surely facilitates but, as Ostrom (1986, 122) points out, cannot per se guarantee that citizens adopt the behavioral attitudes required to sustain effective self-government. Echoing Ostrom's argument, Richard Wagner (2005, 177) speaks of a "congruence between legal arrangements and moral beliefs," noting that the "practice of self-governance requires a proper mental orientation among the participants" (179). As he puts it, "The characteristics of a system of democratic government will depend upon the habits of governance that are cultivated through democratic practice. Good habits result from good practice, with the goodness or badness of the practice arising through political, not market, processes. Desirable norma- tive conduct is reduced to unconscious choice if incentive features contained within a set of institutional arrangements reinforce that conduct" (Wagner 2002, 114).

Addressing the same issues, Sandel discusses the role of decentralization in politics in providing opportunities for practicing citizenship and the concur- rent need for arrangements that encourage citizens to engage in such practice. While emphasizing the role of "dispersed power and multiple sites of civic for- mation" in facilitating participation in self-rule, he equally stresses the need for "agencies of civic education," agencies that cultivate "the 'character of mind' and 'the habits of the heart' a democratic republic requires" (Sandel 1996a, 70).[24]

If indeed, as the authors quoted earlier argue, sustaining an effective system of self-government requires citizens to adopt behavioral attitudes that cannot be trusted to arise as an automatic by-product even within a federalist institu- tional framework most conducive to citizens' participation, this poses an obvi- ous challenge for an economic approach to politics that focuses on reforms in "the rules of the game" as the principal instrument for addressing problems in social organization. How can one "form in citizens habits and dispositions that equip them for self-government" (Sandel 1996b, 242) if this instrument does not suffice?

THE ETHICS OF CITIZENSHIP

In the concluding sections of *The Reason of Rules*, Geoffrey Brennan and James Buchanan ([1985] 2000, 60) discuss the "problem of 'publicness'" that partici- pation in constitutional choice poses:

> Who are to take upon themselves the personal burden of designing provi- sional proposals for basic changes in the rules when the promised benefits accrue *publicly*, that is, to all members of the political community . . . ? . . . The professional economist must look at the governmental-political pro- cess as driven by the same forces that drive the market process. . . .
>
> It should be evident, however, that the basic analytics of "positive public choice" cannot be readily extended to explain changes in the basic rules of political order that are necessarily "public" in scope. . . . To the extent that "investment" in institutional analysis, design, argument, dialogue, discussion, and persuasion is costly in a personal sense, the

individual of the orthodox model will forgo such investment in favor of more immediate gratification of privately directed desires. . . .

Applied to the problem at hand, which is that of deriving some conceptual explanation of why individuals might be expected to seek out, design, argue for, and support changes in the general rules of the sociopolitical order when, by presumption such behavior would be contrary to identifiable self-interest, it is necessary to resort to some version of "general interest" of "public interest" as the embodiment of a shared moral norm. (160–63)

Following "a shared moral norm" means to be guided in one's conduct by a general behavioral disposition to do what is socially appropriate in the kind of problem or situation one confronts, rather than doing what, in terms of one's immediate self-interest, is "rational" given the situational incentives one faces.[25] Institutional framing is an *indirect* method for inducing self-interested individuals to adopt socially desired behavioral dispositions. Yet if, as argued earlier, even participation-friendly institutions of self-government are insufficient to ensure the kind of civic engagement Brennan and Buchanan's "shared moral norm" calls for, the question arises of what method, other than this *indirect* instrument, may serve the intended purpose. An apparent *direct* method for seeking to install in individuals socially desired behavioral dispositions is the "teaching" of moral norms by whatever strategies may prove successful for the purpose.[26]

It is to this direct method of installing moral dispositions that Buchanan refers when he speaks of the role served by "the moral teacher."[27] There exists, Buchanan ([1991] 2001, 222) argues, an "ethical interdependence" in the sense that we are mutually interested in benefiting from others' moral conduct. Persons rationally want "that others behave more cooperatively," which implies "the possible productivity of investment in the promulgation of moral norms," a sort of investment the analysis of which economists "have tended to neglect" (223). Yet, again, a growing group size reduces "the possible direct incentive that each person has to invest privately in the promulgation of moral norms designed to affect the behavior of others,"[28] necessitating "collective organization of the moral persuasion enterprise" (226).

According to Sandel, republican political theory's insistence on the need for a collectively organized "moral persuasion enterprise" is what sharply separates it from its liberal counterpart.[29] Unlike the latter, Sandel (1996b, 25) argues, republican political theory "does not take people's existing preferences, whatever they may be, and try to satisfy them. It seeks instead to cultivate in citizens the qualities of character necessary to the common good of self-government.

Insofar as certain dispositions, attachments, and commitments are essential to the realization of self-government, republican politics regard moral character as a public, not merely private, concern."[30] While Buchanan and Sandel equally insist on the need to resort to a collectively organized "moral persuasion enterprise," the question remains of how, exactly, this indirect method of installing in citizens the behavioral attitudes conducive to self-government is supposed to work.

CONCLUSION: BEHAVIORAL SYMMETRY, SITUATIONAL AND DISPOSITIONAL RATIONALITY

The public-choice postulate of behavioral symmetry in the study of markets and politics must be qualified, as has been argued in this chapter, if one is to account for the behavioral attitudes that a self-governing community requires from its citizens. The "moral persuasion" that Buchanan, like Sandel, invokes as a necessary requisite obviously goes beyond the explanatory tools that choice theorists conventionally employ in their study of politics. While Buchanan speaks of the need to modify the standard *homo economicus* model in order to provide a systematic place for "moral persuasion" as a behavior-influencing instrument, how, exactly, he wants this model to be modified is not quite so obvious. Some of his arguments on the "different conception of human nature" (Buchanan [1982] 2001, 40) that he has in mind sound as if he sees a need for modifying the self-interest assumption. This appears, for instance, to be implied when he speaks of economists having "great difficulty in moving beyond the rather simplistic, if powerful, models of human behavior grounded in self-interest motivation" and notes that to "hold out hope for reform in the basic rules describing the sociopolitical game, we must introduce elements that violate the self-interest postulate" (Brennan and Buchanan [1985] 2000, 162).

There exists, though, a possibility to meet the theoretical challenge of accounting for the behavioral attitudes effective self-government demands— or, more generally, of accounting for any kind of socially desired behavioral attitudes—that is far less demanding than sacrificing the "self-interest postulate." Installing in individuals socially beneficial behavioral attitudes or dispositions by demanding self-sacrifice will surely be a much more difficult task than teaching them that adopting such attitudes may well be a successful longer-term strategy for realizing their self-interest. All that is required for such change in theoretical perspective is to recognize that, in its traditional interpretation, the *homo economicus* model implies a rather limited understanding of what a "rational pursuit of one's self-interest" means, and that adopting the dispositions of which Buchanan and Sandel speak can be "appropriately defined as 'rational' under a more inclusive definition of rationality" (Buchanan [1982] 2001, 49).

As traditionally interpreted, the economic model of man is based on the limited notion of *situational rationality*, understood as case-by-case maximizing choice. According to this notion, to act rationally means that in every single situation one encounters, one chooses the option that, in terms of the present incentive structure, promises the highest payoff. For "rationality" so understood, to follow "moral norms" of citizenship not only when the situational incentive structure renders it beneficial but as a general principle must indeed appear to "violate the self-interest postulate." A quite different outlook of the relation between rationality and self-interest suggests itself, however, if one allows for the concept of *dispositional rationality* or the *rationality of rule-following*. Rather than focusing on the payoffs to be realized in particular individual cases, as the concept of situational rationality does, this concept draws attention to the fact that by adopting a "moral disposition" a person may be able to realize a more attractive *pattern of payoffs* than could be expected from attempted case-by-case maximization.[31] In other words, the concept of dispositional rationality draws attention to the fact that adopting the civic attitudes of which Buchanan and Sandel speak—like adopting other socially desired dispositions—may be a more effective way for citizens to serve their self-interest than following the logic of situational rationality.

To provide for an environment in which citizens are likely to learn that adopting the behavioral attitudes effective self-government requires is certainly a much more manageable task than finding instruments that induce them to sacrifice their self-interest for the "public good."

NOTES

1. Andrew Farrant and Marion Paganelli (2016, 360) speak of the "supposition of motivational homogeneity when analyzing private and public choices."

2. In somewhat different wording, Buchanan ([1983b] 2000, 15–16 distinguishes the "two separate and distinct elements" as "the familiar *Homo economicus* postulate concerning human behavior" and "the generalized *catallactics* approach to economics."

3. "On several occasions I have referred to Public Choice, inclusively defined and as developed largely in the 1960s and 1970s, as 'a theory of government failure' that offsets the 'theory of market failure' that emerged from theoretical welfare economics. Just as the latter contains demonstrations that observed market processes fail to produce results that satisfy the conditions of allocative efficiency, Public Choice theory . . . contains demonstrations that observed political-governmental processes fail to satisfy the requirements for efficiency in the implementation of corrective measures" (Buchanan [1983a] 2000, 113).

4. "With some legitimacy, Public Choice theorists can claim to have advanced the discussion of comparative institutional alternatives. If we acknowledge that *both* markets and government fail against idealized standards for operation . . . what is to be said about organizational structure. How should the interdependencies among persons in society be institutionalized?" (Buchanan [1983a] 2000, 114).

5. "The purpose of the exercise is conceived to be institutional reform, improvement in the *rules* under which political processes operate. . . . Improvement, or hope for improvement, emerges not from any expectation that observed agents will behave differently from the way the existing set of incentives leads them to behave, but from a shift in the rules that defined these incentives" (Buchanan [1988] 2000, 87). "Only by modelling 'private man' as exclusively seeking to maximize net wealth can the legal framework, the 'laws and institutions,' of the marketplace be designed so as to further the 'general interest.' . . . Comparable principles should tell us that 'public man' must be similarly modeled and for the same reasons. The person who is placed in a position to act on behalf of the state must be modelled as a net-wealth maximizer in his own right if the legal-constitutional constraints that define his authorized powers and his behavior within those powers are to be appropriately designed" (Buchanan [1982] 2001, 52).

6. "When persons are modelled as self-interested in politics, as in other aspects of their behavior, the constitutional challenge becomes one of constructing and designing framework institutions or rules that will, to the maximum extent possible, limit the exercise of such interest in exploitative ways and direct such interest to the furtherance of the general interest" (Buchanan [1983b] 2000, 23).

7. "Idealized politics becomes an extension of the reciprocal and voluntary exchange process of the market. . . . In its most abstract sense, politics becomes the complex exchange among all members of a potential political order, who personally and separately enter into the relationship because of shared expectation of mutual gain" (Buchanan and Congleton [1988] 2003, 21).

8. "Since in a democratic society citizens are regarded as free and equal persons, the principles of a democratic conception of justice may be viewed as specifying the fair terms of cooperation between citizens so conceived" (Rawls 2001, 7). About the relations among persons in a "constitutional democracy," Rawls (1963, 99) notes, "These persons . . . are mutually self-interested, that is, their allegiance to their established practices is normally founded on the prospect of self-advantage. . . . Each person will . . . insist on advantage for himself and thus on a common advantage" (Rawls, 103, 106).

9. "This approach . . . draws attention directly to the *process* of exchange. . . . The emphasis shifts, directly and immediately, to all *processes of voluntary agreement* among persons" (Buchanan [1983b] 2000, 16–17.

10. "The direct implication of normative individualism . . . is that the idealized politics must reflect contractarian foundations. . . . The normative stance . . . leads, necessarily in our view, to some sort of contractarian exercise of legitimization or justification for politics" (Buchanan and Congleton [1988] 2003, 21, 24). "What I have attempted to do is to generalize . . . the traditional theory of the social contract. . . . It is this conception, I believe, which . . . constitutes the most appropriate basis for a democratic society" (Rawls 1971, viii).

11. Corporate entities formed as "cooperative ventures" within the legal-institutional framework of the private law society are based on social contracts specifying the terms under which the participants cooperate.

12. "That it is thus ignorance of the future outcome which makes possible agreement on rules which serve as common means for a variety of purposes is recognized by the practice in many instances of deliberately making the outcome unpredictable in order to make agreement on the procedure possible" (Hayek 1976, 4).

13. "Persons are engaged, as natural equals, in a process of conceptualized exchange, in which the separate liberties of individual action are given up. A person gives up his own liberty to act unilaterally against others in exchange for like sacrifices on the part of others, thereby generating social order that is mutually beneficial to all participants" (Buchanan 2005, 43).

14. "If, however, the individual is placed in a genuine *constitutional* choice setting, where the alternatives are differing decision rules under which a whole sequence of particular proposals will be considered, he will evaluate the predicted working properties of rules over the whole anticipated sequence. If, on balance, the operation of a defined rule is expected to yield net benefits over the sequence, the individual may vote to approve the rule, even if he predicts that he must personally be subjected to loss or damage in some particular 'plays' of the political game" (Buchanan [1987] 2001, 73).

15. "It is necessary to distinguish sharply between day-to-day political decision-making . . . and 'constitutional' decision-making. . . . It is precisely at this stage that the individualist model can rescue the 'public interest,' indirectly" (Buchanan [1966] 2001, 255).

16. "The term 'citizen' has, of course, two distinct meanings. A citizen can simply be someone who under the laws and practices of a state has both rights and duties, irrespective of the character of the state. . . . One can be a good citizen in an autocratic state. One can also be *only* a good citizen in a democratic state, that is one can obey the law, pay taxes, drive carefully and behave oneself socially (say minimizing offence to others) but not work with others on any matters that effect public policy. . . . It is this minimalist approach to citizenship that made me, thirty years ago, voice skepticism about an old tradition of citizenship education as Civics which stressed the primacy of 'the rule' of law and learning about the constitution. For citizenship surely involves public discussion of whether laws work badly or are unjust and how they can be changed" (Crick 2007, 243).

17. "Broadly there are two theories of the modern democratic state, mirrored in popular understanding or behavior: that the maintenance of free institutions depends on a high level of popular *participation* in public affairs, both as a practical necessity and as a moral or civic duty; or that competitive elections create governments that can modify and uphold a legal order under which individuals can lead their lives with as little interference as possible from the state and minimal public obligations. . . . Historians and political philosophers call the first 'civic republicanism' and call the second 'the liberal theory of the state'" (Crick 2007, 244).

18. "The popular, everyday conception of democracy is political liberty or free government. Another familiar definition is government by discussion" (Knight [1941] 1982, 219).

19. "The definition of democracy as 'government by discussion' implies that individual values can and do change in the process of decision-making. Men must be free to choose, and they must maintain an open mind if the democratic mechanism is to work at all. . . . The whole period of activity during which temporary majority decisions are reached and reversed, new compromises appear and are approved or overthrown, must be considered as one of genuine discussion" (Buchanan [1954] 1999, 99).

20. In a footnote, Rawls ([1997] 1999, 580) adds, "Deliberative democracy limits the reasons citizens may give in support of their political opinions to reasons consistent with their seeing other citizens as equals."

21. I am paraphrasing Sandel (1996a, 58), who speaks of "economic," not "institutional," arrangements.

22. For "small republics to join in the formation of a larger confederate republic," Ostrom (1986, 118) notes, was seen as a means by which "simultaneous advantage could be gained by recourse to both small and large scales of organization."

23. "Democratic institutions might attain stable forms where the autonomy of diverse self-governing communities could exist in the context of concurrent and overlapping units of government. Such a political order is many-centered and can be characterized as *polycentric*, where no single center exercises dominance over the rest" (Ostrom 1986, 122).

24. "Republican political theory teaches that to be free is to share in governing a political community that controls its own fate. Self-government in this sense requires political communities that control their destinies, and citizens who identify sufficiently with those communities to think and act with a view to the common good. Cultivating in citizens the virtue, independence,

One of the best ways to introduce it is through Friedrich Hayek's work. Hayek defines his position as part of a historical process and as a logical continuation of an intellectual tradition. He writes in the first paragraph of his *Law, Legislation and Liberty* that "the first attempt to secure individual liberty by constitutions has evidently failed" (Hayek 1973, 1). By that he meant that "the pattern set by Montesquieu and the framers of the American constitution has not achieved what it was meant to achieve"—that is to say, it failed to provide institutional safeguards for political freedom. In these circumstances, Hayek saw his task as twofold: on the one hand, to investigate the causes of this failure, and on the other hand, "to ask what those founders of liberal constitutionalism would do today if, pursuing the aims they did, they could command all the experience we have gained in the meantime" (1). To carry out this project requires, admits Hayek, "little less than doing for the twentieth century what Montesquieu had done for the eighteenth" and to focus on issues on which "thought seems to have made little advance since David Hume and Immanuel Kant." In several respects, "it will be at the point at which they left off that our analyses will have to resume" (6).

That being said, the reconstruction of liberal constitutionalism is not meant to be a mere return to classic sources. In Hayek's view, it requires "a critical re-examination not only of current beliefs but of the real meaning of some fundamental conceptions to which we still pay lip service." Moreover, the outcomes of these analyses are nothing else but "suggestions for a radical departure from established traditions," while our greatest advantage in this attempt is that "there is much we ought to have learned from the history of the last two hundred years that those men with all their wisdom could not have known" (Hayek 1973, 2). At the core of this endeavor is the perceived crisis of the Western modern governance system. A profound structural crisis is undermining the societies that are claiming liberal constitutionalism as their basic organizing principle. In Hayek's view, this critical reexamination bolstered by an acute sense of the historical experience leads us to the conclusion that "the aims of those men seem to be as valid as ever. But as their means have proved inadequate, new institutional invention is needed" (2). That institutional invention has to maintain the preeminence of the fundamental principle of the rule of law, which must remain unchallenged. It is the cornerstone and the most important feature of constitutionalism.

From the perspective whose spokesperson is Hayek, the main reason for the failure of the first grand constitutional experiment is precisely the tension between the rule of law and the rule of will incorporated into the modern constitutions via the democratic principle. The actual constitutional arrangements especially in the past 100 years or so, "the original limited Republic has morphed to a significant extent into a nearly unlimited democracy where is little principled limit on the reach of the political into society" (Wagner 2016, vii). He uses the logic of an entangled system of political economy "to explain how a regime founded on a *constitution of liberty*, where citizens pretty much can do as they choose so long as they respect the equivalent rights of other people, can morph into a *constitution of control*, wherein political imperatives come to dominate large swaths of social life" (vii).

To sum up, between the political process and the principles of the rule of law, as embodied in modern constitutional systems, is a tension of radical importance for the present political evolutions. The main problem is how to accommodate democracy and the rule of law in the same constitutional framework. Could both of them be embodied in the same governance system structure, as imagined by the classical liberal-democrat tradition? Could the intrinsic tensions find a solution at the level of principles and at the level of the constitutional structure? Should we, in fact, look outside the formal constitution to the cultural, normative, and social institutions and processes for a possible resolution? Should we rethink the relationship between the economy, society, and the political in our search for a solution? The insights generated by Wagner in his attempt to identify and diagnose the sources of the current crisis, insights based on the notion of entangled political economy, open up a fresh perspective to an alternative way of thinking about constitutional order and its preconditions.

POLITICAL CONSTITUTIONALISM AND ITS DIAGNOSIS OF THE CONSTITUTIONAL-POLITICAL PREDICAMENT

The alternative perspective on constitutional order and the sources of the contemporary governance crisis starts with the criticism of liberal constitutionalism. From the point of view of what has been called "political," "realist," or "republican" constitutionalism, the tensions between the rule of law principle and the political activities of interest groups as manifested in democratic liberal systems are not a pathological phenomenon but an unavoidable matter of fact. They are one basic form of manifestation of the "political." That is the "realist" element of it. At the same time, it considers that the way we currently understand the problem of constitution and constitutionalism is dominated by a specific and limiting view that has its basic source in the 19th century's climate of ideas. In this view, as we have seen, the constitution is the central element in a general strategy of limitation of power as a means to legitimize, regulate, and control it. In emphasizing the negative limits imposed by constitutions, it "mistakenly takes part as a whole." In fact, constitutionalism must be understood as a part of the legal-political system and its associated processes. That is its "political" facet. "Political" constitutionalism claims to be the heir of a tradition that includes Aristotle, Machiavelli, and Rousseau and that implicitly defines constitutionalism with reference to the process of "combining the rule of law with the rule of men." Hence its "republicanism." Moreover, it builds on the nineteenth- and twentieth-century social theory and appeals to social sciences more freely (Castiglione 1996; Bellamy 1996). Drawing on the work of the major sociologists and social theorists of the past 200 years, the political-republican constitutionalism offers an analysis of the past two centuries of constitutional evolution as interesting and challenging as that offered by Hayek or the field of constitutional political economy.

Richard Bellamy (1996) is a good illustration of the political constitutionalist perspective. The basic elements of constitutionalism are in this view rights and the separation of power, plus representative government. In recent years, he says, those elements have managed to predominate, and thus we have a situation in which rights are considered the prime component of a constitution. As a consequence, the normative framework within which politics operates is overestimated. At the same time, the political and institutional mechanisms receive only a secondary recognition. Constitution has been seen as "only a set of legally entrenched rights" that can and must dominate the political process. Politics—seen as real politics—is outside and somehow in tension with the constitutional structure. But if we consider constitutionalism as a form of government, we come to understand that, in fact, the separation between political process and constitution is itself a part of politics: "The protection and the realization of rights and the rule of law fall within politics" (Bellamy 1996, 436). Judicial review plays a role, but this role is subordinate rather than dominant. Bringing to the fore the entangled nature of governance and institutional systems, probably the decisive feature of this view is the point that government serves not only to control and limit power but also to identify, safeguard, and promote values and interests. Constitutional government "is a form of government that brings various groups into dialogue and guarantees the equal participation in the political body and the basis for everyone to pursue their own interests, values and happiness" (Bellamy 1996, 436).

In the political constitutionalist view, the problem of constitutionalism has to be analyzed in the broader context of the impact of the social forces generated by the industrial societies on liberal thought and practice. Constitutional arrangements have to be seen historically and dynamically as part of a larger system of evolving social forces and their associated ideas. In this light, we realize that as a consequence of this historical process, today "no longer a part of the dynamic of history, liberalism has simply been reduced to present himself as a culmination of the historical process in a desperate attempt to circumscribe and contain those social forces which threaten to undermine him" (Bellamy 1992, 2). The contemporary governance crisis has its roots precisely in these developments.

To get a better sense of this diagnostic, we will follow Bellamy's account claiming that we have to go back to the shortcomings of the initial classical liberalism. A closer look, argues Bellamy, reveals that its nature was essentially ethical. Moreover, ethical liberalism had two basic elements—an ethical thesis and a social one, "the latter providing the former with a coherence it otherwise lacked." In spite of other differences between their views, all initial liberal theorists "assumed that a coherent theory of freedom existed and that it was possible to maximize an equal set of harmoniously coexisting liberties for all members of society" (Bellamy 1996, 436–37). They assumed an implicit convergence of preferences and views. Yet, this conjecture or desideratum was more elusive than expected. As years went by, social change increased the social heterogeneity and the diversity of preferences and values. It becomes increasingly problematic to decide between conflicting liberties and values, how to balance them, and how to arrive at the greatest possible liberty in these circumstances. Moreover, the task to discover a criterion for liberty and how a hierarchy of liberties could be construed proved to be even more elusive. Prioritizing liberty over other values is not enough, because a conflict of values remains open within the liberties and their interpretations.

The "social thesis" assumes that as the society develops, "progress" will take place, and this will lead to the harmonization of values and individual life plans. As such, it offered the prospects of a solution to the problem of conflict of values. A built-in convergence mechanism was supposed to operate spontaneously. But, from around 1870, the social evolutions seemed to disconfirm the optimist liberal social thesis. The need for a mechanism that could facilitate the harmonization of different interests and conflicting values *and* the control of the relevant groups over government became more and more stringent. The liberals, explains Bellamy, tried to solve this problem by appealing to the market and the market process. It was assumed that as long as the market is free, the conflicts of values will find a natural and spontaneous solution. Market was considered a neutral and fair mechanism of mediation of the plurality of human values.

However, once more the evolution of social reality challenged liberalism. It looked like the market had some limits in solving the problems created by the conflict of values. In other words, in a functionally and ethically differentiated world, no moral theory could solve the problem, while the spontaneous socioeconomic process put in place by the competitive market could indeed alleviate the problem but was unable to solve it as well. The facts of modern deep pluralism and diversity are too powerful. The result was that between 1880 and 1930 the necessity to rethink the foundations of modern political order became more and more pressing.

From the point of view of political constitutionalism, one could trace how this challenge was met in the works of three great social theorists—Vilfredo Pareto, Emile Durkheim, and Max Weber. All three offered a new account of the nature of political (and implicitly constitutional) order. Each developed in different but complementary ways a redefinition of the political problems, enlightened the social foundations of political order, and articulated the social principles on which they thought to construct a new polity. All pointed toward a pluralism based on an analysis of modern social reality. The increased division of labor, the specialization and fragmentation of the modern world, the ubiquity of social conflict, and the rationalization and bureaucratization of the institutions and human relationships undermined the very possibility of an order based on a classical liberal vision. Even the autonomous capacity of action and choice, so important in the liberal perspective, was weakened by these social evolutions. To neglect this fact in our approach to constitutional order and institutional designs is to invite crisis. A new version of constitutionalism, political and realist in its assumptions and republican in its implications, was necessary.

The conclusion is that in order to respond to the contemporary crisis, we need a renewed realist conception of politics and constitutionalism. This renewed conception has to be more in consonance with the republican tradition than with the ethical-legalistic-economic liberalism of the 19th century. The shift toward social process is a shift from standard rational choice to more socially embedded conceptualizations. Its central feature is that it has to view political order and agreement more as a result of socialization, persuasion, and coercion than as a result of rational convergence of ideals and support of an abstract, neutral legal system. If that is the case, one could clearly see at this point the relevance of Wagner's entangled political economy.

Probably the central concept of the "political" constitutionalist view is "accommodation" with its associated assumption of ongoing negotiations and adjustments. The set of problems covered by the concept of accommodation is as important as the problem of the limits of power is to liberal/legalist constitutionalists. The constitutional structure is the centerpiece for a broad social process of accommodation of liberty and authority. The problem of accommodation is ubiquitous: accommodation of the rule of men with the rule of law, of different values, of different groups, of different interests, and so on (Bellamy 1992, 2). The entanglement of economics, politics, and social actors and forces needs a governance structure. In this view, the liberal approach is open to criticism because it focuses on one limited aspect of the problem. It misses the real dimensions of "entanglement." It overemphasizes in an uncritical way the tension between the rule of men and the rule of law, and overestimates the importance of the second. With its emphasis on rights and judicial process, it fails to take into account the entangled social and political process and the complex set of institutions regulating the distribution of power, rights, and obligations in society.

Again, one can easily see how Wagner's work (1993, 2010, 2016) is more than relevant in this context. His approach is based in the classical liberal tradition, but by using the apparatus of political economy he is in fact drawing attention to the broader social and political forces and processes, and to the ways economics and politics are entangled. In doing this, he builds a bridge between the two perspectives. Constitutions, he explains, "may be construed not so much as a social contract, metaphorically speaking, but as a set of rules and institutions, themselves produced through social processes" (Wagner 1993, 19). The entangled political economy approach allows us to develop analytics of these social processes. At the same time, it allows us to approach the classical liberal perspective from a broader angle and to better understand the limits and the pressure put on it by the current developments.

THE CHALLENGE RESTATED

We now have a clearer view of the difference between the two perspectives, each offering a distinctive take on the current constitutional and political predicament. On the one hand, in the legalist constitutionalism view, we have the departure from the discipline imposed by the rule of law—the outbreak of a political war of redistribution is not an accident. It is a process framed, then fueled, by factors associated with the constitutional structure. Far from being "an umpire which enforces the rule of the game, the state has become the most potent weapon in an incessant political conflict over resources." Corporate interests and pressure groups "are continuously active by lobbying, colonization or co-option of regulatory authorities, or just plain corruption to mold these rules to suit their own interests. . . . Civil life soon comes to resemble the Hobbesian state of nature from which the state was meant to deliver us" (Gray 1993, 12). This is a pathological situation, and the anomie must be dispelled through a solid enforcement of the rule of law principle.

On the other hand, from a political constitutionalism point of view, the situation should not be defined as pathological. It simply is. It is a matter of fact. Given the social order of high modernization, it is unavoidable to have a complex structure with different loci of power and decision-making. Polycentricity has its own dynamics. To curb it under the pressure of a rigid, rights-centered legal and constitutional ideal type, predefined and narrowly conceived, will generate a series of side effects and unintended consequences that have to be addressed. The de facto social trends must be regularized and institutionalized.

From this standpoint, as we have seen, liberal constitutionalism itself may be a source of instability and disorder: "Attempts to devise supposedly neutral legal frameworks, protecting certain rights and liberties, privilege particular points of view at the expense of others of equal importance. As a result, they become a source of conflict rather than of stability" (Bellamy 1992, 261). To avoid this, in place of a doctrine of rights and justice, constitutionalism has to be rethought as "a set of procedures and institutions, which via the redistribution of power become capable of giving expression to a plurality of competing values in society and of securing an accommodation between them" (216). The standard strategy to create and enforce a neutral legal framework meant to restrain and control the groups, with interests or values in conflict, is doomed to fail. In fact, this was plainly demonstrated by reality—constitutional practices and structures reflect these social processes and realities and align with them in spite of the fact that constitutional and political thought is still stuck up at the level of eighteenth- and nineteenth-century political theory. A constitution conceived in classical liberal terms, derived from this thought, is unable to stop or control interest groups and conflicts. An attempt to rethink constitutionalism on the basis of the same assumptions would lead to a dead end. "It is a mistake to think that ethical, rights liberalism represents the only legitimate legal system capable of upholding individual freedom" (257).

One must stress once again that in the realist-constitutionalist's view the basic error of the liberal constitutionalist project is primarily due to a misunderstanding of the social reality. "Societies . . . mirror the balance of power of the various groups within them and the conventions and customs of the economic and political practices in which their members are engaged" (Bellamy

1992, 249). The legalist-constitutionalism approach is wrong about the social reality, about the facts—"Neutralist liberals are especially guilty of failing to see how the institutions of the market and democracy do not operate according to neutral norms of universal rationality but reflect the organizational capacities of different corporate and group interests." The rejection of the liberal error has two important consequences. On the one hand, it challenges the dominant conceptual structures and approaches, and it leads to a reconsideration of the role of social theory in political thought and practice. On the other hand, it offers a "realist" approach to politics that "focuses on conflict and the role of power in holding the community together" (253). "Realism" becomes the key feature of this view.

As Bellamy put it, "A complex plurality of political mechanisms must be devised which facilitates the influence and scrutiny of government policy by all relevant groups and individuals." This requires the decentralization of power and widespread political participation. "Such a system replaces substantive 'moralistic' constitutional constraints on majority rule and government action with 'realistic' procedural democratic checks and controls. Procedures allowing a plurality of views to be expressed, and which encourage their mediation, take place of the pre-political notions of rights and justice" (Bellamy 1992, 259).

In between the two perspectives stands the entangled political economy territory opened up by Wagner's insights. His contribution in this respect may be understood as an attempt to negotiate a path between the two. His solution is to combine a transactional, economic perspective with a social and power-based perspective. He starts, however, in the public-choice tradition with the economic approach. Entangled political economy, he writes, "claims that all processes associated with political economy have a transactional nature." It tries to transcend "the conventional theoretical antinomy wherein economy is treated as organized through market transactions, while politics is organized through teleologically guided planning." Within "the social subsystems denoted as polity and economy each contain many organizations with their precincts and with those organizations interacting among themselves in both cooperative and antagonistic ways" (Wagner 2016, 164). We need to look at social order as an intertwined set of enterprises, some commercial and others political. The power-related process is not totally devoid of a transactional nature. "Those enterprises don't operate independently of one another in separated ponds of activity. They are intertwined in a complex human ecology" (165). This "ecology" is unavoidably a space of polycentric arrangements. The convergence between Wagner's entangled political economy and the Ostroms' polycentricity becomes obvious at this point—so, too, does the relevance of the Ostroms' work regarding the constitutional predicament of modernity and the contemporary crisis of governance and public administration.

We are now, in light of all the above, able to better perceive both (1) the contribution of entangled political economy for our understanding of the tensions behind the constitutional sources of the contemporary crisis of governance and (2) the position of entangled political economy in the broader picture of the tasks ahead in building a bridge between the two perspectives. Indeed, the entangled political economy approach and its associated conceptual apparatus seem to have the potential to maintain the classical liberal tradition while at the same time engaging with elements of the political republican tradition and the criticism mounted by it. The challenge is not an easy one.

These and similar themes and challenges stand before the entangled political economy attempt to redefine and reconstruct our approach to social order, constitutional systems, and the current governance crisis. Wagner's pioneering work has given us new and promising venues and many questions to pursue. Is it possible to develop a combination of systems theory approach and entangled political economy to deal with these issues? Constitutional political economy seems to be more rooted in the liberal constitutionalist tradition. However, if one is looking at the Italian roots of public choice and their realist focus on rent-seeking and competition, one could see a strong potential for integrating some of the sociological and political process aspects claimed by the republican tradition. How should we better use the public choice and constitutional political economy tradition to deal with the competing interpretations of the current predicament? And if that is possible, could the two perspectives be reconciled in a unifying framework? Is it desirable or even possible to bypass them and develop a third, alternative perspective? Could that be done in constitutional political economy terms, as framed by the entangled political economy perspective? Wagner's work has put us in the position to not only ask the key questions and better understand our contemporary predicament but also start thinking about how to respond in systematic ways, leading to a fascinating and very relevant research program.

ACKNOWLEDGMENT

This work was supported by a grant from the Romanian Ministry of Education and Research, CNCS—UEFISCDI, project number PN-III-P4-ID-PCE-2020-1076, within PNCDI III.

REFERENCES

Bellamy, R. 1992. *Liberalism and Modern Society: An Historical Argument*. Oxford: Polity Press.

———. 1996. "The Political Form of the Constitution: The Separation of Powers, Rights and Representative Democracy." *Political Studies* 44, no. 3: 436–56.

Bertalanffy, L. V. 1968. "General Systems Theory as Integrating Factor in Contemporary Science." *Akten des XIV. Internationalen Kongresses für Philosophie* 2: 335–40.

Buchanan, J. M. 1991. *The Economics and Ethics of Constitutional Order*. Ann Arbor: University of Michigan Press.

Castiglione, D. 1996. "The Political Theory of the Constitution." *Political Studies* 44, no. 3: 417–35.

Gray, J. 1993. *Postliberalism: Studies in Political Thought*. London: Routledge.

Hayek, F. A. 1973. *Law, Legislation and Liberty*. Vol. 1. Chicago: University of Chicago Press.

Wagner, R. E. 1993. *Parchment, Guns and Constitutional Order*. Cheltenham, UK: Edward Elgar.

———. 2010. *Mind, Society, and Human Action: Time and Knowledge in a Theory of Social Economy*. London: Routledge.

———. 2016. *Politics as a Peculiar Business: Insights from a Theory of Entangled Political Economy*. Cheltenham, UK: Edward Elgar.

———. 2019. *Public Choice. Introductory Course Notes*. Fairfax, VA: George Mason University.

Chapter 7

The Entangled Mind

James Caton

D uring my years as a graduate student, Richard E. Wagner taught the second Market Process Theory graduate seminar. As his book that he assigned for the class, *Mind, Society, and Human Action* (2010), suggests, Wagner saw his task as conveying a theory of society and its autonomous agents. All societies include markets and government. Members of those societies might be more or less entrepreneurial. Their entrepreneurial efforts, however, are significantly shaped by institutions in the form of shared expectations and systems of rules and enforcement (Baumol 1990; North 1990). Such social systems, while they might experience periods of stability, are continually fraught with conflict at all margins of human interaction.

Wagner brought to my attention the problem of conflicting plans. In one of our many meetings—he was the chair of my dissertation—he mentioned that even individuals are filled with conflicting motivations. An individual may adopt one or another plan, but the road to a plan's implementation is hardly direct, and the victory of any given plan is more or less impermanent. Individuals who attempt to cooperate might find cooperation inhibited by conflicting perspectives. The challenge of a theory of social economy is to describe how individuals and collectives form and execute their plans in spite of conflict pervasive at multiple levels of analysis.

The foil to this research program was equilibrium theory in all its forms. Economic theory's commitment to well-ordered preferences—at least as an analytical device—seemed to assume the answers to the questions that economic theory is tasked with answering. Wagner breathed life into a *very* Austrian research program, asking the same questions concerning assumptions of equilibrium theory that perturbed Hayek (1937, 1962), Lachmann ([1956] 1978), and Kirzner (1966). Plans are continually in flux due to changing objective circumstances as well as changing subjective data.

To tackle these problems, Wagner commonly pointed to the emerging toolset provided by complexity scholars. "Complexity" is an enigmatic term that refers to a mix of nontraditional approaches, including applications of network theory, evolutionary theory, and agent-based models, among other overlapping approaches. It turns out that included under the heading of complex adaptive systems are basically all human social systems. I had been predisposed toward this perspective as I had spent the early part of my graduate career taking a deep dive into Hayek's work. It also helped that Scott Scheall had brought to my attention Hayek's (1962) "Rules, Perception, and Intelligibility" in a recently published volume of more methodologically advanced works, *The Market and Other Orders*. As I studied under Wagner, I began to consider how this methodology could be applied to agent-based models, a pursuit that only a small number of scholars have taken up (e.g., Bylund 2015; Holian and Newell 2017; Keyhani 2016, 2019). These explorations helped me spell out the more general perspective of a theory of entanglement. Between the vision conveyed by Wagner in my meetings with him and that presented by Hayek, I had no shortage of inspiration for thinking through problems that would otherwise be unapproachable.

Projects that I have engaged across my professional career have all been informed by my interaction with Wagner and his work. A consistent theme throughout this development is the significance of agent perception, *thymology* as Ludwig von Mises phrased it, to the evolution of social processes (see also Wagner 2006). The agenda that has unfolded as I have developed this emphasis within Wagner's larger paradigm guides the structure of this chapter and is as follows:

1. Knowledge is partial, skewed, and distributed.

2. Perspective matters. Just as the theorist uses a model of the world, actors also employ models in the form of heuristics rules and narratives to interpret information.

3. Shared mental models transform over the course of conflict, conversation, and cooperation within the arena of social interaction.

4. Communities and the models guiding member action are entangled. Agents subject to multiple affiliations must interface and hierarchically order models from various domains.

These represent key, discrete analytical units that are foundational for an entangled social theory. A theory of entanglement respects methodological individualism while providing a theoretical scaffold that allows collectives and individuals to operate corporately. Economic theory is ultimately useful if its application illuminates our understanding of the world. Theory helps us to abstract from the noisy data of the world. Yet, key components of neoclassical economic theory, like perfect knowledge among agents and the ceteris paribus condition, are convenient analytical devices that obscure the role of knowledge in society. Naive application of this theory can be just as harmful to analysis as the total absence of economic theory from analysis. The strictness of these conditions and the failure to model the conditions of fallible man—*homo fallibilis*—cut short the task of the economist, which is to explain how plans of relatively myopic agents ever develop coherence among one another and coherence with the agent's environment more generally.

The job of the theorist is to develop and apply a theoretical structure that can illuminate the problem of plan coordination in any context. We have a rich inheritance to serve us in this task: Frank Knight elaborated the role of the entrepreneur in bearing uncertainty; Hayek on the role of knowledge, perception, and communication; Ronald Coase on transaction costs; James Buchanan on collective action problems, including pre-constitutional bargaining that shapes our shared perception of the world; and many others who have continued in their footsteps. These are the mainline influences that I believe most strongly shaped Wagner's thought. And, of course, we have Wagner himself, who, even in his early work, continually proclaimed the significance of ideas and models that agents use to frame action. I build from these same foundations in my elaboration of a research program that I received from Wagner. Here I will outline the varying scales of analysis required for theory to cohere to its object of analysis: society with its autonomous members and its institutions.

THE PROBLEM: KNOWLEDGE IS PARTIAL, SKEWED, AND DISTRIBUTED

Wagner's call for development of entangled political economy is recognition of many of the same shortcomings of equilibrium modeling that Hayek also recognized. The object of political economy is human society with its agents and myriad organizations and institutions that they develop and in which they participate. To make analysis tractable, economists often prefer to engage in research using methods that allow them to statistically test hypotheses. This approach constrains the aspects of society and scope of questions that one can consider in analysis. Since this shift, the prevalence of robust economic treatises has waned.

A student of society, however, requires more than a narrow perspective. The operations of society are complex and often hidden from the view of the theorist. Theory is a lens that improves our *understanding* of the object of analysis by moving attention to relevant, generalizable traits of that object while abstracting away from less pertinent details. Statistics, while it might improve our understanding of a given phenomenon, is a tool that contributes to the analysis of the theorist. It should not be a tool that constrains the scope of social theory (Hayek 1952a). Likewise, our job as economists is not to reduce all explanations of social phenomena to application of price theory but, rather, to include price theory as part of our explanations. These are tools that make up a broader toolset.

Perhaps the greatest indicator of Wagner's contribution to Austrian analysis is the consonance of his work with that of Hayek. In his 1976 article in the *American Economic Review*, Wagner asserts that "the prescriptive use of optimality models of local government requires a framework in which the analyst knows *by assumption* the internal mental states of the participants in the economic process. Once the essential privacy of individual minds is recognized, however, the analyst can no longer adhere to such a framework" (Wagner 1976, 110). Wagner cites Hayek (1937, 1945) in defense of an analytical commitment to agent subjectivity that, in the least, respects the variety of viewpoints and the complexity present within a given institutional context. Hayek (1937) recognized many core issues of concern to a theory of entanglement. He identified that equilibrium theory does little to shed light on *how* resources and, more importantly, expectations are coordinated. Equilibrium theory asserts that economic activity tends toward equilibrium. Additional features might be added to models to slow movement toward equilibrium or include the effect of inefficiencies. Yet, key to all this is that the data are known ex ante and that they can be used as input into the equilibrium model.

This picture of the economic world is sorely incomplete. Agent expectations are formed only in terms of prices and quantities of goods in their relation to agent utility. Agent plans are assumed to conform to one another, but in reality, plans often conflict. And even if agents intend to cooperate, differences in interpretation of existing facts are enough to lead to sets of plans that are mutually inconsistent and that are inconsistent with the environment. Hayek's insight suggests that a theory of political economy must explain how knowledge is acquired and how it is shared (Boettke and López 2002). Knowledge is often an inherent part of processes that structure human action. And very often the actors involved are less than fully aware that the processes in which they participate serve the function of generating and sharing knowledge.

The entrepreneur plays a fundamental role in these processes. One need not operate a firm for long to accept Knight's assertion that the entrepreneur's participation in a market is filled with uncertainty. It is the entrepreneur's job to reduce the number and extent of these blind spots, thereby improving the production of value for the consumer. The discoveries made by entrepreneurs cannot be hidden from others into perpetuity. Learning of one tends to promote learning by many. Yet, in equilibrium models, uncertainty cannot be substantively included within agent choices. Uncertainty exists only in terms of shocks that ultimately promote a change in equilibrium conditions, meaning that the shocks generate new equilibria with new resource allocations. There is no discovery process. Responses to changes are automatic as new knowledge of the shock is swiftly provided to all agents so that they immediately respond to events that were not included in their prior set of expectations. They do not in any way anticipate these events if the data concerning them are not given ex ante. As Knight and Hayek have shown, entrepreneurs alleviate uncertainty through a process of trial and error whereby they form a set of plans sufficiently flexible to mitigate losses from unexpected events.

Focus on the entrepreneur enables the analyst to frame the decentralized nature of knowledge and the economic activity supported by that knowledge. Knowledge is distributed across time and place. Hayek spent the decades following his engagement in the socialist calculation debate (Hayek [1935a] 1948, [1935b] 1948, [1940] 1948) identifying the nature of this distribution and its role in economic analysis. Whereas Mises ([1920] 1990) emphasized the role of property rights as prerequisite to price formation, Hayek goes a step further and links decentralized coordination through the price system as enabling integration of disparate knowledge (Lavoie [1985] 2015). The price system communicates investor expectations of relevant scarcities to entrepreneurs, thus influencing the level of profits earned as a result. The fundamental role of the entrepreneur is to bear uncertainty while exercising judgment over the use of resources under control (Knight [1921] 1964; see also Foss and Klein 2012). Hayek (1945) explains that the price system helps profit-seeking entrepreneurs allocate resources away from uses that produce relatively less value as compared with uses that promote relatively greater value. This can only occur under conditions where individuals are granted autonomy that enables local actors to exploit knowledge that can promote net improvements in value creation. Thus, entrepreneurial profits coordinate value-creating activities in a competitive market economy, allowing resources to flow toward entrepreneurs who most efficiently provide value to consumers.

The entrepreneur, the agent that acts to reduce the costs of uncertainty, is a key player in nonequilibrium economic theory, yet the driver of economic change is moved to the background in equilibrium theory. As William Baumol (1968, 66) reminds us, "The prince of Denmark has been expunged from the discussion of Hamlet." By building on substantive microfoundations that include the entrepreneur, one can begin to understand society as a domain where actors attempt to leverage their knowledge of the world in their application of resources under their direct control, as well as influence over resources outside their direct control. And we can understand how markets generate different sorts of outcomes in different contexts—especially under different institutional arrangements. In this frame, conflicting plans suggest conflicting uses of resources that must inevitably be resolved. The market mechanism adjudicates these conflicts in favor of efficiency. One cannot comment on the systematic tendency of nonmarket arrangements for adjudicating between conflicting plans without elaboration of institutional context that exists only in the background of the neoclassical paradigm.

Enter Coase (1937, 1960), who tied the common thread of transactions costs through economic analysis. Coase identifies that a fundamental function of institutions is to reduce the cost of transacting or, put more generally, to reduce the cost of plan coordination. In the Coasean perspective, transaction costs explain why there is a limit to market coordination of resources, thus necessitating the existence of firms and a broad set of institutions, especially clearly defined and enforceable property rights (see also North 1990). The Coasean perspective need not reduce institutions to a neoclassical black box as implied by Solow (1956).

Coase identified that firms incur a cost in accessing markets for resources à la carte. In many cases, entrepreneurs benefit by contracting labor over an extended period of time so as to reallocate workers' efforts as circumstances change. Likewise, a firm might vertically integrate so as to reduce the uncertainty faced in gathering products. This can be quite costly, but it can also improve the flexibility of a firm, improving its ability to exploit emerging profit opportunities and to shift resources away from less profitable opportunities.

Most important for a theory of social economy, Coase (1992, 717) guides us away from a world where interaction is costless, demanding instead that the analyst recognize "the crucial importance of the legal system." This supports shared mental structures that guide human activity and support adjudication of conflict (Denzau and North 1994). In this vein, Coase (1992, 716) continues: "In fact, a large part of what we think of as economic activity is designed to accomplish what high transaction costs would otherwise prevent or to reduce transaction costs so that individuals can freely negotiate and we can take advantage of that diffused knowledge of which Hayek has told us." How can we make an analytical leap from plan coordination within a competitive market to explaining how a competitive market can exist at all? How precisely do entrepreneurs reduce transaction costs in order to facilitate cooperation in market and nonmarket contexts? Here, we must return to Hayek's teacher, Ludwig von Mises, in his consideration of what he termed *thymology* or what is referred to across the Viennese tradition and the broader Kantian tradition as *understanding* (Dekker 2016; Gadamer 1975).[1]

PERSPECTIVE MATTERS, OR AGENT UNDERSTANDING

Long before new institutional scholarship focused on mental models, Mises noted that recognition of internal mental states of acting agents is required for a theory of human action ([1949] 1996, 177): "Thinking and action are inseparable. Every action is always based on a definite idea about causal relations. He who thinks a causal relation thinks a theorem. Action without thinking, practice without theory are unimaginable. The reasoning may be faulty and the theory incorrect; but thinking and theorizing are not lacking in any action." In interpreting history, one necessarily makes assertions about what an agent believes, how those beliefs influence interpretation of data, and how this interpretation motivates agent action (Mises [1957] 2007). Although Mises's assertion flirts with rationalism, his point is generally correct. Mises is really just following in the line of Carl Menger here, whose definition of an economic good requires that the object in question have "such properties as render the thing capable of being brought into a causal connection with the satisfaction of this need" and that there exists "human *knowledge* of this causal connection" (Menger [1871] 2007, 52; emphasis mine).

Human knowledge—or theory—is often embedded in action and ensembles of action. It spans the breadth of human experience. Plans include and interact with one's physiology such that expectations include both a cognitive and an acognitive dimension (Koppl 2002; see also Clark 2016). Perhaps this point is best summed by the observation that, in using economic theory to interpret human action at particular places and times, the economist also acts as historian in accepting the cognitive, and often passion-laden, foundations of human action (Hume [1740] 1896; Wagner 2020, 260, 263). Agents may, with effort, clarify their *understanding* of the world by explicitly elaborating their underlying beliefs concerning causation, but often this is embedded in the manner described by Hayek's (1945, 528) reiteration of Alfred Whitehead that "civilization advances by extending the number of important operations which we can perform without thinking about them." It is not that humans are disinterested in *understanding* the world but that they seek to avoid unnecessary costs of utilizing their knowledge of the world to transform it in a manner valued by the acting agent and those the agent intends to serve.

When we speak of agent *understanding*, we necessarily include this understanding in its physiological totality of action and thought, logic and practice. Like his student Hayek, Mises also recognizes that agent *understanding* is intended to be an aid in reducing uneasiness and that this *understanding* includes choice governing one's habits. Similarly, Buchanan (1979) recognized that man's exercise of autonomy allows him to choose the kind of person he is to become by choosing the rules that guide one's life (see also Lewis and Dold 2020). Commenting on the role of habit in analysis, Mises ([1949] 1996, 47) observes that acting man "indulges in these habits only because he welcomes their effects," and if "he discovers that the pursuit of the habitual way may hinder the attainment of ends considered as more desirable, he changes his attitude." More recently, Gerd Gigerenzer (2008) has spent considerable energy showing that heuristics used to facilitate purposive action are surprisingly accurate (see also Simon and Simon 1962). Claims from Kahneman (2011) and Kahneman and Tversky (1974) that heuristics are prone to error apply to all algorithms for decision-making, no matter how complex. Less burdensome computation in the decision-making process often promotes efficient outcomes. Competitive markets tend to select for relatively efficient sets of strategies, including the habits that underlie them, to guide production and exchange (Caton 2017, 2019). Scholars concerned with a faithful framing of human agency have not isolated that framing from the market process.[2]

The broad view of *understanding* by mainline scholars provides foundations for consideration of the role of the entrepreneur in the operations of the market economy. The enacted plans of one entrepreneur compete with plans enacted by other entrepreneurs. Throughout the process, action guided by such knowledge interacts with the price system, moving, and being moved, by adjustments in relative prices. The ingenuity and creativity of the entrepreneur is a fundamental component of market processes and coordination in society. In referring to the creative innovator, Mises acknowledges "his thoughts and theories," for it is left to individuals to use their imaginations to develop knowledge that ultimately contributes to the cumulative knowledge set made available to humanity in the form of beliefs, institutions, and productive technologies (Mises [1949] 1996, 139).

In providing a robust description of human agency, we set the stage for a robust framing of human action in society. The price system that interfaces belief-driven actions of entrepreneurs with valuations of consumers is always subject to resource and institutional constraints. All of these elements are part of the market process. Elsewhere I have commented on the interaction between market entrepreneurship, mental models, and prices. Here I will elaborate how mental models allow the theorist to include the richness of institutional context in analysis of economy and society.

SHARED MENTAL MODELS AND INSTITUTIONAL CHANGE

Having identified methodological foundations that allow us to remain faithful to agent subjectivity, we can begin to approach Wagner's broader agenda as we investigate mechanisms operating at the systems level in which individual agents play an integral part. Individual decisions play a role in outcomes generated by institutions, as well as the evolution of institutions themselves. Forms of collective decision-making include not only the choice of what goods to produce, a decision mediated by the price system and the profit mechanism, but also which leaders to follow, which moral and legal rules to adhere to, what to believe, and so forth. Formal institutions that facilitate collective decision-making (i.e., elections, law enforcement, judicial process, etc.) may be accessible to the theorist for review; however, when we elevate analysis to the level of formal political selection and political decision-making, we will have skipped a requisite step in our analysis if our goal is to robustly describe institutional evolution. The evolution of formal institutions must be explained in light of the existing nexus of informal institutions that legitimate the authority of the formal institutions. We have access to this level of analysis to the extent that we take seriously agent subjectivity.

These cognitive foundations allow the theorist to elaborate the evolutionary interplay between formal and informal institutions (Leighton and López 2013; Caton and López 2020). One must carefully consider the coordinating role of ideology, or shared mental models (Buchanan and Wagner [1977] 2000; Denzau and North 1994; North 2005). I use ideology here in the sense used by Denzau and North (1994), which is essentially equivalent to what Mises ([1949] 1996, 154) refers to as *worldview*.[3] When ideology changes, formal institutions will likely not be far behind. Formal systems of governance may also influence beliefs of actors subject to them. Formal institutions can only operate effectively if they are coherent with underlying beliefs. In response to this dissonance, either the formal institution or the belief with which it conflicts will likely change to improve coherence between rules-in-use and rules-in-form.

Shared mental models are the building blocks of institutions. They help individuals frame their actions within social context. Their structure also frames thoughts about one's actions and the interpretation of actions by others. To generalize cognitive framing of institutions, we may draw from the most fundamental institutions, language, as a metaphor for all institutions (Hayek 1962; Kripke 1982; Crawford and Ostrom 1995; Searle 1995; Bloor 1997; Koppl 2002). Action has meaning in light of the statuses and associated rules that institutions attribute to different objects, actors, and so forth, in light of context. The meaning of action is a function of its context: its time, physical position, order within a sequence of action, and similar reference to webs of meaning that naturally emerge within a community. Plan coordination among actors is facilitated by shared meanings that help purposive agents interpret and navigate social context.

In this light, Gaetano Mosca (1939) identifies that elites are required to follow a *political formula*, a metamodel that constrains actions of political actors in light of beliefs and institutions embraced within a given cultural milieu (Salter and Wagner 2018). The *political formula* is precisely the sort of shared mental construct described earlier. First, its existence is adjoined to the rules governing political processes. Political players tend to be submitted to a *political formula* that includes a combination of formal rules and informal norms. These bind the actions of players in the political arena in light of shared meanings among actors in that arena. Second, the *political formula* serves to legitimize the operations and interventions of state actors to even those on the fringe of the political system by drawing from generally shared beliefs. It provides a window into the structure and substance of shared mental models. While not strictly religious, the *political formula* is often loaded with explicitly religious content in addition to other symbolic content that relates political processes, agendas, and the scope of acceptable political action to underlying beliefs of the electorate and general populace. It is the means by which one interprets one's political environment, through which one frames the context, meaning, and expected impacts of political action, and in which is implied the social contract governing interaction.

We can see the *political formula* operating within the discussion of Buchanan and Wagner ([1977] 2000) concerning the disposition of Americans toward deficit spending by the federal government. In the decades preceding the Great Depression, there had been a growing progressivist push for increased involvement in the social and economic affairs of American society. The experience of World War I bolstered beliefs that the federal government can and should be involved in coordinating economic activity and should oversee wealth transfers (Higgs 1987).

Political leaders often play a role in transforming the *political formula* in their exercise of sovereignty granted from support of their constituency (Sterpan and Wagner 2017). Elite actors tend to have greater influence over the shared mental models of society than non-elite actors. During the Great Depression, for example, Franklin Delano Roosevelt and other progressive leaders effectively altered American institutions of governance, stretching the bounds of allowable political action. The ascension of Keynes (1936) and his *General Theory* was something of a rubber stamp for this change in political orientation and would guide a new priestly class of economists in the employ of the state. The general result of this change in ideological alignment has been a reinterpretation of constitutional constraints on political action and an increasing tendency toward technocracy where one views development and control of formal institutions as a means of steering society (Koppl 2016). Those steered commonly see the expansion of control exercised by these institutions as appropriate, with the expectation, perhaps in pursuit of one's notion of the "common good," that their faction might influence the operation of these formal institutions. In short, the *political formula* follows an evolutionary path. In the United States, it has integrated beliefs that increasingly treat citizens as subjects who can become qualified for participation in a profession only by pursuing certifications through formal institutions of education.

The *political formula* stands as an exemplar of entanglement. It crosses categorical divisions and bridges both formal and informal institutions. Thus it is an analytical vehicle for understanding entanglement—linking social, economic, and political systems both in the minds of human actors and across the span of formal institutions. In modern society, where, for many, activities involving one's political, religious, and professional affiliations seldom overlap, it may be challenging to imagine such an *entangled mind*.

Interactions between these spheres of activity tend to maintain their independence. No doubt, there can be strong interplay between economic and political activity, but such relations rarely become dogmatized within the modern mind. Religion enters the discussion and might serve as a coordinating force in US party politics, but is otherwise reserved for more innocuous showings like opening prayers and the statement "In God We Trust" on the dollar bill. Political life may for a time inform religious activity, as we have seen in conservative American politics, but there is no rigid alignment between these different kinds of systems. This pluralistic orientation entails its own set of challenges, to which I will return in the next section.

A citizen of antiquity or of medieval society would likely be amused if you attempted to point out distinctions between overlapping systems, whether religious, political, or economic. These societies were thoroughly entangled. Each of these domains operated adjacent one another such that they seemed to operate inseparably. A critic of industrial society, though no high social theorist, Ivan Illich ([1971] 2002, 22) notes that the "traditional society was more like a set of concentric circles" that overlap and inform one another, as compared with modern society, whose institutional structure exhibits a greater degree of modularity (see also Ellul 1964). For example, in the pre-modern neo-Babylonian society, religious temples tended to hold large tracts of land. Output was temporarily allocated to entrepreneurs who provided the service of rent or tax collection. These entrepreneurs sought simultaneously to exploit profit opportunities that improved their own wealth: "The Neo-Babylonian tax farmer often established himself as the go-between accepting commodities for the tax payment for the small rural cultivator [who commonly plowed land owned by temples], converting the crops to cash through transport and sale, thereby linking the producer and consumer, and then delivering the tax money to the crown" (Wunsch 2010, 49). At some point, principalities, and those governed by them, embraced these modes of cooperation as an existential norm, including the window of opportunity used by the tax collector to benefit himself and the taxpayer by bearing uncertainty in accepting payment in kind.

The *political formula* relates various domains, defining what sort of cross-domain behavior is acceptable, or not, and what forms such behavior should manifest. In Stuart England, attempts by King James II to enforce religious tolerance within the Anglican Church deemed unacceptable by religious authorities were sufficient to unite political opposition that ushered in the Glorious Revolution (Kishlansky 1996). Parliament disagreed concerning the acceptability of such action and effectively expanded its own authority by removing the king for a second time within a half century after already disestablishing the Star Chamber. The domain of the king's authority was effectively curtailed. To say that the *political formula* transformed is to say that expectations of economic and political actors integrated this shift in the balance of power. This shift in power is evidenced by a greater willingness of investors to lend to the state, with interest rates falling to as low as 3 percent and the level of borrowing increasing a hundredfold (North and Weingast 1989; Hodgson 2017).

We may generalize the *political formula* as a *social formula*. Varying *formulas* govern different domains. Although those of us not lobbying for political position are not as constrained as politicians, since we do not need general approval that is typically required for victory in election or appointment to a powerful position, we do need to curry some minimum threshold of acceptance among our neighbors, especially those with whom we actively cooperate. Even in the modern context, we see sets of expectations concerning one domain informing another. Thus, businesses commonly launch public relations campaigns. They actively attempt to stay abreast of changing, shared perceptions—for example, concerning acceptable (or unacceptable) forms of religiosity, politically correct speech, and recently, the promotion of equity.

For clarification, we may elaborate the concept using the archetypal institution of language. To transform language that we use to explicate our shared mental models is to transform institutions. Gadamer (1975) notes that tradition shapes our present social reality while participation in that reality shapes our interpretation of such inheritance. Others emphasize the constraint of thought exercised by the form of language (Foucault [1970] 1994; 1980). George Orwell provides a window into such potential with his emphasis on newspeak that constrains the society's elite and the language they use from within formal institutions. And many modern debates concerning language seem to center on the insight that language shapes one's worldview and, consequently, the institutions in which we all participate. This is ultimately a fight over the rudder that steers the evolution of not just one institution but the entire institutional nexus.

The mind shaped by an entangled institutional nexus is necessarily an *entangled mind*. The evolution of a *political formula* within a given milieu of culture, religion, and governance very naturally integrated what, to the modern mind, are often disparate fields of social relations. For us moderns, certain beliefs that one advertises in one social context (e.g., politics) likely will not be warmly greeted or understood in another context (e.g., one's workplace). One who lives in a small community, however, may find that all of these networks overlap. In small, rural communities, one's political opponents often attend the same religious gatherings or frequent the same youth sports activities. Although opponents, they likely share many institutional practices and fundamental beliefs. In such a context, it is easy to imagine how the formula that governs action in one social domain informs the formula governing action in another. And in such a context, it is not uncommon for there to exist a thick set of shared mental models that cohere over the totality of domains pertinent to that particular community.

By leveraging the idea of a formula that acts as a constraint on the range of actions deemed generally acceptable, we contextualize action within existing institutional environments. This action is the driving force of institutional evolution and supports coherence within the entangled mind. To describe the development of institutions, we must first theoretically frame agents acting within those institutions whose experiences and perspectives are substantively defined by these institutions and their participation in them. In reflecting on the modern occurrence of such entanglement, Mauws and Phillips (1995, 332) observe that "organizational members do not experience organizational membership as an external aspect of their life, but rather live it and are shaped by their interactions with the people and objects which make up the organization." There is no contextless perspective in society.

All perspectives manifest in human flesh as agents navigate the nexus of institutions that define their social reality. The job of the social theorist is to make space for this context in the abstractions commonly used to engage in analysis. Shared mental models promote a common conception of social reality whereby potentially diverse members are otherwise unified in their interpretations and status attributions to objects and processes within their shared social domain (Searle 1995, 2005).

THE ENTANGLED MIND WITHIN THE LIBERAL ORDER

The final task of a theory of entangled mind is to relate that mind to the whole institutional nexus. Just as institutions governing a community shape the minds of participants in those communities, so too must the minds of community members submit to hierarchical ordering of institutions as they mediate conflict. Members of a tight-knit community or organization, for example, will avoid inviting outsiders to mediate internal conflict whenever possible. Trade associations and private law courts, for example, perform the role of conflict mediation without a state (Benson 1989; see also Stringham 2015). And property rights, more generally, can arise within a community through the development of mutually corresponding expectations that support relatively low policing costs required to effectively sanction violators (Demsetz 1967). Avner Greif (2006, 120) identifies that similar legal systems coordinated between trade guilds and local rulers "provided the *cognition*, coordination, and information that enabled and guided behavior in the related transactions." Such rules aid plan formation and orient one's activities to be coherent with the expectations of other economic actors.

Without low-cost means of coordinating cooperation, especially in the case of adjudicating conflicts, contracts will be unenforceable and otherwise mutually beneficial exchange will not occur (Coase 1960; Nutter 1968; North 1990). In cases where the state does not actively seek a role in such disputes, state enforcement of commercial law occurs much less often than does voluntary cooperation according to such law, as state mediation is required when privately coordinated action fails to resolve a conflict. While merchants know that state mediation is a possible outcome, they often prefer to avoid it owing to its cost. Following the norms of conduct prevalent among merchants is often sufficient to prevent escalation of most conflict, especially when merchant expectations include potential for higher levels of conflict mediation.

In closing, I will generalize this insight relating private and public ordering to all forms of conflict mediation. The argument so far has provided flesh to the insight from Wagner (1976, 110) that "the prescriptive use of optimality models of local government requires a framework in which the analyst knows *by assumption* the mental states of the participants in the economic process." The generalization that actors seek to maximize the monetary value of resources under their control oversimplifies analysis, ignoring the complexity of structures that agents use to interpret reality and to decide on a course of action within it. While it may be appropriate to apply the neoclassical model under circumstances where economic competition selects for net-value-generating activities, it is wholly inappropriate to interpret the universal applicability of economic theory as the universal applicability of the perfectly competitive model. While the earlier example expands analysis in terms of methodology, it does not move beyond a market context.

There exists the still greater difficulty of coordinating action among diverse participants who may or may not participate in the same community norms and procedures, and who inevitably hold beliefs and preferences unique from their neighbors. Yes, incentives matter, and they must be considered within an institutional context. The resultant market outcomes are a function of institutions, the knowledge set guiding agent interpretation, and the preferences of agents. Often, these institutions lower transaction costs by aligning expectations of market actors from different communities. The challenge, then, is to explain how agents in an institutionally diverse society can form expectations that are mutually coherent.

A liberal society is a society that allows its members a significant scope of freedom to pursue value: "In a very generic sense, liberal values will lead to institutional arrangements where human relationships are governed through the principles of property, contract, and voluntary association. These abstract principles, however, are *always instantiated through specific institutionalized practice.* That practice may, in turn, conflict with the governing principles, perhaps leading to a revision of the underlying values, at least to the extent that normative belief adapts to conventional practice" (Wagner 2006, 523). While it allows for many kinds of traditions to exist within it, members of a liberal society must, in their actions, ultimately be submitted to a belief in the dignity of the autonomous individual. The ideas and actions of any particular individual may seem quite foolish. Yet, anyone familiar with the disposition of impactful entrepreneurs knows that it is exactly such cognitive diversity that guides entrepreneurs, and the organizations in which they participate, to orient the world in a manner that exploits untapped sources of value (Page 2007; see also Page 2011). The challenge always faced by a liberal society is for it to remain *liberal*. It is for society to allow for the cognitive diversity that allows it to function and continually renew itself as its context changes.

A danger faced by a liberal society is that liberal institutions might, through a process of cumulative change, cease to be liberal. Wagner's emphasis on logical and nonlogical action informs our understanding of the problem we face (Wagner 2016). Different kinds of systems for collective decision-making generate different kinds of outcomes. Conflict is endemic in society, so the theorist must be able to explain how it does not persistently lead to destabilizing dynamics. Within the context of the pure market, conflict is resolved through product differentiation—for example, the development of a product ecosystem—and price competition. The end served is ultimately that of the consumer.

Political competitions, on the other hand, do not serve a systematic end as markets do. Expression of preferences through the political system can generate dangers to the liberal society that enables that expression. An example of this is shown clearly through Arrow's (1951) impossibility theorem where three voters must choose from only two of a larger pool of three candidates. If the voters do not agree on their ordering of the candidates, results will cycle through candidates when voters face different pairings, as there is no convergence to a shared choice. Other problems plague political decision-making. For example, voters bear little cost in voting *and* expect to have essentially no impact on the outcome (Buchanan and Tullock [1962] 1999; Caplan 2008; DeCanio 2014).

This is not to say that there are no countervailing forces coordinating decision-making. Political parties, lobbying efforts from political active organizations, whether for-profit or not-for-profit, do influence political outcomes

(Wittman 1995) and therefore serve as intermediaries between voters and politicians that help steer the political process. But even this cannot alleviate the problem that political decision-making is nonlogical. At best, we can hope that the domain of any particular political decision is limited in breadth so as to allow for the rationalizing force of evolutionary selection.

Evaluation of formal institutions of collective decision-making is incomplete. Similar disordering forces impact the breadth of institutional forms, including informal institutions. If the *political formula* and its tandem institutions are constantly subject to pre-constitutional bargaining, what prevents society from unraveling and devolving to the Hobbesian state? This is precisely the concern of Gauthier (1977), who saw that the wholesale adoption of instrumental rationality, free from Kantian categorical imperatives, by members of society in their pursuit of maximizing personal utility would lead to a war of all against all. This, or any other, path to institutional failure is both a theoretical and existential concern.

In a liberal society, the solution to the failure of institutions to effectively coordinate social activity in a manner that integrates the preferences of its participants is the prioritization of liberal principles within the minds of community members.[4] Just as Mises (1949) identifies that agent action is guided by an agent's preference ordering, the models used by an agent are subject to a hierarchy of ordering that is a function of the context of action. A theory of the *entangled mind* elaborates the nature of such a hierarchy in the context of shared mental models, or multilevel morality (Caton 2020; Moehler 2021). The society's individual communities may form a metacommunity with sufficient coherence among shared mental models to enable peaceful interaction in many instances of intercommunal interaction (Buchanan [1983] 2001; Moehler 2018, 2020; see also Gaus 2011).

Different communities in agreement concerning fundamental norms may disagree concerning what processes should adjudicate conflict within the community and determine beliefs more generally. There often is room for variation between communities so long as those communities share fundamental beliefs to which they may defer in the case of intercommunal conflict, even if those same norms are not followed for resolving conflicts that are wholly local within each community (Caton 2020). Some communities hold beliefs that are peculiar, others that are simply incorrect. This is unavoidable. At the very least, liberal society requires tolerance between communities. That tolerance may inform expressions of tolerance within a given community that operates within the larger liberal order. Whether a society's communities form a metacommunity is a matter of degree. Certainly, for a liberal society, the greater the extent to which liberal norms are integrated into local beliefs across all communities, the more accurate it would be to refer to the communities as composing a liberal metacommunity. Without embrace of such an imperative, nonliberal participants and their communities must believe that the benefits of engagement in the liberal order exceed the costs.[5]

Varying levels of institutional analysis are integrated into multilevel legal and moral theories, but there has been little investigation of hierarchical ordering within the mind of the individual. An important step in this respect is the application of Buchanan's constitutional choice to the individual mind by Lewis and Dold (2020). However, the authors do not consider the nature and structure of multiple institutional commitments inherent in a polycentric society (see, for example, Aligica and Tarko 2014; Aligica 2019). Lewis and Dold (2020) investigate the role of free will in selecting the personal constitution governing one's actions. Personal sovereignty, in this view, is the ability to select and alter one's personal constitution. This perspective scales to the level of cooperation within the community and similar contributions between communities and the moral order at large.

Multilevel morality would simply add that rational agents must operate using a hierarchy of models. Any particular mental model within a given community will tend to reflect the shared mental model that more or less defines membership within that community. The choice to join a community represents a choice to adopt the shared mental model of that community, or at least a subset of the model capable of procuring and maintaining membership in the community. Agents from different communities with differing lower-level commitments may reason their way to principles that allow for participation across communities. Some approaches might integrate liberal ideas with one's own tradition; others might choose to prioritize liberal principles only minimally on instrumental grounds. Whereas private law governing the vast majority of commercial exchange operates with an effective commitment to higher levels of adjudication when conflict cannot be resolved internally, a multilevel morality includes an effective commitment to defer to higher-level principles where lower-level approaches fail to orient agent action toward some phenomenon.

Integration of various shared mental models is costly. Models that integrate expectations across various institutions and organizations are subject to different arrays of transaction costs. Successful organizations are able to reduce transactions costs so that participation in them creates net value for participants. Pertinent to our modern context, an attractive mental structure reduces the cost of membership across various communities. In the end, the task that confronts the entangled mind is to coherently interface different domains of action. Integrated models that lower the cost of balancing diverse commitments in different domains will tend to outcompete more costly means of integration and, therefore, are more likely to be selected at the systems level, where they can serve as a shared mental model supporting the same task among many actors. The freedom granted the individual in the liberal order allows for a broad scope of experimentation in the development of such entangled models.

In a world where significant overlap exists between domains of various systems, selecting an entangled model is a more straightforward task since it is, more or less, selected by the entangled community for individual agents. For example, economic activity that is largely contained within an existing religious system will tend not to exhibit features that challenge that system. This sort of alignment, however, greatly inhibits the scope of action within a society and, therefore, limits the scope of experimentation. Such alignment was the source of many conflicts concerning means by which lenders might profit within systems that generally prohibited the charging of interest for loans. So long as the issue remained inadequately resolved in favor of compensating the lender, the society in question failed to allocate unused resources toward their highest-valued uses and economic growth stagnated. As exchange technologies and arrangements have moved outside the bounds of religious systems in the entrepreneurial search for greater efficiency, more sophisticated apologetics is required for existing political and religious systems; so, too, are required more sophisticated linkages between models governing participation in various social domains. In my own sphere of awareness, this challenge is especially pertinent as religious life attempts to deal with modern ideals and political and economic arrangements (Gaus and Vallier 2009). If the work of Callahan and Salter (2018), Salter (forthcoming), and Norcross and Aligica (2020) is of any indication of the merits of such a pursuit, it appears that social visions dreamed from within religious traditions stand to benefit from such interfacing. This is, of course, true of all kinds of social systems that operate within our entangled society.

CONCLUSION

An entangled theory of political economy is an inclusive theory. It does not delimit the domains of entanglement and seeks to include complexities that arise from the interaction of various types of social systems. Analysis of an entangled world requires recognition of the *entangled mind* that is subject to and participates in this process of renewal and reorientation. Human agents truly choose when they exert influence over the mental model that guides their actions. While we are all subject to the status quo of culture on some margins, we can always adapt our existing models by making piecemeal modifications, recombining with other models, or even making a quantum leap of adopting a new model wholesale, as might occur when one joins an exclusive community united by shared practice and beliefs.

The scientistic worldview treats the world as being composed of islands of belief. Yet society is not composed of isolated islands of belief. Incoherence between models that define perspectives within various domains leads, at the very least, to a failure of communication between domains. The entangled mind has no choice but to wrestle with this incoherence or else forfeit value that could be realized by more coherent integration of models. It bears repeating that the problem of entanglement is both a theoretical and an existential difficulty—all the more critical that social theory provide a window into the intricacies of an entangled world.

NOTES

1. Understanding permeates the Kantian tradition, as it was Immanuel Kant who recognized that we build models of the world from our assumptions about it. Hans-Georg Gadamer, for example, describes the relationship between imagination and understanding. Especially informative to the Knightian conception of entrepreneurship, Gadamer reflects on Kant's contribution of "the a priori of judgment": "Judgment is necessary in order to make a correct evaluation of the concrete instance," "judgment provides the bridge between understanding and reason," and this same judgment mediates "between the concepts of nature and of freedom" (Gadamer 1975, 36, 50, 51). Reflective of Viennese intellectual context, Carl Jung (1957), who was both Kantian and an intellectual of the Viennese tradition, consistently draws on *understanding* to highlight the plight of the individual within an increasingly collectivist society.

2. Hayek (1952b) went so far as to provide physiological microfoundations to support the theoretical concepts of *understanding*.

3. According to Mises ([1949] 1996, 154), "A world view is, as a theory, an interpretation of all things, and as a precept for action, an opinion concerning the best means for removing uneasiness as much as possible. . . . Religion, metaphysics, and philosophy aim at providing a world view. They interpret the universe and they advise men how to act."

4. Moehler (2018) refers to this as the weak principle of universalization.

5. Moehler (2018) follows the latter path, attempting to address this problem by an initial administration of distributive justice such as with a universal basic income guarantee.

REFERENCES

Aligica, P. D. 2019. *Public Entrepreneurship, Citizenship, and Self-Governance*. New York: Cambridge University Press.

Aligica, P. D., and V. Tarko. 2014. "Institutional Resilience and Economic Systems: Lessons from Elinor Ostrom's Work." *Comparative Economic Studies* 56: 52–76.

Arrow, K. J. 1951. *Social Choice and Individual Values*. New York: John Wiley and Sons.

Baumol, W. 1968. "Entrepreneurship in Economic Theory." *American Economic Review* 58: 64–71.

———. 1990. "Entrepreneurship: Productive, Unproductive, and Destructive." *Journal of Political Economy* 98, no. 5: 893–921.

Benson, B. 1989. "The Spontaneous Evolution of Commercial Law." *Southern Economic Journal* 55, no. 3: 644–61.

Bloor, D. 1997. *Wittgenstein, Rules and Institutions*. New York: Routledge.

Boettke, P., and E. López. 2002. "Austrian Economics and Public Choice." *Review of Austrian Economics* 15, no. 2/3: 111–19.

Buchanan, J. M. 1979. "Natural and Artifactual Man." In *The Collected Works of James M. Buchanan*, Vol. 1, *The Logical Foundations of Constitutional Liberty*, edited by Geoffrey Brennan, Hartmut Kliemt, and Robert D. Tollison, 246–59. Indianapolis: Liberty Fund:.

———. (1983) 2001. "Moral Community and Moral Order: The Intensive and Extensive Limits of Interaction." In *The Collected Works of James M. Buchanan*, Volume 17, *Moral Science and Moral Order*, edited by Hartmut Kliemt, 202–10. Indianapolis: Liberty Fund.

Buchanan, J. M., and G. Tullock. (1962) 1999. *The Calculus of Consent: Logical Foundations of Constitutional Democracy*. Indianapolis: Liberty Fund.

Buchanan, J. M., and R. E. Wagner. (1977) 2000. *Democracy in Deficit: The Political Legacy of Lord Keynes*. Indianapolis: Liberty Fund.

Bylund, P. 2015. "Signifying Williamson's Contribution to the Transaction Cost Approach: An Agent-Based Simulation of Coasean Transaction Costs and Specialization." *Journal of Management Studies* 52, no. 1: 148–74.

Callahan, E., and A. Salter. 2018. "Dead Ends and Living Currents: Distributism as a Progressive Research Program." *Christian Libertarian Review* 1: 118–39.

Caplan, B. 2008. *The Myth of the Rational Voter: Why Democracies Choose Bad Policies*. Princeton, NJ: Princeton University Press.

Caton, J. 2017. "Entrepreneurship, Search Costs, and Ecological Rationality." *Review of Austrian Economics* 30: 107–30.

———. 2019. "Creativity in a Theory of Entrepreneurship." *Journal of Entrepreneurship and Public Policy* 8, no. 4: 442–69.

———. 2020. "Moral Community and Moral Order: Developing Buchanan's Multilevel Social Contract Theory." *Erasmus Journal for Philosophy and Economics* 13, no. 2: 1–29.

Caton, J., and E. López. 2020. "The Cognitive Dimension of Institutions." In *UFM Companion to Douglass North*, edited by A. Marroquin and N. Wenzel. Guatemala: Universidad Francisco Marroquin.

Clark, A. 2016. *Surfing Uncertainty: Prediction, Action, and Embodied Mind*. Oxford: Oxford University Press.

Coase, R. H. 1937. "The Nature of the Firm." *Economica* 4, no. 16: 386–405.

———. 1960. "The Problem of Social Cost." *Journal of Law and Economics* 56, no. 4: 837–77.

———. 1992. "The Institutional Structure of Production." *American Economic Review* 82, no. 4: 713–19.

Crawford, S. E., and E. Ostrom. 1995. "A Grammar of Institutions." *American Political Science Review* 89, no. 3: 582–600.

DeCanio, S. 2014. "Democracy, the Market, and the Logic of Social Choice." *American Journal of Political Science* 58 no. 3: 537–652.

Dekker, E. 2016. *The Viennese Students of Civilization.* New York: Cambridge University Press.

Demsetz, H. 1967. "Toward a Theory of Property Rights." *American Economic Review* 57, no. 2: 347–59.

Denzau, A. T., and D. North. 1994. "Shared Mental Models: Ideologies and Institutions." *Kyklos* 47, no. 1: 3–31.

Ellul, J. 1964. *The Technological Society.* New York: Vintage Books.

Foss, N., and P. Klein. 2012. *Organizing Entrepreneurial Judgment: A New Approach to the Firm.* New York: Cambridge University Press.

Foucault, M. (1970) 1994. *The Order of Things: An Archeology of the Human Sciences.* New York: Vintage Books.

———. 1980. *Power-Knowledge: Selected Interviews and Other Writings: 1972–1977.* New York: Pantheon Books.

Gadamer, H. 1975. *Truth and Method.* London: Bloomsbury.

Gaus, G. F. 2011. *The Order of Public Reason: A Theory of Freedom and Morality in a Diverse and Bounded World.* New York: Cambridge University Press.

Gaus, G. F., and K. Vallier. 2009. "The Roles of Religious Conviction in a Publicly Justified Polity: The Implications of Convergence, Asymmetry and Political Institutions." *Philosophy and Social Criticism* 35, no. 1–2: 51–76.

Gauthier, D. 1977. "The Social Contract as Ideology." *Philosophy and Public Affairs* 6, no. 2: 130–64.

Gigerenzer, G. 2008. *Rationality for Mortals: How People Cope with Uncertainty.* New York: Oxford University Press.

Greif, A. 2006. *Institutions and the Path to the Modern Economy: Lessons from Medieval Trade.* New York: Cambridge University Press.

Hayek, F. A. (1935a) 1948. "Socialist Calculation I: The Nature and History of the Problem." In *Individualism and Economic Order,* 119–47. Chicago: University of Chicago Press.

———. (1935b) 1948. "Socialist Calculation II: The State of the Debate." In *Individualism and Economic Order,* 148–80. Chicago: University of Chicago Press.

———. 1937. "Economics and Knowledge." *Economica* 4: 33–54.

———. (1940) 1948. "Socialist Calculation III: The Competitive Solution." In *Individualism and Economic Order,* 181–208. Chicago: University of Chicago Press.

———. 1945. "The Use of Knowledge in Society." *American Economic Review* 35 no. 4, 519–30.

———. 1952a. *The Counterrevolution in Science: Studies in the Abuse of Reason.* Glencoe, IL: Free Press.

———. 1952b. *The Sensory Order: An Inquiry into the Foundations of Theoretical Psychology.* Chicago: University of Chicago Press.

———. 1962. "Rules, Perception, and Intelligibility." In *The Market and Other Orders,* edited by B. Caldwell, 232–53. Chicago: University of Chicago Press.

Higgs, R. 1987. *Crisis and Leviathan: Critical Episodes in the Growth of American Government.* New York: Oxford University Press.

Hodgson, G. 2017. "1688 and All That: Property Rights, the Glorious Revolution, and the Rise of British Capitalism." *Journal of Institutional Economics* 13, no. 1: 79–107.

Holian, M., and G. Newell. 2017. "An Agent-Based Model of Entrepreneurship." *Journal of Entrepreneurship and Public Policy* 6 no. 2: 259–70.

Hume, D. (1740) 1896. *Treatise on Human Nature*. Oxford: Clarendon Press.

Illich, I. (1971) 2002. *Deschooling Society*. London: Marion Boyars.

Jung, C. G. 1957. *The Undiscovered Self*. New York: Signet.

Kahneman, D. 2011. *Thinking, Fast and Slow*. New York: Farrar, Straus and Giroux.

Kahneman, D., and A. Tversky. 1974. "Judgment under Uncertainty: Heuristics and Biases." *Science* 185, no. 4157: 1124–31.

Keyhani, M. 2016. "Computer Simulation Studies of the Entrepreneurial Market Process." In *Complexity in Entrepreneurship and Technology Research: Applications of Emergent and Neglected Methods*, edited by E. Berger and A. Kuckertz, 117–37. Springer.

———. 2019. "Computational Modeling of Entrepreneurship Grounded in Austrian Economics: Insights for Strategic Entrepreneurship and the Opportunity Debate." *Strategic Entrepreneurship Journal* 13, no. 2: 221–40.Keynes, John M. (1964) 1936. *The General Theory of Employment, Interest, and Money*. New York: Harcourt.

Kirzner, I. 1966. "An Essay on Capital." In *Essays on Capital*, edited by P. Boettke and F. Sautet, 15–49. Indianapolis: Liberty Fund.

Kishlansky, M. 1996. *A Monarchy Transformed: Britain 1603–1714*. New York: Penguin Books.

Knight, F. (1921) 1964. *Risk, Uncertainty, and Profit*. New York: Augustus M. Kelly.

Koppl, R. 2002. *Big Players and the Economic Theory of Expectations*. New York: Palgrave Macmillan.

———. 2016. *Expert Failure*. New York: Cambridge University Press.

Kripke, S. A. 1982. *Wittgenstein on Rules and Private Language: An Elementary Exposition*. Cambridge, MA: Harvard University Press.

Lachmann, L. M. (1956) 1978. *Capital and Its Structure*. Mission, KS: Andrew and McMeel.

Lavoie, D. (1985) 2015. *Rivalry and Central Planning*. Arlington, VA: Mercatus Center at George Mason University.

Leighton, W., and E. López. 2012. *Madmen, Intellectuals, and Academic Scribblers: The Economic Engine of Political Change*. Stanford, CA: Stanford University Press.

Lewis, P., and M. Dold. 2020. "James Buchanan on the Nature of Choice: Ontology, Artifactual Man and the Constitutional Moment in Political Economy." *Cambridge Journal of Economics* 44, no. 5: 1159–79.

Mauws, M., and N. Phillips. 1995. "Crossroads Understanding Language Games." *Organization Science* 6: 322–34.

Menger, C. (1871) 2007. *Principles of Economics*. Auburn, AL: Ludwig Von Mises Institute.

Mises, L. (1920) 1990. *Calculation in the Socialist Commonwealth*. Auburn, AL: Ludwig von Mises Institute.

———. (1949) 1996. *Human Action*. Indianapolis: Liberty Fund.

———. (1957) 2007. *Theory and History: An Interpretation of Social and Economic Evolution*. Auburn, AL: Ludwig von Mises Institute.Moehler, Michael. 2018. *Minimal Morality: A Multilevel Social Contract Theory*. Oxford, UK: Oxford University Press.

———. 2020. *Contractarianism*. Cambridge: Cambridge University Press.

———. 2021. "Integrated Moral Agency and the Practical Phenomenon of Moral Diversity." *Erasmus Journal for Philosophy and Economics* 14, no. 2: 53–76.

Mosca, G. 1939. *The Ruling Class*. New York: McGraw-Hill.

Norcross, E., and P. Aligica. 2020. "Catholic Social Thought and New Institutional Economics: An Assessment of Their Affinities and Areas of Potential Convergence." *American Journal of Economics and Sociology* 79, no. 4: 1241–69.

North, D. C. 1990. *Institutions, Institutional Change, and Economic Performance*. New York: Cambridge University Press.

———. 2005. *Understanding the Process of Economic Change*. Princeton, NJ: Princeton University Press.

North, D., and N. Weingast. 1989. "Constitutions and Commitment: The Evolution of Institutions Governing Public Choice in Seventeenth-Century England." *Journal of Economic History* 49, no. 4: 803–32.

Nutter, W. 1968. "The Coase Theorem on Social Costs: A Footnote." *Journal of Law and Economics* 11, no. 2: 503–7.

Page, S. E. 2007. "Making the Difference: Applying the Logic of Diversity." *Academy of Management Perspectives* 21, no. 4: 6–20.

———. 2011. *Diversity and Complexity*. Princeton, NJ: Princeton University Press.

Salter, A. Forthcoming. *From Property, Liberty: Distributism and Price Theory in Conversation*. Catholic University of America Press.

Salter, A., and R. Wagner. 2018. "Political Entrepreneurship, Emergent Dynamics, and Constitutional Politics. *Review of Social Economy* 76, no. 3: 281–301.

Searle, J. R. 1995. *The Construction of Social Reality*. New York: Free Press.

———. 2005. "What Is an Institution?" *Journal of Institutional Economics* 1: 1–22.

Simon, H. A. and P. A. Simon. 1962. "Trial and Error Search in Solving Difficult Problems: Evidence from the Game of Chess." *Behavioral Science* 7 no. 4: 425–29.

Solow, R. 1957. "Technical Change and the Aggregate Production Function." *Review of Economics and Statistics* 39, no. 3: 312–20.

Sterpan, I., and R. E. Wagner. 2017. "The Autonomy of the Political within Political Economy." *Advances in Austrian Economics* 17: 147–71.

Stringham, E. 2015. *Private Governance: Creating Order in Economic and Social Life*. New York: Oxford University Press.

Wagner, R. E. 1976. "State and Local Public Finance: Institutional Constraints and Local Community Formation." *American Economic Review* 66, no. 2: 110–15.

———. 2006. "States and the Crafting of Souls: Mind, Society and Fiscal Sociology." *Journal of Economic Behavior and Organization* 59: 516–24.

———. 2010. *Mind, Society, and Human Action: Time and Knowledge in a Theory of Social Economy*. London: Routledge.

———. 2016. *Politics as a Peculiar Business: Insights from a Theory of Entangled Political Economy*. Cheltenham, UK: Edward Elgar.

———. 2020. *Macroeconomics as Systems Theory: Transcending the Micro-Macro Dichotomy*. Cham, Switzerland: Palgrave Macmillan.

Wittman, D. 1995. *The Myth of Democratic Failure: Why Political Institutions Are Efficient*. Chicago: University of Chicago Press.

Wunsch, C. 2010. "Neo-Babylonian Entrepreneurs." In *The Invention of Enterprise*, edited by D. S. Landes, J. Mokyr, and W. J. Baumol, 273–304. Princeton, NJ: Princeton University Press.

Chapter 8
Wagnerian Relationality

Mikayla Novak

With his scholarship spanning over 50 years, Richard E. Wagner has generated novel research insights in fields as diverse as public choice, public finance, fiscal federalism, fiscal sociology, welfare and social services provision, macroeconomic theory, and the study of economic and political institutions. In this chapter I seek to explore the philosophical underpinnings of Wagnerian thought. Specifically, I make the case that Wagner's work on entangled political economy presents a critical, and indeed pathbreaking, application of relational scholarship. It is widely appreciated, and not merely by academics, that relationships serve as a basis for our shared existences as human beings. To accentuate this point, one may consider the social acclimatization, as well as psychological and other, difficulties experienced by individuals who have found themselves in long-term isolation—owing to traumatic experiences such as captivity and imprisonment, as well as to prolonged episodes of loneliness. As has long been emphasized by social psychology and sociology, interpersonal connections, and the human relationships they cultivate, can play an indelible role in shaping appraisals and perceptions of self (Smith [1759] 2002; Cooley [1902] 1983; Mead [1934] 1950; Elias 1991).

In the preface of his *Politics as a Peculiar Business*, Wagner states (2016, ix), "Political and commercial activities take place within the same society, and involve interactions and relationships among the same people. It is thus meaningful to speak of entangled systems of political economy and their properties." I argue that entangled political economy can be seen as an intellectual apparatus that not only fruitfully engages with the scholarly relational turn but also helps resolve certain dilemmas and puzzles that have gripped political economy since its very inception.

The structure of this chapter is as follows. The next section provides an overview of relational thinking in modern social sciences, drawing from a broad range of disciplines including philosophy, economics, and sociology. This is followed by a detailed appraisal of Wagner's entangled political economy through a relational lens, emphasizing the significance of interaction by actors among economic and political domains and the emergent quality of relationships entailed by such interactions. In this chapter, Wagner's relational orientation to scholarship is also applied to the case of equality. I illustrate that an emphasis on relational equality between individuals is consistent with Wagner's long-held support for a liberal economic-political-social order. The final section of this chapter concludes.

RELATIONALITY IN MODERN SOCIAL SCIENCES: AN OVERVIEW

An immense amount of definitional work has been undertaken with regard to human relationships, and it would be impracticable for me to fully encapsulate those efforts in this chapter. For convenience I draw on the *Oxford English Dictionary*, which defines a *relation* as "an attribute denoting or concept expressing a connection, correspondence, or contrast between different things; a particular way in which one thing or idea is connected or associated with another or others." Similarly, a *relationship* is defined as "the state or fact of being related . . . [a] connection formed between two or more people or groups based on social interactions and mutual goals, interests, or feelings."

Social scientists generally concur that relationships denote connections between individuals as well as groups of individuals, as represented by varied collectives. With respect to the latter, relationships are deeply interwoven in our patterns of experiences with others, which, inter alia, give rise to coordination potentials through structures as diverse as families, friendships, associations, organizations, communities, and polities. An acknowledgment of human diversity and societal variety leads to the intuitive observation that relationships may be characterized on the basis of several interrelated criteria. These include (but are not limited to) frequency and duration of engagements between people, extent of relational diversity among people, the degree of dependency built up among relational parties, and reciprocity and voluntariness in relational settings (Duck 1999; Gui and Sugden 2005; August and Rook 2013).

Before proceeding any further, I wish to briefly highlight the distinction between the terms "relationship" and "interaction." "Interaction" often appears, at least in common parlance, to be used interchangeably with "relation" despite their differences in meaning. "Relationship" generically pertains to the state of connection between individuals and their collectives. Alternatively, "interaction" refers to actions or influences of people on—or that otherwise have an effect on—one another (*Oxford English Dictionary*). Again, there is no standardized definition for interaction as testified by ongoing debates about the features and extent of interaction—including the extent of mutual engagement or reciprocity between interactants, the nature of sequencing of interactions between parties, and the extent to which interaction induces change in relational contexts. A pivotal consideration from our perspective is that "social *relationships refer to the connections that exist between people who have recurring interactions* that are perceived by the participants to have personal meaning" (August and Rook 2013; emphasis added).

Relational concepts are represented across a broad spectrum of social science disciplines. Efforts to explicitly bring relationships to the forefront of theoretical and empirical inquiry have been evident in fields such as philosophy and logic (MacBride 2020), psychology (Coats and Feldman 2001; Gergen 2009), and political science (McClurg and Young 2001). Other important contributions to relational thinking are traceable in additional fields, such as anthropology and history (Thelen, Vetters, and von Benda-Beckmann 2014; Blosser 2019). For the remainder of this section, I wish to focus attention on relational studies in economics and sociology, given the perceived proximity of those disciplines to Wagner's entangled political economy scholarship.

Turning first to economics, recent contributions highlight the relational properties of transactions and the importance of shared expectations, norms, and trust between connected individuals in facilitating exchanges of goods and services. Josef Wieland (2020) has outlined a framework of relational economics in which individuals and meso-level collectives, such as firms, develop networks to collaborate on production, distribution, and exchange. Significantly, he sets out a polycontextual environment of heterogeneous actors within multiple systems engaging in discoveries and learnings about how to relate to each other more productively. In the subdiscipline of economic geography, Bathelt and Glückler (2011) develop an interesting relational approach illustrating how economic agents tend to cluster economically and spatially to generate and share knowledge for mutual gain. Both of these studies point to a well-developed literature on "relational contracting," referring to the extent to which trust and other informal norms affect the durability and execution of contractual terms between individuals or enterprises (e.g., Baker, Gibbons, and Murphy 2002; Levin 2003).

Speaking more generally, criticisms of a lack of relational acknowledgment in orthodox (neoclassical) economics is a common feature of a range of heterodox (non-neoclassical) economic approaches. The key target of critique is the presentation of orthodox conceptions of human action and representation that assume the existence of atomistic, or isolated, individuals engaging in production, consumption, and investment decisions. An important contribution within the subdiscipline of evolutionary economics is presented by Potts

(2000), who castigates the *ontological unrealism* and *methodological inapplicability* of orthodox "representative agent" models of humankind that occupy the entire space of economic activity. According to Potts, these orthodox economic models obscure the existence of partial, and specialized, network relations between individuals, as well as private and public enterprises, that coordinate over the means of production and exchange.

It is arguably with sociology that relational concerns have most explicitly assumed intellectual prominence. For forefathers of modern sociology, such as Comte, Spencer, and Durkheim, each considered the influence of relationship patterns on broader societal phenomena. Inspired by the moral philosophy of Adam Smith (e.g., Miller 1973; Creelan 1987; Costelloe 1997), formative figures in American sociology (such as Charles Cooley and George Mead) presented sociopsychological theories of relational selves. In this regard, a given person's self-impressions, and even the actions one undertakes in the world, are seen to be influenced by cognitive models and norms reflecting the imagined judgments, sentiments, and reasons of others.

German sociologist Georg Simmel (1950) also made formative contributions to the study of relationships—in this case, informing the development of social network theory and analysis. An original feature of Simmel's work, of great relevance to the discussion of Wagner's entangled political economy, was his distinction between "dyadic" and "triadic" relational forms. A dyad is a relationship structure consisting of two individuals or groups (with each group consisting of numerous individuals) and is regarded as the sufficiently minimal *social* relation in existence. A triad consists of three (or more) individuals or groups. Dyads and triads are qualitatively distinctive in a number of ways. A dyadic relationship tends to be more intimate or personal in character, involves more affect or emotion in its development and maintenance, and entails a relatively lower threshold of disassociation (Pyyhtinen 2010; Yoon, Thye, and Lawler 2013). The insertion of at least a third person or group in a given triadic relationship is seen to raise the prospect that a majority of participants could opportunistically align to wield influence and power over the minority within the triad.

During the 20th century, social network theory and analysis developed into a key strand of social scientific endeavor in its own right and increasingly assumed a formalistic quality owing to innovations in mathematics and computational science (Freeman 2004). Whereas the study of social networks demonstrated a capacity to produce important theoretical insights and empirical results, pockets of intellectual dissatisfaction emerged in response to perceptions of overformalization of relational inquiry concerning social networks. From the late 1970s these disaffected pockets congealed into a sub-discipline commonly known today as relational sociology, which by now is capably represented by academic associations and other research networks as well as a growing body of scholarly literature.

I wish to note two formative contributions to relational sociology. The first case is a "manifesto" paper, authored by Mustafa Emirbayer. In this paper, he poses the following question: What should be the focal point for social inquiry? For a relationist such as Emirbayer, the answer is that the relationships between actors (be they individuals or organizations and other collectives) should be the focal point. Furthermore, appropriate forms of social inquiry should embrace the possibility that dynamical shifts in relational structures take place among actors over time. Emirbayer's manifesto for relational sociology seeks to undermine the intellectual salience of so-called substantialist approaches, which privilege "*substances* of various kinds (things, beings, essences) . . . [as] . . . fundamental units of all inquiry" (Emirbayer 1997, 282; emphasis in original). Examples of substantialism include the "self-action" of an isolated individual and "inter-action" between distinct actors within a static sociocultural context. Both of these are contrasted with "trans-action," providing both meaning and purpose for actors as a consequence of the relationships they create and manage.

In addition to their ontological and methodological contributions, relational sociologists have advanced a case for deploying relationships as the foundation for examining the empirical content of networks. The second case is that of Harrison White (1992). He points to the efforts of agents within society to justify the generation of ties, and to strengthen the bonds those ties entail, by using persuasive narratives and stories, as well as by creating shared identities. All these strategies are aiming at forging relational meaning and commitment among participants. Associated with White's contributions are those of Tilly (2006), who examined the rationalizations offered by people in the process of forming, perpetuating, and even dissolving their relationships. Within the subdiscipline of economic sociology, Viviana Zelizer (2005, 2011) has coined the concept of "relational work" to describe the forms of claims-making, negotiation, maintenance, and transformation that people undertake when they engage in economic exchange.

What is the objective, if anything, that relational theory is trying to accomplish? In essence, I see two key accomplishments pursuant to the explicit recognition of relationships. The first is that relationality may be regarded as a cornerstone of realist social ontology, and that it provides a methodologically sound frame of social scientific investigation. Elements of the relational turn, as discussed in this section, have emerged as a critique of what are seen to be overly simplistic, indeed unrealistic, conceptions of human agency and decision-making that assume that an individual operates in isolation and divorced from cultural, economic, political, and social contexts. Consideration of relationships is also relevant to discussions about the nature of methodological individualism, as pointed out by Hodgson (2007).

The second point is that an emphasis on relationships opens up analytical vistas on a broad range of societal phenomena that may not be adequately represented by nonrelational frameworks of human action. For example, Emirbayer (1997) speculatively outlines the relevance of relationality for philosophical concepts such as equality, justice, and liberty. All these issues are relevant to Richard Wagner's substantial body of work.

As intellectually efficacious a relational approach may appear, there are risks associated with pursuing especially strong visions of relationality. Some critics of the relational sociology agenda, for example, warn of the potential problems surrounding the *reification* of relations to the exclusion of the study of those individuals that build the connections between one another (e.g., Erikson 2013; Burkitt 2016; Porpora 2018; Vandenberghe 2018). Arguably one of the most robust declarations for retaining individual agency, and the projects they embark on, within academic consideration is given by John Levi Martin (2009, 14), who states,

> Some network theorists in effect declare that the relations themselves, and not the persons, should be the units of analysis. Now this is the kind of change that must be justified on analytic grounds: there is no general philosophic reason for such a preference. This is because if relations become the units, then the relations are connected to one another by the (former) units, which then become the relations! A determination to stand "on the side of relations," however earnest, must only lead to wild catapulting back and forth. For the case of social structures, I do not believe that there are sufficient analytic grounds to treat relations—in this case, interactions—as the things, as opposed to the persons. . . . It strikes me that there is nothing so analytically distasteful about people that we must bend over backward to remove them from our theories, when our theories are, when the day is done, only by, of, and for people—whatever they may be.

My argument, presented in the following sections, is that Wagner's entangled political economy presents a genuine attentiveness toward relational issues without expunging the influence of creative yet fallible individuals in shaping economic and political arrangements. To put it simply, entangled political economy is an apt demonstration of Wagner's intellectual prowess as a *relational social scientist.*

ENTANGLED POLITICAL ECONOMY AS RELATIONAL THEORY: APPRAISING WAGNER'S CONTRIBUTIONS

Orthodox versus Entangled Political Economy: Contrastive Rationalities

As the term implies, "political economy" is a compound noun denoting some form of relation between the distinctive categories of economy and polity. The study of political economy is shrouded in great controversy because, as noted by Wagner, standard interpretations of political economy—including the contemporary form of "political economics" as described by Blankart and Koester (2006)—feature relations between *overly abstracted* categories of economy and polity. By this I mean, and following Potts's (2000) critique, economic and political actors are assumed to be homogenized and united entities that occupy the entire space of economic and political action, respectively. This representative-agent modeling removes from conceptual and analytical scenery the presence of multitudinous, heterogeneous actors (including collective entities such as firms, governments, nonprofit bodies, etc.) that interact and relate among economic-political domains. In its place stand conventional notions of political economy denoted by additive object-to-object relationships.

Several implications arise from this sterilization of relationality in standard, or orthodox, political economy treatments. The representative-agent economic and political actors are modeled to be acting on each other in conceptually predetermined ways. Departures from the presumption that economic activity (conducted by a representative economic actor) reflects an optimal allocation of resources are seen to rationalize sequentially corrective intervention through political means (conducted by a representative economic actor). This idea is synonymous with the well-known paradigm of "market failure," wherein political intervention is held to shift an economy from a suboptimal to an optimal state. As expressed by Wagner (2014, 21), "An economy is conceptualized as an equilibrated entity, which allows it to be treated as possessing point-mass status. A polity is conceptualized as a unified locus of power that stands apart from economy and acts on economy to shift its equilibrium." On several occasions Wagner has metaphorically depicted this economic-political relationship as akin to the impact of a (political) cue ball on an otherwise inert set of (economic) balls on a billiards table, which is strikingly similar to the antisubstantialist language sometimes used by relational scholars.

The vision of politics as a corrective for unsatisfactory, nonoptimal states of the economy is not only apparent in microeconomic theory. In this regard, political actors are viewed as necessary to transition the (micro)economy from conditions of imperfect competition to those reflective of perfect competition. The political impulse for intervention is abundantly evident in macroeconomics, in that the aggregative and unitary system of the (macro)economy is prone to bouts of unemployment, inflation, and other variations of instability in the absence of such political intervention. Macroeconomic approaches that conceive of the economic system as a holistic aggregate is symptomatic, once again, of a lack of ontological realism: "The systems level is just a collection of statistics, projections, and reflections of beliefs, hopes, and ideologies. It is not, however, a place where action occurs" (Wagner 2021, 8).

Over the years Wagner has developed and refined an alternative conception of political economy, one that provides an enriching account of economic and political relationships among actors, and collectives of actors, within the same society. As indicated by Wagner (2020), the substantialist conception of representative agents in orthodox political economy effectively removes interactions and relationships as focal points for investigation, aside from the additive portrait of holistic polity sequentially intervening on holistic economy. The alternative, now commonly known as entangled political economy, serves to substitute "a common individual with variegated individuals and treats the relation between system and individuals as an emergent feature of human interaction" (Wagner 2020, 74).

The connections that emerge within an entangled political economy are as variegated as the individual actors themselves, and the organizations and other collectives they formulate. Indeed, "the connections that run through a society are numerous and dense in places. . . . Society is not encountered as a formless mass but as a structured network of connections and relationships" (Wagner 2013a, 84). Entangled political economy reflects an actor-oriented ontology, similar to that presented in Little (2020), informed by divergent and partial relations among the various individuals and collectives within society. As will be explained in greater detail later in the chapter, the economic, political, and social outcomes are likely to vary in accordance with the structure of connections among entities, as well as the operational and governance properties resident within the various entities (Wagner 2014). Another property that carries especial meaning in entangled political economy is the potential for coeval relationships among actors engaging in crisscrossing economic and political domains of activity. It is here that the potential for emergent order theorizing is accommodated, insofar as interactions and relations at micro- and meso-levels potentially yield arrangements—such as organizational forms and institutional structures—of macro-level coordinative capacity, not to mention varying degrees of societal complexity (Foster 2005).

Entangled political economy is contrasted against orthodox manifestations of political economy that, as mentioned, are informed by the equilibrating logics of separable relations between abstract economic and political categories (Wagner 1993). The entangled approach reinforces that "political and commercial activities take place within the same society, and involve interactions and relationships among the same people. It is thus meaningful to speak of entangled systems of political economy and their properties" (Wagner 2016, ix). This statement implies a methodologically individualistic perspective that is nonatomistic in nature and, consistent with this, is inclusive of those relationships that human beings forge with one another (Hodgson 2007). In response to economic narratives centered on a solitary, Robinson Crusoe–style individual agent, Wagner (2010, 14) observes that "when many Crusoes interact, patterns emerge that would never have occurred through isolated individual action."

The essence of entrepreneurship and innovation for Wagner is inherently relational, invariably entailing entanglements in the form of relational chains of multiperson cooperation. The production of seemingly mundane products, such as pencils, is the product of potentially long-standing interactions between various individuals and, as is more likely the case given the presence of globalized supply chains, various organizational clusters of individuals within firms, industry associations, and other collective participants. Furthermore, these actors would be relationally bound by contracts and similar agreements, which help manage the production and sale of inputs and other relevant materials in complex and uncertain environments. Many economic relationships, in addition to those concerning pencil manufacture, are, indeed, "relational as befits the fixed-cost character that necessarily accompanies the establishment of any relationship. This relational character leads in turn to a strong presumption that the knowledge generated through market interaction will be genuine because both parties are in the position where they must continually attract business in open competition with other potential transactional partners" (Wagner 2013b, 98).

Entangled political economy extends to a consideration of the nature and significance of heterogeneous actors operating within the political domain. As noted, the existence of relationships between fractionalized and distributed political actors sharply contrasts with that of the holistically unified actor conceived in orthodox (additive) political economy frameworks. Actors within the political domain are "tagged" with attributes in accordance with their diverse relational activities and roles—including those that result from the existence of specific offices, as well as those attached to responsibilities assigned to actors among varying levels of government (say, within federal systems of public governance). Wagner's research has directed considerable attention to the "peculiar political business" of legislative assemblies within democracies, wherein their elected members debate and select political initiatives to sponsor (through favorable fiscal, legal, and regulatory measures) (Wagner 2010, 2012a, 2016). A closely associated branch of research is that which characterizes certain agencies within entangled public service ecologies as "Big Players" with discretionary powers that may significantly reorient economic and social relationships (e.g., Koppl 2002; Salter 2012).

Entangled Network Structures: Forms and Implications

For many decades the study of networks has served as a conceptual and analytical centerpiece for investigating an array of human relationships. A network may be described as a set of actors (referred to in network-theoretic terminology as "nodes") connected or joined together by some form of interaction or relationship (referred to as "ties"). Describing networks formally, in mathematical terms, a network consists of a set of objects (the nodes) and a mapping or description of relations between the objects or nodes (Doreian 1970; Kadushin 2012). Network theory and analysis provides a solid basis for an assessment of relationships, for it considers the interdependencies forged between actors (and groups of actors) as giving rise to complicated patterns, or structures, of interaction. As put simply by Little (2020, 84), "Relationships can be represented as a . . . network of interconnections." Furthermore, by emphasizing the existence of relational structures, network theory and analysis avoids the reification of individual actors in social science.

In many of Wagner's works, stylized networks are diagrammatically represented, providing a topographical depiction of actor-nodes and their positions within an abstract space of economic-political activity together with their ties. It is important to reiterate that an ontologically and methodologically nuanced framework, such as entangled political economy, lends itself to a broad-ranging understanding of the character of network nodes and ties. Nodes need not be restricted to a representation of (heterogeneous) individuals but may encompass collective arrangements orchestrated by groups of individuals. As noted by Knoke and Bokun (2020, 71–72), "Relations are interactions among social actors—whether individual natural persons, small groups, organizations, or nation states." In Wagner's own works, nodes have often been represented as commercial and political enterprises, although efforts have been extended to include the likes of nonprofit organizations (Auteri and Wagner 2007; Aligica and Wagner 2020) and, more recently, social movements (Novak 2021).

The analytically admissible set of ties is similarly expansive: "Connections are not singular but entail a structured multiplicity of connections, some surely more foundational than others. . . . We can think of material, legal, and moral levels of connection, all of which operate jointly in generating observable patterns of societal interaction" (Wagner 2010, 46). Similarly, Little (2020, 85) explains that networks can be described "in terms of multiple kinds of social relationship: communication, affinity, loyalty and obligation, economic interdependence, ethnic or religious organization, and many other kinds of social relationship." In large part, ties in entangled political economy studies have been depicted as economic exchanges, but it is possible to extend this to social exchanges, as highlighted by Novak (2018a).

Modern academic inquiry into networks is exemplified by its empirical prowess, with a voluminous amount of research drawing on quantitative frameworks, statistical analysis, and computational modeling capacity to describe the performance of networks. Essentially, the performative properties of networked relations are influenced by the kinds of nodes that carry out actions as well as the patterns of connection among the nodes (Wagner 2020). Space constrains my ability to fully discuss the empirical dimensions of network analysis, although a few remarks are warranted (for a discussion from an economic sociology perspective, see Bleser [2018] and Calder and Storr [2021]). The empirical patterning of ties within a network (Granovetter 1973), and the position of actors within the network space (Burt 1992), is seen to have important implications regarding the diffusion of information and opportunities among actors. In addition, as Austrian economists have explained (Chamlee-Wright 2008), exchange relations within network settings can enable multiple individuals and their groups to engage in a process of social learning. These findings, and more, are of great significance to entangled political economy, as will be explained below.

Entangled political economy recognizes variegated network properties associated with unique relationships forged and retained by a mixture of actors. Wagner's approach emphasizes the phenomenon of entangled commingling between commercial and political enterprises within shared economic and political spaces. There are many abstract and concrete examples that can be nominated in this regard—from Wagner's thought experiments concerning marinas, jitneys, and watercourse draining projects through to his practical discussions about public service systems, credit markets, governmental responses to health and financial crises, and so on. This emphasis transcends a relatively trivial exercise of observation of the kinds of entanglements that have emerged to rather more deeply consider the consequences of such entanglements on the *quality* of relationships in political economy. It is in this respect that I argue that entangled political economy capably addresses the concerns of relational sociologists, such as Harrison White, who argue that network studies have largely ignored the nonmaterialistic meanings underlying relations between actors.

Economic and political enterprises are seen by Wagner to operate in accordance with divergent operating principles and institutional frameworks, and on the basis of contrasting rationalities guiding action. All actors within society are presumed to act rationally, in that they undertake (often costly) actions in the pursuit of material and other gains. Markets are populated by diverse actors (including for-profit, commercial enterprises) aspiring to produce outputs at reasonable prices for their customers. It is presumed these entities are incentivized to generate economic value as a consequence of competitive pressures. Market competition is considered to motivate enterprises to not only minimize transaction costs associated with economic exchange (Coase 1937) but also induce innovations by harnessing the knowledge, skills, and talent of in-house staff and supply chain associates in the quest for betterment (Wagner 2010).

Political enterprises and other actors engaged within the political domain also seek to gain from their activities. However, political enterprises are unable to generate their own revenue and inherently lack a basis for economic calculation, because market prices cannot emerge in the presence of inalienable, collective property (Wagner 2010, 2013a). Specifically, "with collective property being inalienable, the internal economy of the state cannot generate prices. In a technical sense, political entities must act parasitically upon the market economy in using the price information generated through market activity" (Eusepi and Wagner 2011, 578–79). Drawing on the Italian public finance tradition, Wagner indicates that governments compulsorily acquire taxation and other revenues to support their political enterprises and that this process creates a "forced exchange" relationship between political enterprises and the commercial enterprises that furnish revenue. As described in Wagner (2012a), governments also frequently impose regulation to alter the relational landscape of economic exchanges that would otherwise be realized among market participants.

It is in this context that Wagner and his associates draw on a rich vein of sociological literature to distinguish between "dyadic" and "triadic" network relationships. As explained previously, this distinction is commonly attributed to Georg Simmel. In an important paper within the entangled political economy literature, Podemska-Mikluch and Wagner (2013, 180) explain that "triadic exchange arises because sponsors of such exchanges seek to change the pattern created through dyadic exchanges." In a clarifying moment, they outline the difference between "triadic-by-invitation" and "triadic-by-assertion"—with the former arising as a result of a numerical minority of disagreeable parties conceding to the forced (political) exchange in the absence of alternative redress, and the latter arising when political actors and their supporters willingly convert existing dyadic relationships without the consent of those involved in the dyads. The significance of triadic networks is that they are associated with "parasitical and tectonic relationships within a system of political economy" (172) and represent a fount for relational conflict within society.

Emergent in the entangled ecology of relations between commercial and political enterprises is a peculiar mix of relationships. To some extent, voluntaristic relationships remain among some producers, investors, and consumers, insofar as elements of market participation are not unduly rearranged by political ties. Coexisting in an entangled political economy are coercive, forced relations, as political actors exert legal, fiscal, and regulatory rearrangements of economic terms and conditions. All else being equal, a more extensive degree of entanglement between commercial and political enterprises is likely to detrimentally affect economic performance and compromise the exercise of liberties more broadly, as tensions between oppositional interests come to the surface of societal interactions. Economically, the impacts may include the extinguishment of some marginal (including startup, or small size) commercial enterprises and the prospect that some entrepreneurial initiatives may never see the light of day as fiscal and regulatory impositions reshape perceptions of feasible profit opportunities (Kirzner 1997).

Another qualitative aspect of entanglement is the effects of more intensive economic-political commingling on those enterprises that remain. Wagner's scholarship often refers to Jane Jacobs's (1992) warning about the emergence of "monstrous moral hybrids" within the networked landscape of political economy. Commercial and political enterprises operate in accordance with diverging kinds of ethical propensities (or what Jacobs refers to as "syndromes"). Commercial activities are seen to generally correspond with certain properties such as "honesty, rectitude, punctuality, teamwork, and conviviality" (Wagner 2016, 120), not to mention the qualities or virtues of industriousness, adherence to contracts, and respect for property. Political activities may be seen to carry beneficial ethical attributes, such as group protectiveness, fortitude, and solidarity. However, the "guardian" syndromes associated with politics may come in the form of potentially vexing qualities—depending on the circumstances under which they are exercised—such as obedience (including deference to hierarchy) and vengeance in response to (actual or perceived) wrongdoings.

A potential issue with tighter entanglements is the creation of monstrous hybrids as described by both Jacobs and Wagner. Inherent in these peculiar entities is the conduct of activity and the performance of functions, which confound the ethical tendencies typically associated with both economic and political domains. By way of a generic statement, it may be suggested that as commercial enterprises entwine themselves with legislative and bureaucratic actors, whether voluntarily or otherwise, their activities become increasingly dictated by the guardian ethical norms of political prerogative and circumstance. A recent example of this appeared in the shape of Australian policy responses to the 2020–2021 COVID-19 pandemic, pressuring businesses to conduct their affairs contrary to customer service ethical norms. During this period, regulators obliged retailers to actively surveil their customers with QR store entry codes, check for appropriate mask wearing, and discourage the browsing of products in-store (Caisley 2021).

What is especially important to recognize in all this is that political actors, and their enablers and supporters elsewhere within society, significantly partake in communicative strategies to persuade and soothe those who lose from any politically induced lack of choice. Drawing, again, quite freely from the sociological well of insight, Wagner connects with Vilfredo Pareto (1935) in explaining how nonlogical sentiments are deployed to encourage at least communal acquiescence, if not acceptance, of political activity. Witness the common refrains that policy is "good for the country," is "the price of civilization," or, as has been prominently articulated in recent times, helps "keep you, and us, safe," even if those pleadings ideologically deflect from the reality of relational reconfiguration in the support of political enterprise activities.

In the final analysis, "entangled political economy works with network-based representations of relationships and interactions among the relevant entities within a system of political economy" (Wagner 2016, 75). While Wagner embraces an actor-centered perspective of social inquiry, he has embraced conceptual portrayals of human action that include complex guises of relationality. This statement is attested by Wagner's discussions about how structures and forms of relations are qualitatively influenced by differing ordering principles of enterprise activity, and how the assertion of such principles can potentially give rise to contradiction and tension (Wagner 2014). In particular, the assertion of the political pursuit of gain is suggested to lead to tectonic clashes between competing, and often conflicting, activities, as well as the potential for qualitative changes in the character of network nodes themselves in the shape of monstrous hybrids.

Rules and Institutions of (Entangled and Relational) Liberalism

Entangled political economy stresses that individuals and their collective entities pursue actions on the same societal plane. When it comes to commercial and political enterprises, it is highly likely they will intermingle as part of their efforts to reduce the costs and other burdens associated with gainful pursuits, although these varying enterprises operate in accordance with differing operating principles. Strands of contemporary economic thought, such as new institutional economics, public choice, Austrian economics, and law and economics, indicate that economic operations and practices are also influenced by an elaborate tapestry of formal and informal rules and institutional constructs. The prevalence and efficacy of certain institutions are also acknowledged in entangled political economy to affect the condition of economic and political relationships.

Wagner (1997, 162) indicates that "relationships . . . are governed by the principles of property and contract," and I briefly consider these two institutional prerequisites of productive economic activity. As stressed by Liljenberg (2004), market activities are infused with relational obligations that both enable and constrain economic actors in their pursuit of profitable gains. The formulation of contracts is a critical means through which actors coordinate. Although recognizing the potential ambiguities and incompleteness of contracts in evolving and uncertain market contexts, it is generally conceived that contracts can assist in relationally entrenching mutual expectations, especially in relation to the delivery of goods and services at agreed prices over a period of time. Even so, it is also observable that informal practices—such as the exchange of words and handshakes—can relationally connect actors, especially those who have acquired familiarity with one another's behaviors, conduct, and standards.

In a political economy featuring a relatively high degree of entanglement between commercial and political enterprises, governmental entities are afforded great influence regarding the approval and framing of contractual stipulations.

Even the bundles of contracts that constitute commercial enterprises are subject to political scrutiny. To quote Wagner at length on these points:

> Principles of property and contract now operate only as necessary conditions for an enterprise to go forward, but they are no longer sufficient conditions. In many cases, the explicit permission of the state will be required before an enterprise can go forward. This is true in the United States for a wide variety of specific activities, including broadcasting, farming, and many forms of transportation. It is also true for all activities that would use lands designated by the state as wetlands, or even as otherwise environmentally sensitive. Further, the substance of the agreements among enterprise participants is to a significant extent stipulated by the state. (Wagner 1998, 108)

Contracts invariably pertain to the management of property, or at least influence their management, including the terms of control, use, and transfer. A hallmark of Wagner's thought is his acknowledgment of the relational underpinnings of property, and particularly the contestable nature of property given that people are prone to disagree, oftentimes passionately, over how others manage their properties. Specifically, "property rights have meaning only within societies, so a person's rights of property are limited by the willingness of other people to forbear from interfering with any particular person's chosen activity. Where that forbearance ends, public property begins. Once this is recognized, it must also be recognized that dividing lines between state and market are blurry and subject continually to contestation" (Wagner 2016, 26). The presence of societal interest in property, including efforts aiming to sponsor political initiatives to influence the management of (public and private) properties, indicates that property rights are, practically, far from absolute (Novak 2018b).

As a philosophical doctrine, liberalism has long insisted on the desirability of societies to adhere to several institutional prerequisites that are conceived to facilitate material prosperity. This includes, as arguably most clearly articulated by the German ordo-liberal school of political economy (Eucken [1950] 1992; Kolev 2015), the ability of people to establish and enforce contracts and manage their properties, while remaining respectful of the equal liberties of others to conduct similar activity. The implicit presumption here is that voluntaristic relational dealings among heterogeneous economic actors, each with idiosyncratic preferences and knowledge, under these institutional conditions will tend to generate market-tested betterments (Hall and Lawson 2014).

In an effort to guarantee that the equal liberty proviso is maintained, most liberals also give qualified endorsement to a role for political actors, and their political enterprises, to maintain the institutional rules of a liberal economic order. Following the insights of Vincent Ostrom, Wagner (2016, 2021) appreciates that the assignment, and application, of coercive power by political actors represents a Faustian bargain. Specifically, assigning legislators, bureaucrats, and similar political participants the responsibility to uphold liberal institutions in good faith also equips them with the potential to abuse their responsibilities, by using fiscal, legal, and regulatory means to substitute triadic for dyadic relationships. As noted, the proliferation of triads in entangled political economy is consistent with advantaging particularized interests while disadvantaging others. My fundamental point is to, once more, illustrate the inherent relationality of liberal thought—in this respect, liberals have deeply pondered matters concerning the relationship between citizen and state.

Over recent decades, liberal scholars and advocates have noted with concern the tendency in most countries for the size and scope of government to expand. In Wagner's view, this effective transition from liberal democracy toward social democracy is problematic in several respects. Relatively greater political involvement in economic affairs is likely to correspond with an effective departure from "constitution of liberty" institutional settings typified by formal, as well as informal, limitations on governmental spending, taxing, and regulatory authority (Wagner 2012a). Overexploitation of the fiscal commons is one potential consequence of this development (Buchanan and Wagner [1977] 2000). This broader transition likewise risks fomenting tectonic contradictions, which, in turn, arise from the simultaneous existence of private and public property systems: "A regime of social democracy carries with it a set of incongruent institutional arrangements that elicit continuing clashes at the various boundaries where enterprises organized according to two different sets of rules collide" (Wagner 1998, 107). Contrary to sentimental expressions that policy acts to quell economic instability, discretionary political activity that triadically rearranges economic relationships intensifies turbulence and uncertainty for market-situated actors, beyond that turbulence associated with the shifting of the ecology of plans dyadically orchestrated by economic enterprises (Wagner 2012b).

Another trend investigated in depth by Wagner is that of centralization in public administration, especially within federal systems that constitutionally articulate the distribution of policy functions and responsibilities among levels of government. In several insightful contributions, Wagner illustrates that fiscal and regulatory centralization, from lower-level governments to a central government, is consistent with the dulling of significance of polycentrically oriented, and politically competitive, multiple actor-nodes of decision-making

(Eusepi and Wagner 2010; Wagner 2016). In its place emerge monocentric network arrangements within the polity that concentrate political decisions (and, consequently, influence and power) in the possession of fewer nodes. A corollary of this is that "only a subset of citizens will have direct access to . . . members, and the pattern of this access will be systematic and not random: power law distributions will dominate random distributions, which means that a relatively few number of people will dominate direct access to political processes" (Wagner 2016, 77).

ENTANGLED POLITICAL ECONOMY AND RELATIONAL EQUALITY: AGAINST NEO-FEUDALISM

To finalize this exploration of Wagnerian relationality, I wish to briefly sketch out the proposition that liberalism undergirds human action in such a way as to *promote relational equality*. That is to say, the instantiation of substantive liberal commitments—such as competitive markets, open societies, and limited government operating in accordance with the rule of law—would serve to promote the treatment of diverse, heterogeneous individuals as each other's dignified and moral equals. To quote directly from Wagner (2014, 31), "As an ideal type, liberalism envisions society as constituted through horizontal relations among equals. Connective tissue is woven through material created through mutuality."

It is true that temporal inequalities of income and wealth may result as entrepreneurship and innovation are engaged by heterogeneous individuals with diverse talents and endowments. To the extent that economic institutions are oriented to the principles of contract, property, and liability, as discussed previously, most economists suppose that material inequalities would tend to be competed away by the incessant winds of market competition. Furthermore, income and wealth inequalities in an evolving economy are likely to be offset by improvements in consumption equality and the broadening of prosperity's fruits including the least advantaged (Eberstadt 2017).

From the relational perspective outlined in this chapter, it is worthwhile to contextualize these statements. Specifically, we should consider that "the inequalities that arise through market success tend to feed the vanities by exaggerating individual accomplishment relative to what is really due to the supporting nexus of relationships" (Wagner 2013a, 92). Nevertheless, the anticipation is that the greater the freedom bequeathed to actors to choose their partners in economic exchanges, the more likely that relational equality is to be achieved: "The dyadic relationships of market catallaxy are between equals who must continually attract one another in an environment of open competition where there are no entitlements to receive continued support outside of mutual attraction" (Wagner 2016, 125). Hierarchy is out the door, and equality is in, when individuals stand to achieve mutual gains from dyadic economic exchange relations.

The presence, or lack thereof, of relational equality between persons in markets and persons in political environments is synonymized with Martin Buber's (1958) "I-Thou" and "I-It" relational types. This distinction reflects an underlying proposition that "the reality of being for Buber is relation. The I in each of the word pairings is defined in relationship to its pair: It and Thou. These two basic forms of relation for Buber define man's outward behavior" (Brough and Simmons 2019, 11). I-Thou reflects a subject-to-subject relational condition of mutualized feelings of authenticity, empathy, and respect, whereas I-It is considered a subject-to-object relation congruent with patterns of inter-personal abuse, duplicitousness, and insincerity.

Wagner (2010) perceptively argues that most people practically enjoy social experiences consistent with I-Thou relationships. This observation is inclusive of market activity, as noted by Storr (2008). In response to its critics, the market process is seen to have the capacity "to replace the coldness of impersonal exchange with the warmth of personal exchange, creating a friendlier world in the process, or to transform I–It relationships into I–Thou relationships" (Wagner 2010, 110). According to Wagner, I-Thou relationships are synony-mous with market interactions: "Market-based relationships seem typically to be of the I-Thou form, where the focus of the conversation between the parties is on whether they can arrange something that will be for their mutual benefit" (Wagner 2013a, 91).

By contrast, relations through the I-It prism reflect a lack of mutuality and respect from a given participant in relation to another (or others), impart-ing a lack of relational equality. For Wagner, such a malign relational con-ception is more likely to be prevalent in political relationships, in that those who are subject to coercion are seen as objects to be manipulated, controlled, or reformed. This insight bears similarities to Adam Smith's "man of system" conception of subjects as chessboard pieces, and Friedrich Hayek's "synoptic delusion" of top-down societal redesign. Classical liberals also well appreciate that departures from the rule of law, wherein different individuals and groups come to be treated differentially by political actors, induce relational inequali-ties between the governors and the governed. To these criticisms I add the substantialist fantasy, including that which pervades orthodox political econ-omy, conceiving other people as billiard balls to be prodded about the leveled billiards table of society. It follows from this discussion that "political action creates positions of lordship in place of relationships of mutuality, thereby transforming I-Thou relationships into I-It relationships" (Wagner 2013a, 92).

Entangled political economy theorists have also diagnosed a propensity among political actors to stratify those with whom they relate as "friends" or "enemies," along the lines of the notorious German Nazi-era philosopher Carl Schmitt (Wagner 2016; Salter and Wagner 2019). Should the extent of commitment, including by way of self-adherence, to institutional rules wane, the capacity of legislators, bureaucrats, and other influential political actors to create triadic relational exceptions to good public governance is hypothesized to correspondingly increase (Sterpan and Wagner 2017). Transforming the "state into booty," to paraphrase German liberal and statesmen Ludwig Erhard, is a mechanism through which political actors simultaneously reward their friends and punish their enemies. This coalitional tendency is supposed to introduce arbitrariness and discrimination into the conduct of government, all of which depart from the rule of law and equal policy treatment of all (Hayek [1960] 2011; Buchanan and Congleton [1998] 2003).

My basic premise is that much of the empirically and observationally discerned degree of inequality in contemporary societies results from the high degree of entanglement between economy and polity. The liberal schema of equality, liberty, and justice is posited to be underpinned by economic, political, and social relationships "on principles of equality, mutuality, and reciprocity, and not on feudal-like principles involving status relationships of superior and subordinate" (Wagner 2010, 181). In this light, the liberal struggle against neo-feudalism may be similarly framed as a venture opposing the regressive trajectory of societal relations from (voluntary and mutually agreeable) contract to (involuntary and contestable) status. Therefore, liberal thinking aims at generating ideas and proposals with the effect of disentangling forced, triadic relationships that prevent the equalizing effects of market competition and that close off opportunities for upward mobility on the part of the disadvantaged and oppressed (Lindsey and Teles 2017; Novak 2018a).

CONCLUSION

In this chapter honoring Wagner's contributions to political economy, I seek to pay tribute to him as a relational scholar. By this, I mean to say that Wagner provides several landmark contributions advancing our understanding of human relationships. For the most casual reader of Wagner's oeuvre, it might well be sufficient to affirm my claim merely by observing the multiple references to relationships by Wagner himself. When I submit that Wagnerian relationality is both profound and warranting greater attention by social scientists, my argument goes several degrees beyond performing a rudimentary linguistic analysis.

Without exception, Wagner is deeply thoughtful and informative about the human condition and what it means to be free, without resorting to the scholarly dead ends of atomism and holism. I find Wagnerian relationality to be an inspiring point of orientation in my own research, and I suspect other specialists in entangled political economy can attest to a similar experience. In my view it is the humble obligation of Wagner's associates and students to build on his intellectual innovations, in a spirit of genuine inquiry toward better comprehending the nature and significance of that structured living-togetherness that informs our entangled, relational lives.

REFERENCES

Aligica, P. D., and R. E. Wagner. 2020. "Economic Coordination in Environments with Incomplete Pricing." *Review of Austrian Economics* 33, no. 3: 315–29.

August, K. J., and K. S. Rook. 2013. "Social Relationships." In *Encyclopedia of Behavioral Medicine*, edited by M. D. Gellman and J. R. Turner, 1838–42. New York: Springer.

Auteri, M., and R. E. Wagner. 2007. "The Organizational Architecture of Nonprofit Governance: Economic Calculation within an Ecology of Enterprises." *Public Organization Review* 7, no. 1: 57–68.

Baker, G., R. Gibbons, and K. J. Murphy. 2002. "Relational Contracts and the Theory of the Firm." *Quarterly Journal of Economics* 117, no. 1: 39–84.

Bathelt, H., and J. Glückler. 2011. *The Relational Economy: Geographies of Knowing and Learning.* Oxford: Oxford University Press.

Blankart, C. B., and G. B. Koester. 2006. "Political Economics versus Public Choice: Two Views of Political Economy in Competition." *Kyklos* 59, no. 2: 171–200.

Bleser, A. 2018. "Potential Contributions from Sociology to James Buchanan's Theoretical Agenda for Economics." In *Exploring the Political Economy and Social Philosophy of James M. Buchanan,* edited by P. D. Aligica, C. J. Coyne, and S. Haeffele, 215–33. Lanham, MD: Rowman & Littlefield

Blosser, J. 2019. "Relational History: Adam Smith's Types of Human History." *Erasmus Journal for Philosophy and Economics* 12, no. 2: 24–48.

Brough, T. J., and R. T. Simmons. 2019. "Economics as Moral Exchange: James Buchanan Meets Martin Buber." Unpublished manuscript. https://broughtj.github.io/assets/files/Brough -Simmons-Final-Draft-0702-2019.pdf.

Buber, M. 1958. *I and Thou.* 2nd ed. New York: Scribner's.

Buchanan, J. M., and R. D. Congleton. (1998) 2003. *Politics by Principle, Not Interest: Toward Nondiscriminatory Democracy.* Indianapolis: Liberty Fund.

Buchanan, J. M., and R. E. Wagner. (1977) 2000. *Democracy in Deficit: The Political Legacy of Lord Keynes.* Indianapolis: Liberty Fund.

Burkitt, I. 2016. "Relational Agency: Relational Sociology, Agency and Interaction." *European Journal of Social Theory* 19, no. 3: 322–39.

Burt, R. S. 1992. *Structural Holes: The Social Structure of Competition.* Cambridge, MA: Harvard University Press.

Caisley, A. 2021. "Now Is Not the Time to Go to Hardware Stores." *The Australian,* August 18.

Calder, A., and V. H. Storr. 2021. "New Economic Sociology and the Ostroms: A Combined Approach." In *Elinor Ostrom and the Bloomington School: Building a New Approach to Policy and the Social Sciences,* edited by J. Lemke and V. Tarko, 71–86. Montreal, Canada: McGill-Queen's University Press.

Chamlee-Wright, E. 2008. "The Structure of Social Capital: An Austrian Perspective on Its Nature and Development." *Review of Political Economy* 20, no. 1: 41–58.

Coase, R. H. 1937. "The Nature of the Firm." *Economica* 4, no. 16: 386–405.

Coats, E. J., and R. S. Feldman. 2001. *Classic and Contemporary Readings in Social Psychology.* 3rd ed. Upper Saddle River, NJ: Prentice Hall.

Cooley, C. H. (1902) 1983. *Human Nature and the Social Order.* London: Routledge.

Costelloe, T. M. 1997. "Contract or Coincidence: George Herbert Mead and Adam Smith on Self and Society." *History of the Human Sciences* 10, no. 2: 81–109.

Creelan, P. 1987. "The Degradation of the Sacred: Approaches of Cooley and Goffman." *Symbolic Interaction* 10, no. 1: 29–56.

Dépelteau, F. 2018. *The Palgrave Handbook of Relational Sociology.* Cham, Switzerland: Palgrave Macmillan.

Doreian, P. 1970. *Mathematics and the Study of Social Relations.* London: Weidenfeld and Nicholson.

Duck, S. 1999. *Relating to Others.* 2nd ed. Philadelphia: Open University Press.

Eberstadt, N. 2017. "Longevity, Education, and the Huge New Worldwide Increases in Equality." In *Anti-Piketty: Capital for the 21st Century,* edited by J.-P. Delsol, N. Lecaussin, and E. Martin, 19–28. Washington, DC: Cato Institute.

Elias, N. 1991. *The Society of Individuals.* Oxford: Basil Blackwell.

Emirbayer, M. 1997. "Manifesto for a Relational Sociology." *American Journal of Sociology* 103, no. 2: 281–317.

Erikson, E. 2013. "Formalist and Relationalist Theory in Social Network Analysis." *Sociological Theory* 31, no. 3: 219–42.

Eucken, W. (1950) 1992. *The Foundations of Economics: History and Theory in the Analysis of Economic Reality.* Translated by T. W. Hutchinson. Berlin: Springer Verlag.

Eusepi, G., and R. E. Wagner. 2010. "Polycentric Polity: Genuine vs. Spurious Federalism." *Review of Law and Economics* 6, no. 3: 329–45.

———. 2011. "States as Ecologies of Political Enterprises." *Review of Political Economy* 23, no. 4: 573–85.

Foster, J. 2005. "From Simplistic to Complex Systems in Economics." *Cambridge Journal of Economics* 29, no. 6: 873–92.

Freeman, L. C. 2004. *The Development of Social Network Analysis: A Study in the Sociology of Science.* Vancouver: Empirical Press.

Gergen, K. J. 2009. *Relational Being: Beyond Self and Community.* New York: Oxford University Press.

Granovetter, M. S. 1973. "The Strength of Weak Ties." *American Journal of Sociology* 78, no. 6: 1360–80.

Gui, B., and R. Sugden. 2005. *Economics and Social Interaction: Accounting for Interpersonal Relations.* New York: Cambridge University Press.

Hall, J. C., and R. A. Lawson. 2014. "Economic Freedom of the World: An Accounting of the Literature." *Contemporary Economic Policy* 32, no. 1: 1–19.

Hayek, F. A. (1960) 2011. *The Constitution of Liberty: The Definitive Edition*. Chicago: University of Chicago Press.

Hodgson, G. M. 2007. "Meanings of Methodological Individualism." *Journal of Economic Methodology* 14, no. 2: 211–26.

Jacobs, J. 1992. *Systems of Survival*. New York: Random House.

Kadushin, C. 2012. *Understanding Social Networks: Theories, Concepts, and Findings*. New York: Oxford University Press.

Kirzner, I. M. 1997. "Entrepreneurial Discovery and the Competitive Market Process: An Austrian Approach." *Journal of Economic Literature* 35, no. 1: 60–85.

Knoke, D., and A. Bokun. 2020. "Social Relations and Economy: The Effects of Social Ties and Networks on Economic Behavior." In *A Modern Guide to Economic Sociology*, edited by M. Zafirovski, 70–89. Cheltenham, UK: Edward Elgar.

Kolev, S. 2015. "Ordoliberalism and the Austrian School." In *The Oxford Handbook of Austrian Economics*, edited by P. J. Boettke and C. J. Coyne, 419–44. New York: Oxford University Press.

Koppl, R. 2002. *Big Players and the Economic Theory of Expectations*. Basingstoke: Palgrave Macmillan.

Levin, J. 2003. "Relational Incentive Contracts." *American Economic Review* 93, no. 3: 835–57.

Liljenberg, A. 2004. "The Infusion of Relational Market Obligations into the Austrian Agenda: Some Lessons Learned from Economic Sociology." *Review of Austrian Economics* 17, no. 1: 115–33.

Lindsey, B., and S. M. Teles. 2017. *The Captured Economy: How the Powerful Enrich Themselves, Slow Down Growth, and Increase Inequality*. New York: Oxford University Press.

Little, D. 2020. *A New Social Ontology of Government: Consent, Coordination, and Authority*. Cham, Switzerland: Palgrave Macmillan.

MacBride, F. 2020. "Relations." *The Stanford Encyclopedia of Philosophy*. https://plato.stanford.edu/archives/win2020/entries/relations.

Martin, J. L. 2009. *Social Structures*. Princeton, NJ: Princeton University Press.

McClurg, S. D., and J. K. Young. 2011. "Editors' Introduction: A Relational Political Science." *PS: Political Science and Politics* 44, no. 1: 39–43.

Mead, G. H. (1934) 1950. *Mind, Self and Society*. Chicago: University of Chicago Press.

Miller, D. L. 1973. *George Herbert Mead: Self, Language and the World*. Chicago: University of Chicago Press.

Novak, M. 2018a. *Inequality: An Entangled Political Economy Perspective*. Cham, Switzerland: Palgrave Macmillan.

———. 2018b. "Property Rights in an Entangled Political Economy." *Journal des Économistes et des Études Humaines* 24, no. 1. Art. 20160016.

———. 2021. *Freedom in Contention: Social Movements and Liberal Political Economy*. Lanham, MD: Lexington Books.

Oxford English Dictionary. 2nd ed. Oxford: Oxford University Press.

Pareto, V. 1935. *The Mind and Society*. London: Jonathan Cape.

Podemska-Mikluch, M., and R. E. Wagner. 2013. "Dyads, Triads, and the Theory of Exchange: Between Liberty and Coercion." *Review of Austrian Economics* 26, no. 2: 171–82.

Porpora, D. V. 2018. "Critical Realism as Relational Sociology." In *The Palgrave Handbook of Relational Sociology*, edited by F. Dépelteau, 413–30. Cham, Switzerland: Palgrave Macmillan.

Potts, J. 2000. *The New Evolutionary Microeconomics: Complexity, Competence, and Adaptive Behaviour*. Cheltenham, UK: Edward Elgar.

Pyyhtinen, O. 2010. *Simmel and "the Social."* Basingstoke: Palgrave Macmillan.

Salter, A. W. 2012. "A Theory of the Dynamics of Entangled Political Economy with Application to the Federal Reserve." *Journal of Public Finance and Public Choice* 30, nos. 1–3: 77–101.

Salter, A. W., and R. E. Wagner. 2019. "Constitutional Catallaxy: Friends and Enemies in an Open-Ended Social Order." *Journal of Public Finance and Public Choice* 34, no. 1: 83–94.

Simmel, G. 1950. *The Sociology of Georg Simmel*. Translated by K. H. Wolff. Glencoe, IL: Free Press.

Smith, A. (1759) 2002. *The Theory of Moral Sentiments*. In *Cambridge Texts in the History of Philosophy*, edited by K. Haakonssen. Cambridge: Cambridge University Press.

Sterpan, I., and R. E. Wagner. 2017. "The Autonomy of the Political within Political Economy." *Advances in Austrian Economics* 22: 133–57.

Storr, V. H. 2008. "The Market as a Social Space: On the Meaningful Extraeconomic Conversations That Can Occur in Markets." *Review of Austrian Economics* 21, no. 2: 135–50.

Thelen, T., L. Vetters, and K. von Benda-Beckmann. 2014. "Introduction to Stategraphy: Toward a Relational Anthropology of the State." *Social Analysis* 58, no. 3: 1–19.

Tilly, C. 2006. *Why? What Happens When People Give Reasons . . . and Why*. Princeton, NJ: Princeton University Press.

Vandenberghe, F. 2018. "The Relation as Magical Operator: Overcoming the Divide between Relational and Processual Sociology." In *The Palgrave Handbook of Relational Sociology*, edited by F. Dépelteau, 35–57. Cham, Switzerland: Palgrave Macmillan.

Wagner, R. E. 1993. "The Impending Transformation of Public Choice Scholarship." *Public Choice* 77, no. 1: 203–12.

———. 1997. "Choice, Exchange, and Public Finance." *American Economic Review* 87, no. 2: 160–63.

———. 1998. "Social Democracy, Societal Tectonics, and Parasitical Pricing." *Constitutional Political Economy* 9, no. 2: 105–11.

———. 2010. *Mind, Society, and Human Action: Time and Knowledge in a Theory of Social Economy*. London: Routledge.

———. 2012a. *Deficits, Debt, and Democracy: Wrestling with Tragedy on the Fiscal Commons*. Cheltenham, UK: Edward Elgar.

———. 2012b. "Viennese Kaleidics: Why It's Liberty More Than Policy That Calms Turbulence." *Review of Austrian Economics* 25, no. 4: 283–97.

———. 2013a. "Property, Social Order, and Public Finance." In *Essentials of Fiscal Sociology: Conception of an Encyclopedia*, edited by J. G. Backhaus, 79–94. Frankfurt: Peter Lang.

———. 2013b. "What Kind of State in Our Future? Fact and Conjecture in Vito Tanzi's Government versus Markets." *Review of Austrian Economics* 26, no. 1: 93–104.

———. 2014. "Entangled Political Economy: A Keynote Address." *Advances in Austrian Economics* 18: 15–36.

———. 2016. *Politics as a Peculiar Business: Insights from a Theory of Entangled Political Economy*. Cheltenham, UK: Edward Elgar.

———. 2020. *Macroeconomics as Systems Theory: Transcending the Micro-Macro Dichotomy*. Cham, Switzerland: Palgrave Macmillan.

———. 2021. "Emergence and Entanglement in a Theory of Political Economy." In *Emergence, Entanglement, and Political Economy*, edited by D. J. Hebert and D. W. Thomas, 7–25. Cham, Switzerland: Palgrave Macmillan.

White, H. C. 1992. *Identity and Control: A Structural Theory of Social Action*. Princeton, NJ: Princeton University Press.

Wieland, J. 2018. *Relational Economics: A Political Economy*. Cham, Switzerland: Palgrave Macmillan.

Yoon, J., S. R. Thye, and E. J. Lawler. 2013. "Exchange and Cohesion in Dyads and Triads: A Test of Simmel's Hypothesis." *Social Science Research* 42, no. 6: 1457–66.

Zelizer, V. 2005. *The Purchase of Intimacy*. Princeton, NJ: Princeton University Press.

———. 2011. *Economic Lives: How Culture Shapes the Economy*. Princeton, NJ: Princeton University Press.

Chapter 9

Network Effects and the Dynamics of Polity and Economy in Society

Santiago J. Gangotena

One insight that flows from entangled political economy is the possibility of network effects with respect to the different modes of interaction available to individuals for securing cooperation in carrying out their plans. In Richard E. Wagner's (2014, 2016) entangled political economy framework, polity and economy are not independent processes whose outcomes interact; they are different modes of interacting, elements of the same social process where the business of daily life is conducted. Polity and economy are not just interrelated; they are entangled because political and economic plans link to each other, forming an ecology of plans (Wagner 2012) that constitutes social life. Individuals can carry out their plans using political and economic modes of interaction. These modes differ in terms of how interactions are structured and the relative cost of using each mode. Three factors—imitation, investments specific to the use of each mode, and entanglement between these investments—make the cost of using each mode decline in proportion to its relative preponderance in society. The purpose of this chapter is to show how these costs lead to network effects in the choice of modes of interaction. The existence of network effects sheds light on the dynamics of the social configuration of plans along polity and economy, and the substantive traits that are selected for, and prevail in, society.

An important insight from entangled political economy is that the relative preponderance of polity and economy in a society (the societal configuration of polity and economy) is not the object of social choice but the macro-outcome of an emergent process. This contrasts with what Wagner (2016, 35) calls the alternative orthodox formulation, in which equilibrium models of the market determine the extent of the economy. Politics then alters the market equilibrium either in pursuit of some social welfare function or to match the preferences of the median voter (Wagner 2016, 36). The societal configuration of the market is deemed deficient with respect to the provision of public goods and the mitigation of negative externalities, and the normative or positive extent of the polity is an exercise in constrained optimization. In the orthodox formulation, economic and political processes are independent of each other, and the outcomes of each process interact sequentially to yield a societal configuration of polity and economy (Wagner 2016, 36).

When the polity and the economy are viewed as independent entities that act on each other, equilibrium theorizing is plausible if we *assume*, given institutions, given productive capacities, and the pursuit of self-interest. The plausibility of equilibrium theorizing rests on the notion that when faced with scarcity, competition in the pursuit of self-interest will lead to a situation where everyone is as well off as can be, constrained by given institutions and productive capacities. As Kohn (2004, 310) notes, "Maximization is a consequence of trading equilibrium: in equilibrium all individuals must by definition be maximizing." This is true for both polity and economy when viewed independently. However, many (if not most) institutions governing the economy are by and large determined in the polity, while the resources of the polity are determined by the productive capacities of the economy.

What happens to the plausibility of equilibrium theorizing when instead of viewing polity and economy as independent we view them as entangled? We can no longer consider institutions as given when analyzing the economy, nor can we consider productive capacities as given when analyzing the polity. While this hampers our ability to deploy equilibrium theorizing, what happens to its plausibility? While scarcity and competition in the pursuit of self-interest still exist, we can no longer plausibly theorize in terms of overarching societal equilibrium. This is because the rules and productive capacities change as part of the process of competition, and as the constraints needed to deploy these theoretical tools are no longer constraints but the objects of individuals' choices. In general terms, apart from thick descriptions of the social processes, are we limited to noting that societal configurations are path dependent, contingent, and not much more?

In an entangled approach, societal configurations of economy and polity are mutually determined in the course of individuals pursuing their plans. Rather than plans being pursued in different arenas denominated "the polity" and "the economy," there is but one arena of social interaction where polity and economy refer to different modes by which plans can be structured and pursued. The societal configuration of polity and economy at any given moment is the emergent outcome of this bottom up, open-ended process. While there are significant differences between the structure of plans that involve political interactions and those that involve economic interactions, both types of interactions coexist within the same arena of society.

Thinking about what determines societal configurations of economy and polity in terms of process rather than equilibrium leads to thinking about each individual's choice of using each mode of interaction to pursue one's plans. While some plans may be pursued only in the polity or in the economy, many plans can be pursued using either mode. The choice will depend on each individual's anticipation of the chances of successfully carrying out a plan, and the costs and benefits of carrying out a plan employing political or economic modes and structures of interaction. Some costs and benefits of carrying out a plan in either mode are idiosyncratic to the plan and the individual. Other costs and benefits, however, pertain to the societal configuration of these modes of planning and interacting. It is with respect to the latter costs that network effects become relevant. The choice of using each mode of interaction brings us to economizing action in the pursuit of plans and to the presence of network effects based on the costs of using a specific mode of interaction. The basic contention is simple—the relative preponderance of each mode of interaction, polity or economy, is one of the determinants of the cost of using each mode to carry out plans. As more plans are pursued in a given mode (both in number and, more importantly, in scope), the cost of pursuing plans in this mode declines, leading to network effects that are a determinant of the societal configuration of polity and economy.

In order to show how the dynamics of polity and economy are molded by network effects, I will first outline the unit of analysis for each mode of interaction and, following Podemska-Mikluch and Wagner (2013), the unit of interaction in each mode. Here it will be important to note the entanglement between the modes of interaction and the mutual dependence between polity and economy. Starting with the units of analysis and interaction, I will then show how network effects arise as the idiosyncratic costs of using a mode fall in inverse proportion to its preponderance in society. Network effects arise because the costs of using a specific mode depend on imitation, mode-specific investments, and the complementary nature of these investments. Finally, I will show that the mutual dependence between modes can act as a damper on the positive feedback of network effects and offset corner solutions for the societal configuration of polity and economy.

ENTANGLED PLANS, DYADS, AND TRIADS

Consider plans and not individuals as the unit of analysis. Individuals have plans. Individuals choose and act, but the plan is the unit of analysis because it is the plan, and not the individual, that details an expected interaction. Plans are the unit of analysis because they detail the expected interactions that constitute social life. Plans are the means used to attempt to secure aims. A plan can be written as a network of nodes and links that connect players, actions, and goods to each other.[1] For example, the simplest plan of someone who is thirsty may connect the person to a glass of water via the action of pouring it into a glass and bringing it to one's mouth. In this example, the plan does not involve social interactions, because there is only one player, but plans can be more complex and involve a greater number of players, actions, and goods.[2] Plans can be more or less complex but will always involve an interlinked set of players, actions, and goods. However, in a social setting, the level of complexity of plans can be categorized into at least two types of modes of social interactions: the political and the economic. As argued by Podemska-Mikluch and Wagner (2013), these modes of social interaction can be differentiated by the number of players involved: economy modes of interaction have two players (dyadic), and polity modes of interaction have three players (triadic).

As Hayek (1937) points out, individuals' plans are always anticipations, or expectations, of future events. Their formulation depends on individuals' capacities to imagine social interactions and deem them adequate as a means to the achievement of ends. As such, plans are the locus of entrepreneurship (Kirzner 1997). As also noted by Hayek (1937), plans attach to or impinge on each other as the plans of one individual that require the actions of another individual necessarily draw on the other's limited resources (capacity to carry out actions) and plans for those resources. Plans can be either relatively coordinated or uncoordinated, with the coordinating tendency determined by how the knowledge of external events and planned actions agree among individuals (Hayek 1937). The framework of entangled political economy adds to this by identifying two distinct modes of planning and interaction that can be employed by individuals in society, with entrepreneurship being the action that brings planning about (Podemska-Mikluch and Wagner 2010). The formulation of plans depends on an individual's capacity to imagine social interactions consisting of players, actions, and goods, and, as Podemska-Mikluch and Wagner (2013) argue, dyadic and triadic interactions are templates for imagining plans in the economic and political modes of interaction.

Dyads, social plans that involve two players who willingly engage in a game, are the unit of economic interactions. Even multiparty economic interactions can be broken up and analyzed as a set of dyadic interactions between exchanging or contracting parties (Podemska-Mikluch and Wagner 2013). It is the particular structure consisting of two players as willing participants that makes dyads a template for the economic mode of interaction. In general, dyadic interactions can be, ex ante, positive-sum games where both parties expect to gain, zero-sum games where one party gains at the expense of the other, and negative-sum games where both parties lose. However, as explained by Ellsberg (1956) and noted by Podemska-Mikluch and Wagner (2013), players do not willingly engage in what they view ex ante as zero-sum or negative-sum interactions where they expect to lose. This might change in the context of nested games, where while the game itself can be zero-sum or negative-sum, playing the game is valued in itself. For example, a game of chess between two players is a zero-sum game,[3] but if playing the game is valued over its opportunity cost, even though one player wins and one loses, players can engage willingly because of the value of playing the game itself, regardless of the outcome.

Munger and Munger (2015, 31–32) point out that for dyadic interactions to take place at all, a sufficient, although not necessary, condition is third-party enforcement to stamp out cheating and postcontractual opportunism. Third-party enforcement may not be necessary, as explained by Klein, Crawford, and Alchian (1978), with respect to postcontractual opportunism. Although as Munger and Munger (2015) note, there are dyadic interactions that can solve these problems—a credible threat of enforcement is sufficient to make mutually beneficial dyadic interactions possible.

This consideration brings triadic, political plans to the foreground. As explained by Podemska-Mikluch and Wagner (2013), and illustrated by the diagram in Wagner (2016, 118), triadic interactions are the templates for political interactions. The possibility of triadic interactions also entails entrepreneurship and the imaginative capacity of individuals as in Wagner's (2016, 87) discussion of Demsetz's (1967) explanation of how property rights emerge. As in dyadic interactions, individuals must be able to imagine triadic plans in order to secure cooperation to implement them.

Triadic interactions can also be viewed as positive-sum, zero-sum, or negative-sum games for the players. For example, property rights are a prerequisite for the simplest dyadic interaction—mutually beneficial exchange. A sufficient condition for their existence is a triadic interaction where the third party enforces contracts. Players may willingly engage in this triadic game because third-party enforcement allows them to benefit from the fruits of the division of labor. In this case, although coercion is present, the triadic game is a positive-sum interaction, ex ante, and is part of the interactions that make up the polity. A game of corruption is also a triadic interaction, although a negative-sum one, where two players exchange and benefit while a third party loses. Of course, the third party would not enter into this game willingly, and here the "autonomy of political" discussed by Wagner (2016, 93–97) is paramount to explaining how power and coercion are facts of social life.

Buchanan's (1975) distinction of the protective, productive, and redistributive state is related although it is not identical to the notion of positive-, zero-, or negative-sum interactions. What entangled political economy asks of us is to disaggregate the state into particular plans and interactions. Instead of thinking of the activities of the state, distinct interactions involving specific players, actions, and goods are the unit of analysis. Positive-sum triadic interactions can be likened to the protective and productive activities of government in Buchanan's rendering. Redistributive activities can be positive-, zero-, or negative-sum interactions depending on participating individuals' willingness to engage, or not, in these plans. These interactions are imagined by individual entrepreneurs as a means to pursue their goals and are then implemented by securing their participation in these games, willing or unwillingly.

Political and economic triadic and dyadic interactions are the stuff of which the business of social life is made. Much like Lachmann's (1977) structure of production is an interconnected network of economic plans given an institutional framework of private property and freedom and enforcement of contracts, a system view of society entails an interconnected structure of economic and political plans. The significant difference is that by including political plans, the institutional framework is an emergent feature of ongoing individual entrepreneurship in different modes of interaction—for example, as noted by Becchio (2014) and Wagner (2016) with respect to private property and its emergence as a social relation.

Political and economic plans attach to each other as they involve the players, goods, and actions present in other plans. For example, for many types of triadic plans to be carried out, they must attach to willing dyadic plans. Thus, a triadic interaction of coerced redistribution must attach to economic interactions that generate goods to be redistributed. As has already been noted, economic interactions that produce goods and services through the division of labor can be supported by being attached to a productive triadic interaction that secures private property and the freedom and enforcement of contracts. It is the attachment of plans, and not of their outcomes, that creates entanglement rather than mere interdependence.

One particular difference between an additive political economy and an entangled political economy comes into focus when we consider extreme cases. Let us imagine a structure of production (as in Lachmann's [1977] conception of the structure of production as a structure of plans, or Wagner's

[2012] notion of an ecology of plans) that is wholly the result of economic inter-actions and label this "A." This means that the allocation of resources and the network structure of plans are purely the result of dyadic interactions. Now let us imagine for the same set of players, goods, and actions a structure of production that is wholly the result of democratic socialism; we will label this "B." To get here, imagine that the use of all resources is decided through direct voting.[4] This means that the allocation of resources and the network structure of plans are purely the result of triadic interactions. Surely the structure of production that emerges when we allow both triadic and dyadic interactions to coexist is not a linear combination of A and B. The coordinating properties of the structure of production that emerges when we allow both types of interaction are also surely not just a linear combination of the coordinating properties of A and B but something altogether different.

NETWORK EFFECTS IN AN ENTANGLED POLITICAL ECONOMY

Making note of the entanglement of plans of either mode in society allows us to think about the role of network effects in how plans are conceived, imagined, selected, and implemented. As noted earlier, economizing action leads us to consider the costs of using political or economic modes of planning and inter-acting; and all plans have idiosyncratic costs, subject to the substantive content of the plan. The idiosyncratic costs of a plan can be dependent on the mode employed as well. But there are costs to employing each mode that are wholly dependent on the mode of planning itself.

For example, as Coase (1937) realized, there are costs to transacting through economic, dyadic, interactions. As Buchanan and Tullock (1962) show, there are costs to using mechanisms of collective choice—triadic interactions—as well. By placing polity and economy on equal terms and viewing them both as transactions, the costs corresponding to each mode of interaction are in reality just the transaction costs associated with each mode. Rather than treating transaction costs as constant, there are three reasons to view them as being dependent on the societal configuration of plans at any given moment along political and economic modes of interaction in society.

The first reason is due to imitation as a mechanism by which plans are generated. The basic idea is very simple—entrepreneurial discovery entails imagining a plan as a means to achieve a goal. In an open-ended universe, this plan can be imagined "out of the blue"; but given existing templates (dyads and triads) for social interaction, it is also possible, if not more common, to use an existing template to structure one's plan. Imitation lowers the transaction costs of employing a particular mode of planning by making it easier to imagine a plan implemented in that mode. Thus, if I want my neighbor to paint his house a different color and I am more familiar with dyadic interactions because they are more prevalent in society, I may consider a dyadic mutually beneficial plan that involves paying my neighbor to paint his house. On the other hand, if I am more familiar with triadic interactions, I may devise a plan to secure support for a petition to the neighborhood association to pass an ordinance that compels him to paint his house a different color. If no neighborhood association exists, I may formulate a triadic plan to constitute such a group. By providing templates for structuring plans, the costs of devising plans in each mode are dependent on the prevalence of economic and political plans in society. The greater the prevalence and familiarity of one mode of interaction among individuals in society, the lower the cost of imagining and devising plans in this mode, and the greater the chances that it will be implemented in this mode.

A second reason for positing network effects is that some investments made to carry out plans in a given mode of interaction are specific to that mode of interaction and cannot be liquidated without incurring costs. In other words, at the level of each individual, their existing stock of physical and human capital is better adapted to a given mode of interaction. Physical and human capital come together in complementary ways to bring plans to fruition, and part of that complementarity is in how they fit with economic or political means of interaction. This is easier to see in terms of human capital than physical capital. The skills individuals develop to engage in market transactions are not necessarily the same skills an individual would need to carry out political interactions. While honesty and a reputation for honesty are certainly useful skills to develop in market interactions, they may not be as useful in political interactions. In fact, in political interactions, a reputation for honesty would be useful while the practice of honesty may not be so useful. Developing a reputation for honesty while at the same time being able to be dishonest is a skill that is better adapted to political modes of interaction.

Likewise, even though skills of persuasion are useful in both political and economic interactions, the substantive form that persuasion takes in economic and political interactions is different, as noted by Wagner (2016, 125–26). Lawyers are relatively more common in societies where politics prevails than in societies where markets prevail. The stock of human and physical capital at the disposal of each individual depends on its expected efficacy at securing ends—that is, to carry out plans to fruition. Investments are made in capital specific to each mode of interaction on the basis of their expected payoff. The greater the prevalence of a given mode of interaction in society, the greater the stock of capital specific to each mode. The greater the stock of capital specific to each mode, the greater the chance that plans are developed to use the existing stock of human and physical capital specific to that mode.

The third reason is also related to capital—not at the level of each individual's stock of capital but at the level of the structure of capital in society as a whole. In an entangled political economy, unitary political and economic plans are entangled with each other. Relative social coordination entails the relative intersubjective agreement of knowledge used to formulate plans. Changes in the knowledge and expectations of individuals lead to changes in their plans and to the corresponding capital structure. The relative prevalence of one mode of interaction in society will lead to changes in the capital structure adapted to this relative prevalence, not only to the specific capital stock of each individual, but to how the capital stock of each individual is related to other individuals' capital stock in complementary ways to make plans more or less compatible with each other. Thus, the cost of using a mode of interaction declines as a function of not only the prevalence of the stock of capital specific to that mode but also to the structure of complementary capital specific to that mode.

Imitation in the conception of plans, investments in capital specific to a mode of planning and interacting, and the complementary nature of the capital structure in an entangled political economy point to the presence of network effects in the dynamics of societal configurations of polity and economy. However, the real-world relevance of network effects depends on the relative cost between political and economic modes of interaction. If the transaction costs of one mode are much greater than the other, then network effects may be irrelevant for the dynamics of societal configurations. For example, Stigler (1971, 10–11) proposes that some of the transaction costs to democratic political interactions are that decisions "must be made simultaneously by a large number of persons (or their representatives)" and "involve 'all' the community, not simply those who are directly concerned with a decision." In this case, the costs of political interactions relative to economic interactions would seem prohibitively high for network effects to make a significant impact on the dynamics of societal configurations. If we recognize, however, that voting and elections are not the only types of political interactions, and that the government is not unitary but an emergent order of individuals and organizations (as in Wagner 2016, 111), the costs of political interactions may not be so high and network effects can be significant drivers of societal configurations.

THE DYNAMICS OF SOCIETAL CONFIGURATIONS
AND SELECTION FOR SUBSTANTIVE TRAITS

Network effects in the dynamics of societal configurations along polity and economy can lead to corner equilibria if positive feedback is the only driver of the dynamics. Given an initial social configuration of polity and economy, small differences in their relative preponderance accumulate as the more prevalent mode is used with increasing frequency. In the limit, all activity accumulates to one mode of interaction. This markedly contrasts with actual societies, where we observe a mixture of market and political interactions. This contrast points to the presence of dampening effects that diminish or limit the positive feedback from network effects. There are at least two mechanisms that dampen and limit the positive feedback from network effects.

The relative costs of using one mode versus the other are the first mechanism that dampens the positive feedback from network effects. When the relative cost of employing one mode of interaction is relatively much higher than the other, network effects become much less important drivers of the dynamics of societal configurations. As noted earlier, there are different costs to implementing a plan in a given mode. Some costs are idiosyncratic to the plan, others to implementing the plan in a given mode, and others to using the mode for planning and interacting. It is these last costs that are properly transaction costs of using the mode, and the systematic source of network effects as previously explained. When the costs idiosyncratic to a plan, and to the plan being executed in a given mode, are much higher than the transaction costs of the mode, network effects are much less important drivers of societal configurations. This is because the change in costs to using a mode may not lower costs enough for them to be a worthwhile margin of adjustment for individuals.

The second mechanism is the entanglement between plans of different modes. First, let us consider the attachment of political to economic modes of interaction. As Wagner (2016, 136) notes, political plans form parasitical attachments to economic plans, allowing for the extraction of resources for use by political enterprises. Political plans are also attached parasitically to market interaction in the use of the information provided by market prices needed for economic calculation and effective action. Market interactions are necessary for political interactions to take place. Hence, as the political mode becomes more prevalent owing to network effects, the number of economic plans that can be parasitically attached diminishes, lowering the potential value of political plans. Also, as the political mode becomes more prevalent, the information contained in market prices generated by economic interactions deteriorates, leading to greater uncertainty regarding the potential value of political plans.

As an exercise in positive economics,[5] an equilibrium conceptualization might speculate about the optimal prevalence of economic versus political interactions in society. This would be carried out by equating the cost of the marginal political plan in terms of a smaller number of economic plans—the diminished value in economic interactions and the deteriorated information present in market prices with the value provided by the marginal political plan. However, even if we ignore that political plans are heterogeneous, which complicates the marginal analysis somewhat, a descriptive conception of equilibrium cannot be applied to characterize the end state of the process unless a mechanism is found that brings the social process to this equilibrium. This is plausible for economic processes when we hold institutions constant, and for political processes when we hold productive capacities constant, but it is not possible when both are the emergent outcomes of entangled political and economic interactions. Thus, all we can say is that the necessary attachment of political interactions to economic interactions dampens the positive feedback of network effects by diminishing productive capacities and deteriorating information generated in market prices.

At the other end, positive feedback implies that a small initial preponderance of economic interactions would lead to only economic interactions in the limit. However, economic interactions are attached to political interactions as well. In some cases, such as political interactions resulting in the enforcement of rules that act as sufficient conditions for the division of labor and exchange, this attachment is highly productive. It is an interesting and open question as to whether these rules can be wholly enforced through contract, but the autonomy of the political makes it unlikely that political interactions can, or will, be wiped out of existence by network effects. Individuals like playing political games. Both the instability of underdeveloped societies and the remarkable institutional stability of developed societies that have been able to enforce these rules through political modes of interaction, even if the rules themselves are generated spontaneously, attest to the importance of political interactions for the possibility of economic interactions. The autonomy of the political and the usefulness of certain political interactions will also tend to limit the positive feedback from network effects.

Positive feedback, along with the dampening of the relative costs of transacting in each mode and the dampening of attachments between economic and political interactions, is only one set of drivers influencing the dynamics of societal configurations. This framework opens up the possibility for a greater understanding of the dynamics of societal configurations. A potential impli-cation is that in the presence of positive feedback through network effects, and the dampening of positive feedback, self-generated turbulence can be produced (as in, for example, Heinrich 2018) through bifurcations and cusp catastrophes.

Because each mode of interaction is associated with specific substantive traits and qualities (Wagner 2016, 125), the dynamics of societal configura-tions are an important determinant of the prevalence of these traits in soci-ety. If network effects really are a driver of societal configurations of polity and economy, we can expect the preponderance of traits and qualities present in individuals in society to move in step with the dynamics. Rosser (2014) points to the difference between order emerging through natural selection and order emerging through self-organization. Because the positive feedback from network effects is a form of self-organization, the societal configuration of an entangled political economy would, at least from the perspective argued here, be a consequence of self-organization. However, the pattern or order of traits and qualities present in society would be a product of natural selection through competition for substantive traits. This implies that one explanation for the traits and qualities—for example, honesty, deceitfulness, trust, envy—present in the members of society is that they are a product of natural selection, where these traits compete in an order produced by self-organization, driven by positive feedback and dampers. There is no social blank slate; the traits and qualities present in society are not given but instead are the outcome of an emergent process of entangled political and economic interaction.

CONCLUSION

Social processes can never be directly observed, as they are the emergent prod-uct of people's interactions. Social processes must first be conceptualized in order to be comprehended. A common practice in political economy begins with conceptualizations that hold constant either political-institutional con-straints or economic-productive capacities. This is done in order to employ theoretical constructions to make predictions and elucidate underlying mech-anisms. While this may be a useful approximation, it necessarily muddies the lenses through which we view society by making static that which is inherently dynamic. One bold question that Wagner's research program presents to us is, What happens when we stop holding the political or economic constant? What happens when we conceptualize society, in both its political and economic dimensions, as a dynamic entangled process? Wagner's research program only begins with these questions. His many contributions, and those his research program has inspired, provide us with fresh conceptualizations, new lenses, grounded in individuals and their behavior through which we can explore these questions.

A natural concern that arises if we view everything in society as a dynamic entangled process is the role of theory to further our understanding. If political institutions and economic processes generate each other through an entangled web of plans and interactions with turbulent dynamics, what generalizations can we bring to bear other than thick descriptions of the evolution of social systems? While thick descriptions have been, and will continue to be, fruitful empirical avenues to explore the consequences of entangled political economy, Wagner's research program still has much to offer from a theoretical perspective. The lenses provided by the research program can be applied to create theory that orients us toward the general likely patterns and mechanisms governing the evolution of social systems beyond foundational statements about the entanglement of political and economic interactions.

This chapter attempts to bring these lenses to bear in a theoretical direction. Starting from the foundational insights of entangled political economy, we can theorize about how, when viewed through entangled lenses, human interactions can lead to network effects that are a driver of the evolution of social systems and help determine the emergent societal configuration of economic and political interactions. These network effects are dampened by countervailing forces that operate at the level of individual choice, and at a higher emergent level concerning the entanglement of plans along political and economic modes of interaction. Next steps in this direction can be of a theoretical nature as well, especially in the creation of agent-based models that demonstrate this possibility formally and allow us to explore and experiment with the determinants of the trajectories of societal configurations.

Empirical avenues are open as well, including thick descriptions of these processes but not limited to these types of research projects. For example, there has been a good amount of work with respect to the size distribution of economic interactions in the literature on firm size distributions (Axtell 2001, for example). By comparison, relatively little work has been done on the size distribution of political interactions, especially when we expand the meaning of political interactions to be consistent with the triadic interactions that come to the forefront in entangled political economy. The size distribution of political and economic interactions, the possible relationships between these distributions, and their evolution are a natural place to start examining the empirical patterns predicted by network effects in an entangled political economy.

NOTES

1. It may be interesting to note that the elements of a plan (players, actions, and goods) map to the syntax of sentence construction (subject, verb, object), and thus plans can be, and are, expressed and codified in natural language.

2. An open question is how to measure the relative degrees of complexity of a plan.

3. Or negative sum if we consider the opportunity costs of playing to be the missed positive-sum games that could have been played instead, as in Tullock (1967).

4. Another way to get here is to dictate that all social interactions fall into the scope of collective decisions. Of course, to do this we need to abstract away from the feasibility of actually implementing such a scheme as the costs of using direct democracy to decide on the use of all resources are most probably prohibitively high.

5. No doubt this can be carried out as a normative exercise too, if only on paper and assuming given information that is in reality generated by the process itself. Whether an observed societal configuration is optimal is an empirical matter that can hardly be verified. In an entangled political economy, the societal configuration of polity and economy are not the objects of choice but the emergent outcomes of entangled political and economic interactions.

REFERENCES

Axtell, R. L. 2001. "Zipf Distribution of US Firm Sizes." *Science* 293, no. 5536: 1818–20.

Becchio, G. 2014. "Carl Menger on States as Orders, Not Organizations: Entangled Economy into a Neo-Mengerian Approach." In *Entangled Political Economy*, edited by Steven Horwitz and Roger Koppl, 55–66. Emerald, UK: Bingley.

Buchanan, J. M. 1975. *The Limits of Liberty: Between Anarchy and Leviathan*. No. 714. Chicago: University of Chicago Press.

Buchanan, J. M., and G. Tullock. 1962. *The Calculus of Consent: Logical Foundations of Constitutional Democracy*. Ann Arbor: University of Michigan Press.

Coase, R. H. 1937. "The Nature of the Firm." *Economica* 4, no. 16: 386–405.

Demsetz, H. 1967. "Towards a Theory of Property Rights." *American Economic Review* 57, no. 2: 347–59.

Ellsberg, D. 1956. "Theory of the Reluctant Duelist." *American Economic Review* 46, no. 5: 909–23.

Hayek, F. A. 1937. "Economics and Knowledge." *Economica* 4, no. 13: 33–54.

Heinrich, T. 2018. "A Discontinuity Model of Technological Change: Catastrophe Theory and Network Structure." *Computational Economics* 51, no. 3: 407–25.

Kirzner, I. M. 1997. "Entrepreneurial Discovery and the Competitive Market Process: An Austrian Approach." *Journal of Economic Literature* 35, no. 1: 60–85.

Klein, B., R. G. Crawford, and A. A. Alchian. 1978. "Vertical Integration, Appropriable Rents, and the Competitive Contracting Process." *Journal of Law and Economics* 21, no. 2: 297–326.

Kohn, M. 2004. "Value and Exchange." *Cato Journal* 24: 303.

Lachmann, L. M. 1977. *Capital and Its Structure*. Kansas City, MO: Sheed Andrews and McMeel.

Munger, M. C., and K. M. Munger. 2015. *Choosing in Groups: Analytical Politics Revisited*. New York: Cambridge University Press.

Podemska-Mikluch, M., and R. E. Wagner. 2010. "Entangled Political Economy and the Two Faces of Entrepreneurship." *Journal of Public Finance and Public Choice* 28, no. 2–3: 99–114.

———. 2013. "Dyads, Triads, and the Theory of Exchange: Between Liberty and Coercion." *Review of Austrian Economics* 26, no. 2: 171–82.

Rosser, J. B. 2014. "Natural Selection versus Emergent Self-Organization in Evolutionary Political Economy." In *Entangled Political Economy*, edited by Steven Horwitz and Roger Koppl, 67–91. Emerald, UK: Bingley.

Stigler, G. J. 1971. "The Theory of Economic Regulation." *Bell Journal of Economics and Management Science*: 3–21.

Tullock, G. 1967. "The Welfare Costs of Tariffs, Monopolies, and Theft." *Economic Inquiry* 5, no. 3: 224–32.

Wagner, R. E. 2012. "A Macro Economy as an Ecology of Plans." *Journal of Economic Behavior & Organization* 82, no. 2–3: 433–44.

———. 2014. "Entangled Political Economy: A Keynote Address." In *Entangled Political Economy*, edited by Steven Horwitz and Roger Koppl, 15–36. Emerald, UK: Bingley.

———. 2016. *Politics as a Peculiar Business: Insights from a Theory of Entangled Political Economy.* Cheltenham, UK: Edward Elgar.

Chapter 10

Seven Stepping Stones to a Systems Theory of Economics

Abigail N. Devereaux

It takes a theory to beat a theory: if there is a theory that is right
51 per cent of the time, it will be used until a better one comes along.

—George Stigler, *The Theory of Price*

Essentially, all models are wrong, but some are useful.

—attributed to G.E.P. Box

The first paper of Richard E. Wagner's that I came across as a graduate student, the paper that made me knock on his door in the fall of 2016, was his 2012 paper in the *Journal of Economic Behavior and Organization* titled "A Macro Economy as an Ecology of Plans." It was the first place I saw Dick lay out his vision of a systems theoretic economics. Dick and I have since worked on various aspects of a systems theory of economics. In 2020, Dick wove a variety of his ideas about a systems theoretic economics into his book *Macroeconomics as Systems Theory*. In keeping with Dick's scholarly habit of looking ever forward instead of backward, I hope with this chapter to extend his exposition: to envision not just *macroeconomics* as a systems theory but the entire program of economics itself.

Dick and I are theorists in an age where economic theory has been declared dead. Theoretical analyses constitute a historically small fraction of the articles published in top economics journals. Daniel Hamermesh (2013) published a time series of top journal publications from 1963 to 2011 showing that the publication of pure theory papers is under 20 percent—an all-time low. Empirical papers are at an all-time high, constituting 64 percent of all publications in top economics journals. The empirical age focusing particularly on research design (and not theory) is the incarnation of the credibility revolution in economics. Research rooted in the credibility revolution has won several of the most recent Nobel Prizes in economics: Esther Duflo and Abhijit Banerjee for randomized control trials (2019), and David Card, Joshua Angrist, and Guido Imbens for their theoretical role in the credibility revolution (2021). Rather than the credibility revolution, it should be called the causality revolution, for its contribution of putting questions of causality at the forefront, and especially for how it engendered the belief by working economists that they could, with clever-enough research design, suss out causality and thus become *useful* by providing instructions on how to control some socially relevant variable by means of tweaking others.

The credibility revolution is accompanied by two assumptions. The primary assumption of the credibility revolution is that economic theory in general is not defensible in its own right, and that any and all theoretical statements require evidence, garnered through either large, randomized control trials or clever-enough research design. The secondary, typically unstated, assumption of the credibility revolution is that econometric theory suitably substitutes for the missing rigor of the traditional analytical theory of economics. It is perhaps no surprise that the credibility revolution occurred during and after the publication of a series of results calling into question the rigor of general equilibrium theory in terms of uniqueness (Sonnenschein 1973; Mantel 1974; Debreu 1974), aggregate representations (Kirman 1992), and individual optimization (Lewis 1985, 1992). It is also no surprise that the credibility revolution occurred alongside another revolution in the sciences—namely, the complex systems revolution (Wolfram 1984; Wolfram 2002; Helbing, and Kirman 2013).

For simplicity, I define "traditional economic theory" as the theoretical bundle based on Debreu's *Theory of Value* (1959), centered on fixed-point equilibrium analysis both at the individual and social levels and including traditional game theory (in particular, Nash's theorem). Traditional economic theory constitutes the textbook exposition of economic systems in virtually all university economics programs at all levels and has for at least the past 70 years. The traditional economic approach is so hegemonous that it is often conflated with what it means to be a working economist. Also, for simplicity, I will refer to the current trend of replacing theory with data analysis as "econometrics," even though the field is converging with the applied theory of data analytics.

Consider the quote by George Stigler at the beginning of this chapter. I am going to combine Stigler's quote with G. E. P. Box's quote in order to consider how we understand the incentives of academia—an exercise Stigler would doubtless approve. It takes a theory to beat a theory: if there is a theory that is *useful* 51 percent of the time, it will be used until a *more useful* theory comes along. One might quibble that the usefulness of a theory implies correctness, and while this may be true in materials engineering, it is much less true in the social sciences, regardless of how closely economic theory apes physics. As Josh Angrist and Jörn-Steffen Pischke (2010, 4) put it when describing the success of empirical economics, the usefulness of a theory is embodied in both "policy relevance and scientific impact." *Useful* means useful to the consumers of economic theories, who are not academic economists but beneficiaries—the vast majority of whom operate in the public policy world[1]—of predictions and analyses made by professional, academic, and public economists (White 2005).

This chapter is not intended to cast judgment on economic theorists, who, by behavioral symmetry, face a set of incentives that create the tendency for their ends to coordinate with the ends of the primary consumers of economic theorizing. The incentives in structured scholarly life lead to a process of preferential attachment to more highly cited papers (Jeong, Néda, and Barabási 2003; Wang, Yu, and Yu 2008). Degree of influence is determined not only by merit but also without regard to merit in favor of the apparently novel. Science is not necessarily self-correcting (Ioannidis 2012). Nonreplicable economic studies with novel results are published and cited at higher rates than are replicable studies, even after a recognition of nonreplicability (Serra-Garcia and Gneezy 2021). The reason economic theory is dead or dying in the top journals is not because economists are in a golden age of correct theories and bankrupt theoretical contenders.

For a while now, I have told everyone who listens—including Dick—that economic theory is not over, closed for business, or no longer taking applications. Economic theory is a wide-open frontier. The traditional theoretical edifice has deteriorated so badly as to be the topic of casual apologism at any professional conference. "Well, yes, the theory's wrong," nearly everyone admits off the record, "but all models are wrong, and there isn't a better theory out there right now."

It is time—well past time—to build a better theory of economics. This chapter represents the tip of a massive iceberg of work (some mine, mostly others') on that better theory.

I organize the chapter as a metaphor, a path laid with stones one after the other, leading in succession toward a coherent and *useful* systems theory of economics. I have identified seven of these "stepping stones" to a systems theory of economics, which I have listed below, and whose description serves as the main body of this chapter. As with any path, the ordering of the stones is important: one cannot get to a further stone without traversing a nearer.

Without further ado, here are the seven stepping stones to a systems theory of economics:

1. Economic dynamics are rich and exhibit organized complexity.

2. Relationships are irreducible.

3. Computation is costly.

4. The use of knowledge by an agent within the system matters at the process level.

5. Causality in economic systems is complex.

6. The evolution of economic systems is open-ended and nonergodic.

7. Intervention must occur from within the system and is theoretically incomplete.

The second section motivates a systems theory of economics. The third section describes the stepping stones in sequence. The fourth section discusses what is required to develop a robust systems theory of economics and, importantly, what kinds of questions are natural to answer within the theory that are difficult or impossible to answer within traditional economic theory. I conclude at the end of the fourth section.

MOTIVATING A SYSTEMS THEORY OF ECONOMICS: LOOKING FOR SELF-ORGANIZED COMPLEXITY

Why do we need a systems theory of economics? Who is going to use it? Is there anything already being done along these lines? Understanding the motivation to develop a systems theory of economics requires what I call the Zeroth Stepping Stone: economists are *scientists*, not mechanics or engineers, though this was not always considered the case.

In 1949, the economist Bill Phillips created the Monetary National Income Analogue Computer (MONIAC). MONIAC worked as a circular flow machine, with dials representing policy-controlled variables like tax, savings and investments rates that released fluid into chambers representing stocks like the national treasury or healthcare spending. But there are problems with modeling economies as analog or digital MONIAC-like machines, and economists as controllers standing outside the system, next to the machine. Economists are *embedded* within the systems they set out to control. Social systems present fundamental constraints to control from within, owing to their complex open-ended evolution (Koppl et al. 2015; Devereaux and Wagner

2020), inherent and ineliminable bias and information loss in social data sets (Calude and Longo 2017), and combinatorial richness. Furthermore, economists are inextricably embedded in non-scientific-influence networks and thus subject to nonscientific incentives (White 2005). The Zeroth Stepping Stone implies that whether, and by whom, social systems can be designed is an open question that economic science has not yet answered in the affirmative.

Since economists are scientists, they need scientific tools—theories and applied methods—that are most suited to the study of social systems given the inherent characteristics of those social systems. The tractability of one's methods is a secondary concern and should not be allowed to define the science. The tractability represents a tradeoff between having *an* explanation and having explanatory *power*. The explanatory power of a method is an estimate, a calculation that can be, and often is (especially at first), incorrect. As sciences progress, their practitioners get a better sense of what the existing methods actually explain, and develop new methods in the interest of increasing explanatory power.

Economists deal with complex problems in complex systems where an explanation may seem plausible and, if it gains consensus within the academy, may stand unchallenged long past the point where the explanation has been disproved by the academy's margins: economists persist in citing nonreplicable results even after nonreplicability is established (Serra-Garcia and Gneezy 2021). Traditional economic theory and econometrics are powerful because they are fully synthesized methods that provide an explanation with apparent explanatory power in particular situations. Both theories have gone through crises of confidence at various points of their development, where they have been forced to negatively reevaluate the apparent explanatory power of their methods and develop new methods to improve actual explanatory power.

The credibility revolution in econometrics represents one such reevaluation and redevelopment (Angrist and Pischke 2010). Expectations theory, experimental economics, and behavioral economics (Kahneman et al. 1982) were developed to explain deficits in the explanatory power of traditional economic theory in certain situations. Complex systems theory, whose main concepts and tools were developed primarily in the 1980s, 1990s, and 2000s (though drawing on theoretical and computational advancements beginning in the 1930s), roared to life due in part to the deficits[2] in explanatory power in the computation control theories of mechanism design and cybernetics, both postwar theories, and both serving as logical successors to economic theory in the age of computation.[3]

For all that economists have resisted engaging in systems thinking even after it was apparent that the deficits in their theories were signposts pointing toward a more suitable framework for their subject matter, systems thinking in the social sciences is not new.[4] Systems theory in its inception was highly interdisciplinary and remains so today. To some extent, that is the point. General systems theory, as coined by Ludwig von Bertanlaffy (1951), was supposed to be a theory about defining formal structures, relationships, and dynamics that are exemplified in many fields. The example of a closed, self-reproducing system of agents, with some kind of food source, waste, and catalysts, represents existing and important concepts and systems in biochemistry (autocatalytic set), ecology (ecological equilibria), the social sciences (a self-sustaining community), and computer science (a cybernetic system). As Kenneth Boulding (1956, 200) describes and warns, general systems theory cuts a swath across many disciplines, but "to be productive, however, [interdisciplinary excitement] must operate within a certain framework of coherence. It is all too easy for the interdisciplinary to degenerate into the undisciplined."

What motivates a systems theory of economics is the largest formal deficits in a field with over a century of formalism: the inability of economic theory to explain either spontaneous order or innovation. As Wagner has discussed in several of his books and papers, understanding order without design requires a synthesis of micro-meso-macro built on an explicit acknowledgment of relationships and feedback between individual choosers, controllers, intermediate-level social structures, and system-level indicators (Wagner 2010, 2020; Devereaux and Wagner 2020; Lewis and Wagner 2017). Further motivation for a systems theory of economics arises out of the failure of economic theory to produce an adequate theory of deliberate social alteration, despite its earnest attempts. Dick has addressed this point as well in his book on entangled political economy (Wagner 2016).

A systems theory of economics is a candidate theory to both explain spontaneous orders and innovation and provide a formal intuition for the limits of control of social systems. I will begin by discussing what I consider the most exigent motivation for a systems theory of economics: formally characterizing organized complexity.

That economics deals with phenomena that exhibit organized complexity was expressed in the seminal tract on organized complexity, Warren Weaver's ([1948] 1991) "Science and Complexity." Weaver points out that up until that point, science had done a good job describing systems of two or fewer variables as in classical mechanics or high-variable disorganized systems as in statistical mechanics. But "science has as yet little explored or conquered" systems with three to many variables, since "these problems, as contrasted with the disorganized situations with which statistics can cope, show the essential feature of *organization*. In fact, one can refer to this group of problems as those of *organized complexity*" (4; italics in original).

While Weaver ([1948] 1991, 7) hoped that computers would make progress into complex problems—in other fields of scientific study they certainly have (Wolfram 2002)—systems of two or fewer variables, and statistical analyses, still form the core of scholarly economic inquiry. This is despite the fact that, as Weaver ([1948] 1991, 5) observes, questions of currency stabilization, regulation, planning, cycle prevention, labor unions, economic discrimination, and industrial organization all exhibit organized complexity and are more properly understood as complex problems ill suited to approaches based on very small or very large numbers of variables.

This chapter and its stepping stones represent a journey to *center* the discovery and explanation of organized complexity in economics. I begin by delineating a heuristic for categorizing systems dynamics in economics, and by discussing which theoretical paradigms are capable of generating phenomena in each dynamical category.

THE STEPPING STONES OF A SYSTEMS THEORY OF ECONOMICS

The Evolutionary Richness of Economic Systems: Four Dynamical Categories

> And yet this statistical method of dealing with disorganized complexity, so powerful an advance over the earlier two-variable methods, leaves a great field untouched. One is tempted to oversimplify and say that scientific methodology went from one extreme to the other—from two variables to an astronomical number—and left untouched a great middle region. . . . The importance of this middle region . . . which science has as yet little explored or conquered lies in the fact that these problems, as contrasted with the disorganized situations with which statistics can cope, show the essential feature of organization. We will therefore refer to this group of problems as those of organized complexity. (Weaver 1961, 59)

Since the mid-20th century, and more so in the 1980s and afterward, theorists have been trying to define, categorize, and model complexity in economic systems. As noted in Rosser (2006), Richard Day attempted to define complex phenomena as phenomena that do not converge to a point or a limit cycle, explode, or implode. Organized complexity seems to fit this bill.

Traditional economic theory treats spontaneously generated system-level patterns as if they are either entirely reducible to microlevel interactions (so, not spontaneous) or entirely disembodied from micro action (so, not ordered). But spontaneous order, also known as organized complexity, is all around us. Theorists have known for a long time that advancing the complex biological and social sciences requires an understanding of organized complexity, as we see from Weaver's 1961 quote earlier. The job of the economic theorist, then, is to seek out theories capable of exhibiting organized complexity in a manner consistent with an intuitive understanding of individual and social phenomena.

Social systems are characterized by recursive functions.[5] Recursive functions define an agent's or system's state at a given time and are functions both of relevant data and of some previous value(s) of the function itself, at some previous state(s). Examples of recursivity in modeling human action and social systems include familiar concepts like feedback and ex ante / ex post error correction common in the entrepreneurship literature, search over NK landscapes, and algorithmic decision-making and search as in the application of genetic algorithms and locally game theoretic decision-making in agent-based models (Tesfatsion 2017).

Recursive functions interacting within a system—even very simple functions and systems—evolve in a rich variety of ways. Equilibrium, or stationarity, is but one and the most trivial of evolutionary categories. A simple heuristic to categorize the evolution of systems of recursive functions is the four Wolfram-Chomsky categories: stationarity (class 1), periodic (class 2), chaotic (class 3), and self-organized complex (class 4) (Wolfram 1984, 2002; Adamtzky and Martinez 2010).

In Figure 10.1, I illustrate these classes using the evolution of a simple system: a two-state, one-dimensional cellular automaton (what are called "elementary"

Figure 10.1. Examples of elementary cellular automata and their Wolfram-Chomksy classes

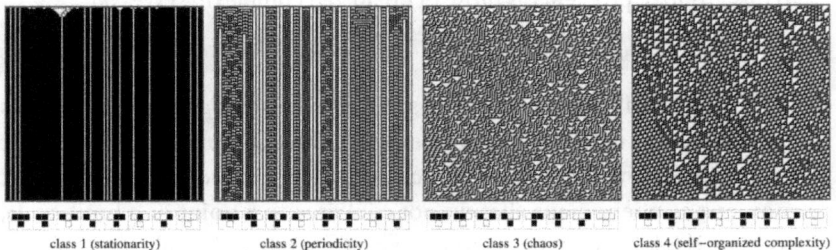

| class 1 (stationarity) | class 2 (periodicity) | class 3 (chaos) | class 4 (self-organized complexity) |

cellular automata). The first state of the system is the top row of black and white cells. The system then updates according to nearest-neighbor rules that tell a given cell whether to remain in its current state or flip to the other state depending on its current state and the current states of its nearest neighbors.

Each row represents an overall system state for that time step, with the agents of the system shown as black or white cells arranged side by side in the row. The system evolves from top to bottom for 175 steps. The initial step of the system, shown at the top of each evolution, assigns a random black or white state to each agent of the system. Then each state of the system is determined by that system's update rule, shown below the evolution, where the three cells on the first line correspond to the state of the leftmost neighbor of a given agent, the state of the agent, and the state of the rightmost neighbor of the agent. The second line corresponds to how the given agent updates its state on the next step of the evolution based on its own state and the states of its nearest neighbors in the current state of the evolution. In the class 1 and class 2 systems, we see that initially and sometimes for a good chunk of steps, the system's dynamics are not apparent. But, after enough time, the system settles down into a stable state or pattern of states.

Figure 10.2 shows a cross-section of the two-dimensional "Game of Life," where I have taken the mean of the evolution from a particular set of initial conditions for 400 steps. The outer totalistic cellular automaton that codes the Game of Life is provably computationally universal—that is, its behavior is so rich that it can emulate any other computational evolution, no matter how complex (Wolfram 2002). The Game of Life is a classic example of organized complexity.

Traditional economic theory concerns itself with class 1 stationarity, anxiously noting cases in which stationarity cannot be obtained as in the "impossibility" theorems due to Arrow (1950). Classifying the "exceptional" cases is still largely an open problem requiring a different theoretical framework not solely focused on the discovery of fixed points.

Figure 10.2. A cross-section of the two-dimensional "Game of Life"

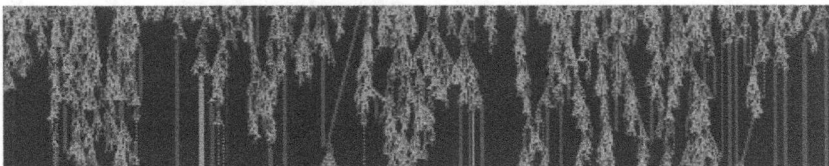

Class 1 stationarity—what economists call equilibrium—is hegemonous and overrepresented in economic theory owing to the relative analytical tractability of models that resolve into stationary states. I include both unique equilibria and multiple stable equilibria with no cycling in this category. All economic optimization methods that require solutions to be "in the core" (existence, uniqueness, stability) are stationarity. Microeconomics is stationary (Mas-Collel, Whinston, and Green 1995), as is game theory (Fudenberg and Tirole 1991). Traditional macroeconomic theory is generally stationary, including Austrian Business Cycle Theory, modern growth theory (Acemoglu 2012), and theories based on rational expectations. Dynamic stochastic general equilibrium (DSGE) models are the modern macroeconomics stationarity workhorses. The foundational DSGE models are Smets and Wouters (2003, 2007).

Class 2 periodicity—what is alternately called possessing stable limit cycles—arises in the analytical investigation of intertemporal optimization models and other optimal control models with at least two parameters (Benhabib and Nishimura 1979; Feichtinger and Sorger 1988; Feichtinger 1992; Steindl et al. 1986; Sethi and Thompson 2000; Bosi and Desmarchelier 2018). The most famous and possibly the first representative of this category was Knut Wicksell's "rocking horse" business cycle (Wicksell 1918). Nonlinear dynamical systems exhibit parametric regions that produce limit cycles, as in the phase space of the Simonovits model describing investment cycles in a centrally planned economy (Jakimowicz 2016). Voting often resolves into limit cycles in both two- and multiparty systems (Coleman 1992), as can dynamic evolutionary games that feature multiple equilibria (Platkowski and Zakrzewski 2011).

Class 3 chaos—what we might think of as white noise, random walks, or other kinds of endogenous systemic randomness—arises in economics in the analysis of nonlinear differential equations as in the Simonovits model, or as stock market "jutter" similar to random-walk (path-dependent) white noise. Rosser (1999, 174) discusses the relevance of chaotic dynamics in economic analysis, noting McCloskey's several historical examples of sensitive independence on initial conditions (losing the kingdom for want of a nail). The kind of randomness we associate with chaos in systems dynamics emerges endogenously, not in a driven or stochastic fashion, as that randomness is effectively exported from outside the system.

Class 4 organized complexity—what economists call spontaneous order, order without design, or self-ordering systems—has a long history in the economics and philosophy literature. It was of particular interest to the authors of the Scottish Enlightenment, such as Adam Smith ([1759] 2010) and Adam Ferguson (1768), and later to the French liberals, such as Alexis de Tocqueville ([1835] 2003), who was fascinated by spontaneous orders in poesy and language. Adam Ferguson is credited with coining the definition of a spontaneous social order in his passage from *An Essay on the History of Civil Society* (1768, 187): "Every step and every movement of the multitude, even in what are termed enlightened ages, are made with equal blindness to the future; and nations stumble upon establishments, which are indeed the result of human action, but not the execution of any human design."

Theories of spontaneous orders remained (largely) unmathematized up to the 20th century, though they were of interest to both mathematicians and philosophers. The philosopher Henri Bergson (1913) discusses creation as a nonteleological becoming that makes itself during its evolution and cannot be written in any functional form, which anticipates Stepping Stones 6 and 7. In economics, spontaneous ordering is taken up primarily by the Austrian school, particularly in the postwar period, and also by mathematicians like John von Neumann, who worked closely with economists. Finite automata were of interest to cyberneticists and mechanism designers, but though analogous to strategic choice in a traditional game theoretic setting, they were incapable of producing much in the way of complex behavior.

Instead, cellular automata, a level more complex than finite automata, were able to produce with relative ease evolutions that seemed to exhibit organized complexity. Using cellular automata to illustrate frameworks that easily and intuitively account for organized complexity leads into the most popular framework with which to model organized complexity in the social sciences: agent-based modeling. Agent-based models consist of sets of heterogeneous agents with certain characteristics (typically) placed somewhere with respect to each other in space, where interactions that can alter the characteristics of agents based on some set of update rules occur between agents based (typically) on geographic adjacency to the agent in question. Agent-based modeling in the paradigm, called agent-based computational economics, has become the framework of choice of economists seeking to develop models capable of exhibiting organized complexity (Tesfatsion 2002, 2006).

Cellular automata are themselves very simple agent-based models. Each cell is an agent, and its neighborhood consists of the agents to its direct right and left. Agents have two characteristics: their binary state and their location. Interactions are between an agent and its neighbors, and an agent's state updates based on an update rule that specifies what triple of states resolves into which state on the next step. There are eight total combinations of binary-state triples ($2 * 2 * 2 = 8$) and two possible states (0/white or 1/black) to assign to each triple determining a current agent's state on the next step of the system's evolution, for a total of $2^8 = 256$ possible systems. Not all of these systems are unique, as update rules are white-black symmetric, and some rules are mirror images of other rules. All told, there are 88 unique nearest-neighbor two-state cellular automata (Weisstein 2021). That is a mind-bogglingly rich amount of behavior for such a simple system.

Increasing the number of characteristics of agents (states), expanding the diversity of agent neighborhoods, and adding dynamic elements quickly result in a very large space of unique systems. One of the primary failings of economic theory in its current configuration is its inability to explain the combinatorial richness of social systems. Traditional analytical models are constrained to an extremely small number of agents, goods, and other sources of heterogeneity in the interest of analytical tractability (Wagner 2020). Cellular automata and agent-based models, owing to their locally constructive nature (see Stepping Stone 4), require relatively low information for agents to make efficient decisions (as well as present lower thresholds of transaction and computation costs—see Stepping Stone 3).

Cellular automata were first developed by von Neumann, the mathematician behind the development of game theory. It is interesting that game theory took hold in economic theory while cellular automata did not—it is an open question as to why this is. Game theoretic models under the assumption that they should obtain solutions in the core could be solved analytically, while the modal cellular automaton could not. Time would take care of these issues, however, with the advent of the computer age making coding and cataloging these systems simple (Wolfram 1984). Basic agent-based models were utilized more by noneconomist social scientists, like Herbert Simon (1952), who published in the management sciences, and the strategist Thomas Schelling (1978). Other early-use cases in economics are evolutionary games on lines or grids (Axelrod 1997).

Relationships Are Irreducible

We are located not just in space with relation to each other but also in terms of our memberships in different secular or religious groups. Memberships can also define in- and between-group influence (and vice versa). Influence matters a great deal in social systems. Information (both true and false) flows according to influence, can become echo chambers inside community clusters, and can even cascade like a contagion throughout a social network

(Granovetter 1973; Bikhchandani, Hirshleifer, and Welch 1992, 1998; Burt 2004; Palla et al. 2005; Jackson 2008).

The infrastructure of a social network reveals a great deal about the social system. How well an intervention works can depend on a detailed understanding of an underlying network or relationships (Haldane and May 2011; Tedeschi et al. 2012; Acemoglu, Ozdaglar, and Tahbez-Salehi 2015). At the level of a firm, whether a group is able to work well together depends on the structure of the who-knows-what network within the firm (Lee, Bachrach, and Lewis 2014; Peltokorpi 2008). Despite the importance of relationships, traditional economic theory does not take relationships into account. One need only read the *Theory of Value* or a PhD-level introductory microeconomics textbook (like Mas-Collel, Whinston, and Greene 1995) to see the formal lack of specific relationships.

Consider an economic possibility space inhabited by choosing agents, governing institutions, and choice bundles. In physics, we call a space *integral* if all elements of the spaces are connected to all other elements (i.e., what network theorists call "complete"). If we think of it in terms of information flow, then a random particle A knows the state of any other random particle B in an integral system, regardless of their relationship to each other in space. We call a space *nonintegral* if connections between elements of the system are anything less than complete. The trivial nonintegral space is one where there are zero connections, what network theorists call "completely disconnected." In practice, the connectivity of social systems lies somewhere between completely connected and completely disconnected, but certainly squarely in the realm of being nonintegral rather than integral (as discussed at length in Potts 2001).

I am going to call the explicit modeling of relationships between agent-individuals, firms, institutions, and other social structures *sociotopological infrastructure*. I do this in order to not conflate the specific study of individual social networks, institutional and bipartite individual-institutional networks, or interaction-direction networks like those for multiple games theories (Bednar and Page 2007; Bednar 2018; Devereaux 2020; Frey et al. 2021). Sociotopological infrastructure is an umbrella term that contains all ways in which social systems can be modeled using graph theoretic techniques, with the idea that any social system has multiple graph-theoretic formulations in terms of some kind of underlying way of specifying relationships between agents.[6]

Models being simplifications, it is important to understand what we gain by integrating sociotopological infrastructure into our modeling, and to emphasize what we lose when embracing the analytical simplicity of integrality's everywhere connectedness:

1. *Epistemological heterogeneity*: By simplifying social systems as fully connected, we lose the natural epistemological heterogeneity afforded through the relational perspective of one's position in a network. Epistemological heterogeneity can be added back in, but doing so requires a less intuitive argument that classifies and distributes various groups whose members, in the economist's argument, know more or less about such and such for some arguable reason. Explaining epistemological heterogeneity then requires its own methodological infrastructure, like search or private/public research investment or education. Theorists are always fighting against the tide of their heroic knowledge assumptions.

2. *Path-dependent and perverse social orders*: Ignoring connections by aggregating outcomes destroys information not only about how a perverse or seemingly suboptimal order may have arisen but also about how to possibly ameliorate it. Note that no after-the-fact rationalization in terms of fully connected rational choice theory is required to understand how path dependence or perverse orders occur. Explicitly modeling a traditional economic problem with a sociotopological infrastructure can be enough to demonstrate path-dependent and apparently suboptimal patterns (Jackson and Zenou 2015).

3. *Endogenous externalities*: Economists using integral analysis are tempted to treat the sociotopological infrastructure as a nondefault deviation to be intervened upon and controlled, without conducting a complete reckoning in terms of knowledge division (Peltokorpi 2008; Lee, Bachrach, and Lewis 2014; Devereaux and Yuan 2016), costs of calculation (see Stepping Stone 3), and other factors of why the sociotopology looks the way it does. This confusion is particularly prevalent in the naive integral analyses of externalities and economic networks (Haldane and May 2011; Jackson and Zenou 2015; Acemoglu, Ozdaglar, and Tahbaz-Salehi 2015).

4. *System-embedded intervention and governance*: By ignoring the sociotopological infrastructure and particularly influence networks in which policymakers themselves are embedded, a theorist may be tempted to mischaracterize intervention as affecting a system from the outside. This can lead to improper cost-benefit accounting and missing obvious unintended consequences. Furthermore, ignoring the sociotopological infrastructure erases a model-level intuitive foundation for how people and groups organize—or are already

organized—to solve social and governance problems. Polycentric governance can be intuitively modeled by visualizing where nodes of influence are placed in relationship to other nodes (Ostrom, Tiebout, and Warren 1961; V. Ostrom 2006; E. Ostrom 2010).

5. *Contextual choice*: In a nonintegral social system, action is necessarily embedded in a context. The relational context, defined by the sociotopological infrastructure, imposes a set of constraints on action, calculation, and knowledge. Amending a choice context comes with explicit costs that can be calculated based on costs of transforming one (less efficient/desirable) sociotopology into another (more efficient/desirable) sociotopology.

Calculation Is Costly

That calculation is costly is no more clearly evidenced than by work from the winners of the 2020 Nobel Prize in economics, Paul Milgrom and Robert Wilson, who won for their work on auction theory. Massive online auctions drove the revenue streams of the top internet companies of the aughts and 2010s.

Calculation is costly. Moreover, the costs of calculation are *endogenous* to understanding and predicting decision-making in social systems. This is different from observing that transaction costs are usually not zero. Recognizing that calculation is costly does not presume transaction costs have been precalculated. Recognizing that calculation is costly endogenizes the process of knowledge generation and acquisition and acknowledges that this process is costly.

The recognition that calculation is costly does not conflate the generation of *novel* knowledge with the acquisition of knowledge *already present* in the system. One cannot reduce the calculation of the costs of knowledge generation to a question of search costs. Even search costs come with an associated calculation that presumes agents somehow know the average cost of generating an answer to a *novel* question, and that agents calculate all possible modes of knowledge acquisition (for a *novel* question!) and choose the most efficient. If our agent is rational, then the calculation costs of this endeavor quickly become enormous. Not only must agents categorize their questions, but they must decide among the numerous ways that people like themselves approach such questions, carefully associating their personal skills, resources, and search context with a known set of exemplars who have approached similar questions enough times to generate a reliable error ratio. If this is starting to sound like the kind of complex creative problem that entrepreneurs attempt and fail to solve, it is not by accident.

Unfortunately, a recognition that calculation is costly, particularly in an open-ended evolutionary system, is tricky to fully represent mathematically. Consider a utility function U over some bundle $\mathbf{x}$. An explicit recognition that calculation is costly in this framework requires inserting a term in the utility function that represents the cost of calculating one's utility. This cost could be represented as first a calculation of the time it would take for an agent to compute their utility given a particular functional representation of the utility, then an assignment in real-valued units to represent the opportunity cost of the highest-utility alternative use of that time.

So, if f is the functional form of a naive utility calculation where $U(x) = f(x)$, and C a cost-of-calculation function that takes $f(x)$ as its argument, then the true utility calculation U_C, which incorporates the costs of calculation as a function of time t, is

$$U_C(x, f(x)) = f(x) - C(f(x), t) \qquad (1)$$

There are two cases to consider when analyzing equation (1), if we assume the costs of calculation are anything but trivial (as they would be under a literal interpretation of rational choice theory in any realistic setting).

The first case is when one's utility and the costs of calculating one's utility are estimable, or when a guess over a small sample works well (that is, when the error rate of guessing is estimable). In that case, agents can estimate how much effort goes into calculating their utility using some simpler method than actually conducting the calculation, and also estimate the expected gain in utility from a precise calculation relative to using some computationally less costly, inexact method. A simple application of case 1 is "rational irrationality." If calculating the true costs of making a utility calculation over the bundle $\mathbf{x}$ is known or suspected to be high relative to the utility of action $f(x)$, then guessing one's own utility, or acting in ways that seem not to take the as-if-calculated utility into account, could be (strictly speaking) rational.

The second case to consider when analyzing equation (1) is when there are no known less computationally costly methods to infer or estimate $C(f(x), t)$. Take, for example, a culture stuck in what seems to be a suboptimal equilibrium—where mores that apparently make some groups in the culture worse off continue to perpetuate themselves, despite those mores making individuals worse off than they would be if the mores were different. Suppose $\mathbf{x}$ is the bundle that refers to a representative agent choosing to reinforce the negative mores, $\mathbf{x}^*$ is the bundle associated with actions that go against the mores, and $\mathbf{x}^*$ is *not* a network good. But suppose that $C(f(x^*), t)$ is inestimable, perhaps because there is no example of individuals choosing $\mathbf{x}^*$ inside cultures where most people are still choosing $\mathbf{x}$. A given agent must explicitly calculate $f(x^*)$ to have a sense of what $C(f(x^*), t)$ is, which requires the agent to know the true, full, realistic form of $f(x^*)$.

And, of course, rational individuals would not embark on such a calculation unless they know that the calculation is feasible—that is, it contains no undecidable disjunctions or other calculational obstacles that result in a computation of the calculation being unable to halt (and thus, resulting in $C(f(x^*), t) = \infty$). But they *cannot* know that since they have not yet generated this knowledge, and it does not yet exist in the system in a way it can be acquired except through its generation. The risk of essentially finding no definitive answer when embarking on complex calculations, particularly those featuring moral conundrums that may not be answerable outside some accepted ad hoc interpretation, may be so great as to deter most people from the attempt. A social system might be stuck in a suboptimal cultural state, even though the answer (in retrospect) lies in the direct adjacent possible to the social system, owing to the high calculational costs of *imagining* forging into the unknown.

Incorporating the costs of utility calculation into a calculation of utility as in equation (1) calls into question a mechanistic interpretation of human decision-making. Neither are experts, dedicated to modeling possible social systems and calculating the utility of an individual, the answer to the conundrum of costly calculation, as I shall explain further in Stepping Stones 6 and 7. Experts have even less knowledge of the individual than an individual has of oneself, and though they may have a greater corpus of examples with which to estimate $f(x^*)$ or $C(f(x^*), t)$, they are constrained by the nonergodicity of social systems (Koppl et al. 2015) and the fundamental incompleteness of *any* deductive or inferential theoretical framework (Devereaux et al. 2021). Recognizing that calculation is costly is a fundamental stepping stone leading one away from a mechanistic interpretation and toward a systems theoretic interpretation of economics.

The Use of Knowledge by an Agent within the System Matters at the Process Level

Why don't economic agents "flock"?

Flocking behavior in birds is one of the fundamental ecological examples of self-organization. Fish schooling is another example of the same phenomenon. Neither birds nor fish have complicated enough brains to compute the complicated trajectory of their flock or school (any doubts about the complicatedness of these trajectories can be erased by watching a flock of starlings at sunset). Even extremely simple robots can be programmed to flock (Mataric 1992).

People in social systems *do* flock, and flock often. People literally flock on roller- and ice-skating rinks. They also metaphorically flock, forming groups based on high homophily (characteristic-level similarity to other people). Herding effects, a way to frame the phenomenon of flocking in terms of informational cascades, can be used to explain behaviors that can lead to stock market bubbles and crashes, bank runs, toilet paper shortages, moral panics that result in the ban of certain products and services, riots and social unrest, and economic booms and busts (Bikhchandani, Hirshleifer and Welch 1992; Devenow and Welch 1996; Helbing and Kirman 2013). Herding is not necessarily inefficient, even if it is not predicted by rational choice theory (Devenow and Welch 1996).

Wagner often invokes the metaphor comparing a parade to a piazza. You cannot model a parade as if it were a piazza, for a few reasons. First, utilizing Stepping Stone 2, we know that the sociotopological structure is entirely different, like comparing a hierarchical tree graph to semi-torn mesh. Relationships between marching band members are mediated through a parade master, which in piazza relationships are nearest neighbor and transient. Second, the piazza economizes on the use of knowledge in ways the parade cannot: Stepping Stones 3 and 4.

Flocking and herding behavior cannot be reduced at the process level to any one agent calculating the trajectory of the system. That is, and importantly, *the flocking process does not occur "as if" each agent were calculating a place in the trajectory of the system.* Flocking concerns itself with nearest neighbors. The agent alters its velocity vector with respect to the position of its nearest neighbors. The agent rarely has more than a handful of nearest neighbors. It is, at most, calculating a three-dimensional average distance and solving for the velocity that produces that average distance. True flocking can be programmed even more easily: if the agent is flocking correctly, it should appear to not move relative to its nearest neighbors. So, the agent does not really have to calculate anything beyond simple angles, as it can merely speed up (or slow down) in a particular direction if it sees its nearest neighbors going a bit faster (or slower). If it really flubs up and ends up flying out of the flock, it need not return to its original position but to the flock's edge. Error does not necessarily generate catastrophe in local, feedback-oriented processes.

Trajectory calculations, even if computationally feasible (and there is no guarantee they are), feature completely different cost and epistemological profiles and are brittle to systemic changes in a way that local, feedback-oriented processes are not. If an ice-skater falls down, rink-goers nearby alter their trajectories. These alterations cascade through the system until there emerges a new systemic trajectory that avoids the downed skater without resulting in more downed skaters or devolving into chaos. Contrast feedback-oriented, process-level alterations with a trajectory calculation: not only must individuals calculate their own trajectories, but in order to calculate a safe trajectory around the downed skater that does not result in rink-goers bumping into each other, falling down, and causing general chaos, they must calculate every *other* person's new trajectory too. They must also know that other people are doing this and that everyone is making the same calculations at the same time. Now comes the problematic part: How do agents implement these changes in a coordinated way, so that if Susie has to elongate her ellipsoid by 10 percent and Rocky by 30 percent, Rocky does not crash into Susie by moving before she does?

In summary, for a trajectory calculation to emulate the final pattern brought about by flocking, individuals are *not* calculating individual trajectories but rather their optimal trajectory through time given the calculated trajectories of all others in the system through time such that the system comes to a new equilibrium as quickly as possible all the while skirting chaos and destruction. If this calculation is of the order of the traveling salesman problem, I suspect its computational costs to be astronomical in all cases featuring more than a small handful of agents. Costly calculation and processes that economize on knowledge are very important to explaining and modeling organized complexity. As we saw in Stepping Stone 1, simple systems programmed to take only their nearest neighbors into account when deciding their next state can produce extremely complex behavior at the systems level. The memory needed to run even large systems of this sort is in the kilobytes, at most. If agents are rational, we will expect them to economize on knowledge acquisition at the process level, not solve for fixed trajectories of the complicated linear or nonlinear differential equations that characterize the system as a whole. Having an expert solve for the system and tell agents what to do will not improve anyone's lot: as we will see in Stepping Stones 6 and 7 in particular, the expert is effectively epistemologically symmetric to agents within the system, and even at a (local) disadvantage.

Causality in Economic Systems Is Complex

"It takes a theory to beat a theory." Or does it? If we have large enough data sets, can't economists (and other scientists) simply ignore theory in favor of evidence and experiment?[7]

The perceived success of the credibility revolution and the foothold of statistical methods in economics is at its peak, with two of the past three Nobel Prizes in economics credited to the movement. In their seminal paper summarizing the credibility revolution in econometrics, Angrist and Pischke (2010, 18) dismiss calibrated computational modeling in macroeconomics as (too) theoretical: "An effort to put reasonable numbers on theoretical relations is harmless and may even be helpful. But it's still theory," as if associating statements about causality to a linear decomposition of variable effect intensities from data is not, itself, a theory.

As Karl Popper ([1953] 2014, 61) notes, data analysis is inherently theory-laden: "Observation is always selective. It needs a chosen object, a definite task, an interest, a point of view, a problem. And its description presupposes a descriptive language, with property words; it presupposes similarity and classification, which in their turn presuppose interests, points of view, and problems."

Social science experiments and their statistical analyses are based on several layers of theoretical assumptions. Intervention research, the mother of econometrics, associates an outcome or effect with a set of independent variables or treatments whose mathematical relationship constitutes the model of the outcome/effect, with the assumption that the independent variables cause the observed outcome/effect. The vast majority of econometric modeling attempts represent an outcome in terms of a linear composition of linearly independent effects. That is, the assumption is that the response is subject to decomposition into independent causal mechanisms that can be manipulated in order to effectively control the response (Hausman and Woodward 2004). Econometric results intended to inform policy include at least one independent variable that can be manipulated through policy.

While all this sounds perhaps more straightforward than a complex analytical or computational model, it is accompanied by a number of theoretical choices and assumptions:

a.   Most econometric models are linear, with neither too few variables so as to underspecify the effect nor too many so as to overfit. Curvature is utilized sparingly.

b.   The relationship between outcomes and independent variables is assumed constant down to some periodic or discernibly process-specific pattern.

c.   The direction of causality emanates from the treatments/independent variables to the effect.

d. More data improves the significance of the observed effects (if the effects are significant).

e. Differences between groups can be effectively controlled for through randomization (either explicit or synthetic).

It is true that models are simplifications. But policies can have a wide reach and deep impact on the lives of individuals. And while models are simplifications, it is important to, *at the very least,* utilize models of effects that are appropriate to the level of complexity represented by the system in which a set of effects is embedded. Social systems are complex, as discussed in Stepping Stone 1. Interventions into complex systems are complex. So, we must ask: Are (a)–(e) appropriate theoretical choices and assumptions for credibly and reliably intervening in complex social systems?

Linearity (a): In order for a linear decomposition to be the true model, it must take into account all salient effects and attain a stable set of relationships that unmask true causal relationships. Any changes in the relationships between the variables must have been accounted for in the research design. But complex social systems are characterized by strong and irreducible interdependence between variables—that is, "the whole is greater than the sum of its parts,"[8] which, when inverted, implies that the whole is not reducible to a sum of its parts (Simon 1996; Arthur 2014; Cioffi-Revilla 2014). In Day's (1994) definition, complex economic dynamics do not converge to a point or limit cycle, nor do they catastrophically diverge (explode, implode). That is, some nonlinearity is indicated to characterize complexity in economic systems (Rosser 2006).

Dynamics (b): In traditional econometrics, models represent a linear decomposition of effects that are relatively stationary or, at their most complicated, follow some process-level pattern. Already, one should start to worry—can't such assumptions only account for economic phenomena that are either Wolfram-Chomsky class 1 or class 2?

Causality (c): Correlation is not causation, and the strength of correlations between modeled explanatory variables is not enough to establish those variables as causes of the effect/response, rather than the other way around (Pearl 2002). Intervention in this case amounts to treating the symptoms rather than finding a cure. But the credibility revolution was a revolution primarily because it sought to get to the heart of the direction of the possibly causal link surfaced by noting a strong correlation between variables. Intervention in the form of an experiment—a quasi-randomized control trial in the social science setting—can determine what manipulation of which variable is prior to which outcome. Difference-in-difference, regression discontinuity, synthetic control, and fieldwork random control trial research designs represent an attempt to first suss out actual correlations, then get at causality.

Big Data (d): Sampling a model over more data is generally considered to improve the quality of the study and to isolate truly significant correlations. But it can be proved mathematically even in very large data sets that increasing the sample size also increases the amount of spurious or apparent correlations between variables with no causal link—so much so that in very large data sets we expect a veritable "deluge" of spurious correlations (Calude and Longo 2017). Furthermore, in Bayesian probability, priors must be formally taken into account at each step of the updating process. This requires an ability both to list all relevant priors and to form a probability distribution over their relative likelihoods. Listability of relevant possibilities is not fact but a theoretical assumption, one that the unbounded nature of evolution in an open-ended social system heavily calls into question (see Stepping Stone 7). The ability to form a probability distribution typically assumes low or no computation costs to doing so, which the combinatorial richness of the economic possibility space heavily calls into question (see Stepping Stone 3).

Econometric analyses are often intended to advise on some kind of intervention into an economy, an intervention that is, by the nature of the subject matter, complex. A complex intervention deals with interventions that have complex and sensitive causal chains and processes, as opposed to simple interventions, where the causal chains are less complex and more insensitive (Rickles 2009, 81). That is, we would expect the relationship between saving more in one's youth and, say, happiness in later life to be complex and not straightforward. There are several avenues through which savings behavior could be connected to happiness in later life (straightforward investment; having enough wealth to save implies having enough wealth to take care of one's health and other needs, which has a cumulative happiness effect, lowering lifelong stress by knowing one has savings and thus having a happier personal and professional life), just as there are several avenues through which savings behavior could *reduce* happiness in later life (saving more when younger signals risk aversion, which could result in fewer bigger successes in life; the opportunity cost of saving is spending on items that could make someone happier or wiser or lead to more professional and personal success in the long term). Any intervention to change savings behavior in young adults, therefore, represents a complex intervention.

Randomization (e): In complex systems under complex interventions, randomization can be extremely difficult owing to the nonlinear interconnectivity of control variables. Even very small differences between control and treatment groups can lead to significant observable differences (Altman 1985; Rickles 2009), an effect that gets worse with smaller sample sizes (as one might have in a policy setting). And, of course, randomization can only be conducted with respect to readily identifiable characteristics. The ways in which we categorize people in particular are faulty, biased toward available and visible data, based on theories that are likely to look outmoded to the next generation (like inherent intelligence). Synthetic control deepens this issue, giving the designer of the study yet another way to insert possibly faulty theory and bias into the design.

The Evolution of Economic Systems Is Open-Ended and Nonergodic

In his 1889 essay, "The Decay of Lying," Oscar Wilde sorrowfully describes how artists of his age lost their ability to create life and beauty and strove merely to copy it. By adhering too closely to fact, Wilde laments, art is unable to create anything new. While his is a warning directed mainly at writers, I do not believe it is mere coincidence that scientific management and rationalization of social systems was gaining popularity at the same time Wilde wrote this piece. Wilde (1889) writes, "The public imagine that, because they are interested in their immediate surroundings, Art should be interested in them also, and should take them as her subject matter. But the mere fact that they are interested in these things makes them unsuitable subjects for Art."

Similarly, economists imagine that because they can observe particular data or possess certain tractable mathematical tools, the evolution of social systems must somehow be based on that particular data or be largely describable with a clever enough application of those tractable tools. Wilde believed that art was bigger than what we can observe—that art's very purpose was to describe what we cannot observe.

The evolution of social systems—which contain art—does not reflect merely what we can observe; more importantly, it reflects the unobservable, the unmodelable, and the inapprehensible elements that cannot be ignored or approximated away without ignoring the very engine of human development. This is another of Wagner's points, rephrased. Dick remains simple and concrete, pressing home to the attentive student that the 5 percent of human activity that economists ignore or approximate away without a second thought constitutes the very engine of the world (Wagner 2010).

Understanding the evolution of economic systems cannot be done without acknowledging the creation and the generation of unpredictable novelty. And this is where approaching social science from the perspective of mechanism fails the theorist, as this sort of novelty, by definition, lies outside mechanistic description (Banzhaf et al. 2016). Economic systems are characterized by open-ended and nonergodic evolution (Koppl et al. 2015; Devereaux and Wagner 2020; Devereaux 2021; Kauffman and Roli 2021). Alfred J. Lotka (1925) argues that evolution is teleologically directed toward greater entropy via the law of entropy (Rosser 2020). This creates a spectrum of economic complexity that increases as economies become more diverse and economic choice more combinatorially complex.

Neither is the issue solvable through a Bayesian approach where unknown states are assigned some tiny cumulative probability, as this presupposes the ability of an agent to list all possibilities. As Kauffman and Roli (2021) argue, the nature of complex systems like biochemical systems and social systems is that all possibilities are inherently unlistable. One need only consider all the uses of a screwdriver throughout all possible histories of the universe. Even if deterministic, the sheer combinatorial size of the possibility space makes listability computationally unreasonable when we acknowledge that calculation is costly (Stepping Stone 3).

The open-ended evolution of a system can be defined as having a system-generated evolution of states that is both unbounded and innovative (Adams et al. 2017). The ensuing discussion summarizes points I made in an earlier article (Devereaux 2021). Novelty has three characteristic types, whose definitions I take from Banzhaf et al. (2016) to discipline the discussion of evolution in economic systems: Type 0 (variation), Type 1 (innovation), Type 2 (emergence). As one can guess, the search for organized complexity means dealing directly with the difficulties of engaging with theories that are capable of characterizing emergence (Type 2). One of the primary difficulties is in listing possibilities in the system. If economic theories are based on epistemological grounds with some notion of rationality and deterministic choice over known or knowable possibilities, then these theories require prelisted or listable possibility spaces over and within which agents choose. As I note (Devereaux 2021, 10–11), possibilities in Type 0 variational novelty are prelisted, possibilities in Type 1 innovative novelty are listable, but possibilities in Type 2 emergent novelty are not listable.

But aren't all models—even systems theoretic models—deterministic? A tension arises between the closure of a systems theory of economics and the nonergodic nature of the system. But it is not a tension faced by systems theory alone. In our search for organized complexity, we must be content with a fundamental constraint on our ability to generate all possible system states. We cannot generate all possible system states, which implies that neither systems theorists nor any other kinds of theorists can be engineers. Scientists of complex social systems must content themselves with striving for explanatory rather than predictive power. And, as we will see in the next stepping stone, this limitation is even more fundamental than recognizing the open-ended evolutionary nature of complex social systems.

Intervention Must Occur from within the System, and It Is Theoretically Incomplete

The most recent scientific eras can be roughly described as the era of mechanism, which began with Newton, and the era of probability, based on discoveries in thermodynamics and quantum dynamics. Economic theory reflects each era with somewhat of a lag, the Debreuvian *Theory of Value* its *Principia*, and the credibility revolution representing an all-is-statistics approach.

However, scientists like Kauffman and Roli (2021) claim we are on the verge of a third scientific era of understanding physical, biological, and sociological systems in terms that transcend mechanism and probability. A systems theory of economics is at home in this third scientific era in a way that traditional economic theory and econometrics cannot be. I will explain why in this last—and most controversial—stepping stone.

Stepping Stone 7 is based on recent discoveries in mathematics, physics, and chemistry that together herald a set of constraints on conducting science from mechanistic and probabilistic frames, as discussed in the previous stepping stones. Mechanistic thinking about goals requires some theory of "mind" inhabiting and controlling a system. Spontaneous and self-ordering, on the other hand, requires "no mind." That is, there are changes within and to a system that require or afford the use of (human, but possibly artificial) mind, and there are those that do not. Socioecological systems produce themselves, so understanding a system cannot be synonymous with design.

Attempts to affect a future state of the system can never be completely designed because minds are embedded inside the system and are unavoidably ignorant of some aspects of the system that are used to determine its next state. F. A. Hayek described the latter reality in terms of the epistemological deficit of mind (1937, 1945, 1955) and later attempted a diagonal proof to demonstrate that a complete characterization of complex systems inevitably lies outside the reach of mind ([1964] 2018).

While Hayek's diagonal proof was not sufficient to demonstrate this, a second attempt of this proof was made in 2021 using meta-mathematical techniques (Devereaux et al. 2021). The proof is of a principle called "frame relativity." The original statement of this principle, that agents who reside within a system that has met a low and reasonably realistic threshold of complexity cannot generate a complete theory of the system, is credited to Roger Koppl (Devereaux et al. 2021, 3). Relying primarily on results derived from Gödel's incompleteness theorem, the authors prove that "mind" is at a distinct and insurmountable disadvantage when it comes to apprehending the complete possibility set of a system over all possible histories of that system.

DISCUSSION

> If . . . we regard Nature as the collection of phenomena external to man, people only discover in her what they bring to her. She has no suggestions of her own.
>
> —*Oscar Wilde, "The Decay of Lying: A Dialogue"*

I am both a frontiersman and a surveyor; most economists who choose to engage in systems thinking will be both, at this early stage of the theory. Those who choose to forge into the frontier must tolerate a high risk of failure. In terms of selection effects, it is likely that the extremes of the field will generate frontiersmen: those insulated from failure by having played the game to the satisfaction of their peers, and those with less of an incentive to conform by already having established themselves outside of the mainstream.

In this final section, I will briefly map out the frontier of a systems theory of economics given the stepping stones that have led us closer to understanding how a systems theory of economics needs to work, what it is able to say, and what it is not able to say. There are systems theorists in economics, and economics has had a brush or two with systems theoretic ideas in its time. We should understand the existing efforts and how (and whether) to incorporate them.

Mapping the Frontier

Each one of the stepping stones of a systems theory of economics requires a certain level—and perhaps a great deal—of theoretical infrastructure. Some of this infrastructure has already been built by scholars, sometimes explicitly with respect to augmenting or rewriting parts of economic theory, and more often to deal with theoretical issues in other fields. Systems theory, as discussed in Stepping Stone 1, represents a cross-disciplinary synthesis of ontologies and approaches. The act of building an explicitly systems theoretic economics requires synthesizing the results from other fields, filling the gaps where salient mathematical results and modeling approaches do not yet exist, and developing a body of examples that fruitfully apply elements of the systems theory of economics to existing economic questions.

Thankfully, a few decades of work in complex social systems have provided the budding economic systems theorist with a variety of tools. I have already discussed agent-based modeling at some length, but I encourage readers nonetheless to read Axtell and Farmer (2022), which is an excellent survey of the use and usefulness of agent-based modeling in economics. I have also already discussed the theory of networks in social science, with Jackson (2008) serving as a well-rounded introduction to the reasoning, theory, and tools.

When it comes to extending existing approaches in economics, several complexity economists (including me) are excited about the potential for game theory to be extended beyond its narrow definition in economic theory, in particular the need for games to have solutions in the core (or fixed points, period). Once again, Wagner was my primary influence in this respect. While his 2012 paper was based on the idea of the macro economy as an ecology of *plans*, we quickly found ourselves talking in his office about how plans can be seen as chains of games. We then progressed to researching the ecology of games literature (which is rather sparse but has good entries by Norton Long [1958] and Mark Lubell [2013]) and envisioning an economy as some kind of ecology of games. Our initial paper on the subject, "Contrasting Visions for Macroeconomic Theory" (Devereaux and Wagner 2020), lays out many of these ideas for the interested reader.

Building on these ideas, I demonstrate the possibility for emergent solutions in the theory of multiple games (Devereaux 2020). As for other interesting work on a systems approach to multiple games theory, I recommend Bednar and Page (2007), Bednar (2018), and Frey et al. (2021). There is a great deal of enthusiasm in multiple games work at the moment. For related work that explicitly takes an Ostromian tack and integrates both games and networks, I recommend Michael McGinnis (2011). Elinor Ostrom's (1990, 2010) work on governing the commons and Vincent Ostrom's (2006) work on polycentric governance in particular are two areas ripe for the introduction of systems theoretic methods.

Interdisciplinary opportunities abound for any systems theorist of economics. I have already mentioned the extent to which a systems theory of economics borrows, and would continue to do so, from ecological theories and results. But did you know that biochemistry provides great insights that could be both more explanatory and more useful to a systems theorist of economics? Insights from theoretical biology and chemistry are seeping into papers that discuss the nonergodicity of the evolution of economic systems (Koppl et al. 2015). Equations used to model the combinatorial richness of biochemical systems have turned up in growth theory models (Koppl et al. 2021) and have provided frameworks for comparing production to chemistry (Padgett, McMahan, and Zhong 2012).

Note that while I mostly made the case for a systems theory of economics with respect to equilibrium and optimal control theories of economics and econometric analyses, these are not the only ontological traditions in economics. A systems theory of economics is the ontological predecessor of the process-based narrative method of classical theorists such as Smith,[9] Hayek, and Ludwig von Mises and the interaction-focused game theoretic and computational methods of John von Neumann, Oskar Morgenstern, and Herbert Simon (1996) (Hayek [1964] 2018; Vaughn 1999; Koppl 2006; Rosser 2015; Lewis and Wagner 2017). While the latter was subsumed by rational choice methods, and the former dismissed owing to lack of devotion to mechanism, their discoveries and conclusions are independently consistent with a systems theoretic economics.

Forging into the Frontier

Next, I outline a few early areas and open questions ripe for exploration by the frontiersmen of systems economics. I do not categorize these questions as macro, micro, or meso, because I want to encourage readers to adopt an entangled and synthesized systems thinking with respect to individual action and social ordering, though my questions do touch on traditional topics in both macro and micro. I have generated these questions primarily as working paper drafts or idea stubs over the past seven or so years of being both a surveyor and frontiersman of systems economics.

Modeling the Emergence and Entanglement of Economic Indicators

Economic indicators are heavily used in economic modeling, forecasting, and public policy. Some of the first modern social indicators—in particular, growth, productivity, employment, and inflation—were developed in the 1930s as New Deal exigencies and reflect a high degree of entanglement with leading business concerns and professional associations in their creation

(President's Research Committee on Social Trends 1933: I). Economic indicators represent *models*. To be meaningful, indicators must establish a set of fundamental laws inferred by the internal structure of the statistic (Sheldon and Parke 1975, 696; De Solla 1978, 72). Indicators by definition are theory-laden and subject to choice within an entangled political economy. Using graph and systems theory, can one model the emergence and entanglement of economic indicators?

My work so far on this subject has used the theory of the formation of special interest groups—in particular a paper by Hebert and Wagner (2017)—to represent economic indicators as emergent from the division of knowledge in society and the strategic positioning of experts tasked with delivering knowledge (Devereaux 2018). A small amount of unknown bias can, in a position of enough influence, ramify through the system via cascade effects and alter the normative preferences of one group to conform with the normative preferences of another group by adopting an indicator unwittingly biased in favor of the second.

Reconsidering Behavioral Economics under Explicit Calculation-Costing

Behavioral economists have been more open than most traditional economists to the idea that choice requires some degree of disutility-generating calculation. Experimental economists have shown in a variety of settings that people do not choose as we would expect a rational calculus user to choose. Behavioral economics tends to use experimental observation to discern the "heuristics and biases" that people actually use to make choices—but what if we recast rational choice in terms of the recursive utility function?

Recall the functional form of the recursive utility function (equation [1]):

$$U_C(x, f(x)) = f(x) - C(f(x), t)$$

What we should see is that people tend to stick with a known *estimate* of their utility if they are facing a complex problem whose computational complexity would make it too costly (if not impossible) to explicitly calculate. The most computationally complex choice settings should have the most prevalence of ecological rationality (V. Smith 2003) and dependence on other sources of knowledge, like from history, or embedded in society as norms, hierarchies, folklore, and common wisdom (Koppl 2018). A great deal of work in this area can be done to understand how estimates form, emerge, and propagate through a social system, and dovetails with work on information choice theory (Levy and Peart 2004), path dependence, and perverse social orders (Martin and Storr 2008).

Furthermore, using equation (1), we can show that guessing behavior is rationally indicated in "Buridan's ass" situations. Jean Buridan, a logician and philosopher, uses the example of an ass (donkey) that stands perfectly equidistant from two piles of hay. A traditional rational choice theory that does not take the cost of calculating one's utility into account will founder on what is logically an undecidable disjunction. But if $C(f(x), t) = DNE$, then the choosing agent is rationally justified in using any heuristic, even an ad hoc one, to make its choice.

Comparing Different Sociotopological Infrastructures in Economic Terms

In a systems theory, a proposed transformation from one state to another must be made explicit and demonstrated to work. For instance, it is not enough to simply compare two apparent sociotopologies in terms of indicators like robustness and informational efficiency—particularly when comparing partial informational connectedness, as in asymmetric information. It is simpler to understand this point by recalling that particular partially connected topologies mean a space is nonintegral, and that integral spaces, the spaces used in traditional economic theory, imply *full connectedness*, not zero connectedness. Traditional economic theory has an implied topology of action, where all elements of the system are fully (informationally) connected. Reducing the number of connections between elements of the system is synonymous with imposing additional constraints that are costly to remove.

Naive use of contextual theorizing by economists has led to such odd results as positing that action in any nonintegral space is suboptimal to action in integral space, without explaining why and how it was possible or near costless to remove the contextual constraints in a nonintegral choice space (Akerlof 1978; Grossman and Stiglitz 1980; Stiglitz 2002), and such comparisons are still being made despite the relatively advanced theory of social networks (as in Acemoglu, Ozdaglar, and Tahbaz-Salehi 2015).

The open questions relevant here that could be addressable in a systems theory of economics are the relative efficiency of different sociotopological infrastructures (markets along some spectrum of regulatory activity, for instance); how the sociotopological infrastructure creates or mitigates principal agent problems; whether *problems* as identified in traditional economic theory really are problematic given an explicit sociotopological infrastructure (Stepping Stone 2), how agents use knowledge at the process level (Stepping Stone 4), endogenizing calculational costs (Stepping Stone 3), fundamental interventional constraints (Stepping Stone 7), and under the kind of uncertainty that defies calculation (Stepping Stone 6).

CONCLUSION: THOUGHTS FROM A SURVEYOR AND FRONTIERSMAN

Often, while chatting in his office, Wagner and I would reflect on what drives a theorist to theorize, despite the opportunity costs of theorizing in a field that ostracizes theorists to its margins. As I recall, we concluded that theorizing relieves some form of uneasiness: we feel better when we have come to an answer, or even a direction if before we had none. Theorizing is hard. If you do not have the knowledge you need to answer your question, there is no way around the hard work of obtaining it. One can coauthor, and I am grateful for the ways Dick and my other coauthors have complemented my strengths over the years, but one of the difficulties in choosing theory is the need to synthesize apparently different methods, to understand the methods of other fields and apply them to your own, to see the true similarities and differences between the myriad ways one can approach a problem, and, most importantly, to understand which are the artifacts of one's theory versus the objects about which one theorizes.

Will a systems theory of economics "beat" traditional economic and econometric theory? I suppose it depends on whether it becomes useful, in terms of the combined sentiment of Stigler and Box from the introduction. But there is a great deal of frontier yet to explore. Adopting systems theoretic tools, even if you are not on board with the whole theory, is a good strategy for any economic theorist who wants to be at the forefront of this change. I think both Wagner and I would agree on the idea that change at the institutional level of academia is a nonlinear incremental process subject to unexpected cascades and phase transitions.[10]

NOTES

1. In 2005, economist Larry White (2005, 325) determined that "some 74 percent of the articles on monetary policy published by US-based economists in US-edited journals appear in Fed-published journals or are co-authored by Fed staff economists."

2. In the early 1980s, the edifice of fixed-point control theory, which was postulated to be able to engineer entire economies and military strategies, was discovered by Kenneth Arrow's protégé Alain Lewis to have been built on sand (Lewis 1985). The writing had been on the Cowles Foundation wall since the late 1960s (Kramer 1967). Noncomputability of fixed points was a fatal blow to a mechanism design theory built on the discovery and proof of existence of fixed points, and cybernetics premised on the computational attainment of goals that had been theoretically envisioned as fixed points.

3. For an overview of complexity ideas in economics up until the early aughts, I recommend Rosser (2006).

4. For a good overview of the history of systems thinking in the social sciences, refer to Hammond (2002).

5. Note that these functions are not necessarily well defined. Also, as we will see in a later section, open-endedness obliterates listability, which means all recursive functions have errors that are not mean-zero or themselves well defined.

6. It is an open question whether all possible ways of specifying relationships between agents is listable; my intuition is that it would not be difficult to demonstrate an analogy between the listability of all possible relationships and the listability of all possible uses of a screwdriver (that is, a phenomenon that is unlistable). One need only create a mapping between the set of all possible relationships and an unlistable phenomenon.

7. As Calude and Longo (2017: 596) note, the declaration that theory is dead in the face of big enough data sets was made by C. Anderson (2008) in an essay titled "The End of Theory: The Data Deluge Makes the Scientific Method Obsolete."

8. It's interesting to note that this quote, originally attributed to Aristotle, was also *mis*-attributed to the German Gestalt psychologist Kurt Koffka. Koffka's quote is, rather, "the whole is something else than the sum of its parts," which is an even more apt characterization of complex social systems.

9. Note especially that Smith's *Theory of Moral Sentiments* was more systems theoretic than *Wealth of Nations*.

10. I refer here of course to the popularity of DSGE modeling in the aughts compared with the teens, after the fallout of the financial recession and the inability of DSGE theory to apprehend such an event.

REFERENCES

Acemoglu, D. 2012. "Introduction to Economic Growth." *Journal of Economic Theory* 147, no. 2: 545–50.

Acemoglu, D., A. Ozdaglar, and A. Tahbaz-Salehi. 2015. "Systemic Risk and Stability in Financial Networks." *American Economic Review* 105, no. 2: 564–608.

Adamatzky, A., and G. J. Martinez. 2010. "On Generative Morphological Diversity of Elementary Cellular Automata." *Kybernetes* 39, no. 1: 72–82.

Adams, A., H. Zenil, P. C. W. Davies, and S. I. Walker. 2017. "Formal Definitions of Unbounded Evolution and Innovation Reveal Universal Mechanisms for Open-Ended Evolution in Dynamical Systems." *Scientific Reports* 7, no. 1: 997.

Akerlof, G. A. 1978. "The Market for 'Lemons': Quality Uncertainty and the Market Mechanism." In *Uncertainty in Economics*, edited by P. Diamond and M. Rothschild, 235–51. Cambridge, MA: Academic Press.

Altman, D. G. 1985. "Comparability of Randomised Groups." *The Statistician* 34, no. 1: 125–36.

Anderson, C. 2008. "The End of Theory: The Data Deluge Makes the Scientific Method Obsolete." *Wired Magazine*, June 23, 2008.

Angrist, J. D., and J. S. Pischke. 2010. "The Credibility Revolution in Empirical Economics: How Better Research Design Is Taking the Con out of Econometrics." *Journal of Economic Perspectives* 24, no. 2: 3–30.

Arrow, K. J. 1950. "A Difficulty in the Concept of Social Welfare." *Journal of Political Economy* 58, no. 4: 328–46.

Arthur, W. B. 2014. *Complexity and the Economy*. Oxford, UK: Oxford University Press.

Axelrod, R. 1997. *The Complexity of Cooperation: Agent-Based Models of Competition and Collaboration*. Princeton, NJ: Princeton University Press.

Axtell, R. L., and J. D. Farmer. 2022. "Agent-based Modeling in Economics and Finance: Past, Present, and Future." *Journal of Economic Literature*. Online.

Banzhaf, W., B. Baumgaertner, G. Beslon, R. Doursat, J. A. Foster, B. McMullin, V. V. de Melo, T. Miconi, L. Spector, S. Stepney, and R. White. 2016. "Defining and Simulating Open-Ended Novelty: Requirements, Guidelines, and Challenges." *Theory in Biosciences* 135, no. 3: 131–61.

Bednar, J. 2018. "Modeling the Institutional Matrix: Norms, Culture, and Robust Design." In *A Research Agenda for New Institutional Economics*, edited by C. Ménard and M. Shirley, 162–70. Cheltenham, UK: Edward Elgar.

Bednar, J., and S. Page. 2007. "Can Game(s) Theory Explain Culture? The Emergence of Cultural Behavior within Multiple Games." *Rationality and Society* 19, no. 1: 65–97.

Benhabib, J., and K. Nishimura. 1979. "The Hopf Bifurcation and Existence and Stability of Closed Orbits in Multisector Models of Optimal Economic Growth." *Journal of Economic Theory* 21: 421–44.

Bergson, H. 1913. *L'evolution Creatrice*. Paris: F. Alcan.

Bertalanffy, L. V. 1951. "General System Theory, a New Approach to Unity of Science. 5. Conclusion." *Human Biology* 23, no. 4: 337–45.

Bikhchandani, S., D. Hirshleifer, and I. Welch. 1992. "A Theory of Fads, Fashion, Custom, and Cultural Change as Informational Cascades." *Journal of Political Economy* 100, no. 5: 992–1026.

———. 1998. "Learning from the Behavior of Others: Conformity, Fads, and Informational Cascades." *Journal of Economic Perspectives* 12, no. 3: 151–70.

Bosi, S., and D. Desmarchelier. 2018. "Limit Cycles Under a Negative Effect of Pollution on Consumption Demand: the Role of an Environmental Kuznets Curve." *Environmental and Resource Economics* 69, no. 2: 343–63.

Boulding, K. E. 1956. "General Systems Theory: The Skeleton of Science." *Management Science* 2, no. 3: 197–208.

Burt, R. S. 2004. "Structural Holes and Good Ideas." *American Journal of Sociology* 110, no. 2: 349–99.

Calude, C. S., and G. Longo. 2017. "The Deluge of Spurious Correlations in Big Data." *Foundations of Science* 22, no. 3: 595–612.

Cioffi-Revilla, C. 2014. *Introduction to Computational Social Science*. London: Springer.

Coleman, S. 1993. "Cycles and Chaos in Political Party Voting: A Research Note." *Journal of Mathematical Sociology* 18, no. 1: 47–64.

Day, R. H. 1994. *Complex Economic Dynamics*, Vol. 1, *An Introduction to Dynamical Systems and Market Mechanisms*. Cambridge, MA: MIT Press.

Debreu, G. 1959. *Theory of Value: An Axiomatic Analysis of Economic Equilibrium*. New Haven, CT: Yale University Press.

———. 1974. "Excess Demand Functions." *Journal of Mathematical Economics* 1, no. 1: 15–21.

Devenow, A., and I. Welch. 1996. "Rational Herding in Financial Economics." *European Economic Review* 40, nos. 3–5: 603–15.

Devereaux, A. 2020. "Synecological Systems Theory: An Alternative Foundation for Economic Inquiry." Doctoral diss., George Mason University.

———. 2021. "The Limits of Control in the Face of Accelerating Growth: A Complexity Economist's View." Working paper.

Devereaux, A., R. Koppl, S. Kauffman, and A. Roli. 2021. "An Incompleteness Result Regarding Within-System Modeling." Working paper.

Devereaux, A. N., and R. E. Wagner. 2020. "Contrasting Visions for Macroeconomic Theory: DSGE and OEE." *American Economist* 65, no. 1: 28–50.

Doria, F. A. 2017. *The Limits of Mathematical Modeling in the Social Sciences: The Significance of Gödel's Incompleteness Phenomenon*. Singapore: World Scientific.

Feichtinger, G. 1992. "Limit Cycles in Dynamic Economic Systems." *Annals of Operations Research* 37, no. 1: 313–44.

Feichtinger, G., and G. Sorger. 1988. "Periodic Research and Development." In *Optimal Control Theory and Economic Analysis*, edited by G. Feichtinger, 3:121. North-Holland, Amsterdam: Elsevier Science.

Ferguson, A. 1768. *An Essay on the History of Civil Society*. Edinburgh: A. Millar and T. Cadell in the Strand, and A. Kincaid and J. Bell.

Frey, S., J. Hedges, J. Tan, and P. Zahn. 2021. "Composing Games into Complex Institutions." August 2021. https://arxiv.org/abs/2108.05318v1.

Fudenberg, D., and J. Tirole. 1991. *Game Theory*. Cambridge, MA: MIT Press.

Granovetter, M. S. 1973. "The Strength of Weak Ties." *American Journal of Sociology* 78, no. 6: 1360–80.

Grossman, S. J., and J. E. Stiglitz. 1980. "On the Impossibility of Informationally Efficient Markets." *American Economic Review* 70, no. 3: 16.

Haldane, A. G., and R. M. May. 2011. "Systemic Risk in Banking Ecosystems." *Nature* 469, no. 7330: 351–55.

Hamermesh, D. S. 2013. "Six Decades of Top Economics Publishing: Who and How?" *Journal of Economic Literature* 51, no. 1: 162–72.

Hammond, D. 2002. "Exploring the Genealogy of Systems Thinking." *Systems Research and Behavioral Science* 19: 429–39.

Hausman, D. M., and J. Woodward. 2004. "Manipulation and the Causal Markov Condition." *Philosophy of Science* 71: 846–56.

Hayek, F. A. 1937. "Economics and Knowledge." *Economica* 4, no. 13: 33.

———. 1945. "The Use of Knowledge in Society." *American Economic Review* 35: 519–30.

———. 1955. "Degrees of Explanation." *British Journal for the Philosophy of Science* 6, no. 23: 209–25.

———. (1964) 2018. "The Theory of Complex Phenomena." In *Critical Approaches to Science & Philosophy*, edited by M. Bunge, 332–49. New York, NY: Routledge.

Hebert, D. J., and R. E. Wagner. 2017. "Political Parties: Insights from a Tri-Planar Model of Political Economy." *GMU Working Paper in Economics* 15, no. 23.

Helbing, D., and A. Kirman. 2013. "Rethinking Economics Using Complexity Theory." *Real-World Economics Review*, no. 64: 23–52.

Ioannidis, J. P. A. 2012. "Why Science Is Not Necessarily Self-Correcting." *Perspectives on Psychological Science* 7, no. 6: 645–54.

Jackson, M. O. 2008. *Social and Economic Networks*. Princeton, NJ: Princeton University Press.

Jackson, M. O., and Y. Zenou. 2015. "Games on Networks." In *Handbook of Game Theory with Economic Applications*, edited by H. P. Young and S. Zamir, 95–163. Amsterdam: Elsevier.

Jakimowicz, A. 2016. "Fundamental Sources of Economic Complexity." *International Journal of Nonlinear Sciences and Numerical Simulation* 17, no. 1: 1–13.

Jeong, H., Z. Néda, and A. L. Barabási. 2003. "Measuring Preferential Attachment in Evolving Networks." *Europhysics Letters* 61, no. 4: 567.

Kahneman, D., S. P. Slovic, P. Slovic, and A. Tversky, eds. 1982. *Judgment under Uncertainty: Heuristics and Biases*. Cambridge: Cambridge University Press.

Kauffman, S. A., and A. Roli. 2021. "The Third Transition in Science: Beyond Newton and Quantum Mechanics—a Statistical Mechanics of Emergence." May. https://arxiv.org/abs/2106.15271v4.

Kirman, A. P. 1992. "Whom or What Does the Representative Individual Represent?" *Journal of Economic Perspectives* 6, no. 2: 117–36.

Koppl, R. 2006. "Austrian Economics at the Cutting Edge." *Review of Austrian Economics* 19, no. 4: 231–41.

———. 2018. *Expert Failure.* Cambridge: Cambridge University Press.

Koppl, R., A. Devereaux, S. Valverde, R. Solé, S. Kauffman, and J. Herriot. 2021. "Explaining Technology." Working paper.

Koppl, R., S. Kauffman, T. Felin, and G. Longo. 2015. "Economics for a Creative World." *Journal of Institutional Economics* 11, no. 1: 1–31.

Kramer, G. H. 1967. "An Impossibility Result Concerning the Theory of Decision-Making." Cowles Foundation Discussion Papers 218. Cowles Foundation for Research in Economics, Yale University.

Lee, J., D. G. Bachrach, and K. Lewis. 2014. "Social Network Ties, Transactive Memory, and Performance in Groups." *Organization Science* 25, no. 3: 951–67.

Levy, D. M., and S. J. Peart. 2004. "Analytical Egalitarianism, Anecdotal Evidence and Information Aggregation via Proverbial Wisdom." *Journal of Economic Methodology* 11, no. 4: 411–35.

Lewis, A. A. 1985. "On Effectively Computable Realizations of Choice Functions." *Mathematical Social Sciences* 10, no. 1: 43–80.

———. 1992. "On Turing Degrees of Walrasian Models and a General Impossibility Result in the Theory of Decision-Making." *Mathematical Social Sciences* 24, no. 2–3: 141–71.

Lewis, P., and R. E. Wagner. 2017. "New Austrian Macro Theory: A Call for Inquiry." *Review of Austrian Economics* 30, no. 1: 1–18.

Long, N. E. 1958. "The Local Community as an Ecology of Games." *American Journal of Sociology* 64, no. 3: 251–61.

Lotka, A. J. 1925. *Elements of Physical Biology.* Baltimore: Williams and Wilkins.

Lubell, M. 2013. "Governing Institutional Complexity: The Ecology of Games Framework." *Policy Studies Journal* 41, no. 3: 537–59.

Mantel, R. R. 1974. "On the Characterization of Aggregate Excess Demand." *Journal of Economic Theory* 7, no. 3: 348–53.

Martin, N. P., and V. H. Storr. 2008. "On Perverse Emergent Orders." *Studies in Emergent Order* 1, no. 1: 73–91.

Mas-Colell, A., M. D. Whinston, and J. R. Green. 1995. *Microeconomic Theory*, Vol. 1. New York: Oxford University Press.

Mataric, M. J. 1992. "Minimizing Complexity in Controlling a Mobile Robot Population." In *Proceedings 1992 IEEE International Conference on Robotics and Automation*, 830–31. IEEE Computer Society.

McGinnis, M. D. 2011. "Networks of Adjacent Action Situations in Polycentric Governance: McGinnis: Adjacent Action Situations." *Policy Studies Journal* 39, no. 1: 51–78.

Ostrom, E. 1990. *Governing the Commons: The Evolution of Institutions for Collective Action.* Cambridge: Cambridge University Press.

———. 2010. "Beyond Markets and States: Polycentric Governance of Complex Economic Systems." *American Economic Review* 100, no. 3: 641–72.

Ostrom, V. 2006. "Citizen-Sovereigns: The Source of Contestability, the Rule of Law, and the Conduct of Public Entrepreneurship." *PS: Political Science & Politics* 39, no. 1: 13–17.

Ostrom, V., C. M. Tiebout, and R. Warren. 1961. "The Organization of Government in Metropolitan Areas: A Theoretical Inquiry." *American Political Science Review* 55, no. 4: 831–42.

Padgett, J. F., P. McMahan, and X. Zhong. 2012. "3. Economic Production as Chemistry II." In *The Emergence of Organizations and Markets*, edited by J. F. Padgett and W. W. Powell, 70–91. Princeton, NJ: Princeton University Press.

Palla, G., I. Derenyi, I. Farkas, and T. Vicsek. 2005. "Uncovering the Overlapping Community Structure of Complex Networks in Nature and Society." *Nature* 435, no. 7043: 814–18.

Pearl, J. 2002. "Reasoning With Cause and Effect." *AI Magazine* 23, no. 1: 95–112.

Peltokorpi, V. 2008. "Transactive Memory Systems." *Review of General Psychology* 12, no. 4: 378–94.

Platkowski, T., and J. Zakrzewski. 2011. "Asymptotically Stable Equilibrium and Limit Cycles in the Rock–Paper–Scissors Game in a Population of Players with Complex Personalities." *Physica A: Statistical Mechanics and Its Applications* 390, no. 23–24: 4219–26.

Popper, Karl. (1953) 2014. *Conjectures and Refutations: The Growth of Scientific Knowledge.* London: Routledge.

Potts, J. 2001. *The New Evolutionary Microeconomics: Complexity, Competence and Adaptive Behaviour.* Cheltenham, UK: Edward Elgar.

Rickles, D. 2009. "Causality in Complex Interventions." *Medicine, Health Care and Philosophy* 12, no. 1: 77–90.

Rosser, J. B. 1999. "On the Complexities of Complex Economic Dynamics." *Journal of Economic Perspectives* 13, no. 4: 169–92.

———. 2006. "Complex Dynamics and Post Keynesian Economics." In *Complexity, Endogenous Money and Macroeconomic Theory*, edited by M. Setterfield, 3552. Cheltenham, UK: Edward Elgar.

———. 2015. "Complexity and Austrian Economics." In *The Oxford Handbook of Austrian Economics*, edited by C. J. Coyne and P. Boettke, 593–611. Oxford: Oxford University Press.

———. 2020. "The Minsky Moment as the Revenge of Entropy." *Macroeconomic Dynamics* 24, no. 1: 7–23.

Schelling, T. C. 1978. *Micromotives and Macrobehavior.* New York: Norton.

Serra-Garcia, M., and U. Gneezy. 2021. "Nonreplicable Publications Are Cited More Than Replicable Ones." *Science Advances* 7, no. 21, eabd1705.

Sethi, S. P., and G. L. Thompson. 2000. *Optimal Control Theory: Applications to Management Science and Economics.* New York, NY: Springer Nature.

Sheldon, E. B., and R. Parke. 1975. "Social Indicators: Social Science Researchers are Developing Concepts and Measures of Changes in Society." *Science* 188, no. 4189: 693–99.

Simon, H. A. 1952. "On the Application of Servomechanism Theory in the Study of Production Control." *Econometrica* 20, no. 2: 247.

———. 1996. *The Sciences of the Artificial.* Cambridge, MA: MIT Press.

Smets, F., and R. Wouters. 2003. "An Estimated Dynamic Stochastic General Equilibrium Model of the Euro Area." *Journal of the European Economic Association* 1, no. 5: 1123–75.

———. 2007. "Shocks and Frictions in US Business Cycles: A Bayesian DSGE Approach." *American Economic Review* 97, no. 3: 586–606.

Smith, A. (1759) 2010. *The Theory of Moral Sentiments.* London: Penguin.

Smith, V. L. 2003. "Constructivist and Ecological Rationality in Economics." *American Economic Review* 93, no. 3: 465–508.

Solla Price, D de. 1978. "Cumulative Advantage Urn Games Explained: A Reply to Kantor." *American Society for Information Science* 29, no. 4: 204.

Sonnenschein, H. 1973. "Do Walras' Identity and Continuity Characterize the Class of Community Excess Demand Functions?" *Journal of Economic Theory* 6, no. 4: 345–54.

Steindl, A., G. Feichtinger, R. F. Hartl, and G. Sorger. 1986. "On the Optimality of Cyclical Employment Policies: A Numerical Investigation." *Journal of Economic Dynamics and Control* 10, no. 4: 457–66.

Stiglitz, J. E. 2002. "Information and the Change in the Paradigm in Economics." *American Economic Review* 92, no. 3: 460–501.

Tedeschi, G., A. Mazloumian, M. Gallegati, and D. Helbing. 2012. "Bankruptcy Cascades in Interbank Markets." *PLoS ONE* 7, no. 12: e52749.

Tesfatsion, L. 2002. "Agent-Based Computational Economics: Growing Economies from the Bottom Up." *Artificial Life* 8, no. 1: 55–82.

———. 2006. "Agent-Based Computational Economics: A Constructive Approach to Economic Theory." *Handbook of Computational Economics* 2: 831–80.

———. 2017. "Modeling Economic Systems as Locally-Constructive Sequential Games." *Journal of Economic Methodology* 24, no. 4: 384–409.

Tocqueville, A. (1835) 2003. *Democracy in America: and Two Essays on America*. London: Penguin.

Vaughn, K. I. 1999. "Hayek's Theory of the Market Order as an Instance of the Theory of Complex, Adaptive Systems." *Journal Des Économistes et Des Études Humaines* 9, no. 2–3: 241–56.

Wagner, R. E. 2010. *Mind, Society, and Human Action: Time and Knowledge in a Theory of Social-Economy*. London: Routledge.

———. 2012. "A Macro Economy as an Ecology of Plans." *Journal of Economic Behavior & Organization* 82, no. 2–3: 433–44.

———. 2016. *Politics as a Peculiar Business: Insights from a Theory of Entangled Political Economy*. Cheltenham, UK: Edward Elgar.

———. 2020. *Macroeconomics as Systems Theory: Transcending the Micro-Macro Dichotomy*. Cham, Switzerland: Palgrave-Macmillan.

Wang, M., G. Yu, and D. Yu. 2008. "Measuring the Preferential Attachment Mechanism in Citation Networks." *Physica A: Statistical Mechanics and its Applications* 387, no. 18: 4692–98.

Weaver, W. (1948) 1991. "Science and Complexity." In *Facets of Systems Science*, edited by G. J. Klir, 449–56. Boston: Springer US.

———. 1961. "A Quarter Century in the Natural Sciences." *Public Health Reports (1896–1970)* 76, no. 1: 57–65.

Weisstein, E. W. 2021. "Elementary Cellular Automaton." *MathWorld*. https://mathworld.wolfram.com/ElementaryCellularAutomaton.html.

White, L. H. 2005. "The Federal Reserve System's Influence on Research in Monetary Economics." *Econ Journal Watch* 2, no. 2: 325–55

Wicksell, K. 1918. Ett bidrag till krisernas teori [A contribution to the theory of crises]. *Ekonomisk Tidskrift* no. 20: 66–75.

Wilde, O. 1889. "The Decay of Lying: A Dialogue." *Nineteenth Century and After: A Monthly Review* 25, no. 143: 35–56.

Wolfram, S. 1984. "Cellular Automata as Models of Complexity." *Nature* 311, no. 5985: 419–24.

———. 2002. *A New Kind of Science*. Champaign, IL: Wolfram Media.

Chapter 11

Crypto-macroeconomics

Jason Potts, Chris Berg, and Sinclair Davidson

WHAT IS MACROECONOMICS IN A DIGITAL ECONOMY?

Macroeconomics is the subfield of economics that studies the whole economy. This is usually understood to mean the total economic activity of a nation-state or country, with the specific intent of being able to provide policy-relevant advice in order to guide the economic design, intervention, and operational governance of that economy. Macroeconomics is intended as a practical, useful field of study. Macroeconomic theory is the core of that undertaking, as an applied science that builds models to analytically represent and simulate the behavior of a complex, open dynamical system. This is supported with constructed macroeconomic measures to calibrate models built from macroeconomic theory.

It should also be noted that macroeconomies—that is, the object of study for macroeconomics—are not merely complex systems analogous to the complexity observed in physics and biology, but what Foster (2005) calls 4th-order complex systems, where complexity arises not just from interactions between people but from those interactions being mediated by internal models of the whole system, which itself includes models of agents themselves with models (i.e., recursive interactive knowledge). More difficult still, macroeconomies are not real objects, unlike the elements of microeconomics (people, firms and goods, or markets and prices). A macroeconomy is an emergent phenomenon that is only understood through shared mental constructs. It has an abstract, conceptual identity. Its measures (such as GDP or price levels) are all indices or aggregations. Still, these measures are persistent and meaningful constructions for theory. However, a consequence of this reification is that there are several different coherent frameworks with which to analytically represent and understand a macroeconomy. These are sometimes called different *models* of a macroeconomy, such as when emphasizing empirical testing. Other times they are called different *schools of thought*, such as when emphasizing theoretical assumptions.

The various schools of macroeconomic thought evolved as departures from classical economics. The Keynesian schools, for instance, built models that emphasized the new analytic concept of aggregate demand, and then built micro-foundations under that using information-constrained rational choice models. Heterodox macroeconomics—for example, post-Keynesian, Austrian, and evolutionary—covers a range of models of a macroeconomy as an emergent complex system in which institutions coordinate interactions between agents. Each school of macroeconomic thought makes different assumptions about the constituent elements and structural dynamics of a macroeconomy and seeks to answer somewhat different questions (e.g., in relation to causes of growth or collapse, or how to stabilize volatility in different markets). Each model or school of thought emphasizes different things and therefore has different uses.

The definition of macroeconomics is also closely linked to the nature of modern economies. For the past 400 or so years, these have been synonymous with the Westphalian nation-state, and for the past 200 or so years with growth through industrialization, capital investment, and technological change. An industrial economy in a nation-state has economic activity guided by markets, production and innovation done by industrial firms, and economic and administrative infrastructure supplied by the government. Macroeconomic policy levers are public spending and taxation, control of money and trade, supply of public goods (including law and order), and design of regulation and economic institutions.

With industrial technologies, the main change was the shape of different economic sectors and markets, with the main impact on overall economic productivity and output (i.e., economic growth). A key feature of industrial economic dynamics was that they mostly did not affect economic institutions, and so the fundamental nature of a macroeconomy was not much disrupted even through massive periods of economic growth and transformation (Freeman and Soete 1995; Perez 2002).

But technological change continued, and the latest long wave of technologies associated with digital technologies (computers, internet, etc.) has ushered in not only revolutionary new communications technologies but also transformative institutional technologies such as new digital forms of money, identity, assets, markets, and even organizations. These new digital technologies, including cryptocurrencies, blockchains, artificial intelligence (AI), the metaverse, and so forth, are beginning to disrupt and transform the types of economic coordination that can occur, as well as the scale and speed at which that can happen. As this economic evolution continues to reshape macroeconomies, the question becomes, What sort of macroeconomics is needed to understand these transformations?

What, specifically, is the aggregate effect of these new digital and computational technologies—these *institutional technologies* (Davidson et al. 2018)—on the way a macroeconomy works and the sort of policies that might help control it? Specific macroeconomic questions include the following: How do these new technologies affect how money works? What effect do they have on prices and inflation? How do they affect jobs and employment, and long-run growth? What changes will they have on industrial and market dynamics? What changes will they have on policy levers and instruments? Do macroeconomic models calibrated on an industrial economy also apply to a digital economy?

These questions matter because we are now, in most countries and especially since 2020, in a period of rapid transition from an industrial to a digital economy. One important seeming difference is innovation. For instance, innovation in a digital economy occurs in institutional technologies as well as industrial technologies. This process lowers transaction costs in economic infrastructure, including private-order economic institutions, which in turn facilitates the rise of the commons and other nonhierarchical organizational forms. Data are a more important resource in a digital economy, and more economic activity is devoted to its production and use in innovation. Innovation in a digital economy is more distributed and decentralized, and this structural shift alone has deep and profound macroeconomic consequences. What, then, is a macroeconomy in a digital economy that is in many ways fundamentally instantiated on the (global, borderless) internet rather than in a nation-state? We explore a proposal that there is, currently, an explosion of new types of macroeconomies that approximately correspond to layer 1 (L1) blockchains.

We proceed as follows. In the second section we review Wagnerian macroeconomics, which corresponds to an open-ended evolutionary framework. In the third section we review how crypto and blockchain map onto different types of economic analysis, and in fourth section we argue that institutional cryptoeconomics (e.g., Berg, Davidson, and Potts 2019b) is the meso foundation for a Wagnerian approach to crypto-macroeconomics. In the fifth section we set out four research topics for crypto-macroeconomics: technology, constitutions, money, and policy. The sixth section concludes.

WAGNER ON MACRO

The purpose of this chapter is not only to seek to identify new types of emergent *macroeconomies* (an economic object, as a technological affordance) but also to explore the meaning of *macroeconomics* (a subject domain, a type of science) in a digital economy. Our claim is that a Wagnerian approach to macroeconomics is especially useful to make sense of this. Indeed, several of Richard Wagner's own students, including Abigail Devereaux and James Caton, have already opened this pathway. Let us start with what we mean by "Wagnerian macro."

As a student of James Buchanan, Wagner built his macroeconomics on public finance in the Wicksellian tradition and a hybrid of constitutional economics, public choice theory, Austrian economics, and institutional economics (Wagner 1988; Lewis and Wagner 2017). The Wagnerian macro perspective, best represented in works like "A Macro Economy as an Ecology of Plans" (Wagner 2012), *Macroeconomics as Systems Theory* (Wagner (2020), and "Contrasting Visions for Macroeconomics" (Devereaux and Wagner 2018), is an eclectic hybrid of a number of different but analytically compatible and only partially overlapping frameworks or schools of thought. As indicated, Wagner's approach to macroeconomics has strong classical economics foundations, built on an evolutionary Schumpeterian understanding of dynamics and a Buchanan-type public finance and public choice theory understanding of governance (Runst and Wagner 2011).

The Wagnerian macro theory of coordination is fundamentally Hayekian/ Austrian in its market-process-centered analytic approach. However, it also seeks to integrate Robert Clower and Axel Leijonhufvud (1975) on disequilibrium coordination (also called post-Walrasian macro; Colander 2006) with the dynamic coordination frameworks of George Shackle, Thomas Schelling, and Brian Loasby on expectations and intersubjective knowledge and coordination (also called post-Keynesian macro). A further support pillar of Wagnerian macro is institutional "meso-foundations" in an Elinor Ostrom understanding of private-order governance and Douglass North–type models of institutional evolution. We define meso in the context of micro-meso-macro in the fourth section, but as an analytic category, meso refers to the institutional layer that intermediates between micro (which refers to economic agents) and macro (which refers to interacting populations of meso units). Institutional economics is meso (rules as coordinating structure and populations), and so is innovation or evolutionary economics (rules as processes and adoption-diffusion trajectories).

However, running through the heart of Wagnerian macroeconomics is a braid of complexity economics and evolutionary macroeconomics—of the type advanced by Metcalfe (1998), Potts (2000), Epstein (2006), Dopfer, Foster, and Potts (2004), Foster (2005), Potts and Morrison (2007), Dopfer and Potts (2008), and Koppl et al. (2015), Potts (2019)—that analytically represents an economy as a complex adaptive system that is made of rules, knowledge, institutions, and technology.

This integration of complex systems coordination and evolutionary dynamics powered by entrepreneurship and innovation furnishes a model of the macroeconomy as a complex ecology and an open, evolving historical process. It emphasizes the concept of emergent rationality. It also locates complex emergent systems as analytic units of macroeconomics and thus eschews an approach to microfoundations that reduces analysis to representative agent choice theory (an approach also argued by Alan Kirman [1992]). While dressed in modern analytic and theoretical formulations of agent-based computational modeling, nonlinear dynamics, and complexity science, Wagnerian macro has themes similar to those of classical economics (Smith, Ricardo, Marx, Mill, Menger), seeking to understand the driving forces and institutional ordering of an entire market society.

Wagner has come to call this perspective by a number of names. In some writings he refers to a *systems ecology* or *complex systems* view of macroeconomics, and at other times to a *meso-centered* or *evolutionary* approach to macro (e.g., Wagner 2012; Devereaux and Wagner 2018). In his more recent work, which has been developed by numerous students and colleagues (e.g., Novak 2018), this approach is called *entangled political economy* (Wagner 2016), which is the most manifestly classical description.

CRYPTO IN MODERN ECONOMICS

The central premise of this chapter is that in a digital economy, the relevant macroeconomic unit is not a nation-state but the semi-discrete space created by digital economic infrastructure and its ecosystem(s). While the digital infrastructure on which economically valuable activity is conducted has existed (as the internet) since at least the 1970s, blockchains since Nakamoto (2008) have created a domain with identifiably macroeconomic features, with boundaries determined by technical standardization and network interoperability.

At a technical level, a blockchain is a deterministic distributed *state machine* (Nakamoto 2008) for time-ordered data. A "state" is a bitstring that represents, for example, a fact, a token, a transaction, or a contract (i.e., an economic primitive). A cryptocurrency is a digital money that is recorded and secured by a blockchain. As such, it provides the ability to make many of the base layer components of an economy digital, secure, and decentralized. That property is what makes it such a powerful and valuable technology, and why it is a revolutionary *institutional technology*.

Blockchains are a new technology that enables digital scarcity and is some-times described as the *third generation of the internet* (i.e., web3). This genera-tion brings economic primitives such as money, contracts, property rights, organizations, and so forth natively to the internet to create the "internet of value." (The first generation of the internet was networked communication [e.g., email], and the second generation was networked social [e.g., Facebook].)

Blockchain is also described as a *trustless technology* or as a new *architec-ture of trust* (Werbach 2018; De Filippi, Mannan, and Reijers 2020), or less figuratively as a new technology to automate trust by facilitating peer-to-peer (P2P) interactions to disintermediate many parts of the industrial econ-omy. Automating trust using a new institutional architecture enables eco-nomic agents to economize on trust, which is the source of economic gains. Blockchains lower the specific costs associated with transactions relating to verifying information and networking (Catalini and Gans 2017). This is the argument that cryptocurrencies, for instance, disintermediate banks with P2P transactions, thus substituting one type of economic coordination (central-ized intermediation in transactions) with a different institutional structure (blockchain protocol to facilitate decentralized P2P exchange). The produc-tivity gains and therefore economic value of the new technology accrue to the cost differentials between the two forms of economic organization.

Others describe blockchain as a technology that enables *common knowledge* (Micali 2021) to work at scale. Common knowledge is information that I know that you know and you know that I know, and so we can coordinate on that. A technology that increases the range and scope of common knowledge enables people who might not know or even trust each other to neverthe-less have agreement (and therefore mutual expectations) about common knowledge such as identity, agreements, ownership, promises, and so on. The provision of common knowledge is easy in small-scale societies but is dif-ficult to scale and is normally what governments provide through registries and administration, all of which are the foundations of a modern economy. Blockchain is a much better, faster, cheaper way of providing that base layer administrative and record-keeping infrastructure for an economic and social order. This is why blockchains can be the foundation of a macroeconomy.

Blockchain and cryptocurrencies are a computer science and database tech-nology, as well as an application of advanced mathematics (i.e., cryptography). But they are also an economic technology, making use of game theory and mechanism design, both of which are branches of modern microeconomics. This is called *cryptoeconomics*, and it studies how incentives and competition work in distributed ledger technology systems (Abadi and Brunnermeier

2018; Schilling and Uhlig 2018; Cong, Li and Wang 2020). The use of crypto-economics to design blockchain-based protocols is sometimes called *tokenomics* (Cong, Li, and Wang 2018), because the protocol system usually has native tokens, and the cryptoeconomic design seeks to incorporate incentives into the economic system so that it works without needing to rely on internal or central human control. Thus, microeconomics (especially mechanism design) is used in the design of blockchain protocols.

A further range of applied economics (i.e., microeconomics) of crypto addresses the blockchain use cases as cryptocurrencies (i.e., as private money) and as a new technology of finance, trade, and other industrial dynamics. There is both a monetary economics component to this (e.g., Luther 2015) and an industrial economics component. The monetary component builds from Hayek's theory of private money and extends to analysis of competition between cryptocurrencies and digital versions of government money (e.g., central bank digital currencies [CBDCs]). This line of analysis is usually based in Austrian economics and monetary economics.

The industrial economics research line considers such factors as how block-chain technologies will disrupt existing industrial sectors, how investment will drive productivity change in existing firms, how that disruption will affect job creation and separation, and aggregate effects on trade patterns, price levels, and so on. This is analogous to analysis of the effect of any new technology (computers, AI, etc.) and is in essence applied neoclassical analysis of the effect of a novel technology shock.

Davidson, de Filippi, and Potts (2018) and Berg, Davidson, and Potts (2019a), along with a suite of other work by colleagues at the Blockchain Innovation Hub (e.g., Allen et al. 2019), have introduced the idea of *institutional cryptoeconomics*. This new research program in new institutional economics builds on Coase-Williamson foundations to define blockchain as a disruptive but potentially transformative *institutional technology* that is specifically interesting to economists because of its effect on transaction costs and the cost of trust associated with economic exchange and coordination (Novak, Davidson, and Potts 2018).

An argument that this school of cryptoeconomics makes is that before the arrival of the institutional innovation of blockchain technology, the major economic institutions were classified in terms of markets and hierarchies, with hierarchies further classified into organizations and governments, and with a residual of clubs and commons. But after blockchain, the elemental types of economic organization are markets, firms, governments, clubs, commons, and blockchains. Building on this institutional foundation, a further set of questions then extends through other applied branches of economics, considering the effect of distributed ledger technology on trade, on tax and public finance, and on economic policy (see, e.g., Berg, Davidson, and Potts [2019c], who write about capitalism after Satoshi).

Institutional cryptoeconomics also has foundations in the Alchian-Demsetz approach to property rights (see Demsetz 1967). In Alchian-Demsetz, property rights emerge when they are economically valuable, as compared with the standard legal-centric view of property rights originating owing to government decree. (It is an argument analogous to the Mengerian theory of the origin of money, emerging from trade, rather than the standard neoclassical theory of money originating from government.) The significance of this is that blockchain technology can facilitate the emergence of private-order property rights systems (e.g., with token curated registries, or NFTs) where it is economically worthwhile to do so.

Institutional cryptoeconomics emphasizes the parallel development of base layer economic infrastructure (e.g., money, identity, assets and property registries, contracts and governance, standards, marketplaces) for a global market economy that is emerging from private order (i.e., from the commons) rather than from government action.

So, we have a microeconomic conception of cryptoeconomics—of which a great number of papers have already been written exploring game theory and mechanism design applications, network theory applications, industrial organization applications, and monetary economics applications. And we also have a "meso-economic" conception of cryptoeconomics (institutional cryptoeconomics) that focuses on blockchains as a new coordinating institution that economizes on transaction costs of using both markets and hierarchies. What, then, is crypto-macroeconomics?

THE MESO FOUNDATIONS OF CRYPTO-MACROECONOMICS

The difference between early and modern macroeconomics (e.g., 1930s–1950s macro versus modern graduate school macro) is microfoundations. Old macro models were aggregate models; they had no foundations in choice theory or price theory. Modern macroeconomic models have foundations that are consistent with rational agents making choices guided by price signals. However, we argue that crypto-macroeconomics does not have microfoundations. Instead, it has meso foundations. But the broad heterodox approach to macroeconomics associated with the knowledge-centered, complex systems-based, institutional, and evolutionary approaches discussed earlier (Wagnerian macro) does not actually have microfoundations; rather, it has meso foundations. In turn, as outlined in Dopfer, Foster, and Potts (2004), both micro and macro are explained in terms of meso. We argue that crypto-macroeconomics also has meso foundations, but first let us recap what we mean by the micro-meso-macro framework.

Micro-meso-macro (e.g., Dopfer, Foster, and Potts 2004; Dopfer and Potts 2008) is a generalization and integration of both the *evolutionary economic framework* (e.g., Joseph Schumpeter, Richard Nelson and Sidney Winter, et al.) and the *complexity economics framework* (e.g., Friedrich Hayek, Thomas Schelling, Brian Arthur, et al.), by integrating the historical process aspect of a general theory of economic dynamics with the connections and network aspect of a general theory of economic structure. Meso is the foundational unit of both structure and dynamics. Micro refers to agents that carry knowledge and interact with each other to constitute the meso structure and dynamics. And macro is the emergent consequence of the meso structure and the meso dynamics. An institution, which is a set of rules carried by a population of agents, is a meso unit. But so is a technology, which is knowledge (i.e., a deductive rule) that is carried by a population of agents.

Both technology and institutions are gathered into a single analytic concept called meso. A macroeconomy is in this sense "made of" meso, or rule populations, and it is those rule populations that are constituted by micro carriers (a person or organization carries an idea or rule). An economy is not made of people or organizations per se, but rather is made of knowledge or ideas. In evolutionary and complexity economics, both micro and macro have meso foundations. In other words, we seek to understand economic agents as being made of knowledge, and we also understand a macroeconomy as a complex structure of knowledge and its dynamics.

As theory: an economy is fundamentally/ontologically made of knowledge, of rules, of ideas. Each idea or rule has a population of actualizations. A rule plus population is a *meso unit*. The process by which a meso unit forms is called a *meso trajectory*. These are the basic elements of economic structure and dynamics. An economic agent (micro) is a carrier of an economic rule. This could be a person or a firm. There are many such micro agents. Each micro unit carries many different rules. Thus, a population of rules (a meso unit) is distributed across a population of micro carriers. The process by which each micro agent acquires a new rule is a micro trajectory. A meso trajectory forms as many such micro agents adopt and use a rule. A meso unit (which is an element of a structure) and a meso trajectory (which is a process) are the central analytic concepts in a general framework of open system macroeconomics. The complex structure of a macroeconomy is formed by the connections between meso units. The evolutionary dynamics of a macroeconomy are due to new meso trajectories. Meso is a general analytic concept that integrates both evolutionary theorizing and complexity theorizing about economic structure and change.

By this definition, a blockchain protocol is a meso unit, and the adoption and use of a protocol (e.g., Bitcoin) is a meso trajectory. Each agent that has adopted and uses the protocol is a micro carrier, and the origination, adoption, and retention of a blockchain protocol across a population of micro agents forms a meso trajectory, which begins the process of macro disruption and change. This approach is entirely consistent with a definition of institutional crypto-economics as the analysis of the economic logic of a single meso unit in terms of how costs and benefits shape the differential use and application of the rule. The micro-meso-macro framework then mostly abstracts from the operational level of analysis (i.e., resource scarcity) to focus on the underlying economics of knowledge and rules in terms of a selection environment of *generic complementarity*, or how rules and knowledge fit together into complex systems.

What, then, is crypto-macroeconomics? It is the study of the effect of a new meso unit and meso trajectory (e.g., a new L1 blockchain protocol) on the structure and dynamics of a macroeconomy. Critically, it is the study of this structure and dynamics given a conception of a macroeconomy with meso foundations (i.e., as a complex evolving structure of meso units experiencing ongoing disruption from meso trajectories).

FOUR APPLICATIONS OF CRYPTO-MACROECONOMICS

With this framework and definition of crypto-macroeconomics outlined, we consider four applications of crypto-macroeconomics: (1) general dimensional technologies, (2) constitutional orders in crypto-macroeconomics, (3) monetary crypto-macroeconomics, and (4) economic policy after Satoshi.

General Dimensional Technologies

Crypto-macroeconomics helps us understand and analytically formulate the reason that a digital economy has a different structure and dynamics than an industrial economy. This argument follows from the distinction between general-purpose technologies (GPTs) and what Kurt Dopfer and Jason Potts (see Potts 2021) call general dimensional technologies.

The adoption dynamics of digital technologies is fundamentally different from that of industrial technologies because it is a systems process that requires systems-level coordination. It is therefore useful to distinguish between economic evolution in an industrial economy with GPTs (e.g., steam, steel, electricity, plastics) that evolve as consumers and firms adopt the technology along a Schumpeterian S-shaped adoption-diffusion trajectory, and economic evolution in a digital-platform-based economy with general dimensional technologies. The key distinction is that digital is not just the mechanism of work or computation but also a lingua franca in which anything digital can connect and interact with anything else digital. Digital technologies are in this structural coordination and evolutionary dynamic sense general dimensional (i.e., in their spatial and temporal scale). Digital evolution can therefore occur both faster and at a greater scale than industrial evolutionary technology dynamics, making digital evolution a qualitatively different process of economic transformation.

The basic economic policy problem with GPTs is market failure, from which the innovation policy response is support or subsidy. However, the economic problems arising from general dimensional technologies are due to the interconnectedness and feedback amplification in space and time, which means that economic problems mostly relate to coordination problems and problems associated with platform (i.e., multisided market) economics, especially where parts of the system have zero prices or require cross-subsidies. In general, dimensional technologies, early users, and user communities are critically important to the evolutionary trajectory and often play a significant entrepreneurial, financial, and governance role. A further aspect is that general dimensional technologies have more choice automation built into the technology, such that consumer pathways are shaped by the technology and its network effects (including data and privacy) rather than consumer preferences. Rationality is somewhat more endogenous to the technological system and an emergent outcome of group dynamics. Moreover, general dimensional technologies are "consumed in public" far more than are industrial technologies and so require more social coordination of technological choice.

A further aspect typical of general dimensional digital technologies is that trust works somewhat differently, requiring more ex ante trust in the platform or protocol before use rather than an ex post trust in the good or service that can be redressed through third-party institutions such as government regulation, courts, or media. Digital general dimensional technologies face a higher implicit initial trust hurdle for adoption and therefore need to build upward from that. Observe that this is exactly why consensus protocol security such as Proof of Work is foundational for the success of the Bitcoin blockchain, and why blockchain security is the prime consideration for crypto adoption and is far more salient than other considerations such as ease of use or cost.

The upshot is that general dimensional technologies are not a series of microeconomic goods or markets but are closer to a digital macroeconomy that is threaded by the full range and domain of interconnectedness. Each L1 blockchain protocol is the potential basis of an entire macroeconomy that can be built on it. Each digital macroeconomy, or general dimensional technology, competes with others based not only on operational factors such as speed, cost, security, user simplicity, and so on but also on more general structural properties that we associate with entire economies. One important dimension is the extent and scope for protocol level automation (i.e., by machine substitution especially with respect to smart decision-making and agency). Another concerns the integrated design to facilitate complete information communication and feedback to enable globally coordinated action—for instance, to facilitate circular economy applications or general social welfare insurance that is operated at the level of the protocol.

Many current socioeconomic problems—such as inequality and structural unemployment, populism in politics, ecological stresses and risks of environmental catastrophe, growth of corruption of economic administration and protectionism—are often characterized as emergent consequences of late-stage capitalism. The implication is that better regulation of capitalism will help solve these problems. Yet solutions to these problems might be better advanced by framing them as opportunities for a digital economy to resolve through the smart application of general dimensional technologies.

Constitutional Crypto-macroeconomics

Modern macroeconomics is focused on analysis of aggregate economic production and consumption and largely abstracts from political institutional choice or comparative institutional analysis or constitutional economics, which is to say that macroeconomics is a different field of study from political economy. However, building on the work of Knut Wicksell and Frank Knight, Buchanan and Tullock (1962) and Buchanan (1990) set out a research program of constitutional economics, as a branch of public choice theory, that emphasizes the exchange theory of politics. Rather than seeing economics as the study of voluntary cooperation in society, and politics as the study of coercion and power, in Buchanan's view, both politics and economics are different domains of voluntary exchange between individuals.

The import of this idea for macroeconomics is a focus on rule-based economic policy and central concern with the choice of rules and institutions that govern political decision-making in the economic context (a perspective also argued by Hayek 1960 and Ostrom 1990). Buchanan thought that economists should cease proffering policy advice as if they were employed by a benevolent despot and instead focus on the constitutional rules governing how collective decision-making occurs. Buchanan is critical of an approach to macroeconomic policy making through a lens of maximizing social welfare because of its failure to reflect individual justice and likelihood to produce benefits for dominant majorities and coalitions. (Tyranny of the majority is a central theme in Buchanan and Tullock [1962], and tyranny of the organized minority is the core idea in Olson [1965].) Instead, following Wicksell, Buchanan emphasizes the importance of unanimity in agreement to rules as the only true test of efficiency in political exchange. This idea extends to the notion that the process of reaching supermajority or ideally unanimous agreement will ensure that bargaining to compensate individual losses from new rules is accounted for (an exchange-theory concept that underpins the theory of logrolling and the existence of political parties in public choice theory). The underlying insight on the importance of agreement is also expressed in the theory of fiscal federalism (Tiebout 1956), in which free exit (i.e., voluntary movement between jurisdictions) ensures efficient sorting over different political bundles (i.e., systems of rules plus a fiscal package of taxes and benefits).

This Wicksell-Buchanan-Hayek-Olson-Tiebout theory of the significance of constitutional agreement as a criterion for efficiency in macroeconomic policy finds a clear parallel in the explicit attention to constitutional agreements and conventions in blockchains (see Berg, Davidson, and Potts 2018). Blockchains are a prime instance of a new type of macroeconomic order emerging that clearly illustrates the Wicksellian-Buchanan et al. conjecture about unanimity and consensus in constitutional orders mattering more than social welfare maximizing policy.

Blockchains are constitutional orders that have explicit and publicly transparent rules and systems of governance for changing those rules (core developers and committees, improvement proposals, decentralized autonomous organizations (or DAOs), open forums and communication channels in social media apps, etc.). Blockchains are not just software protocols but also social and political communities that exert governance over the protocol (see pioneering work on this by Miller and Drexler 1988). The specific structure and instantiations of these rules and institutions, and the way they issue from the stakeholder community, are critical for understanding and shaping the overall social benefits that the blockchain, as a macroeconomic order, can bring.

Trent MacDonald (2019) has extended this argument to observe that competition between blockchains is like Tiebout competition, in that free exit ensures voluntary and efficient sorting, and is analogous to the Wicksell-Buchanan unanimity criterion. But MacDonald further notes that because blockchains are digital and exist in cyberspace, but people live in physical space in nation-states, *nonterritorial secession* is now possible; this unbundles economic governance from political governance and raises interesting new possibilities. For instance, blockchains are now able to compete for citizens by offering bundles of economic governance (identity, property rights, and security that are token controlled, for example, by crypto startup Kong, which issues passports for citizenship in Kong Land). As the metaverse continues to develop, there will be basic tension between corporate-controlled versions (e.g., Facebook's Meta) and more decentralized protocol-controlled versions (e.g., Decentraland). A critical difference between these two conceptions is the way in which the rules governing the digital economy are able to be constitutionally reformed by community agreement (commons model), or whether rules and institutions are imposed from above (corporate model) or externally (regulatory model).

In the external regulatory model of blockchain governance, the legislative and institutional rules of a nation-state and its various regulatory agencies are hardcoded into a blockchain. This enables a nation-state to export its institutional infrastructure through blockchain scale and growth, such that blockchain users in another sovereign nation using a blockchain with hardcoded rules from an external nation are in effect being institutionally governed by that foreign nation. This may be particularly salient for digital trade infrastructure.

Monetary Crypto-macroeconomics and Entangled Political Economy

Monetary economics is integral to modern macroeconomics in two ways. The first is the analytic distinction between a real and nominal economy, separated by money, which is variously neutral or nonneutral depending on theoretical assumptions. This broadly differentiates aggregate supply-side approaches (in which money is a neutral veil) from aggregate demand-side approaches that deal with a macroeconomy with money prices. The second is the role of monetary policy, with control over the money supply or interest rates as policy instruments to target aggregate price level and/or nominal aggregate economic activity. Cryptocurrencies and blockchain infrastructure increase the complexity of these analytic formulations by introducing multiplicity and competition into the monetary units in an economy that otherwise tends to have monopoly conditions in the market for money.

Cryptocurrencies fragment and decouple money from the whole economy, enabling particular parts of an economy to have a monetary base and supply of venture finance that is independent of government and central bank policy settings. This weakens the power of monetary policy and introduces an exogenous supply shock of money. Privately supplied money competes with government (fiat) money. As Hayek (1976) pointed out long ago, the denationalization of money is likely to have socially beneficial effects by breaking up a monopoly and disrupting the harm that it brings. As with all competition, the primary beneficiaries are consumers (i.e., citizens), who now have access to and choice among competing technologies for money services. If citizens in a nation-state have an alternative technology for store of value or payments, then it is harder and more costly for the government to debase the money supply for its own benefit (i.e., instead of raising taxes) or to interfere in the price of money for political ends.

New cryptocurrencies can be units of account themselves (i.e., a digital commodity money with its own supply schedule, such as bitcoin). But they can also be synthetic versions of fiat currencies, called stablecoins, which are tokenized versions of government money (e.g., stablecoins such as USDT or USDC). The benefit of stablecoins is that they can work as a global internet money that is decoupled from a national banking system. Central banks can also seek to create CBDCs, which enable citizens to have direct accounts with the central bank, bypassing the commercial or private banking system. From the government's perspective, this enables complete surveillance over all transactions in an economy, which is beneficial from the government's perspective. Among other things, it minimizes opportunities for tax evasion and allows the welfare state to operate through the money system. However, CBDCs impose huge privacy and control costs on citizens, who may therefore prefer choice in money. The interests of citizens and governments diverge with governments benefiting from seeking to maintain monopoly privileges on the issuance and control of money. To achieve this, they will perhaps seek to make cryptocurrencies illegal or heavily licensed.

Blockchains and other tokenized applications have what is often considered their own "monetary policy." A tokenized project can be created with a fixed supply (e.g., 1 billion tokens) and distributed to buyers and stakeholders or can be subject to a minting or burning function that adds or subtracts the number of tokens in existence. Many of the early advocates of blockchain as a monetary phenomenon emphasized the fact that Bitcoin has a minting schedule that fixes the total number of bitcoins at 21 million. Unlike fiat currency, the figure of 21 million is fixed into the code of Bitcoin—it is a hard rule rather than a target—and changing it would require an extremely difficult network-wide change to Bitcoin's consensus protocol.

Subsequent blockchain protocols have varied these parameters (e.g., Dogecoin will mint 5 billion new tokens each year in perpetuity, some proof of stake chains algorithmically vary the minting of new tokens in order to encourage holders to stake their tokens, and so forth). Many applications built on top of blockchains have their own tokens that represent ownership claims over the application or a medium of exchange for the payment of fees. Each of these tokens has its own issuance schedule depending on the cryptoeconomic design of the protocol, from simple fixed supply to extremely complicated (such as the so-called rebasing algorithmic stablecoins like Olympus DAO).

Wagner's entangled political economy is a useful framework to understand the interface between monetary economics and the "monetary policies" of cryptocurrencies. Entangled political economy is a rejection of the false divide between distinct "public" and "private" spheres; rather, political and market forces are systemically intertwined, producing deep complexity. This is highly evident in the crypto macroeconomy. The "moneyness" of cryptocurrencies has been much debated (Ólafsson 2014; Umlauft 2018; Luther 2015; Berg, Davidson, and Potts 2019d). Cryptocurrencies can be variously used as a medium of exchange and unit of account within blockchain ecosystems but are only a store of value under particular definitions of the word "value." These cryptocurrencies increasingly interface with each other—consumers and investors can move between tokens that have different issuance rates without trading between fiat currency or using a centralized cryptocurrency exchange. Fiat currency denominated stablecoins provide an interface between crypto-currency issuance rates and government monetary policies.

Even just over a decade after the invention of Bitcoin, these networks of entangled monetary policies are staggeringly complex and intertwined. Until recently, blockchain networks were relatively siloed as discrete environments that could only be accessed (i.e., funds transferred in and out of them) through an intermediary such as a centralized exchange like Coinbase, FTX, or Binance. Now the cryptoeconomy features networks of bridges between so-called L1 blockchains (such as Bitcoin and Ethereum), which have their own independent consensus mechanisms, and layer 2 (L2) blockchains, which are built on top of L1 chains to provide greater speed and lower transaction costs (such Bitcoin's Lightning Network and the Arbitrum and Immutable X networks being built on Ethereum). These L2 chains typically use the relevant L1 chain's token as the base for their own semi-independent cryptoeconomy.

The macroeconomic complexity thus can involve an application on an L2 blockchain that requires payment for use in a local token with a given issuance rate that settles onto an L1 blockchain with a native token (such as Ethereum's ETH). The supply conditions of the former affect price dynamics and inflation in the derivative economies such as L2 decentralized finance applications. The monetary policies in these derivative economies are to a considerable extent decoupled from monetary conditions and policy in the external macroeconomy, although at the same time they have the ability to move in between fiat currencies in the form of stablecoins.

MACROECONOMIC POLICY AFTER SATOSHI

A digital economy with blockchain-based economic infrastructure will require new macroeconomic policy—not just to regulate the new technology but to unwind the regulations that were necessary to constrain the institutional consequences of industrial technologies, particularly monopolistic hierarchicalization. Institutional cryptoeconomics makes three broad predictions about the structural consequences of widespread blockchain adoption:

- disintermediation in markets,
- dehierarchicalization of organizations, and
- increasing private provision of public economic infrastructure.

Each of these trends in adoption of institutional technologies reverses the effects of industrial technologies, which broadly since the beginning of modern capitalism saw the growth of market intermediation, tendencies for monopolistic growth in industrial corporations, and generalized market failure in local public goods resulting in the need for publicly supplied economic infrastructure, including not just physical infrastructure for trade (e.g., roads, ports) but especially administrative infrastructure (e.g., money, property registries, identity, commercial courts). The first wave of progressive reform in the late 19th and early 20th centuries focused on mitigating these problems. Shareholder protection laws were introduced to protect shareholders from managerial opportunism. Labor laws sought to prevent workers from being exploited by firms. Consumer protection laws sought to protect consumers from corporate opportunism. Prudential laws sought to protect taxpayers from banking crises. And so, capitalism became regulated.

However, as economic policy sought to deal with the negative consequences of intermediation, monopolistic corporate growth, and the public supply of economic infrastructure—that is, policy that was originally formulated to enable capitalism to cope with market power, to control hierarchy, and to furnish public infrastructure for trust—this had increasingly negative consequences on innovation. This then required an additional realm of policy—called innovation policy—to counteract the innovation-chilling consequences of competition policy, social welfare policy, and industrial policy. There are both first-order and second-order effects to consider here in order to understand how new technologies and innovation set up deep structural changes in the economy (first order) that then induce (second order) policy responses.

The following are first-order structural economic effects of an industrial economy:

1. New technologies (industrial machines) cause economic growth.

2. Economic growth fosters economic complexity.

3. This complexity was governed in hierarchically organized firms and governments.

The following are second-order consequences for economic policy:

4. The costs of hierarchy induce demand for policy responses to reduce those costs.

5. Policy responses to hierarchy reduce innovation.

6. Reduced innovation induces demand for innovation policy to compensate.

The upshot (represented in these six effects) is that industrial capitalism is not just a series of regulatory corrections to a free-market economy but a complex skein of policy, many of the top layers dealing with problems and unintended consequences of the bottom layers. The origin of much modern economic policy is an adaptive counterbalancing response to market and organizational externalities of the dynamics of industrial capitalism. Therefore, if the externalities that caused the policy response are removed, then so too is the policy rationale. Because blockchain technology unwinds some of the rationale for the top or bottom layers, it also mitigates the need for the subsequent layers. We can therefore predict the effect of blockchain adoption (as new plat-form infrastructure for trade and other forms of economic cooperation) will reduce overall demand for economic policy.

The long-run historical effect of blockchain technology is to disrupt the economic value of hierarchy. This predicts reduced demand for economic pol-icy to redress the negative consequences of industrial capitalism in the specific context of macroeconomic policy, competition policy, industrial regulation, and industry and innovation policy. Capitalism after Satoshi will be flatter, more distributed, and less regulated.

CONCLUSION

Wagner's scholarship has built an evolutionary and complexity-based analytic framework for macroeconomics. This framework emphasizes the fundamen-tal centrality of information and coordination problems in the context of the growth of knowledge in open systems, as well as the irreducible coevolution (or entanglement) of behavioral, technological, market, institutional, and political rules. Wagner has been critical of aggregate models that utterly fail to recognize the extent of complexity in open economic systems.

Yet we may reasonably ask, What benefits do we obtain from a more com-plex and general analytic framework? Wagner's answer, also given by his stu-dents, is a better understanding and deeper appreciation of macroeconomic structure and dynamics. The answer we have given in this chapter is more specific: it gives us a better insight into the nature of the historical transforma-tion from an industrial to a digital economy and an outline of a framework for macroeconomics for a digital cryptoeconomy—a *crypto-macroeconomics*, as we have called it here. Crypto-macroeconomics is an analytic framework designed to organize a research program around the macroeconomics of a digital economy with blockchain infrastructure. To this we can add analysis of the effects of other digital technologies, such as AI, the metaverse (virtual reality), cloud data, and so on.

The core insight we have emphasized here is that crypto-macroeconomics shifts the definition of a macroeconomy from a nation-state (which is cen-tral in an industrial economy) to something closer to an L1 blockchain and everything that is built upon that, which is analytically defined as a meso unit and meso trajectory. Crypto-macroeconomics, therefore, has meso analytic foundations. A research program for crypto-macroeconomics can then be for-mulated in these terms, examining topics such as long-run growth dynamics, policy proposals and analysis, constitutional governance, and money and inflation, among other domains.

REFERENCES

Abadi, J., and M. Brunnermeier. 2018. "Blockchain economics" available at SSRN: https://papers .ssrn.com/sol3/papers.cfm?abstract_id=3310346.

Allen, D., C. Berg, S. Davidson, and J. Potts. 2021. "Property Rights, Knowledge Commons and Blockchain Governance." In *Governing Markets and Knowledge Commons*, edited by Dekker and Kuchar, 159–75. Cambridge: Cambridge University Press.

Allen, D., C. Berg, M. Novak, B. Markey-Towler, and J. Potts. 2019. "Blockchain and the Evolution of Institutional Technologies: Implications for Innovation Policy." *Research Policy* 49, no. 1: 103865.

Berg, C., S. Davidson, and J. Potts. 2018. "Blockchains as Constitutional Orders." In *James M. Buchanan: A Theorist of Political Economy and Social Philosophy*, edited by R. Wagner, 383–98. New York: Palgrave Macmillan.

———. 2019a. "Blockchain Innovation and Public Policy." *Journal of Entrepreneurship and Public Policy* 9, no. 2: 149–51.

———. 2019b. "Blockchain Technology as Economic Infrastructure: Revisiting the Electronic Markets Hypothesis." *Frontiers in Blockchain* 2, no. 22.

———. 2019c. "Capitalism after Satoshi: Blockchains, Dehierarchicalisation, Innovation Policy, and the Regulatory State." *Journal of Entrepreneurship and Public Policy* 9, no. 2: 152–64.

———. 2019d. *Understanding the Blockchain Economy: An Introduction to Institutional Cryptoeconomics*. Cheltenham, UK: Edward Elgar.

Buchanan, J. M. 1990. "The Domain of Constitution Economics." *Constitutional Political Economy* 1, no. 1: 1–18.

Buchanan, J. M., and G. Tullock. 1962. *The Calculus of Consent*. Ann Arbor: University of Michigan.

Catalini, C., and J. Gans. 2017. "Some Simple Economics of the Blockchain." https://j2-capital.com /wp-content/uploads/2017/11/Some-Simple-Economics-of-the-Blockchain.pdf.

Clower, R., and A. Leijonhufvud. 1975. "The Coordination of Economic Activities: A Keynesian Perspective." *American Economic Review* 65: 182–88.

Colander, D., ed. 2006. *Post-Walrasian Macroeconomics*. Cambridge: Cambridge University Press.

Cong, W., Y. Li, and N. Wang. 2018. "Tokenomics: Dynamic Adoption and Valuation." NBER Working Papers Series. http://www.nber.org/papers/w27222.

Davidson, S., P. de Filippi, and J. Potts. 2018. "Blockchains and the Economic Institutions of Capitalism." *Journal of Institutional Economics* 14, no. 4: 639–58.

De Filippi, P., M. Mannan, and W. Reijers. 2020. "Blockchain as a Confidence Machine: The Problem of Trust & Challenges of Governance." *Technology in Society* 62: 101284.

Demsetz, H. 1967. "Towards a Theory of Property Rights." *American Economic Review* 57, no. 2: 347–59.

Devereaux, A., and R. Wagner. 2018. "Contrasting Visions for Macroeconomics: DSGE and OEE." *American Economist* 65, no. 1. https://journals.sagepub.com/doi/full/10.1177 /0569434518810506.

Dopfer, K., J. Foster, and J. Potts. 2004. "Micro-Meso-Macro." *Journal of Evolutionary Economics* 14: 263–79.

Dopfer, K., and J. Potts. 2008. *The General Theory of Economic Evolution.* London: Routledge.

Epstein, J. 2006. *Generative Social Science.* Princeton, NJ: Princeton University Press.

Foster, J. 2005. "From Simplistic to Complex Systems in Economics." *Cambridge Journal of Economics* 29, no. 6: 873–92.

Freeman, C., and L. Soete. 1995. *Economics of Industrial Innovation.* Cambridge: Cambridge University Press.

Hayek, F. A. 1960. *The Constitution of Liberty.* Chicago: University of Chicago Press.

———. 1976. *The Denationalization of Money.* London: IEA.

Kirman, A. 1992. "Whom or What Does the Representative Agent Represent." *Journal of Economic Perspectives* 6, no. 2: 117–36.

Koppl, R., S. Kauffman, T. Felin, and G. Longo. 2015. "Economics for a Creative World." *Journal of Institutional Economics* 11: 1–31.

Lewis, P., and R. Wagner. 2017. "New Austrian Macro Theory: A Call for Inquiry." *Review of Austrian Economics* 30: 1–18.

Luther, W. 2015. "Cryptocurrencies, Network Effects and Switching Costs." *Contemporary Economic Policy* 34, no. 3: 554–73.

MacDonald, T. 2019. *The Political Economy of Non-Territorial Exit.* Cheltenham, UK: Edward Elgar.

Metcalfe, J. 1998. *Evolutionary Economics and Creative Destruction.* London: Routledge.

Micali, S. 2021. "Cryptocurrency, Blockchain, Algorand, Bitcoin & Ethereum." Podcast with Lex Fridman. https://www.youtube.com/watch?v=zNdhgOk4-fE.

Miller, M., and K. E. Drexler. 1988. "Markets and Computation: Agoric Open Systems." In *The Ecology of Computation,* edited by B. Huberman, 133–76. North-Holland: Elsevier.

Nakamoto, S. 2008. "Bitcoin: A Peer-to-Peer Electronic Cash System." https://bitcoin.org/bitcoin.pdf.

Novak, M. 2018. *Inequality: An Entangled Political Economy Approach.* London: Palgrave.

Novak, M., S. Davidson, and J. Potts. 2018. "The Cost of Trust: A Pilot Study." *Journal of British Blockchain Association* 1, no. 2. https://doi.org/10.31585/jbba-1-2-(5)2018.

Ólafsson, I. A. 2014. "Is Bitcoin Money? An Analysis from the Austrian School of Economic Thought." MS, University of Iceland.

Olson, M. 1965. *The Logic of Collective Action.* Cambridge, MA: Harvard University Press.

Ostrom, E. 1990. *Governing the Commons.* Cambridge: Cambridge University Press.

Perez, C. 2002. *Technological Revolutions and Financial Capital.* Cheltenham, UK: Edward Elgar.

Potts, J. 2019. *Innovation Commons: The Origin of Economic Growth.* Oxford: Oxford University Press.

———. 2000. *The New Evolutionary Microeconomics.* Cheltenham, UK: Edward Elgar.

———. Forthcoming. "Evolution of the Digital Economy." In *The Research Agenda for Evolutionary Economics,* edited by K. Dopfer. Cheltenham, UK: Edward Elgar.

Potts, J., and K. Morrison. 2007. "Meso Comes to Markets." *Journal of Economic Behavior and Organization* 63, no. 2: 307–12.

Runst, P., and R. Wagner. 2011. "Choice, Emergence, and Constitutional Process: A Framework for Positive Analysis." *Journal of Institutional Economics* 7, no. 1: 131–45.

Schilling, L., and H. Uhlig. 2018. "Some Simple Bitcoin Economics." Working paper.

Tiebout, C. 1956. "A Pure Theory of Local Expenditures." *Journal of Political Economy* 64: 416–26.

Umlauft, T. S. 2018. "Is Bitcoin Money? An Economic-Historical Analysis of Money, Its Functions and Its Prerequisites." Working paper.

Wagner, R. 1988. "The 'Calculus of Consent': A Wicksellian Retrospective." *Public Choice* 56: 153–66.

———. 2012. "A Macro Economy as an Ecology of Plans." *Journal of Economic Behavior and Organization* 82, no. 2–3: 433–44.

———. 2016. *Politics as a Peculiar Business: Insights from a Theory of Entangled Political Economy.* Cheltenham, UK: Edward Elgar.

———. 2020. *Macroeconomics as Systems Theory: Transcending the Micro-Macro Dichotomy.* Cham, Switzerland: Palgrave-Macmillan.

Werbach, K. 2018. *The Blockchain and the New Architecture of Trust.* Cambridge, MA: MIT Press.

Chapter 12
Finance in a Theory of Money

Cameron Harwick

T he idea that economic fluctuations can be explained mainly by changes in the quantity of money rose to prominence during the inflation of the 1970s, buoyed by the failure of then prominent Keynesian theories, which had themselves displaced less money-centric explanations in the 1930s. The monetarist theory was a great deal simpler than the Keynesian theory it replaced and was able to gain prominence in large part because of new monetary aggregates that had just started to be reliably collected in the previous few decades. It was a mechanical theory with a few simple equations, but, based as they were on rational expectations, they did not rely on *individuals* behaving mechanically, as the Keynesian theory did.

Then, in the 1980s, monetarism lost currency nearly as quickly as it had gained it in the 1970s. The Volcker disinflation was a high-profile win for monetarism against rival theories of inflation, but in the following years, monetary aggregates started to lose power as predictors of aggregate economic activity. In principle, monetarists could chalk this up to changes in velocity—that is, in the demand to hold money—but in practice it was hardly possible to use the money supply as a policy instrument without stable velocity (Friedman and Kuttner 1992). Monetarism, though never dealt a fatal theoretical blow, was rendered at least empirically nonoperational.

The mechanical nature of monetarist theory, like the mechanical nature of Keynesian and Ricardian theory before it, proved to be its undoing. But rather than content ourselves with the postmonetarist discretionary inflation-targeting regime, which despite a strong start in the 1990s has performed rather poorly since 2008, this chapter aims to reforge the conceptual building blocks of monetary theory in an *ecological* mold. As Wagner (2020, 65) argues, "Observed spending is an output of a plan, and changes in patterns of spending reflect changes in the plans of economizing agents. To understand the macro-level properties of an economic system, it is necessary to understand the properties of the ecology of plans out of which economic observations derive." The basic argument of this chapter is that the same is true of the money supply, *especially* in financially developed economies, where the same asset can be demanded for both liquidity and investment purposes. Monetarist theory was not wrong to note the causal importance of monetary aggregates for the plans that constitute aggregate economic activity: even if that causal line was not necessarily explicit in the formal models, monetarists had a story in the back of their minds where money's role in coordinating economic plans was the key mediating link (Friedman [1969] is a canonical parable). Instead, monetarists failed to note that *money itself was also the output of an ecology of plans* and not simply a policy given.

This chapter draws on more recent work in monetary aggregation to explore the relevance of the network structure of economic agents in the construction of monetary aggregates, especially across countries. This approach enables us to disentangle the link between liquidity and investment, *even when the same asset often serves both purposes*. After the conceptual groundwork is laid in the following two sections, we argue that theoretically crucial details about this network structure, oft ignored by monetarists but not by other heterodox perspectives, are captured in a Divisia-type aggregate but not in simple-sum aggregates like M2. While work on Divisia aggregation has already resolved a number of apparent paradoxes in monetary theory, the final section uses the network structure of the economic agents involved in creating liquidity both within and between countries to resolve the more recent empirical puzzle that domestic inflation seems to depend more on global liquidity than on domestic liquidity.

THE ECONOMIC MEANING OF THE MONEY SUPPLY

Aggregation is not an illegitimate enterprise in economics. But it is crucial to be clear on *what* is being aggregated. In the first place, no meaningful aggregate can be constructed from unlike elements. Two pounds plus five miles is simply two pounds plus five miles. To add together two quantities, they must first have the same units. Theoretical work on index numbers and aggregates must be understood, not as finding a way to add together unlike elements, but as *finding the commonality* in apparently unlike elements such that they can be meaningfully summed.

In the case of monetary theory, to call something "money" is not to make a statement about the good itself, but about the expectations in a community that might lead individuals in it to employ the good at a certain juncture in their plans. To wit, when an individual holds a good not because it provides any direct utility or financial return, but because of a prevailing expectation that the good can be alienated in exchange for a good desired at some point in the future, that good is money. The usefulness of money in this capacity is called liquidity services. A "unit" of money, in its economically meaningful sense, is a value unit of liquidity provision.

This is a circuitous way to express the common claim that "money is a medium of exchange," but it is vital for the question of aggregation that we peel back the "veil" of essentialist language, so to speak. Notice that in defining money we have not started with "what is money?" and built up (i.e., with the money good); rather, we have started with "what is a monetary economy?" (i.e., with the plans and expectations that constitute it) and worked *down* to the question of a "unit" of money. The money supply can never be "atomized"— that is, it cannot be considered as individual units in isolation. To posit one unit of money *presupposes* a quantity of other units sufficient to ensure general acceptability in the population. Singular items cannot be considered to provide liquidity services, as the very definition of liquidity entails a widespread market for a homogeneous good.

A macro aggregate like "the money supply," in order to be economically meaningful, must therefore preserve the meaningfulness of the micro concept of money. Such an aggregate would carry the meaning of "the total nominal value of the liquidity services being provided in an economy." While this value itself may or may not factor directly into the plans of economic agents in a money economy, any failure of the market for liquidity to clear—if quantity supplied exceeds quantity demanded, or vice versa—will impinge on individuals' plans with respect to exchange using money, which is to say, nearly all of their economic plans.

In order to preserve this meaningfulness as we aggregate, several complications immediately arise that will take us beyond the textbook conception of the money supply. In the first place, there are goods that may provide liquidity services *in addition to* a financial return or direct utility. The monetary value of these goods, therefore, will reflect their *joint* services and must be treated as a composite good consisting of (1) direct utility (consumption), (2) the present discounted value of a financial return (investment), and (3) liquidity services.

Imagine, for example, a noninflationary economy with three financial assets: a "pure" money (call it cash), valued entirely for its liquidity services; a "pure" bond, valued entirely for its financial return; and a hybrid asset, one that provides a rate of return but is also valued to some extent for liquidity services. Standard portfolio balance theory dictates that, on the margin, consumers must be indifferent between holding each of the three assets. This being the case, the price of bonds will be bid to the level at which their rate of return is equal to the implicit liquidity return of cash (Gurley and Shaw 1960), hence the familiar short-run interest rate effects of monetary policy: a scarcity of liquidity services raises their value on the margin, therefore also raising the rate of return on bonds. But provided that the quantity of cash demanded equals the quantity supplied (that is to say, once prices of goods have adjusted to a level consistent with long-run spending plans), the rate of return on bonds—and the implicit value of liquidity services on the margin—will tend to be determined in the usual Fisherian way as the relative valuation of present and future consumption.

But what of our hybrid asset? Clearly it too must be bid to a price where consumers are indifferent between it and the other two assets. Its explicit return, however, will be lower than that of the bond, as its liquidity services induce consumers to bid its price beyond that of the bond. This difference, the explicit return given up on an asset as a compensating differential for its liquidity services, is its *user cost* (Barnett 1978).

Such hybrid assets make up a not inconsiderable fraction of a modern financialized economy's liquidity services. Money market mutual funds, for example, are one such semiliquid asset. Consider now the aggregation problem. An aggregate that takes the money supply as simply the quantity of cash in the economy will understate the liquidity services being provided. A broader aggregate that simply adds together the quantity of cash with the total value of our hybrid asset, on the other hand, will overstate the liquidity services. A simple-sum aggregate like M2, therefore, will both overstate the liquidity contribution of a number of its component assets *and* miss entirely the contribution of a variety of less liquid assets—for example, the use of Treasury bonds as collateral. This problem becomes more severe (1) the wider the variety of such hybrid assets and (2) the more complex an asset-liability structure they form, meaning that the reaction of the *actual economic total* of liquidity services to a change in the quantity of cash may be quite different from the reaction of a simple sum aggregate, *especially if the liquidity services being provided by some of these assets vary over time.*

Correcting these problems is the purpose of a Divisia index of monetary services (Barnett 1980). Essentially, a Divisia index[1] identifies a risk-free "benchmark asset" like the pure bond[2] and estimates the liquidity services of other assets by their user cost in relation to the benchmark (see Barnett et al. 2012 for details). This can then be used to construct an index of monetary services that reflects the *actual meaning* that money has in economic agents' plans, rather than simply summing up the value of a variety of incommensurable assets.

Using a Divisia index in place of the standard simple-sum aggregates resolves a number of apparent paradoxes where experience seemed to

Figure 12.1. Divisia M4+ compared to the monetary base and simple sum M2

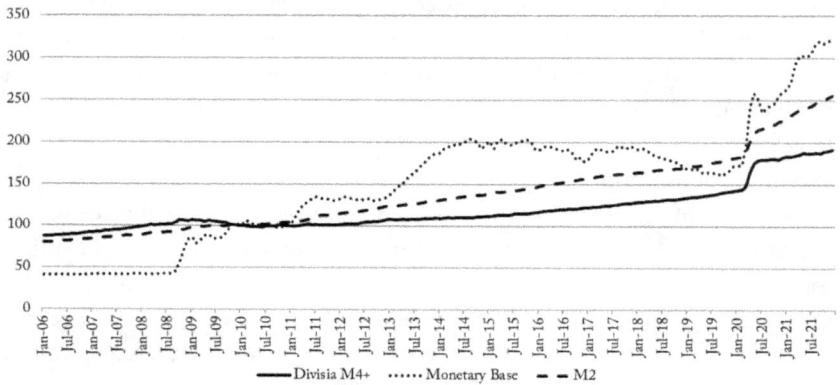

Note: From Jan 2006– Dec 2021, normalized to January 2010 = 100

Source: Monetary base and M2 data from FRED; Divisia M4+ from the Center for Financial Stability.

contradict theory, most importantly, the connection between monetary aggregates and economic activity (Barnett 2016; Belongia and Ireland 2019; Harwick 2019), which had seemed to falter after the financial deregulation of the 1980s.

Correlating figure 12.1 to the events of the past 15 years in the United States makes it clear how much more closely a Divisia index accounts for the place of money in people's economic plans than does the monetary base or M2. In the first place, the quintupling of the monetary base following several rounds of quantitative easing, even the relatively steady increase of M2 throughout the 2008 financial crisis, masked a contraction in broader monies, a liquidity crunch, and therefore a classic spending crash (Beckworth and Hendrickson 2012).

Second, the 2017–2019 economic boom was occurring at the same time that the monetary base was *declining*. Nevertheless, private suppliers of liquidity were expanding more than enough to compensate. And finally, the more recent inflation of 2021–2022 is no surprise in light of the fact that the dramatic expansion of the monetary base in 2020 *did* have a material effect on the Divisia aggregate, unlike in 2008. As the growth rate did not rise, however (5.08 percent in 2021 vs. 6.67 percent in 2019), we can expect a one time jump in the price level rather than permanently higher inflation—though perhaps one that takes time to work its way through the economy as the demand for money returns to normal, pre-pandemic levels.

A COORDINATIONIST PERSPECTIVE ON LIQUIDITY

The individual perspective on liquidity does not, of course, exhaust its economic meaning: while our explanations must be *reducible* to individual plans, all the real interest in economics is in discerning patterns that arise out of these which *no one* intended (Wagner 2010, ch. 3). This dualism between individual and overall perspectives has been a recurring feature of monetary theory since its inception (Yeager 1997). It will be worth briefly considering what our individual perspective on liquidity entails about the role of *aggregate* liquidity in the pattern and coordination of resource use in an economy from a bird's-eye view.

The availability of liquidity services in an economy—that is, of money—is, functionally, a way for money holders to coordinate their use of resources (Horwitz 2008; Harwick 2018b). This is not to say that money is, as the classical economists put it, a "veil" over some more fundamental relationships that might be understood as isomorphic to a barter economy. Rather, money *constitutively coordinates* resource use in a way that would not be possible under alternative coordinating mechanisms (and recourse to "frictionless" barter is question-begging with respect to the question of alternative coordinating mechanisms for reasons we will explore later).

Essentially, monetary coordination takes advantage of the law of large numbers to allow individuals to make plans as if production and consumption were separate (I can consume very different things from what I produce, and I can save consumption potential in liquid form for later), even as production and consumption *overall* are mostly synchronous (nothing can be consumed that has not been produced, and in normal circumstances, little time elapses between the production of a resource by someone and its consumption by someone else). Liquidity, in other words, is the creation of *optionality* in consumption through improved coordination.[3]

Consider premonetary economic coordination. When exchange is rigid and mostly stereotyped, it will be necessary to carry large buffer stocks of goods in order to weather potential shocks. In a small economic community, a drought can be fatal without a well-stocked granary. Stocking said granary requires abstinence from consumption in normal times. But in a larger economy, coordinated by monetary exchange, shocks are less likely to affect the entire economic community. A local drought, in this case, induces economic agents to import grain from elsewhere. They may spend down existing balances that have been built up from providing goods or services to others in the past, or they may borrow with a promise to repay by providing goods or services to others in the future. But in either case, they do not have to abstain from the consumption *of grain*. Their ability to provide *other* services in exchange, whether past or future, improves their option set dramatically versus being forced to store up or repay *in grain* (and it is this crucial point that Ricardian wage-fund/corn-economy models elide; see Harwick 2018a).

In this sense, the significance of money's optionality for economic welfare is that the marginal utility of money diminishes much more slowly than the marginal utility of any particular good, simply because money can be used to purchase *any* good (de Jasay 1985, 152). From the perspective of the rest of the economic area, the demand for grain rises, bidding up its price, inducing those in grain-rich areas to restrict their consumption, an imposition voluntarily taken on by those most willing to suffer it rather than being forced on the community beforehand or afterward. Not only do no stocks of grain need to be accumulated before or after, by the affected community or by anyone else, but the drought-stricken community will even consume *fresher* grain than if it had stored up its own grain from previous surplus. In essence, a large market coordinated by monetary exchange improves welfare by *allowing buffer stocks to be reduced*.

Thus far we have been considering liquidity in its orthodox sense, as "money" simpliciter. But now consider how this argument is affected by considering liquidity in all its variety of forms, not only money but also the huge variety of semiliquid assets available in a financially developed economy that a Divisia index takes into account.

Imagine a financial innovation that increases liquidity. To take the most basic example, compared to a world with only cash, the ability of fractional-reserve banks to issue nearly perfectly liquid liabilities on the basis of illiquid and idiosyncratic loans increases both the availability of credit (an asset to the bank, and a liability to the borrower) and the availability of liquidity (a liability to the bank, and an asset to the holder). From the consumer's perspective, both of these increase optionality: when wealth can be more easily converted from one form to another, more exchanges can be made on demand, as opposed to requiring past or future abstinence. From an overall perspective, this increase in the real availability of liquidity represents an intermediary's use of the law of large numbers to squeeze an increase in optionality from the existing plans of economic agents, to coordinate them more effectively, and thus to allow additional buffer stocks to be used for present consumption—a "free lunch" from improved coordination. From the perspective of the consumer-investor, this is a windfall reduction in the price of liquidity in terms of foregone consumption.

Moving further toward the financialized present, and by analogy to the use of fractional-reserve banking to issue circulating liquid liabilities by pooling (largely) business loans, a great deal of financial innovation over the past few decades has consisted in the issue of standardized semiliquid liabilities on the basis of a great variety of risky, illiquid, and otherwise nonstandardized assets. For example, the securitization of risky and idiosyncratic mortgage loans increased their liquidity both by standardizing them and by reducing their overall risk through diversification (Coval, Jurek, and Stafford 2009), allowing both mortgage borrowers and securities holders to maintain a greater degree of optionality in their plans while in fact committing more resources to present use.[4] Fundamentally this is simply a generalization, with the same economic significance, of the same operation that orthodox monetary theory has long appreciated in the concrete form of fractional-reserve banking. Similarly, in terms of concrete reductions in buffer stocks, it is no accident that the use of just-in-time inventory systems, which aim to minimize buffer stocks in the course of production and distribution, rose to prominence around the same time as the explosion in financial innovation from the 1970s to the 1990s.

This perspective allows a straightforward comparison between the process of financial innovation and the process of a spending boom caused by an increase in the nominal money supply, both of which initially increase the real supply of liquidity. In the former case, the real demand for liquidity services rises pari passu with its supply, reflecting the provision of liquidity in different and more desired forms, and allowing buffer stocks to be permanently reduced. Thus financial innovation will not generally be inflationary, provided it does indeed result from a real improvement in coordination. In the latter case, a spending boom has the same initial effects of reducing buffer stocks. The difference is that without real improvements in coordination, economic agents will eventually desire similar buffer stocks of real goods, bidding up their price, driving inflationary pressure and—per orthodox monetary theory—a return to the initial real supply of liquidity services.[5]

The reduction of buffer stocks might be thought of as an economy's "leverage," the analog in terms of real resources to a financial intermediary's balance sheet in monetary terms. As a bank subject to less predictable withdrawals will require a higher reserve ratio, an economy subject to more unpredictable shocks will be able to support a lower real supply of liquidity compared with an otherwise equivalent economy with more predictable shocks. In this sense an overprovision of liquidity (whether from unexpected monetary expansion or from overoptimistic financial innovation) makes the economy less resilient to shocks that might deplete its now-scarcer buffer stocks. The 2008 financial crisis was plausibly the result of this sort of overoptimistic innovation in housing securities, not, apparently—again contrary to some hardline Austrians—the inevitable result of previous monetary expansion. The turn from boom to bust, therefore, must be understood not as illusory (as Friedman [1993] would have it) and not as inevitable and mechanical (as Hayek [1933] would have it), but as stochastic, through increased vulnerability to unpredictable shocks.

The "coordinationist perspective" on macroeconomics that Wagner (1999) called for can, therefore, be reconciled after all to the bulk of orthodox monetary theory, provided that we are sensitive to the role of the variety of concrete liquid and semiliquid assets that facilitate consumers' spending plans. A Divisia index, because it represents the economic meaning of money in terms of money holders' plans and ability to buffer economic shocks, points us to a full view of the ecology of liquid assets in a financially developed economy, and a rather more subtle perspective on monetary shocks and the real-nominal distinction than simple-sum aggregation allows.[6]

NETWORK STRUCTURE AND THE MONEY SUPPLY

So far, we have focused on the aggregation problem from the perspective of consumers' plans to acquire and dispose of liquidity, plans that are constitutive of the assets' liquidity. But the provision of these assets is itself the outcome, not merely of policy choices, but also of an ecology of interlocking plans by providers of financial services.

Liquidity, as we have argued, is an abstract composite good, the demand for which is satisfied by a number of partially substituting assets to varying degrees. The supply of and demand for liquidity is an abstraction, taking into its purview certain similarities that various financial assets have in consumer plans. We must, therefore, carefully distinguish between the supply of and demand for *particular assets* (including cash) and the supply of and demand for *liquidity in general*—a distinction that monetary theory usually neglects in talking about the supply of and demand for *money*. A change in the demand for a particular asset can affect not only the price and quantity of that asset but, depending on the reasons for that change, the liquidity of that asset too, and therefore the *entire supply schedule for liquidity.*

Harwick (2019), following Mehrling (2012) and Hayek (1937), conceptualized the supply side of the market for liquidity as an inverted pyramid, with cash at the base, reflecting the asset-liability structure of financial assets as promises to pay. The pyramid shape indicates leverage ratios, in that bank deposits (for example) may be issued by banks as promises to pay cash, but in quantities exceeding the quantity of cash. Further securities may in addition be pyramided atop bank deposits and upon other securities, in value quantities far exceeding their "backing" under conditions of reasonably predictable flow redemption demand.

The pyramid, however, is a rather blunt metaphor. It collapses a rich and open-ended asset-liability structure into a diagram with only a continuous quantity dimension and a discrete "layer" dimension indicating how many redemptions must be made to return to cash. Complex securities, however, may securitize arbitrary sets of other assets, and—as Harwick (2019) noted—an asset's liquidity does not necessarily bear a simple relation to the layer dimension. We can better capture this richness by replacing the pyramid metaphor with a directed and weighted network, with financial firms as nodes, their liquid liabilities as outbound nodes, and their liquid assets as inbound nodes. A firm with a leverage ratio greater than one, a net liquidity *creator*, will have a total outbound weight greater than its total inbound weight.

In figure 12.2, the Federal Reserve (FR) issues base money, which is held by the government (G), various financial institutions, and the general public (dotted lines). The government issues Treasury bonds as a promise to pay base money. The first three private banks hold a mix of base money and Treasury bonds on the asset side of their balance sheets, and issue deposits to the general public as a promise to pay cash. Some of these assets are held by further financial institutions, such as the fourth (AIG), which in this example securitizes assets (e.g., mortgages) held by the general public and issues its own assets (e.g., mortgage-backed securities), which may be more liquid than the originating assets. These may also be collateralized by assets originating with financial institutions further back in the network, or with Treasury bonds.

Conceptualizing financial markets with this kind of diagram gives us a straightforward way to think about the effects on the money supply—and therefore on economic agents' plans to hold and dispose of liquidity—of various kinds of economic shocks, starting from the most conventional to the least.

1. For starters, take expansionary monetary policy. The central bank purchases a less liquid asset by issuing a more liquid asset, easing the liquidity constraint on financial firms that can then increase their own issues, and so on throughout the network. This is the standard "money multiplier" effect. The ultimate effect on output (in the short run) and prices (in the long run) of a given expansion depends on the *liquidity differential* between cash and the asset purchased by the central bank.

Figure 12.2. A sample network of liquidity services

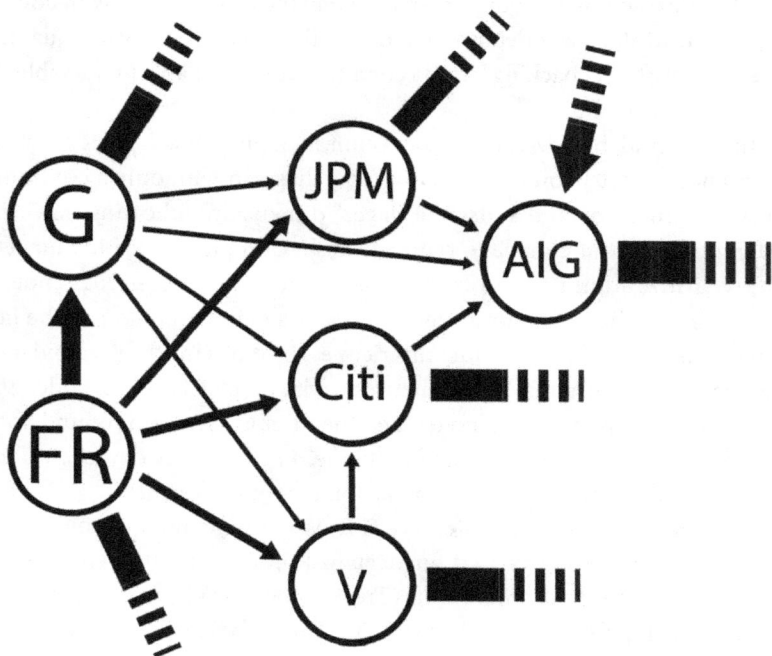

2. But now take the issue of government debt. In a pure monetarist story, debt-financed fiscal policy should have no stimulative effect: if neither money supply nor money demand is changed, any increase in government spending can only displace private investment spending (i.e., Treasury bonds must outbid private investments in risk-adjusted rate-of-return terms). But to the extent that Treasury bonds serve a liquidity role—in particular, to the extent that they are more liquid than the private investments they displace—government bonds *can* increase the supply of liquidity in the economy, though not to the full extent of their value. This is the basic logic of the "safe asset" argument for government debt, at least in countries (particularly the United States) where government debt is indeed regarded as sufficiently safe to serve a liquidity purpose (Caballero, Fahri, and Gourinchas 2017).

   To what extent this increased liquidity indeed improves coordination like financial innovation versus gets washed out in inflation like monetary expansion is a complex question. On the one hand, the fact that the revenue stream behind government bonds is derived from future taxation and/or monetization means that a government's ability to float increased debt should not ordinarily be presumed to improve coordination, and may therefore be inflationary to the extent of that debt's liquidity. On the other hand, *the creation of a market* that would not otherwise exist or would otherwise be illiquid—for example, one for safe assets—may be classed with welfare-enhancing liquidity provision and will therefore *not* be inflationary.[7]

3. As noted in the previous section, financial innovation that increases liquidity through an improvement in coordination allowing buffer stocks of real resources to be reduced will be a windfall in the sense of a "free" increase in optionality from the perspective of any given consumer and will thus not ordinarily be inflationary.

4. A change in consumer-investor demand for the issues of any particular issuer will have different effects depending on how the change figures into consumers' plans with respect to the asset. If consumers become more willing to accept the asset in payment or as collateral for other assets—even holding total demand constant—its liquidity premium will increase, along with its contribution to the money stock for a given value (Beckworth and Hendrickson 2018).

   Imagine what kinds of situations might lead to such a change: not simply an increased willingness to hold the asset (as might result from an increase in its return, all else equal) but an increase in the perceived *marketability* of the asset or its issuing institution, including the availability of productive investment opportunities. This can also be the case during a speculative boom: an increase in the perceived safety of the financial system *as a whole* increases the liquidity of existing assets. Separately, a decline in systemic risk expectations can also lead financial institutions to increase their leverage ratios and thereby increase the quantity of assets. These effects can compound each other and lead to an inflationary boom even in the absence of expansionary monetary policy (Harwick 2019). This boom may then turn to bust if those perceptions turn out to be unwarranted and it becomes necessary to reaccumulate buffer stocks, which will manifest as a scramble for liquidity.

5. The failure of a node can initiate what has been called a "multiple contraction"—that is, a deleveraging from the perspective of the

financial system as a whole. Holders of a failed firm's assets must now hold substitute assets, either assets from other firms redeemable for the same assets as the original or those assets for which it was redeemable. The total quantity, however, will as a rule be lower, at least in the short run. All else equal, this creates an opportunity for competing firms to satisfy the demand by expanding their own issues, and to the extent that the failure is isolated and that other nodes can provide close substitutes, there will typically be no wider ramifications in consumers' liquidity plans. But if the failure is part of a general downturn, if the failure causes investors to update their expectations of the safety of other firms, then the process in (4) can reverse: consumer-investors refuse to accept some assets in exchange or as collateral, their value comes to reflect purely on their return, the liquidity premium falls, and consumers who held these assets for liquidity purposes will need to find other sources, raising the price of liquidity in terms of foregone consumption.

A network perspective may also contextualize the relevance of more exotic theories of financial downturns, such as Bernanke and Gertler's (1995) "credit channel" of monetary policy transmission, and reconcile them to orthodox quantity-theoretic approaches. In the credit channel story, internal and external finance are imperfect substitutes owing to informational imperfections—the same sort of imperfections that financial intermediaries are supposed to smooth over. When a node fails as in (5), its credit relationships cannot be easily taken up by rival firms, thus impairing its ability to satisfy the liquidity demands of its erstwhile customers. That is to say, the coordination managed by one firm cannot necessarily be easily taken over by another, and the aggregate supply of liquidity will be correspondingly lower until a similar level of coordination can be reestablished. It is not that the aggregates are irrelevant (as many advocates of detailed microstructure models might argue), nor is it the case that monetary aggregates are the end of the story (as strict quantity theorists might argue), but rather that the aggregates *emerge from the network microstructure* as an important indicator of individuals' abilities to accomplish their economic plans in a monetary economy.

GLOBAL LIQUIDITY AND LOCAL MONIES

A plan-centric network perspective on liquidity provision and consumption also gives us a useful angle from which to explore the puzzle that, as Ciccarelli and Mojon (2010, 524) observe, "inflations of 22 OECD countries have a common factor that accounts for nearly 70% of their variance [. . . including] fluctuations at business cycle frequencies." This idea was popularized by the president of the European Central Bank in a speech in 2015, noting that "in a globalized world, inflation is becoming less responsive to domestic economic conditions, and is instead increasingly determined by global factors" (Draghi 2015), and a mostly DSGE-inspired cottage literature has sprung up, with output gaps as the mediating variable, to explore implications for monetary policy (Kabukçuoğlu and Martínez-García 2018; Dur and Martínez-García 2020, Martínez-García and Wynne 2021).

The approach taken here suggests that it is not so much that we should replace domestic liquidity with global liquidity in our models, but that the relationship between global liquidity and domestic liquidity is more complicated than existing models have accounted for. In other words, it is not that domestic liquidity fails to predict domestic inflation, but that we have *failed to adequately measure* domestic liquidity (which is operationalized in these papers as simple-sum M2) and that the relatively better predictive power of global liquidity is an artifact of that failure. In any case, we are more interested in a *mechanism* than mere statistical prediction.

Unfortunately, micro data sufficient to construct the necessary Divisia indices in a wide variety of countries are lacking, hence the use of simple-sum M2 for availability reasons. So here I will only suggest a plausible and plan-centric mechanism by which the availability of global liquidity might dominate domestic monetary policy as a predictor of domestic inflation, and leave a more rigorous empirical investigation to future research.

In the first place, we must be clear as to what will be a satisfying explanation, and why foreign expansion under normal circumstances does *not* cause domestic inflation.

1. Under a fixed exchange rate regime where the domestic currency is pegged to a foreign currency, foreign expansion can force domestic expansion: as the foreign currency depreciates, investors will want to exchange it at the fixed rate for new domestic currency, which will expand its issues passively until the arbitrage opportunity is eliminated. Under a gold standard, therefore, it was sensible to talk about global liquidity (i.e., the supply of gold) as a direct determinant of international inflation. There is *no* analogous mechanism today under a regime of floating exchange rates, and so we cannot have recourse to this explanation.

2. Currencies that are *close substitutes* can have pecuniary externalities on one another and diminish each other's value through expansion. In the limit, if consumers make no distinction between two or more currencies, its value is a commons that any issuer will have an incentive to deplete through expansion. Selgin (1988, 42) considers this a reductio ad absurdum that establishes that consumers *must* distinguish between different issuers, even those denominated in the same currency. Or consider the proliferation of "altcoins" in the crypto market in recent years. No doubt some amount of substitutability among coins in the long tail has kept their price down. On the other hand, *lack* of substitutability has staunched any inflationary pressure that this proliferation might have had on the larger players such as Bitcoin or Ethereum.

Such an explanation might be a viable explanation for the global liquidity observation in a regime of floating exchange rates *if* consumers were relatively indifferent to holding domestic versus foreign currency—that is, if domestic and foreign currency provided subjectively identical (or at any rate close) services. Empirically, this is certainly not true of investors, who distinguish between currencies based on risk and rate of return; it is not true of consumers in border towns who may desire to hold both currencies for mostly disjunct sets of transactions but do not regard them as substitutes; and it is certainly not true of ordinary consumers who face prices denominated in one unit of account, and for whom foreign currency has essentially no liquidity value.

Note that both of these explanations involve only a (public or private) liquidity issuer and a representative consumer. If neither of these explanations is adequate to account for the observed relationship between global liquidity and domestic inflation across a variety of countries, a disaggregated network view of liquidity provision might hold promise.

In the first place, the purported failure of domestic liquidity to predict domestic inflation in the United States is remedied when using a Divisia index rather than simple-sum M2 (Hendrickson 2013; Barnett 2016). Financial development, which increases both the variety and the complexity of liquid assets available to consumers, vitiates the usefulness of simple-sum measures of liquidity in any reasonably financialized economy. In the United States in particular, a "decoupling" of M2 from economic aggregates followed the financial deregulation of the 1970s. This decoupling led to a spurious rejection of monetary aggregates from the usual conduct of monetary policy, not because liquidity became a worse predictor of economic activity, but because the orthodox measure of liquidity became less reliable.

In light of the continued adequacy of our more economically meaningful liquidity aggregate, it still remains to explain why global liquidity would predict domestic inflation *better* than a highly imperfect measure of domestic liquidity (but not better than our improved measure of domestic liquidity). This implies that a Divisia index will track global liquidity more closely than M2 does.

A network perspective helps explain why this might be the case. For starters, note that there is no requirement that inbound edges share the same unit of account. That is, a firm's issues may be "backed" by liquid reserves, illiquid loans, or semiliquid assets from other issuers, including issuers in other countries. Indeed, larger financial firms—especially those operating in multiple countries—will find it advantageous to diversify away from exchange rate risk by holding foreign assets. Some of these may be relatively liquid in the sense that they can be reliably used in exchange or as collateral with a subset of other nodes in that country or that deal with nodes in that country. Note that this does not mean that consumers have to deal with foreign currencies, and it does not mean that foreign assets are a *substitute* for domestic assets— certainly not perfect substitutes. Indeed, they may be complements in a well-diversified portfolio.

In short, more abundant global liquidity eases the balance sheet constraints of domestic issuers of liquidity who hold foreign assets. Consider the scenarios from the previous section across international borders:

1. Suppose the European Central Bank engages in expansionary monetary policy. The supply of liquidity increases, European bonds become more liquid, and their rate of return falls. This represents a windfall to holders of European bonds, including American financial firms, which may now—without any expansion on the part of the Federal Reserve—safely expand their own issues for a given level of risk tolerance.

2. An increase in the supply of "safe assets" in Europe through the increase of government debt might have similar effects on the liquidity of American firms holding European bonds, particularly to the extent that the legal definition of "safe asset" for the purposes of financial regulation is standardized internationally, as in the Basel accords.

3. Models of crisis contagion generally focus on currency risk in fixed exchange rate scenarios, when the failure of one fixed exchange rate

raises doubts about the viability of the fixed exchange rate commitment in other countries, as during the Asian financial crisis of the 1990s. But the global financial crisis of 2008 highlights the extent to which even countries with floating exchange rates are linked, not through a base money channel, but through liquidity issuers holding portfolios of international assets. Major shocks in one country can force financial firms in other countries that hold its assets to contract liquidity there too.

4. Exchange rate movements can similarly constitute balance sheet shocks in either direction, inducing expansion or contraction of liquidity quite independently of both domestic monetary policy and the direct effect of a terms-of-trade shock on consumption.

To see why these effects would show up in a Divisia index but *not* in M2, consider the portfolios of the issuers whose assets are included in a Divisia index but not in M2. Issuers of checkable deposits and money market mutual funds included in M2 are commercial banks issuing monies of near-zero risk and near-perfect liquidity. The asset side of their balance sheets, therefore, must be relatively safe and insulated. It is only those less-but-still-partially-liquid assets included in a broader Divisia index but not in M2, particularly where rate of return considerations begin to play a role (though not a dominating role), whose issuers will be more exposed to foreign shocks.

Several implications of this transmission mechanism for both monetary policy and monetary regimes suggest themselves. First, in terms of the Mundell trilemma,[8] if vulnerability to foreign shocks can enter "through the back door" via free capital flow rather than through a fixed exchange rate, one crucial purported advantage of floating exchange rates—namely, insulation from foreign shocks—is muted. This will tip the balance of costs and benefits toward fixed exchange rates on the margin.

Second, the fact that domestic liquidity *providers* satisfy their own liquidity demands with systematically different assets than consumers do can lead the former to propagate shocks that the latter are ill-equipped to accommodate. In other words, the fact that consumer nodes generally connect only to nodes issuing liquidity in their domestic unit of account, while producer nodes are linked transnationally, forces domestic consumers to respond in socially unproductive ways to foreign liquidity shocks. By orthodox optimum currency area logic (Mundell 1961), this linkage through liquidity providers should tip the balance on the margin toward larger rather than smaller currency areas. In addition, while end consumers are likely to continue satisfying their demand for liquidity in a single unit of accounts for reasons of calculative convenience, provided that liquidity providers are allowed to diversify across currency boundaries (and there are good reasons for them to continue being able to), barriers to consumers being able to do the same should be removed.

CONCLUSION

Too often coordinationist-process and mainstream model-test approaches to macroeconomics find themselves at loggerheads: if a model's primitives do not correspond to real causal forces, or if empirical observations do not correspond well to variables of theoretical interest, what Bayesian would be moved by the bulk of empirical literature? But this quite valid concern must be understood as a call for *better* quantification, and theoretically informed aggregation, not as a call for giving up on quantification or aggregation. In particular, we must aggregate with the commonality among the underlying plans firmly in mind.

This chapter has argued that a Divisia index is such a theoretically informed aggregate, on both theoretical and empirical grounds. Unlike the predominant strategy of simply choosing a list of liquid assets and adding up their values, a broad Divisia index is faithful to the *ecological* nature of both the provision of and the demand for liquidity. While this by no means opposes us to the bulk of orthodox monetary theory, firmly anchoring to an ecological perspective provides us with a path through the murky forest of monetary theory, the subtle contours of the border between the "real" and the "nominal" sides of the economy, and where they might interpenetrate each other.

NOTES

With apologies to Gurley and Shaw (1960).

1. A Divisia index can be proved to track a hypothetical Divisia quantity aggregate, without needing to estimate certain parameters necessary to construct an exact quantity aggregate (Barnett 2012, 197). Thus, while the exact nominal value of the liquidity services of the economy is more difficult to estimate, the *rate of growth* can be estimated more easily and summarized as a chained index number.

2. Both simple-sum and Divisia aggregates ignore the possibility of direct utility from holding assets. While this may be an important factor in things like cryptocurrency valuation (Graf 2013) or "meme stocks," which became important during the GameStop incident of 2021, I am not aware of any dollar-denominated assets whose liquidity services would be greatly changed by considering direct utility.

3. This is a similar perspective to Lachmann's (1956, ch. 6) discussion of money's place in a firm's capital structure.

4. As with the *Titanic*, the fact that a portentous misestimation of risk famously put mortgage-backed securities at the center of a salient disaster should not overshadow the fruitfulness of the idea as an innovation.

5. Buffer stocks play a role here that is similar to that of "savings" in the classical Austro-Ricardian parable of inflation-led capital consumption, but it should be noted that the meaning of "savings" in that parable (real resources set aside for future consumption) is exactly what liquidity *obviates*: economic progress consists in the *reduction* of buffer stocks, not in the increase of "savings." If economic agents were perfectly coordinated, there should be no need for "savings" at all in that sense (hence the incoherence of telling a boom-bust story starting from a frictionless equilibrium).

6. In this, we pursue a line of questioning similar to—though perhaps less iconoclastic than—that in Bilo and Wagner (2015).

7. North and Weingast's (1989) argument that the establishment of the Bank of England as a market maker for government debt contributed to England's financial development seems another example of this latter phenomenon.

8. The Mundell trilemma states that an exchange rate regime can achieve at most two of the following: (1) free capital flow, (2) autonomous monetary policy, and (3) a fixed exchange rate. With free capital flow, a fixed exchange rate is conventionally regarded to expose a country to foreign shocks that could be better accommodated with a floating exchange rate.

REFERENCES

Barnett, W. A. 1978. "The User Cost of Money." *Economics Letters* 1: 145–49.

———. 1980. "Economic Monetary Aggregates: An Application of Index Number and Aggregation Theory." *Journal of Econometrics* 14: 11–48.

———. 2012. *Getting It Wrong: How Faulty Monetary Statistics Undermine the Fed, the Financial System, and the Economy.* Cambridge, MA: MIT Press.

———. 2016. "Friedman and Divisia Monetary Measures." In *Milton Friedman: Contributions to Economics and Public Policy*, edited by R. A. Cord and D. Hammond, 265–91. Oxford: Oxford University Press.

Barnett, W. A., J. Liu, R. Marrson, and J. Van Den Noort. 2012. "The New CFS Divisia Monetary Aggregates: Design, Construction, and Data Sources." *Open Economies Review* 24, no. 1: 101–24.

Beckworth, D., and J. R. Hendrickson. 2012. "Great Spending Crashes." *B.E. Journal of Macroeconomics* 12, no. 1: 1–28.

———. 2018. "Transaction Asset Shortages." AIER Sound Money Project Working Paper 2018-08.

Belongia, M. T., and P. N. Ireland. 2019. "The Demand for Divisia Money: Theory and Evidence." *Journal of Macroeconomics* 61: 1–24.

Bernanke, B. S., and M. Gertler. 1995. "Inside the Black Box: The Credit Channel of Monetary Policy Transmission." *Journal of Economic Perspectives* 9, no. 4: 27–48.

Bilo, S. and R. E. Wagner. 2015. "Neutral Money: Historical Fact or Analytical Illusion?" *Review of Austrian Economics* 28: 139–50.

Caballero, R. J., E. Fahri, and P. O. Gourinchas. 2017. "The Safe Assets Shortage Conundrum." *Journal of Economic Perspectives* 31, no. 3: 29–46.

Ciccarelli, M., and B. Mojon. 2010. "Global Inflation." *Review of Economics and Statistics* 92, no. 3: 524–35.

Coval, J., J. Jurek, and E. Stafford. 2009. "The Economics of Structured Finance." *Journal of Economic Perspectives* 23, no. 1: 3–25.

de Jasay, A. 1985. *The State*. Oxford: Basil Blackwell.

Draghi, M. 2015. "Global and Domestic Inflation." Speech by Mario Draghi, President of the ECB, Economic Club of New York, December 4.

Dur, A., and E. Martínez-García. 2020. "Mind the Gap! A Monetarist View of the Open-Economy Phillips Curve." Working paper.

Friedman, M. 1969. "The Optimum Quantity of Money." In *The Optimum Quantity of Money and Other Essays*, ed. M. Friedman, 1–50. London: Macmillan Press.

———. 1993. "The 'Plucking Model' of Business Fluctuations Revisited." *Economic Inquiry* 31: 171–77.

Friedman, B. M., and K. Kuttner. 1992. "Money, Income, Prices, and Interest Rates." *American Economic Review* 82, no. 3: 472–92.

Graf, K. 2013. *On the Origins of Bitcoin*. Nakamoto Institute.

Gurley, J. G., and E. S. Shaw. 1960. *Money in a Theory of Finance*. Washington, DC: Brookings Institution.

Harwick, C. 2018a. "Against Savings: A Suggested Exposition of the Markets for Money and Credit." Working paper.

———. 2018b. "Money and Its Institutional Substitutes: The Role of Exchange Institutions in Human Cooperation." *Journal of Institutional Economics* 14, no. 4: 689–714.

———. 2019. "Bubbles and Broad Monetary Aggregates: Toward a Consensus Approach to Business Cycles." *Eastern Economic Journal* 45, no. 2: 250–68.

Hayek, F. A. 1933. *Monetary Theory and The Trade Cycle*. London: Jonathan Cape.

———. 1937. *Monetary Nationalism and International Stability*. Fairfield, NJ: Kelley.

Hendrickson, J. R. 2013. "Redundancy or Mismeasurement? A Reappraisal of Money." *Macroeconomic Dynamics* 18, no. 7: 1437–65.

Horwitz, S. 2008. "Monetary Calculation and the Extension of Social Cooperation into Anonymity." *Journal of Private Enterprise* 23, no. 2: 81–93.

Kabukçuoğlu, A., and E. Martínez-García. 2018. "Inflation as a Global Phenomenon: Some Implications for Inflation Modeling and Forecasting." *Journal of Economic Dynamics and Control* 87: 46–73.

Lachmann, L. 1956. *Capital and Its Structure*. Kansas City, MO: Sheed Andrews and McMeel.

Martínez-García, E., and M. Wynne. 2021. "Global Slack as a Determinant of U.S. Inflation." Globalization and Monetary Policy Institute Working Paper no. 123.

Mehrling, P. 2012. "The Inherent Hierarchy of Money." In *Social Fairness and Economics: Economic Essays in the Spirit of Duncan Foley*, edited by L. Taylor, A. Rezai, and T. Michl, 394–404. New York: Routledge.

Mundell, R. A. 1961. "A Theory of Optimum Currency Areas." *American Economic Review* 51, no. 4: 657–65.

North, D. C., and B. R. Weingast. 1989. "Constitutions and Commitment: The Evolution of Institutions Governing Public Choice in Seventeenth-Century England." *Journal of Economic History* 49, no. 4: 803–32.

Selgin, G. A. 1988. *The Theory of Free Banking: Money Supply under Competitive Note Issue*. Lanham, MD: Rowman and Littlefield.

Wagner, R. E. 1999. "Austrian Cycle Theory: Saving the Wheat While Discarding the Chaff." *Review of Austrian Economics* 12, no. 1: 65–80.

———. 2010. *Mind, Society, and Human Action: Time and Knowledge in a Theory of Social Economy*. New York: Routledge.

———. 2020. *Macroeconomics as Systems Theory: Transcending the Micro-Macro Dichotomy*. Cham, Switzerland: Palgrave Macmillan.

Yeager, L. B. 1997. "Individual and Overall Viewpoints in Monetary Theory." In *The Fluttering Veil: Essays on Monetary Disequilibrium*, edited by G. Selgin, 137–62. Indianapolis: Liberty Fund.

Chapter 13
Expressive Entrepreneurship

Adam Martin and Vincent Miozzi

E conomics touches on all aspects of human action, including the doing of economics. Human action springs from a "felt uneasiness" (Mises 1949, 14). Richard Wagner often describes the process of writing to his students as "articulating your way through your uneasiness." Scholars write with many overlapping purposes. Some are instrumental, such as trying to get tenure. Others are positional, as when one scholar simply seeks to outpublish a friend or rival (we will not name names). Some seek to satisfy their curiosity or to establish a reputation. In all these cases, the scholar utilizes scarce means for the achievement of some end.

We argue that an important scholarly motivation that is often overlooked is best characterized as *expressive entrepreneurship*. By "entrepreneurship," we mean the attempt to discover new opportunities for and means of persuasion. By "expressive," we invoke the work of Brennan and Lomasky (1993) on expressive preferences. Just as an individual voter is unlikely to change the outcome of a large election, an individual scholar is unlikely to swing the opinion of a scholarly field or of society at large. Most academic papers are read by a scant few people. Nonetheless, we persist. The uneasiness that scholars often feel is alleviated (temporarily) by expressing certain commitments in various forms. We illustrate this theory by examining the scholarly work of James Buchanan and Richard Wagner as expressive entrepreneurs.

This chapter proceeds as follows. The first section develops the theory of expressive entrepreneurship, building on Martin and Thomas's (2013) two-tiered approach to understanding political entrepreneurship. We contrast this view with other economic approaches to scholarship or expertise. The second section examines Buchanan's key analytic and normative commitments. At the risk of going too meta, we rely on Wagner's interpretation of Buchanan's scholarly vision to argue that while individual scholarly works argue for particular conclusions, they also often express a deeper commitment to a particular "window on the world." These sorts of commitments characterize all sorts of scholarship across the natural, social, and humanistic sciences. The third section explores Buchanan's normative commitment to a vision of the good society and the corresponding role of the economist. This form of commitment is often absent in the natural sciences. But in the social and humanistic sciences, these normative commitments drive a great deal of scholarly practice. The fourth and fifth sections explore Wagner's positive and normative commitments. The final section concludes by discussing the tension that scholars of political economy inevitably face between holding both normative and analytic commitments.

ECONOMISTS IN THE MODEL. BUT WHICH MODEL?

Public choice economics aims to put political agents "inside the model" (Levy 2001, 58). Rather than taking public policy as an exogenous imposition on a market system, public choice examines the incentives and rules that give rise to policy. David Levy and Sandra Peart likewise urge economists and other scholars to put themselves inside the model. The ideas and predictions that economists generate are as subject to constellations of social structures and individual characteristics as any other form of human activity. Those interactions between the pursuit of individual purposes and the constraints and opportunities offered by various social settings in turn have a powerful influence on whether scholarship produces useful results.

Levy (2001) posits what can best be thought of as a Stiglerian model of expertise. Like anyone else, the expert is a utility maximizer. It is just as unfounded to assume that scholars are disinterested truth seekers as it is to assume that politicians or bureaucrats disinterestedly seek the public good. In typical Stiglerian fashion, explaining the difference between reliable and unreliable scholarship is largely a function of the constraints that scholars face. *De gustibus non est disputandum*, so to the budget line we must look.

Levy and Peart (2017, ch. 2) expand on this narrow model by adding a Smithian conception of sympathy to the utility function of experts. Experts value approbation and fear disapprobation from their clients, which may include external audiences such as policymakers or scientific peers. They show how such sympathy can lead to biased accounts of social phenomena, perhaps even generating diverging beliefs of different groups, and offer some potential institutional mechanisms to help deal with these biases and make experts more democratically accountable.

In direct contrast with the public choice-inspired view of Levy and Peart is the older view of expertise associated with Keynes (if you thought you were going to get out of this chapter without reading *that* quote, well, you can just skip to the next paragraph):

> At the present moment people are unusually expectant of a more funda-mental diagnosis; more particularly ready to receive it; eager to try it out, if it should be even plausible. But apart from this contemporary mood, the ideas of economists and political philosophers, both when they are right and when they are wrong, are more powerful than is commonly understood. Indeed the world is ruled by little else. Practical men, who believe themselves to be quite exempt from any intellectual influences, are usually the slaves of some defunct economist. Madmen in authority, who hear voices in the air, are distilling their frenzy from some academic scribbler of a few years back. I am sure that the power of vested inter-ests is vastly exaggerated compared with the gradual encroachment of ideas. Not, indeed, immediately, but after a certain interval; for in the field of economic and political philosophy there are not many who are influenced by new theories after they are twenty-five or thirty years of age, so that the ideas which civil servants and politicians and even agita-tors apply to current events are not likely to be the newest. But, soon or late, it is ideas, not vested interests, which are dangerous for good or evil. (Keynes 1936, 383–84)

This quote is well known, in part because it paints a flattering picture of the importance of scholarship. And there can be little doubt that Keynes himself wielded tremendous influence on practical affairs over the course of his life. Buchanan and Wagner (1977), following R. F. Harrod, label this view of the relationship between academic economics and public policy "the presuppositions of Harvey Road." The key precept of this view of economic scholarship is that technical policy proposals can be translated more or less directly into public policy, and thus effect social change for the better. Robert Skidelsky (1995), writing with a far more sympathetic take on Keynes, phrases this view even more starkly: "the economist as savior."

But not every scholar is as influential as Keynes. It is well known that a small percentage of academic work attracts the bulk of attention. Larivière, Gingras, and Archambault (2009) find that, after five years, 30 percent of articles pub-lished in social science journals have no citations at all. Less than 30 percent of articles account for 80 percent of all citations. While the concentration of cita-tions is falling over time, this is due largely to the exponential increase in the number of journals and articles published over the 20th and 21st centuries.

The reality is that the vast majority of academic publications attract the attention of but a scant few readers.

The obvious explanation for these mountains of unread papers is that universities require publications in order to grant tenure. We do not dispute that this motivation looms large. However, these incentives explain only part of the pattern of scholarly output because they leave ambiguous the *content* of scholarship. While it is true that some choose to focus on narrower and more parochial issues, scholars who maintain active publication records often focus on big, important questions, even though they are competing for attention with far more prominent scholars. If their sole goal in selecting topics is to influence policy or effect other sorts of social change, they would do better to focus on issues of local importance. Finally, it beggars belief that scholars as productive as Buchanan and Wagner are writing for strictly instrumental purposes. For purposes of external rewards, the marginal instrumental benefit of an extra publication likely hits zero well before generating 20 volumes of academic scribbling.

One way to explain this behavior is that it is like buying a lottery ticket. All it takes is one landmark paper to massively improve one's career prospects or even to help shape a better world. The probability that any one paper will land big is small, but the payoff is large. Not everyone gets to be Keynes, but maybe I do.

While the self-importance of many academics cannot be doubted, we doubt that the lottery ticket motivation explains the bulk of scholars writing articles that few read on topics that they are deeply passionate about. We propose an alternative explanation, building on the taxonomy of different forms of political entrepreneurship in Martin and Thomas (2013). They distinguish between ordinary political entrepreneurship over policy and various forms of constitutional entrepreneurship over the rules of the political game.

Constitutional entrepreneurship properly conforms to Buchanan's ideas regarding the role of the economist: in a state of relative uncertainty about the future, individuals propose changes in the rules of the political game aimed at securing broad-based agreement based on the belief that they are mutually beneficial. Uncertainty is the key feature that makes such rule changes likely to serve broad-based rather than sectional interests. But while Buchanan's view (articulated in more detail later) is a noble one, it ignores the reality of "post-constitutional rules," such as the congressional committee system. In between constitutional rules and policy lies another layer of rules that govern the day-to-day activity of policy making. So political entrepreneurs have some scope for altering the rules of the game for narrow, instrumental purposes.

Constitutional rules are also not the ultimate, most foundational rules. Every constitutional order is situated in a broader cultural and social context that Martin and Thomas label "pre-constitutional" rules. These rules, including language and social mores, shape how individuals interpret and understand the requirements of formal constitutions. Pre-constitutional entrepreneurship affects policy indirectly by changing what policy outcomes individuals perceive as justified, what they view as within the government's legitimate realm of authority, and what they think government is even capable of. Pre-constitutional entrepreneurs are those who change the pre-constitutional environment within which more formal rules and policies exist.

Since pre-constitutional ideas touch on individuals' core beliefs, Martin and Thomas refer to the motivations for pre-constitutional entrepreneurship as *expressive*, following Brennan and Lomasky (1993). By calling voting "expressive," Brennan and Lomasky distinguish between the motivation to express one's preference for a party or platform and the motivation to actually influence the results of an election. Expressive activities more generally include actions like cheering at sporting events: individuals cheer for their favored team even if they think this has no impact on the outcome. We follow that usage here.

Why entrepreneurship? Levy and Peart treat economists and other experts as estimators of the truth of propositions. This is an apt description of part of what economists do. But economists also propose novel questions, propositions, arguments, theories, and methods. In order to capture this *creative* aspect of scholarly activity, we must add Knightian-Kirznerian uncertainty and discovery to Stiglerian rational ignorance and search. And while scholarship is one important form of pre-constitutional entrepreneurship, not all scholarship is aimed at effecting social change. Consequently, we refer to our theory as *expressive entrepreneurship*. Expressive entrepreneurs change the parameters of a conversation (scholarly or otherwise) but are *motivated* at least in part by expressive rather than instrumental concerns.[1]

Considering two objections to this view of scholarship will help clarify our stance. The first objection is that explaining an action as expressive may denigrate the motives of those engaged in it. Some critics of the expressive theory of voting take umbrage with the idea that voting is like cheering for a sports team, arguing that it may be motivated by a strong sense of civic duty. Framing actions as expressive may also be taken to imply that individuals are acting under the cloud of social desirability bias. They may be saying things that others will find appealing and may even be insincere.

We deny that there is any contradiction between expressive action and sincere commitment to some principle. In fact, one of the prime candidates for expressive behavior is sincerely held commitments. In using the term "commitment," we follow Sen (1977), who characterizes commitment as a form of motivation independent of the individual's welfare. Expressive actions can be either consistent or inconsistent with commitment, just as instrumental actions can. Many voters aim to express sincerely held commitments to moral principles, which *may or may not* include a civic duty to vote. Similarly, many scholars pursue their writing and teaching to express their own commitments.

Commitments to what? Sen's work on commitment typically focuses on moral principles that individuals might endorse over and above their effects on utility or welfare (Sen 2005). Commitments also sometimes refer to various notions of identity, such as membership in particular groups (Sen 1985). Here the close link between expressive action and commitment is clear: allegiance to a group is an iconic object of expressive activity. Group allegiance informs a great deal of scholarship. As Levy and Peart recognize, this can often be a source of bias and error when it takes the form of partisanship or ideological sorting. Commitment can have a dark side. But, we argue, there are forms of commitment that are not only benign but even complementary to fruitful scholarly endeavors.

Even the least dogmatic approaches to scholarship require commitment to some *analytical principles*. "Politics as exchange." "Individuals optimize subject to constraints." "Observations are reflections of plans in progress." Abstract theories not only suggest hypotheses for testing but tell us what would count as an answer to a question and what sort of evidence counts in favor of or against a proposition. The principles that inform these considerations may not be certain, but on some level they function, as Buchanan would say, as "relatively absolute absolutes."

Scholars working in the field of social philosophy or political economy also carry normative commitments. There is legitimate concern that these normative commitments are often the tail that wags the dog of positive analysis. But while it is certainly possible and desirable to engage in dispassionate analysis that puts descriptive reality first, the reality is that even the strictly positive questions we ask are often raised by normative considerations. We want to know how political and social systems work, in part due to basic human curiosity, but also—even if we have no desire to play social engineer or activist—because of their momentous import for human well-being. Work that engages with these questions, whether positive or not, often reflects an expressive commitment to certain normative ideals.

In the next four sections, we explore the commitments to both normative and positive principles that motivate the work of Buchanan and Wagner.

Since they both work more on the theoretical side of political economy, these are the commitments that we find relevant. But it is worth noting that applied work in social science also expresses commitments. There are theories behind what counts as good data and what techniques allow for plausible causal inferences. There are also norms of scientific interaction that aim to generate results that are more plausible. So, while we focus on commitments to more abstract principles, we do not mean to exclude applied social scientists from the realm of expressive entrepreneurship.

The second objection to our view is that scholarship is necessarily instrumental in some sense: it aims to convince. This objection suffers from two main problems. First, it is true that scholarship includes actions that *can* persuade. It is also true that voting involves actions that *can* change the outcome of an election. It does not follow that such possible outcomes rule out expressive motivations providing a partial or even primary explanation for voting or for scholarship. Second, this objection ignores the idea that expressive behavior is often about proving something to oneself rather than to others. In the case of both Buchanan and Wagner, formulating the implications of a particular principle is often a way of articulating away uneasiness. There is some tension between a normative or analytic principle that they are committed to and the dominant way of discussing some issue. This form of alleviating felt uneasiness. is purposive in the broadest sense, but not necessarily instrumental in the way that Brennan and Lomasky use the term.

Despite the overall success of their scholarly careers, even Buchanan and Wagner have produced some scholarly works with very few readers. One might interpret their actions simply as buying raffle tickets for a house on Harvey Road. We think this is a poor explanation of their work habits and scholarly pursuits. Rather, we posit that they have commitments (both shared and unique) to certain analytic and normative principles of political economy. Much of their work can be explained as an expressive attempt to understand, articulate, and defend those principles both to themselves and to others. These principles are tied up not only with their understanding of the world but also with what they see as the essence of their own work. And these expressive acts of scholarship are entrepreneurial, pointing to new ways of framing issues and of understanding the social world around us.

Again, in claiming that expressive commitments help motivate scholarly activity, we are not claiming that they are the sole motivators. Many of our day-to-day actions spring from a complex of different motivations. Any scholar who enjoys teaching or writing is engaged in both consumption and production. While instrumental concerns absolutely play a role in scholarship and other forms of expressive entrepreneurship, it is nonetheless a mistake to ignore these commitments. We hope to illustrate why they are powerful by exploring their role in the work of Buchanan and Wagner.

BUCHANAN'S POSITIVE COMMITMENTS

Buchanan's collected works span more than 20 volumes over six decades of active scholarship. He was beyond prolific. Yet, Wagner (2017) argues, the core vision that would underwrite that was already in place in "The Pure Theory of Government Finance" in 1949. Buchanan (1949) distinguishes between two models of government finance: the "organismic" and the "individualistic." The organismic model sees the state as a single decision maker acting on behalf of society. Fiscal theory is reduced to a maximization problem of social welfare. On the other hand, the individualistic model rejects the maximization approach of fiscal policy, since the state represents only the collective will of a sum of individuals, and not the origin of action in an abstract sense. In the individualistic approach, the fiscal system acts as "one channel through which certain collective desires may be accomplished" (Buchanan 1949, 505). Governments are composed of individuals, and any explanation of fiscal outcomes must be understood as the products of interaction among a set of individuals within a society.

Choices under democratic regimes cannot be explained in the organismic model since there is no single choice made by the regime. The outcomes of the regime are the products of interaction among many agents. Yet, the theory of government finance is often understood in a dictatorial sense—that is, outcomes are the product of a single decision. The individualistic approach is a better method to explain democratic regimes. This argument laid the foundation for Buchanan's entire academic career, with Wagner (2017, 25) referring to it as "the sapling from which grew nearly the entire corpus of his subsequent work, which 64 years later had grown into a mighty oak tree that cast a large shadow over the territory of political economy."

Buchanan's vision stood in stark contrast to the popular approach to political economy of his day. The greatest difference between twentieth-century economists and the eighteenth-century philosophers such as Adam Smith was a methodological one. Smith and the other philosophers emphasized structural and institutional changes rather than the particular policies. Modern economics has split political economy into two parts—politics and economics—and this has created confusion. Nowhere is this confusion more evident, for Buchanan, than in the search for a social welfare function by thinkers such as Paul Samuelson and Kenneth Arrow. They attempted to salvage an organismic understanding of democracy by establishing some canonical method for aggregating individual preferences. Arrow's attempt to find principles of democratic decision-making that could generate group preferences in conformity to standards of rationality and minimal democratic norms—monotonicity, transitivity, Pareto optimality, independence from irrelevant alternatives, and nondictatorial—famously failed, resulting in the "impossibility theorem." Attempts to satisfy all these standards were simply not robust, especially in complex decision environments.

Buchanan, at least at some point, was aware of this fundamental divide between his own views and those of the profession. In his presidential address to the Southern Economic Association, Buchanan borrows Nietzsche's metaphor and encourages economists to "look at the same phenomena through another window" and place exchange rather than choice in the foreground (Buchanan 1964). In fact, Buchanan goes so far as to say that economists should change their vocabulary, emphasizing catallactics or symbiotics. Since Lionel Robbins, the profession has focused on allocation and choice problems. But the term "problem" implies a knowable, correct solution that reduces economics to computational work. Instead, by focusing on exchange, economists can study institutions and how they affect the processes characterized by incessant change.

The centrality of exchange carries over to Buchanan's understanding of politics. Because he could not conceive of government as a singular, coherent entity, Buchanan was driven to adopt a paradigm of "politics as exchange." The alternative to "politics as exchange" is "politics as truth-seeking," the "truth" in this case being what is good for society, or the "will of the people." Buchanan (1954) argues that Arrow's quest was doomed from the start. Without interpersonal comparisons of utility, there was never any reason to suspect that individual preferences could be aggregated into some coherent will of society as a whole. Just as we do not seek coherence when analyzing markets—the market does not "add up" to a set of social preferences but is rather an arena in which individuals pursue their own several ends—it is a mistake to seek coherence when analyzing democracy.

Politics as exchange is implied by Buchanan's individualistic theory of government. Individuals pursue their several purposes in the context of democratic institutions just as they do in the context of market institutions. Because there is no general will of the people to discover, the whole enterprise of politics can be seen only as a complex many-person system of exchanges or contracts. These exchanges may appear undesirable, taking the form of practices like bribery, corruption, or logrolling. But they may also take forms that many find desirable, such as individuals agreeing, in contract-like fashion, to produce public goods or recognize one another's rights (Buchanan 1975). But in both instances, the social scientist should not appeal to what is "good for society" as the explanatory principle by which we understand collective decision-making.

Understanding politics as an exchange process also requires understanding the rules under which political exchanges take place. Buchanan (1990, 1) defines constitutional political economy as a "research program that directs inquiry to the working properties of rules, and institutions within which individuals interact, and the process through which these rules and institutions are chosen or come into being." What distinguishes this program from the conventional economics of the profession is the emphasis of choice among constraints, rather than choice within constraints.

Individuals can benefit tremendously by living within communities. But communities can also inflict great harm. The test for whether communities are beneficial is the same as the test for any other exchange: Does the individual agree to the rules that constitute that community? In order to analyze the value of such rules, Buchanan distinguishes between two separate stages of the political process: the constitutional stage and the post-constitutional stage. The constitutional stage is where the rules of the game are decided, and the post-constitutional stage is where choices are made under the governing rules. The logic of exchange is present at both stages.

This basic stream of thought leads to Buchanan's emphasis on spontaneous order. He contends that "order is defined in the process of its emergence" (Buchanan 1982). That is, the order of the market is defined as the outcome of the process that generates it. The outcome in a market cannot, and does not, exist in the absence of the exchange process that gives rise to it. This further emphasizes Buchanan's call for catallactics over economics.

BUCHANAN'S NORMATIVE COMMITMENTS

Buchanan's normative commitments are closely related to his analytic commitments. As he recognized early on, to have a theory of public finance is to have an implicit or explicit political theory. He preferred that it be made explicit. Any theory of public finance necessarily rests on a political foundation. Thus, when economists speak of the taxing and spending of governments, they are engaging political theory (Wagner 2017). Buchanan's 1949 piece sought to bring those political presuppositions forward.

Buchanan consistently criticized the implicit utilitarianism of mainstream public finance (Buchanan 1959, 1962). According to Buchanan, standard economics has become the study of market failures and analyzing interventions that can fix them. We do things in piecemeal. We look at incremental margins and diagnose market failure or market power, ignoring the underlying structure, constitution, and rules of the game. The program is top-down oriented, and Buchanan argues that we must move beyond it to address the foundational framework within which social cooperation takes place.

Moreover, Arrow's concern that democracy has multiple possible outcomes is a strength according to Buchanan's understanding of politics (Buchanan 1954). In some domains, especially those in which there is widespread disagreement, the possibility of vote cycling is desirable. The fact that coalitions are unstable allows for a form of intertemporal power sharing, preventing an indefinite tyranny of the majority. In the absence of a coherent social welfare function, cycling can be understood as a feature rather than a bug.

The positive understanding of politics as exchange becomes normative when it is married to the idea that exchange is mutually beneficial. Buchanan aims to apply that core belief, shared with most economists, more consistently. Market exchanges only occur if both parties expect to benefit. Moreover, through voluntary exchange, individuals are forced to acknowledge the individual values of others. The difference between political and market exchange is that political exchange is often less than unanimous. Following Knut Wicksell, Buchanan argues that unanimously approved public works are beneficial for the same reason that market exchange is beneficial. While he recognizes that actual unanimity is not on the table in most political situations, it serves as a normative benchmark for evaluating actual political processes. The closer to unanimity we get, the more confident we can be that a political decision is good.

Spinning out the implications of the idea that politics should be understood as exchange, Buchanan (1986, 243) counseled against the tendency of economists to "proffer advice as if they were employed by a benevolent despot" for two reasons. First, the actual political exchange process can produce very different policies, whatever a clever technician might imagine. One example of this concern is Buchanan and Wagner's (1977) worry that Keynesianism in combination with democratic politics would lead to a regime of permanent deficits. Politicians facing reelection have every incentive to boost spending when the economy is sluggish, but little reason to cut spending in good times. Second, the economist is not normatively authorized to simply guess what people would like and make policies based on it. This approach shortcuts the democratic process of garnering consent. Economic theory may be invaluable in trying to discover further gains from political trade, but the test of whether those gains have been discovered is only ever carried out through the democratic process itself. "When politics is wrongly interpreted as being analogous to science, coercion may find moral legitimation for those who claim enlightenment" (Buchanan 1986, 154).

Buchanan's view is not that economics has nothing to offer in making the world a better place, but rather that political economy should address citizens at large rather than focusing on elite policymakers. In other work, Buchanan (1977, 96) also emphasizes that economists have an important role to play in teaching the principles of spontaneous order, referring to it as the "one principle in economics that is worth stressing." This is a clear example of pre-constitutional entrepreneurship: the economist aims to shift the way in which individuals think about social processes generally. The downstream consequences of this might be quite unpredictable.

But while popularizing the intellectual apparatus of spontaneous order is necessary, it is not sufficient. Buchanan (2000) argues that in order to have any positive effect on the world, political economists must revive "the soul of classical liberalism." This soul offers "a vision of what might be" and was approachable, and realistic enough, so as to "offer the animating principle or moving spirit for constructive institutional change" (112–13). According to Buchanan, Adam Smith and his successors created a coherent vision of an extended order of human cooperation that was sufficiently attractive to motivate institutional change. It is with this vision that Buchanan approached—and called for others to approach—scholarship. Rather than speaking in dry terms of "efficiency" and "bundles of goods," the classical liberal economist must operate in a coherent, philosophical fashion by holding true to the soul of classical liberalism.

WAGNER'S POSITIVE COMMITMENTS

While Buchanan's individual arguments were often persuasive to his peers, his analytic vision inspired many fewer scholars. Even a Nobel Prize winner was unable to shift the core analytic commitments of the profession. Wagner is among those who took inspiration from Buchanan's vision rather than just from particular arguments. Like Buchanan, Wagner's work moves beyond particular policies and propositions and is often nested in an overarching analytical research program with normative implications. Wagner's work has attempted to push the public choice tradition in a more radical direction.

As Wagner himself argues about Buchanan, one can find hints of his radical direction from the very beginning of Wagner's corpus. In his first publication, reviewing Mancur Olson's *The Logic of Collective Action*, Wagner argues that Olson's theory of large pressure groups focuses on particular features of large lobbying organizations while neglecting the more general causes underlying them (Wagner 1966). Even when the conditions for the existence of pressure groups are absent, there remain political profit opportunities for large groups to increase their own incomes. Just as the market for corporate control emerges in response to the collective action problem of investors monitoring managers, political entrepreneurs will always remain alert to opportunities to seek special favors from the government. The institutional features of democratic governance create profit opportunities that political entrepreneurs seek to exploit.

Throughout his extremely productive career, Wagner has continually deployed signature Austrian concepts such as entrepreneurship, time, and spontaneous order in public-choice analysis. Wagner makes free use of Buchanan's appropriation of Nietzschean windows. Consider his distinction between the Mengerian and Walrasian windows on society (Wagner 2010, ch. 1). Both windows allow the viewing of the same social phenomena but reveal different things about them. The Walrasian window follows the standard economic end-state, equilibrium framework. It illuminates the time-invariant relationships between economic variables. In contrast, the Mengerian window focuses on causal processes that unfold through time. This window follows the catallactic approach highlighted by Buchanan and the Austrian school and focuses on social life generally as opposed to a narrow look at "the market."

Wagner draws similar distinctions in other work, distinguishing between additive and entangled political economy (Wagner 2016, ch. 2) or between conjunctive and disjunctive approaches to public finance (Wagner 2007, ch. 1). Additive political economy treats politics and economics as two separate spheres. The market equilibrium exists theoretically before and independent of political action, and the policy world acts on the economy. This view operates as if a car is broken down and the mechanic (policy) is called in to fix it. Policy can alter the end state that would otherwise have been reached by a pure market. An entangled political economy treats society as a complex ecology of both public and private enterprises that are thoroughly enmeshed with one another. Similarly, the disjunctive view of public finance treats private goods as provided by markets and public goods as provided by the state, while the reality is that markets and states play a role in the provision of both forms of goods.

In making these distinctions, it is always obvious which approach Wagner finds more fruitful. He has a principled commitment to the analytic principles embodied in the Mengerian, entangled, and conjunctive views of the social process.[2] These distinctions aim to articulate the distinctive contours of an analytic vision that guides theorizing. Wagner expresses his commitment to a particular view of the social world by attempting to make clear what distinguishes that view from more common approaches. He is the model of a scholar who uses one's commitments as fuel for an engine of inquiry, constantly asking readers to consider what questions and answers are prematurely ruled out by the standard approach to public economics.

Wagner (2007) likewise offers criticisms of standard public finance, especially its foundation in welfare economics using the same strand of thought outlined above. He argues that the standard approach presumes a teleological view of how public policy is made. Rather than accepting the state as intervening in a preexisting market order, the dominant strand of thought in the public finance profession, Wagner argues that the state is itself a social space that has its roots deep in human nature. Like the market, the state consists of individual agents who pursue their own ends. Further, the state and the market are interdependent and offer each other complex feedback and exchange networks.

WAGNER'S NORMATIVE COMMITMENTS

Like Buchanan, Wagner focuses his normative attention on the constitutional level. But unlike Buchanan, he does not ground his normative approach in social contract theory. Politics is a "peculiar business" (Wagner 2016). That is, politics does not function the exact way a private-sector company may, but entrepreneurship is still an omnipresent feature. Entrepreneurship is an inherent feature of all human action, and since Wagner—like Buchanan— sees the state as a sum of its individual members, political activity can be, and often is, entrepreneurial. However, what makes politics peculiar is that the profit and loss mechanisms do not operate the same way they do in the market. Most obviously, the controllers of state enterprises are not residual claimants. Market enterprises rely on competitively determined money prices for calculating profitability. This is not so for the state. With at least one foot in the fiscal commons, political enterprises lack a profit and loss test of the enterprise's success. Prices are still present within the sphere of public finance, just not in the way they are in the market. Fiscal decisions have some sort of meaning based on the knowledge of prices. However, in the context of the state and public finance, prices are parasitic. That is, prices reflect both the profit-and-loss accounting of the private sector and any associated fiscal decisions.

Thinking of policy formation as an unfolding, entangled process means that the rules governing that process are likewise in flux (Wagner 2007). Because the state is made up of individuals seeking their own ends, the sphere of public finance is subject to rent-seeking (lobbying for special favors and privileges) and discriminatory policy. The rules governing the entangled process are always subject to change since political entrepreneurs may be incentivized to alter the rules in their favor. Fiscal and policy outcomes emerge from social interaction, "wherein people are continually engaged in activities that are generating the reality they will live with and experience, and with no end in sight for this process" (Wagner 2016, 190).

Wagner alludes to Arthur Lovejoy to offer an illustration of the contrasting views of social theories. Lovejoy (1936, ch. 1) distinguishes between two general visions: other-worldly and this-worldly. The "other-worldly" vision follows the simple scheme of thought that postulates a vision of societal perfection, a north star or maxim to strive for. The "this-worldly" vision accepts the complex, nonequilibrium scheme of thought that postulates a vision of movement, change, and experimentation. Buchanan's vision embraces the other-worldly orientation, which sets forth a path of learning and perfection, with an understanding that society will undoubtedly fall short. Yet, this vision is meant to serve as a guide and inspiration for the preservation of liberty.

Wagner's vision, by contrast, embraces the this-worldly orientation where experimentation and change are in the foreground, and the maxim to strive for is created within—as a result of—this theoretical construct. In this vision, "there is no source for the injection of power into society because power is always resident within society" (Wagner 2016, 190). While Buchanan's vision offers an ideal outside-in view of democratic consensus, Wagner's vision offers an inside-out perspective on human creativity in both its democratic and despotic forms. People are curious and adventurous. They experiment and learn in both competing and cooperating ways. Understanding a constitutional order appropriate to such individuals requires peering through the Mengerian window.

Unlike Buchanan's approach to constitutional political economy, there is no clean picture of a two-stage process in Wagner's thought. There is constant feedback between the levels of rules, policies, and outcomes. The way in which processes unfold will in turn be shaped by more sociological factors, such as individuals' moral imaginations and moral sentiments (Wagner 2016, ch. 8). Indeed, Wagner does contend that entrepreneurs can, through their market activities, create the momentum for societies to move toward new arrangements (Podemska-Mikluch and Wagner, 2012). Moreover, this sort of environment must be fostered and encouraged by the relevant institutions. A normative vision must inquire into both the ability of institutions to promote individual liberty and the ability of moral imagination and fiscal culture to support those institutions.

CONCLUSION: TENSIONS AND TRUTH-SEEKING

Both Buchanan's and Wagner's scholarly output is wildly creative, constantly seeking out and discovering new arguments concerning a wide range of issues in political economy and social philosophy. But this entrepreneurial spirit was motivated by their relatively constant core commitments to a few basic principles. In his positive scholarship, Buchanan's individualist approach casts a shadow over his long career. In his normative scholarship, Buchanan's presumption of liberty and the centrality of exchange underscore his work as an academic and political economist. In his positive scholarship, Wagner's commitment to the entangled nature of social interaction influenced his approach to political and economic analysis. In his normative work, Wagner's commitment to the centrality of entrepreneurship and human creativity led him in a more sociological direction. While they both faced various institutional and instrumental incentives, their expressive commitments had a profound impact on both the volume and substance of their intellectual contributions.

Once the issue of scholars holding both normative and positive commitments is raised, an obvious concern is whether the normative tail is wagging the positive dog. Economists in general have an analytic commitment to a value-free science of economics and a desire to avoid (at least the appearance of) ideology. We only wish to raise two points in response to this concern. First, as Buchanan noted in 1949, normative assumptions are incredibly difficult to avoid in public economics especially. Concepts such as welfare, efficiency, equity, and consent have obvious normative content. But as both Buchanan and Wagner note, there are also implicit normative differences regarding to whom public economic arguments are addressed. Discussions of an "optimal tax rate" can easily veer into what Wagner (2012, ch. 8) calls a "public finance of control," which he distinguishes from his own preferred "constitution of liberty." Better to have such commitments out in the open, where their relationship to positive analysis can be easily scrutinized.

Second, we should be concerned about our normative commitments, however well considered, leading us to put a finger on the scale in formulating and responding to arguments. This is an unavoidable tension of the honest pursuit of scholarship in social science. A central message of Wagner's analytical apparatus is that ignoring such tensions does nothing to eliminate bias in political economy and social philosophy. In order to productively live with that tension, we need commitment not only to ideas but also to principles and practices of sound scholarship.

How can we bolster our commitments to sound scholarship? Together, just as Wagner has taught us. Emphasizing the deeply social nature of human beings is perhaps Wagner's most profound contribution to the public-choice project. Both for better and for worse, we take an interest in one another's affairs. Contestation and cooperation are partly in response to institutionally structured incentives, but they also reside deep within our sentiments and imagination. Scholarship is no less social than politics in this regard. Vigilance against motivated errors requires more than clever design of incentives; it also requires our cultivating a shared moral imagination that asks better of us. Wagner's scholarly legacy will extend beyond his intellectual contributions and to the ethic of an open, spirited, provocative, and sometimes raucous process of shared inquiry that he has helped instill within his students and colleagues.

NOTES

1. Our argument frames Buchanan's *intellectual contributions* as entrepreneurial. This is distinct from but related to his academic entrepreneurship in program building explored by Boettke and Kroencke (2020).

2. At a conference held at the Foundation for Economic Education at which he presented the Mengerian versus Walrasian distinction, one of the participants asked what value the Walrasian approach had, arguing that the Mengerian approach could do everything the Walrasian approach could and more. Wagner responded, "I'm a lover, not a fighter."

REFERENCES

Boettke, P., and J. Kroencke. 2020. "The Real Purpose of the Program: A Case Study in James M. Buchanan's Efforts at Academic Entrepreneurship to 'Save the Books' in Economics." *Public Choice* 183: 227–45.

Brennan, G., and L. Lomaksy. 1993. *Democracy and Decision: The Pure Theory of Electoral Preference*. Cambridge: Cambridge University Press.

Buchanan, J. M. 1949. "The Pure Theory of Government Finance: A Suggested Approach." *Journal of Political Economy* 57: 496–505.

———. 1954. "Individual Choice in Voting and the Market." *Journal of Political Economy* 62: 334.

———. 1959. "Positive Economics, Welfare Economics, and Political Economy." *Journal of Law and Economics* 2: 124–38.

———. 1962. "Politics, Policy, and the Pigouvian Margins." *Economica* 29: 17–28.

———. 1964. "What Should Economists Do?" *Southern Economic Journal* 30: 213–22.

———. 1975. *The Limits of Liberty: Between Anarchy and Leviathan*. Chicago: University of Chicago Press.

———. (1977) 2001. "Law and the Invisible Hand." *The Collected Works of James M. Buchanan*, Vol. 17, Indianapolis: Liberty Fund.

———. 1986. "The Constitution of Economic Policy." Nobel Prize Lecture. Republished in 1987, *American Economic Review* 77: 243–50.

———. 1990. "The Domain of Constitutional Economics." *Constitutional Political Economy* 1: 1–18.

———. 2000. "The Soul of Classical Liberalism." *Independent Review* 5: 111–19.

Buchanan, J. M., and R. Wagner. 1977. *Democracy in Deficit: The Political Legacy of Lord Keynes.* New York: Academic Press.

Keynes, J. M. 1936. *The General Theory of Employment, Interest, and Money.* New York: Harcourt, Brace & Company

———. 1937. "The General Theory of Employment." *Quarterly Journal of Economics* 51: 209–23.

Larivière, V., Y. Gingras, and É. Archambault. 2009. "The Decline in the Concentration of Citations, 1900–2007." *Journal of the American Society for Information Science and Technology* 60: 858–62.

Levy, D. M. 2001. *How the Dismal Science Got Its Name: Classical Economics and the Ur-Text of Racial Politics.* Ann Arbor: University of Michigan Press.

Levy, D. M., and S. J. Peart 2017. *Escape from Democracy: The Role of Experts and the Public in Economic Policy.* Cambridge: Cambridge University Press.

Lovejoy, A. O. 1936. *The Great Chain of Being: A Study of the History of an Idea.* Cambridge, MA: Harvard University Press.

Martin, A., and D. Thomas. 2013. "Two-Tiered Political Entrepreneurship and the Congressional Committee System." *Public Choice* 154: 21–37.

Mises, L. 1949. *Human Action: A Treatise on Economics.* New Haven, CT: Yale University Press.

Podemska-Mikluch, M., and R. E. Wagner. 2010. "Entangled Political Economy and the Two Faces of Entrepreneurship." *Journal of Public Finance and Public Choice* 28, no. 2–3: 99–114.

Sen, A. 1977. "Rational Fools: A Critique of the Behavioral Foundations of Economic Theory." *Philosophy & Public Affairs* 6: 317–44.

———. 1985. "Goals, Commitment, and Identity." *Journal of Law, Economics, and Organization* 1: 341–55.

———. 2005. "Why Exactly Is Commitment Important for Rationality?" *Economics and Philosophy* 21: 5–14.

Skidelsky, R. 1995. *John Maynard Keynes,* Vol. 2, *The Economist as Savior, 1920–1937.* London: Penguin Books.

Wagner, R. 1966. "Pressure Groups and Political Entrepreneurs: A Review Article." *Papers on Non-Market Decision Making* 1: 161–70.

———. 2007. *Fiscal Sociology and the Theory of Public Finance: An Exploratory Essay.* Cheltenham, UK: Edward Elgar.

———. 2010. *Mind, Society, and Human Action: Time and Knowledge in a Theory of Social Economy.* London: Routledge.

———. 2012. *Deficits, Debt, and Democracy: Wrestling with Tragedy on the Fiscal Commons.* Cheltenham, UK: Edward Elgar.

———. 2016. *Politics as a Peculiar Business: Insights from a Theory of Entangled Political Economy.* Cheltenham, UK: Edward Elgar.

———. 2017. *James M. Buchanan and Liberal Political Economy: A rational Reconstruction.* London: Lexington Books.

Richard E. Wagner: Published Works

BOOKS AND MONOGRAPHS

The Fiscal Organization of American Federalism. Chicago: Markham, 1971.

The Public Economy. Chicago: Markham, 1973.

Democracy in Deficit: The Political Legacy of Lord Keynes (with James M. Buchanan). New York: Academic Press, 1977.

Inheritance and the State: Tax Principles for a Free and Prosperous Commonwealth. Washington, DC: American Enterprise Institute, 1977.

Public Finance: Revenues and Expenditures in a Democratic Society. Boston: Little, Brown, 1983.

Smoking and the State: Social Costs, Rent Seeking, and Public Policy (with Robert D. Tollison). Lexington, MA: D.C. Heath, 1988.

To Promote the General Welfare: Market Processes vs. Political Transfers. San Francisco: Pacific Research Institute, 1989.

The Economics of Smoking (with Robert D. Tollison). Boston: Kluwer Nijhoff, 1991.

Trade Protection in the United States (with Charles K. Rowley and Willem Thorbecke). Cheltenham, UK: Edward Elgar, 1995.

Fiscal Sociology and the Theory of Public Finance: An Exploratory Essay. Cheltenham, UK: Edward Elgar, 2007.

Mind, Society, and Human Action: Time and Knowledge in a Theory of Social Economy. London: Routledge, 2010.

Deficits, Debt, and Democracy: Wrestling with Tragedy on the Fiscal Commons. Cheltenham, UK: Edward Elgar, 2012.

Politics as a Peculiar Business: Insights from a Theory of Entangled Political Economy. Cheltenham, UK: Edward Elgar, 2016.

James M. Buchanan and Liberal Political Economy: A Rational Reconstruction. Lanham, MD: Lexington, 2017.

Public Debt: An illusion of Democratic Political Economy (with Giuseppe Eusepi). Cheltenham, UK: Edward Elgar, 2017.

Macroeconomics as Systems Theory: Transcending the Micro-Macro Dichotomy. London: Palgrave Macmillan, 2020.

Rethinking Public Choice. Cheltenham, UK: Edward Elgar, 2022.

Rethinking Economics as Social Theory. Cheltenham, UK: Edward Elgar, forthcoming.

PAMPHLETS AND OTHER OCCASIONAL ITEMS

Public Debt in a Democratic Society (with James M. Buchanan). Washington, DC: American Enterprise Institute, 1967.

Death and Taxes: Some Perspectives on Inheritance, Inequality, and Progressive Taxation. Washington, DC: American Enterprise Institute, 1973.

The Consequences of Mr. Keynes (with James M. Buchanan and John Burton). London: Institute of Economic Affairs, 1978.

The Tax-Expenditure Budget: An Exercise in Fiscal Impressionism. Washington, DC: Tax Foundation, 1979.

Balanced Budgets, Fiscal Responsibility, and the Constitution (with Robert D. Tollison). Washington, DC: Cato Institute, 1980.

The Federal Budget Process: Why It Is Broken and How It Can Be Fixed. Tallahassee, FL: James Madison Institute, 1988.

Federal Transfer Taxation: A Study in Social Cost. Washington, DC: Institute for Research in the Economics of Taxation, 1993.

Who Benefits from WHO? The Decline of the World Health Organization (with Robert D. Tollison). Social Affairs Unit, 1993.

Parchment, Guns, and Constitutional Order. Hants, UK: Edward Elgar, 1993.

Economic Policy in a Liberal Democracy. Hants, UK: Edward Elgar, 1996.

Taxation and the Price of Civilization: An Essay on Federal Tax Reform. Washington, DC: National Legal Center for the Public Interest, 1998.

State Excise Taxation: Horse-and-Buggy Taxes in an Electronic Age. Washington, DC: Tax Foundation, 2005.

American Federalism: How Well Does It Support Liberty? Arlington, VA: Mercatus Center at George Mason University, 2014.

Public Debt and the Corruption of Contract: Excising the Keynesian Cancer. Milan: Bruno Leoni Institute, 2017.

Public Debt as a Form of Public Finance: Overcoming a Category Mistake and Its Vices. Cambridge: Cambridge University Press, 2019.

BOOKS AND MONOGRAPHS EDITED

Perspectives on Tax Reform. New York: Praeger, 1974.

Fiscal Responsibility in Constitutional Democracy (with James M. Buchanan). Leiden: Martinus Nijhoff, 1978.

Policy Analysis and Deductive Reasoning (with Gordon Tullock). Lexington, MA: D.C. Heath, 1978.

Government Aid to Private Schools: Is It a Trojan Horse? Wichita, KS: Center for Independent Education, 1979.

Public Choice and Constitutional Economics (with James D. Gwartney). Greenwich, CT: JAI Press, 1988.

Charging for Government: User Charges and Earmarked Taxes in Principle and Practice. London: Routledge, 1991.

Limiting Leviathan (with Donald P. Racheter). Cheltenham, UK: Edward Elgar, 1999.

Federalist Government in Principle and Practice (with Donald P. Racheter). Norwell, MA: Kluwer Academic Publishers, 2001.

Politics, Taxation, and the Rule of Law (with Donald P. Racheter). Norwell, MA: Kluwer Academic Publishers, 2002.

Handbook of Public Finance (with Jürgen G. Backhaus). Boston: Kluwer Academic Publishers, 2004.

Debt Default and Democracy (with Giuseppe Eusepi). Cheltenham, UK: Edward Elgar, 2018.

James M. Buchanan: A Theorist of Political Economy and Social Philosophy. London: Palgrave Macmillan, 2019.

ARTICLES IN ACADEMIC AND PROFESSIONAL JOURNALS

"Pressure Groups and Entrepreneurs: A Review Article." *Public Choice* 1 (Fall 1966): 161–70.

"Optimality in Local Debt Limitation." *National Tax Journal* 23 (September 1970): 297–305.

"Optimality in Local Debt Limitation: Reply." *National Tax Journal* 24 (March 1971): 109–11.

"Politics, Bureaucracy, and Budgetary Choice: A Review of the Brooking's Budget for 1974." *Journal of Money, Credit, and Banking* 16 (August 1974): 367–83.

"The Antisocial Activities of the Public Sector." *The Banker* 125 (December 1975): 1503–11.

"Competition, Monopoly, and the Organization of Government in Metropolitan Areas" (with Warren E. Weber). *Journal of Law and Economics* 18 (December 1975): 661–84.

"Revenue Structure, Fiscal Illusion, and Budgetary Choice." *Public Choice* 25 (Spring 1976): 45–61.

"Institutional Constraints and Local Community Formation." *American Economic Review*, Proceedings, 66 (May 1976): 110–15.

"Rational Models, Politics, and Policy Analysis" (with Gordon Tullock). *Policy Studies Journal* 4 (Summer 1976): 408–16.

"Wagner's Law, Fiscal Institutions, and the Growth of Government" (with Warren E. Weber). *National Tax Journal* 30 (March 1977): 314–19.

"Tax Policy toward Private Foundations: Confused Principles and Unfortunate Legislation." *Policy Studies Journal* 5 (Spring 1977): 314–19.

"Revenue Structure, Fiscal Illusion, and Budgetary Choice: Reply." *Public Choice* 29 (Spring 1977): 131–32.

"Economic Manipulation for Political Profit: Macroeconomic Consequences and Constitutional Implications." *Kyklos* 30, no. 3 (1977): 395–410.

"Dialogues Concerning Fiscal Religion" (with James M. Buchanan). *Journal of Monetary Economics* 4 (July 1978): 627–36.

"Carl Menger's Contributions to Economics: Introduction." *Atlantic Economic Journal* 6 (September 1978): 1–2.

"Carl Menger's Contribution to Economics: Final Remarks." *Atlantic Economic Journal* 6 (September 1978): 65–69.

"The Institutional Framework for Municipal Incorporation: An Economic Analysis of Local Agency Formation Commissions in California" (with Delores T. Martin). *Journal of Law and Economics* 21 (October 1978): 409–25.

"The Tax Reform Fraud" (with Paul Craig Roberts). *Policy Review* (Summer 1979): 121–39.

"Spending Limitation, the Constitution, and Productivity: A Response to James Tobin." *Journal of Contemporary Studies* 3 (Winter 1980): 59–67.

"Sense versus Sensibility in the Taxation of Personal Wealth." *Canadian Taxation: A Journal of Tax Policy* 2 (Spring 1980): 23–30.

"Boom and Bust: The Political Economy of Economic Disorder." *Journal of Libertarian Studies* 4 (Winter 1980): 1–37.

"Funded Social Security: Collective and Private Options." *Cato Journal* 3 (Fall 1983): 581–602.

"On Economics, Political Science, and Public Policy." *Policy Studies Journal* 12 (December 1983): 251–57.

"A Reconsideration of Some Principles of Tax Reform." *Florida Policy Review* 1 (Spring 1985): 13–18.

"Tax Reform through Constitutional Limitation: A Sympathetic Critique." *Cumberland Law Review* 15, no. 2 (1985): 475–97.

"Normative and Positive Foundations of Tax Reform." *Cato Journal* 5 (Fall 1985): 385–99.

"The Experimental Search for Free Riders: Some Reflections and Observations" (with Thomas S. McCaleb). *Public Choice* 47, no. 3 (1985): 479–90.

"Wealth Transfers in a Rent-Seeking Polity." *Cato Journal* 6 (Spring/Summer 1986): 155–71.

"Rationalization versus Explanation in the Political Economy of Wealth Transfers." *Florida Policy Review* 2 (Summer 1986): 30–37.

"Central Banking and the Fed: A Public Choice Perspective." *Cato Journal* 6 (Fall 1986): 519–38.

"James M. Buchanan: Constitutional Political Economist." *Regulation* 11 (February 1987): 13–17.

"The Cameralists: A Public Choice Perspective" (with Jürgen G. Backhaus). *Public Choice* 53, no. 1 (1987): 3–20.

"Courts, Legislatures, and Constitutional Maintenance." *Cato Journal* 7 (Fall 1987): 323–29.

"The Public Choice Revolution" (with James D. Gwartney). *Intercollegiate Review* 23 (Spring 1988): 17–26.

"The *Calculus of Consent*: A Wicksellian Retrospective." *Public Choice* 56 (February 1988): 153–66.

"Morals, Interests, and Constitutional Order." *Oregon Law Review* 67, no. 1 (1988): 73–92.

"Social Cost, Rent Seeking, and Smoking" (with Robert D. Tollison). *Journal of Public Finance and Public Choice* 6 (December 1988): 171–86.

"Constitutional Order in a Federal Republic." *Public Choice* 61 (May 1989): 187–92.

"Politics, Central Banking, and Economic Order." *Critical Review* 3 (Summer/Fall 1989): 11–22.

"Choosing Freedom: Public Choice and the Libertarian Idea" (with Charles K. Rowley). *Liberty* 3 (January 1990): 43–45.

"Regulatory Finance in Alternative Models of Regulation: General Fund Financing versus Earmarked Taxes" (with Mwangi S. Kimenyi and Robert D. Tollison). *European Journal of Political Economy* 6, no. 4 (1990): 519–29.

"Romance, Realism, and Economic Reform" (with Robert D. Tollison). *Kyklos* 44, no. 1 (1991): 57–70.

"Self Interest, Public Interest, and Public Health" (with Robert D. Tollison). *Public Choice* 69, no. 3 (1991): 323–43.

"The Logic of Natural Monopoly Regulation" (with Robert D. Tollison). *Eastern Economic Journal* 17, no. 4 (1991): 483–90.

"Public Debt Controversies: An Essay in Reconciliation" (with Karen I. Vaughn). *Kyklos* 45, no. 1 (1992): 57–70.

"Grazing the Budgetary Commons: The Rational Politics of Budgetary Irresponsibility." *Journal of Law and Politics* 9 (Fall 1992): 105–19.

"Crafting Social Rules: Common Law vs. Statute Law, Once Again." *Constitutional Political Economy* 3 (Fall 1992): 381–97.

"The Impending Transformation of Public Choice Scholarship." *Public Choice* 77 (1993): 203–12.

"A Competitive Federalism for the New Century." *Madison Review* 1 (Fall 1995): 34–40.

"Who Chooses What, and for Whom? Public Debt, Ricardian Equivalence, and Governmental Form." *Review of Austrian Economics* 9, no. 2 (1996): 143–57.

"Federal Transfer Taxation: The Effect on Saving, Capital Accumulation, and Economic Dissipation." *Family Business Review* 9 (Fall 1996): 169–83.

"Choice, Exchange, and Public Finance." *American Economic Review*, Proceedings, 77, no. 2 (May 1997): 160–63.

"Smoking, Insurance, and Social Cost" (with Robert E. McCormick and Robert D. Tollison). *Regulation* 20 (Summer 1997): 33–37.

"Politics, Public Capital, and the Structure of Production" (with Mark Crain). *Journal of Public Finance and Public Choice* 15, no. 1 (1997): 3–24.

"Parasitical Political Pricing, Economic Calculation, and the Size of Government: Variations on a Theme by Maffeo Pantaleoni." *Journal of Public Finance and Public Choice* 15, no. 2–3 (1997): 135–46.

"Social Democracy, Societal Tectonics and Parasitical Pricing." *Constitutional Political Economy* 9, no. 2 (1998): 105–11.

"Austrian Cycle Theory: Saving the Wheat While Discarding the Chaff." *Review of Austrian Economics* 12, no. 1 (1999): 65–80.

"Understanding the Tobacco Settlement: The State as a Partisan Plaintiff." *Regulation* 22, no. 4 (1999): 38–41.

"A Bipartisan Declaration of Independence from Death Taxation" (with Edward J. McCaffrey). *Tax Notes* 88, no. 6 (2000): 801–14.

"Competition as a Rivalrous Process: Attilio da Empoli and the Years of High Theory That Might Have Been." *Journal of Economic Studies* 28, no. 4/5 (2001): 337–45.

"Complexity, Governance, and Constitutional Craftsmanship." *American Journal of Economics and Sociology* 61 (January 2002): 105–22.

"Custom, Legislation, and Market Order." *American Journal of Economics and Sociology* 61 (April 2002): 563–69.

"Polycentric Public Finance and the Organization of Governance." *European Journal of Management and Public Policy* 2 (2002): 3–15.

"Some Institutional Problematics of Excess Burden Analytics." *Public Finance Review* 30 (November 2002): 531–45.

"Institutions, Emergence, and Macro Theorizing: A Review Essay on Roger Garrison's Time and Money" (with Ryan D. Oprea). *Review of Austrian Economics* 16, no. 1 (2003): 97–109.

"Happy Anniversary? Ninety Years of the Income Tax." *World and I* (April 2003): 28–33.

"Public Choice and the Diffusion of Classic Italian Public Finance." *Il pensiero economico italiano* 11, no. 1 (2003): 271–82.

"Public Choice as an Academic Enterprise: Charlottesville, Blacksburg, and Fairfax Retrospectively Viewed." *American Journal of Economics and Sociology* 63 (January 2004): 55–74.

"Inefficient Market Pricing: An Illusory Economic Box" (with Kevin Brancato). *Journal of Public Finance and Public Choice* 22 (2004): 3–13.

"Self-Governance, Polycentrism, and Federalism: Recurring Themes in Vincent Ostrom's Scholarly Oeuvre." *Journal of Economic Behavior and Organization* 57 (2005): 173–88.

"From Continental Public Finance to Public Choice: Mapping Continuity" (with Jürgen G. Backhaus). *History of Political Economy*, Annual Supplement 37 (2005): 314–32.

"Continental Public Finance: Mapping and Recovering a Tradition" (with Jürgen G. Backhaus). *Journal of Public Finance and Public Choice* 23 (2005): 43–67.

"States and the Crafting of Souls: Mind, Society, and Fiscal Sociology." *Journal of Economic Behavior and Organization* 59 (2006): 516–24.

"Choice, Catallaxy, and Just Taxation: Contrasting Architectures for Fiscal Theorizing." *Social Philosophy and Policy* 23 (2006): 235–54.

"Retrogressive Regime Drift within a Theory of Emergent Order." *Review of Austrian Economics* 19 (2006): 113–23.

"Katrina and the Social Organization of Disaster Recovery: Dissolving a Theoretical Antinomy." *Journal of Public Finance and Public Choice* 24 (2006): 143–61.

"The Organizational Architecture of Nonprofit Governance: Economic Calculation within an Ecology of Enterprises" (with Monica Auteri). *Public Organization Review* 7 (2007): 57–68.

"Value and Exchange: Two Windows for Economic Theorizing." *Review of Austrian Economics* 20 (2007): 97–103.

"Finding Social Dilemma: West of Babel, not East of Eden." *Public Choice* 135 (2008): 55–66.

"Polycentricity, Political Economy, and the Welfare State." *Public Finance and Management* 8 (2008): 141–67.

"From Scholarly Idea to Budgetary Institution: The Emergence of Cost-Benefit Analysis" (with Michael D. Makowsky). *Constitutional Political Economy* 20 (2009): 57–70.

"Elections as Take-Over Bids: Some Agonistics concerning Good Government." *Review of Austrian Economics* 22 (2009): 145–50.

"Heterogeneity, Voting, and the Political Economy of Public Policy" (with Adam Martin). *Public Finance and Management* 9 (2009): 393–415.

"Spontaneous Order and Positive Legislation: Ruminating on Daniel Shapiro's Justification of the Welfare State." *Review of Austrian Economics* 23 (2010): 97–102.

"Polycentric Polity: Genuine vs. Spurious Federalism" (with Giuseppe Eusepi). *Review of Law and Economics* 6 (2010): 329–45.

"Raising vs. Leveling in the Social Organization of Welfare." *Review of Law & Economics* 6 (2010): 421–39.

"Change within Permanence: Time and the Bivalent Language of Economic Analysis." *Advances in Austrian Economics* 14 (2010): 181–203.

"Entangled Political Economy and the Two Faces of Entrepreneurship" (with Marta Podemska-Mikluch). *Journal of Public Finance and Public Choice* 28 (2010): 99–114.

"Choice, Emergence, and Constitutional Process: A Framework for Positive Analysis" (with Petrik Runst). *Journal of Institutional Economics* 7 (2011): 131–45.

"A Theory of Entangled Political Economy, with Applications to TARP and NRA" (with Adam Smith and Bruce Yandle). *Public Choice* 148 (2011): 45–66.

"States as Ecologies of Political Enterprises" (with Giuseppe Eusepi). *Review of Political Economy* 23 (2011): 573–85.

"Municipal Corporations, Economic Calculation, and Political Pricing: Exploring a Theoretical Antinomy." *Public Choice* 149 (2011): 151–65.

"Spontaneous Order, Liberty, and Austrian Economics." *Studies in Emergent Order* 4 (2011): 209–23.

"A Macro Economy as an Ecology of Plans." *Journal of Economic Behavior and Organization* 82 (2012): 433–44.

"The Institutional Framework for Shared Consumption: Deemphasizing Taxation in the Theory of Public Finance." *Public Finance and Management* 12 (2012): 5–20.

"Indebted State versus Intermediary State: Who Owes What to Whom?" (with Giuseppe Eusepi). *Constitutional Political Economy* 23 (2012): 199–212.

"Rationality, Political Economy, and Fiscal Responsibility: Wrestling with Tragedy on the Fiscal Commons." *Constitutional Political Economy* 23 (2012): 261–77.

"*The Calculus of Consent*: A Compass for My Professional Journey." *Public Choice* 152 (2012): 393–96.

"Viennese Kaleidics: Why It's Liberty More Than Policy That Calms Turbulence." *Review of Austrian Economics* 25 (2012): 283–97.

"Remembering Bill Niskanen: Pursuing Economics as a Public Science in the Service of Liberty." *Public Choice* 153 (2012): 1–7.

"The Social Construction of Theoretical Landscapes: Some Economics of Economic Theories." *American Journal of Economics and Sociology* 71 (2012): 1185–204.

"Democracy and the Theory of Public Finance: A Polycentric, Invisible-Hand Framework." *Public Finance and Management* 12 (2012): 298–325.

"Public Finance without Taxation: Free Riding as Institutional Artifact." *Journal of Public Finance and Public Choice* 30 (2012): 191–202.

"Political Entrepreneurship and the Formation of Special Districts" (with Alexander Fink). *European Journal of Law and Economics* 35 (2013): 427–39.

"Tax Prices in a Democratic Polity: The Continuing Relevance of Antonio de Viti de Marco" (with Giuseppe Eusepi). *History of Political Economy* 45 (2013): 99–121.

"What Kind of State in Our Future? Fact and Conjecture in Vito Tanzi's Government versus Markets." *Review of Austrian Economics* 26 (2013): 93–104.

"Dyads, Triads, and the Theory of Exchange: Between Liberty and Coercion" (with Marta Podemska-Mikluch). *Review of Austrian Economics* 26 (2013): 171–82.

"Legal Entrepreneurship within a System of Entangled Political Economy" (with Shruti Rajagopalan). *American Journal of Entrepreneurship* 6 (2013): 24–36.

"Constitutional Craftsmanship and the Rule of Law" (with Shruti Rajagopalan). *Constitutional Political Economy* 24 (2013): 295–309.

"James M. Buchanan and Me: Reminiscing about a 50-Year Association." *Journal of Public Finance and Public Choice* 31 (2013): 43–59.

"Taxation as a Quasi-market Process: Explanation, Exhortation, and the Choice of Analytical Windows" (with David Hebert). *Journal of Public Finance and Public Choice* 31 (2013): 163–77.

"Polycentrism, Federalism, and Liberty: A Comparative Systems Perspective" (with Akira Yokoyama). *Journal of Public Finance and Public Choice* 31 (2013): 179–97.

"Form vs. Substance in Selection through Competition: Elections, Markets, and Political Economy" (with Deema Yazigi [Shamoun]). *Public Choice* 159 (2014): 503–14.

"Default without Capital Account: The Economics of Municipal Bankruptcy" (with Lota Moberg). *Public Finance and Management* 14 (2014): 30–47.

"James Buchanan's Public Debt Theory: A Rational Reconstruction." *Constitutional Political Economy* 25 (2014): 253–64.

"Game Theory and the Architecture of Social Theory: Reflections on Luigino Bruni's *Ethos of the Market*." *Studies in Spontaneous Order* 7 (2014): 225–38.

"Richard Epstein's Classical Liberal Constitution: A Public Choice Refraction." *New York University Journal of Law and Liberty* 8 (2014): 961–90.

"Entangled Political Economy: A Keynote Address." *Advances in Austrian Economics* 18 (2014): 15–36.

"Design vs. Emergence in a Theory of Federalism: Toward Institutional Reconciliation." *Journal of Public Finance and Public Choice* 32 (2014): 197–213.

"Virginia Political Economy: A Rational Reconstruction." *Public Choice* 163 (2015): 15–29.

"Welfare Economics and Second-Best Theory: Filling Imaginary Economic Boxes." *Cato Journal* 35 (2015): 133–46.

"Neutral Money: Historical Fact or Analytical Artifact?" (with Simon Bilo). *Review of Austrian Economics* 28 (2015): 139–50.

"Gordon Tullock: A Conspectus on His Life's Work." *History of Economic Ideas* 23 (2015): 11–21.

"From Mixed Economy to Entangled Political Economy: A Paretian Social-Theoretic Orientation" (with Meg Patrick-Tuszynski). *Public Choice* 164 (2015): 103–16.

"Volatility in Catallactical Systems: Austrian Cycle Theory Revisited" (with James Caton). *Advances in Austrian Economics* 19 (2015): 95–117.

"Treating Macro Theory as Systems Theory: How Might It Matter?" (with Vipin P. Veetil). *Advances in Austrian Economics* 19 (2015): 119–43.

"The Peculiar Business of Politics." *Cato Journal* 36 (Fall 2016): 535–56.

"Vilfredo Pareto's Theory of Action: An Alternative to Behavioral Economics" (with Rosolino Candela). *Il pensiero economico italiano* 24 (2016): 15–29.

"New Austrian Macro Theory: A Call for Inquiry" (with Paul Lewis). *Review of Austrian Economics* 30 (2017): 1–18.

"Economic Coordination across Divergent Institutional Frameworks: Dissolving a Theoretical Antinomy" (with Marta Podemska-Mikluch). *Review of Political Economy* 29 (2017): 249–66.

"The Autonomy of the Political in Political Economy" (with Ion Sterpan). *Advances in Austrian Economics* 22 (2017): 133–57.

"James M. Buchanan and the *Journal of Public Finance and Public Choice*: Extending the Italian Tradition of Public Finance." *Journal of Public Finance and Public Choice* 33 (2018): 5–17.

"Trade, Power, and Political Economy: Reason vs. Ideology in Edward Stringham's *Private Governance*." *Review of Austrian Economics* 31 (2018): 245–55.

"Nominal GDP Stabilization: Chasing a Mirage" (with Vipin P. Veetil). *Quarterly Journal of Economics and Finance* 67 (2018): 227–36.

"Gordon Tullock's Scholarly Legacy: Extracting It from Buchanan's Shadow." *Independent Review* 23 (Fall 2018): 187–207.

"Political Entrepreneurship, Emergent Dynamics, and Constitutional Politics" (with Alexander Salter). *Review of Social Economy* 76 (2018): 253–67.

"Political Parties: Insights from a Tri-Planer Model of Political Economy" (with David Hebert). *Constitutional Political Economy* 29 (2018): 253–67.

"Bankruptcies, Bailouts, and Some Political Economy of Corporate Reorganization" (with Dylan DelliSanti). *Journal of Institutional Economics* 14 (2018): 833–51.

"Inequality within a System of Entangled Political Economy: Reflections on Mikayla Novak's Disentanglement of Fact and Value." *Cosmos & Taxis* 6 (2019): 32–39.

"Constitutional Catallaxy: Friends and Enemies in an Open-Ended Social Order" (with Alexander Salter). *Journal of Public Finance and Public Choice* 34 (2019): 83–94.

"Arrogance and Humility in the Governance of Human Interaction: A Reflection on Roger Koppl's *Expert Failure*." *Cosmos & Taxis* 7 (2019): 57–62.

"The Oxford Handbook of Public Choice: A Masterful Compendium." *Constitutional Political Economy* 30 (2019): 467–79.

"Governance within a System of Entangled Political Economy." *Forest Policy and Economics* 107 (October 2019): article 101918.

"Private-Public Partnership as Remedy for Crumbling Infrastructure: Is This Hope Looking for Reason?" *Journal of Infrastructure, Policy, and Development* 3 (2019): 233–43.

"American Democracy and the Problem of Fiscal Deficits." *Public Policy Review* (Ministry of Finance of Japan) 15 (2019): 199–216.

"Economic Theory and 'The Social Question': Some Dialectics Regarding the Work-Dependency Relationship." *Journal of Contextual Economics* 139, nos. 2–4 (2019).

"Contrasting Visions for Macroeconomic Theory: DSGE and OEE" (with Abigail Devereaux). *American Economist* 65 (2020): 28–50.

"Economic Coordination in Environments with Incomplete Pricing" (with Paul Dragos Aligica). *Review of Austrian Economics* 33 (2020): 315–29.

"Pandemic Politics within a System of Entangled Political Economy" (with Marta Podemska-Mikluch). *Journal of Contextual Economics* 140 (2020): 87–109.

"Giuseppe Eusepi: A Courageous and Cheerful Countenance for the Ages." *Public Choice* 186 (2021): 7–8.

"Economics, Covid-19, and the Entangled Political Economy of Public Health." *Independent Review* 25 (Spring 2021): 1–13.

"Deconstructing Public Debt: Who Owes What to Whom?" *Homo Oeconomicus*, forthcoming.

"Ethics as a Topic of Economic Inquiry: The Social-Theoretic Context" (with Jonathan Plante). *Journal of Private Enterprise*, forthcoming.

"State-Market Entanglement: Some Implications for the Theory of Public Finance" (with Zachary Kessler). *Journal of Public Finance and Public Choice*, forthcoming.

"The Vitality of Animal Spirits for Market Economies" (with Sarah Moore). *Review of Austrian Economics*, forthcoming.

ARTICLES IN SYMPOSIA AND CONFERENCE PROCEEDINGS

"The Efficiency Basis for Federal Fiscal Equalization" (with James M. Buchanan). In *The Analysis of Public Output*, edited by Julius Margolis, 139–58. New York: Columbia University Press, 1970.

"Conscription, Voluntary Choice, and Democratic Fiscal Choice." In *The Theory of Public Choice*, edited by James M. Buchanan and Robert D. Tollison, 136–52. Ann Arbor: University of Michigan Press, 1972.

"The Division of Responsibility for Housing Policy in a Federal System of Government." In *Housing in the Seventies*, Vol. 1, *Department of Housing and Urban Development*, 474–83. Washington, DC: US Government Printing Office, 1977.

"Death, Taxes, and Charitable Bequests: A Survey of Issues and Options." In *Research Papers Sponsored by the Commission on Private Philanthropy and Public Needs*, Vol. 4, *Taxes*, pp. 2337–53. Washington, DC: US Department of the Treasury, 1977.

"American Education and the Economics of Caring." In *Parents, Teachers, and Children: Prospects for Choice in American Education*, 111–25. San Francisco: Institute for Contemporary Studies, 1977.

"Some Aspects of Tax Policy toward Private Philanthropy." In *Policy Analysis and Deductive Reasoning*, edited by Gordon Tullock and Richard E. Wagner, 77–92. Lexington, MA: D.C. Heath, 1978.

"Advertising and the Public Economy: Some Preliminary Ruminations." In *The Political Economy of Advertising*, edited by David G. Tuerck, 81–100. Washington, DC: American Enterprise Institute, 1978.

"Contemporary Democracy and the Prospects for Fiscal Control: Initial Thoughts about and Final Reactions to the Conference" (with James M. Buchanan). In *Fiscal Responsibility in Constitutional Democracy*, edited by James M. Buchanan and Richard E. Wagner, 1–8. Leiden: Martinus Nijhoff, 1978.

"The Political Biases of Keynesian Economics" (with James M. Buchanan). In *Fiscal Responsibility in Constitutional Democracy*, edited by James M. Buchanan and Richard E. Wagner, 79–100. Leiden: Martinus Nijhoff, 1978.

Foreword to Stephen C. Littlechild, *The Fallacy of the Mixed Economy*. San Francisco: Cato Institute, 1978, xi–xiv.

"State Aid to Private Education: Curse or Blessing, and for Whom?" In *Government Aid to Private Schools: Is It a Trojan Horse?*, edited by Richard E. Wagner, 38–46. Wichita, KS: Center for Independent Education, 1979.

"Politics, Monetary Control, and Economic Performance." In *Time, Uncertainty, and Disequilibrium*, edited by Mario J. Rizzo, 177–86. Lexington, MA: D.C. Heath, 1979.

Foreword to Paul Whiteley, ed., *Models of Political Economy*. London: Sage, 1980, 1–6.

"Public Choice, Monetary Control, and Economic Disruption." In *Models of Political Economy*, edited by Paul Whiteley, 201–20. London: Sage, 1980.

"Finanzpolitik in der Demokratie: Eine Neo-Kameralistische Einschatzung der Zeitgenossischen Haushaltswirtschaft" (with Jürgen G. Backhaus). Appendix to *Zum Wirtschaftsrecht den Funktionen und Rechtsformen öffentlicher Unternehmen*. Frankfurt: Haag und Herchen, 1980, 457–84.

"Federal Aid to State and Local Governments." In *Agenda for Progress*, edited by Eugene McAllister, 303–15. Washington, DC: Heritage Foundation, 1980.

"The Enterprise System, Democracy, and the General Welfare: An Approach to Reconciliation." In *Essays in Supply Side Economics*, edited by David G. Raboy, 93–118. Washington, DC: Institute for Research on the Economics of Taxation, 1982.

"Estate Gift Duty and the Family." In *Taxing the Family*, edited by Rudolph G. Penner, 127–33. Washington, DC: American Enterprise Institute, 1983.

"Democracy and the Market Economy: A Contradiction for Liberal Society?" In *Free Enterprise: 15 Commentaries*, edited by Burt Elwert, 67–71. Chicago: University of Illinois Press, 1983.

"The Political Economy of the Sheltered Sector." In *The Sheltered Sector, the Use of Resources, and Inflation*, edited by Karl Brunner, 7–28. Rochester, NY: Center for Research in Government Policy and Business, 1983.

"Christianity and the Problem of Political Economy: One Economist's Ruminations." In *Economics, Theology, and the Social Order*, edited by Ronald W. Hansen, 23–45. Rochester, NY: Center for Research in Government Policy and Business, 1986.

"The Welfare State, Capital Formation, and Tax-Transfer Politics." In *Taxation and the Deficit Economy*, edited by Dwight R. Lee, 241–73. San Francisco: Pacific Research Institute for Public Policy, 1986.

"Limiting Government Spending: Alternative Constitutional Perspectives." In *The Growth of Government*, edited by Karl Brunner, 5–24. Rochester, NY: Center for Research in Government Policy and Business, 1986.

"The Agent-Principal Relationship in the Public Sector." In *The Growth of Government*, edited by Karl Brunner, 37–53. Rochester, NY: Center for Research in Government Policy and Business, 1986.

"Liability Rules, Fiscal Institutions, and Public Debt." In *Deficits*, edited by James M. Buchanan, Charles K. Rowley, and Robert D. Tollison, 199–217. Oxford: Basil Blackwell, 1986.

"Balanced Budgets and Beyond" (with Robert D. Tollison). In *Deficits*, edited by James M. Buchanan, Charles K. Rowley, and Robert D. Tollison, 374–90. Oxford: Basil Blackwell, 1986.

"Constitutional Remedies for Democratic Budget Tragedies." In *The Federal Budget: The Economic, Political, and Moral Implications for a Free Society*, 123–41. Hillsdale, MI: Hillsdale College Press, 1987.

"Gordon Tullock as Rhetorical Economist." In *Democracy and Public Choice: Essays in Honor of Gordon Tullock*, edited by Charles K. Rowley, 27–38. Oxford: Basil Blackwell, 1987.

"Parchment, Guns, and the Maintenance of Constitutional Contract." In *Democracy and Public Choice: Essays in Honor of Gordon Tullock*, edited by Charles K. Rowley, 105–21. Oxford: Basil Blackwell, 1987.

"Agency, Economic Calculation, and Constitutional Construction." In *The Political Economy of Rent Seeking*, edited by Charles K. Rowley, Robert D. Tollison, and Gordon Tullock, 423–45. Boston: Kluwer Academic Publishers, 1988.

"Public Choice and the Conduct of Representative Government" (with James D. Gwartney). In *Public Choice and Constitutional Economics*, edited by James D. Gwartney and Richard E. Wagner, 3–28. Greenwich, CT: JAI Press, 1988.

"Public Choice and Constitutional Order" (with James D. Gwartney). In *Public Choice and Constitutional Economics*, edited by James D. Gwartney and Richard E. Wagner, 29–56. Greenwich, CT: JAI Press, 1988.

"Political Economy and the Problem of Rules and Order in a Shrunken World" (with Jack High). In *Northeast Asia in the Changing World Perspective*, 23–37. Taegu: Kyungpook National University, 1989.

"Fiscal Principle, Fiscal Politics, and Consumption Taxation." In *Heidelberg Congress on Taxing Consumption*, edited by Manfred Rose, 247–69. Heidelberg: Springer, 1990.

"Tax Norms, Fiscal Reality, and the Democratic State: User Charges and Earmarked Taxes in Principle and Practice." In *Charging for Government*, edited by Richard E. Wagner, 1–12. London: Routledge, 1991.

"Subjective Cost, Property Rights, and Public Pricing." In *Charging for Government*, edited by Richard E. Wagner, 75–89. London: Routledge, 1991.

"The Political Economy of Tax Earmarking" (with Dwight R. Lee). In *Charging for Government*, edited by Richard E. Wagner, 110–24. London: Routledge, 1991.

"User Fees and Earmarked Taxes in Constitutional Perspective." In *Charging for Government*, edited by Richard E. Wagner, 179–94. London: Routledge, 1991.

"Economic Efficiency, Rent Seeking, and Democracy: Zenoistic Variations on Coasian Themes." In *Advances in Austrian Economics I*, edited by Peter J. Boettke and Mario J. Rizzo, 129–44. Greenwich, CT: JAI Press, 1994.

"ORDO Liberalism and the Social Market Economy." In *Economics and Religion*, edited by H. G. Brennan and A. Waterman, 121–38. Boston: Kluwer, 1994.

"Political Business Cycles." In *Edward Elgar Companion to Austrian Economics*, edited by Peter J. Boettke, 425–30. Cheltenham, UK: Edward Elgar, 1994.

"Progress, Poverty, and Democracy." In *American Perestroika: The Demise of the Welfare State*, 113–29. Hillsdale, MI: Hillsdale College Press, 1995.

"Complexity, Governance, and Economic Policy." In *Economic Directions*. Latrobe, PA: Saint Vincent College, Vol. 7, No. 1, 1997.

"The Taxation of Alcohol and the Control of Social Cost." In *Taxing Choice: The Predatory Politics of Fiscal Discrimination*, edited by William Shughart II, 227–46. New Brunswick, NJ: Transactions Publishers, 1997.

"Does the World Health Organization Return Good Value to American Taxpayers?" In *Delusions of Grandeur: The United Nations and Global Intervention*, edited by Ted Galen Carpenter, 191–99. Washington, DC: Cato Institute, 1997.

"Common Law, Statute Law, and Economic Efficiency." In *The New Palgrave Dictionary of Economics and the Law*, edited by Peter Newman, 1:313–17. London: Macmillan, 1998.

"Inheritance Taxation." In *The New Palgrave Dictionary of Economics and the Law*, edited by Peter Newman, 2:321–26. London: Macmillan, 1998.

"The Constitutional Protection of Private Property." In *Who Owns the Environment?* edited by Peter J. Hill and Roger E. Meiners, 315–36. Lanham, MD: Rowman and Littlefield, 1998.

"Faustian Bargains and Constitutional Governance" (with Donald P. Racheter). In *Limiting Leviathan,* edited by Donald P. Racheter and Richard E. Wagner, 1–9. Cheltenham, UK: Edward Elgar, 1999.

"Inheritance." In *The Elgar Companion to Law and Economics,* edited by Jürgen G. Backhaus, 77–84. Cheltenham, UK: Edward Elgar, 1999.

"Carl Menger." In *The Elgar Companion to Law and Economics,* edited by Jürgen G. Backhaus, 412–19. Cheltenham, UK: Edward Elgar, 1999.

"Georg Simmel's Philosophy of Money: Some Points of Relevance for Contemporary Monetary Scholarship." In *Georg Simmel's Philosophy of Money: A Centenary Appraisal,* edited by Jürgen G. Backhaus and Hans-Joachim Stadermann, 13–32. Marburg: Metropolis, 2000.

"Competitive Federalism in Institutional Perspective." In *Federalist Government in Principle and Practice,* edited by Donald P. Racheter and Richard E. Wagner, 19–37. Norwell, MA: Kluwer, 2001.

"Taxation, Free Markets, and the Use of Agricultural Land." In *Agriculture and the Environment: Searching for Greener Pastures,* edited by Terry L. Anderson and Bruce Yandle, 47–64. Stanford, CA: Hoover Institution Press, 2001.

"Politics and the Macro Economy." In *The Elgar Companion to Public Choice,* edited by William F. Shughart and Laura Razzolini, 422–39. Cheltenham, UK: 2002.

"The Constitutional Framework for Democratic Taxation" (with Donald P. Racheter). In *Property, Taxation, and the Rule of Law,* edited by Donald P. Racheter and Richard E. Wagner, 1–7. Norwell, MA: Kluwer, 2002.

"Property, Taxation, and the Budgetary Commons." In *Property, Taxation, and the Rule of Law,* edited by Donald P. Racheter and Richard E. Wagner, 33–47. Norwell, MA: Kluwer, 2002.

"Federalism, Democracy, and Liberty." In *Cooperative vs. Competitive Federalism,* 21–31. Washington, DC: Friedrich Naumann Foundation, 2002.

"Meddlesome Preferences and Rent Extraction: The Tobacco Settlement." In *The Encyclopedia of Public Choice,* edited by Charles K. Rowley and Friedrich Schneider, 2:378–80. Dordrecht: Kluwer, 2004.

"Parchment versus Guns." In *The Encyclopedia of Public Choice,* edited by Charles K. Rowley and Friedrich Schneider, 2:406–9. Dordrecht: Kluwer, 2004.

"Public Finance in Democratic Process." In *The Encyclopedia of Public Choice,* edited by Charles K. Rowley and Friedrich Schneider, 2:455–57. Dordrecht: Kluwer, 2004.

"Society, State, and Public Finance: Setting the Analytical Stage" (with Jürgen G. Backhaus). In *Handbook of Public Finance,* edited by Jürgen G. Backhaus and Richard E. Wagner, 1–18. Boston: Kluwer, 2004.

"Debt, Money, and Public Finance." In *Handbook of Public Finance,* edited by Jürgen G. Backhaus and Richard E. Wagner, 195–215. Boston: Kluwer, 2004.

"Redistribution, Poor Relief, and the Welfare State." In *Handbook of Public Finance,* edited by Jürgen G. Backhaus and Richard E. Wagner, 385–405. Boston: Kluwer, 2004.

"Austrian Cycle Theory and the Prospect of a Coordinationist Macroeconomics." In *Modern Applications of Austrian Thought,* edited by Jürgen G. Backhaus, 77–92. London: Routledge, 2005.

The following eight articles appear in *American Conservatism: An Encyclopedia,* edited by Bruce Frohen, Jeremy Beer, and Jeffrey O. Nelson. Wilmington, DE: ISI Books, 2006.

"Anti-Federalists," 42–44.
"Capital Punishment," 122–24.

"Capitalism," 124–26.
"Entitlements," 273–74.
"Poverty," 670–71.
"Protectionism," 684–86.
"Regulation," 723–26
"Socialism," 789–92.

The following three articles appear in the *Encyclopedia of Law and Society*, 3 vols., edited by David S. Clark. Thousand Oaks, CA: Sage, 2007.

"Auction Theory," 1:106–7.
"Carl Menger," 2:1014–15.
"Tobacco," 3:1485–87.

"Public Finance." In *International Encyclopedia of the Social Sciences*, 2nd ed. London: Macmillan, 2008.

"The World Health Organization: A Time for Reconstitution." In *Fighting the Diseases of Poverty*, edited by Philip Stevens, 239–64. New Brunswick, NJ: Transaction, 2008.

"James M. Buchanan." In *The New Palgrave Dictionary of Economics*, 2nd ed., edited by Larry Blume and Steven Durlauf, 584–88. London: Palgrave Macmillan, 2008.

"Taxation." In *Encyclopedia of Libertarianism*, edited by Ronald Hamoway, 499–501. Los Angeles: Sage, 2008.

"Knut Wicksell." In *Encyclopedia of Libertarianism*, edited by Ronald Hamoway, 543–44. Los Angeles: Sage, 2008.

"Property, State, and Entangled Political Economy." In *Markets and Politics: Insights from a Political Economy Perspective*, edited by Wolf Schäfer, Andrea Schneider, and Tobias Thomas, 37–49. Marburg: Metropolis, 2009.

"Promoting the General Welfare: Political Economy for a Free Republic." In *Rediscovering Political Economy*, edited by Joseph Postell and Bradley C. S. Watson, 135–57. Lanham, MD: Lexington Books, 2011.

"The Cameralists: Fertile Sources for a New Science of Public Finance." In *Handbook for the History of Economic Thought*, edited by Jürgen G. Backhaus, 123–35. Dordrecht: Springer, 2012.

"Knut Wicksell and Contemporary Political Economy." In *Handbook for the History of Economic Thought*, edited by Jürgen G. Backhaus, 513–25. Dordrecht: Springer, 2012.

"The State as a Peculiar Investment Bank: Attilio da Empoli's Fiscal Theorizing in Light of Contemporary Theorizing about Complex Adaptive Systems." In *Attilio Da Empoli (1904–1948): Una economista partecipe del suo tempo*, edited by Massimo Di Matteo and Ernesto Longobardi, 139–50. Milan: Franco Angeli, 2012.

"Choice vs. Interaction in Public Choice: Discerning the Legacy of *The Calculus of Consent*." In *Public Choice, Past and Present: The Legacy of James. M. Buchanan and Gordon Tullock*, edited by Dwight R. Lee, 65–79. New York: Springer, 2013.

"The Tax State as Creator of Perpetual Crisis." In *Oxford Handbook of Austrian Economics*, edited by Peter J. Boettke and Christopher J. Coyne, 445–63. Oxford: Oxford University Press, 2015.

"Collaboration vs. Imposition as Motifs for a Theory of Public Finance: Transcending the Goldscheid-Schumpeter Debate." In *Taking Up the Challenge! Festschrift in Honor of Jürgen Backhaus*, edited by Helge Peukert, 211–28. Marburg: Metropolis, 2015.

"Gordon Tullock: A Maverick Scholar of Law and Economics." In *Springer Encyclopedia of Law and Economics*, edited by A. Marciano and G. Ramello. Berlin: Springer, 2016.

"Public Finance: Entrepreneurial or Parasitical?" (with Steve Hanke). In *An Enterprising Liberal and Generous Mind: Essays in Honor of H.S.H Prince Michael of Liechtenstein*, 53–59. Triesen, Liechtenstein: Van Eck, 2016.

"Fiscal Crisis as a Quality of Progressivist Democracy." In *Economic and Political Change after Crisis*, edited by Stephen H. Balch and Benjamin Powell, 73–94. London: Routledge, 2017.

"Economic Efficiency and the Law: Distinguishing Form from Substance." In *Law and Economics in Europe and the U.S.: The Legacy of Jürgen Backhaus*, edited by Alan Marciano and Giovanni Ramello, 17–30. Berlin: Springer, 2017.

"The Language of Taxation: Ideology Masquerading as Science." In *For Your Own Good: Taxes, Paternalism, and Fiscal Discrimination in the Twenty-First Century*, edited by Adam Hoffer and Todd Nisbit, 77–96. Arlington, VA: Mercatus Center at George Mason University, 2018.

"James Buchanan's Liberal Theory of Political Economy: A Valiant but Failed Effort to Square the Circle." In *Buchanan's Tensions: Reexamining the Political Economy and Philosophy of James M. Buchanan*, edited by Peter Boettke and Solomon Stein, 9–33. Arlington, VA: Mercatus Center at George Mason University, 2018.

"Dispute Resolution When Rationalities Conflict: Cost and Choice in a Market Economy." In *Research Handbook on Austrian Law and Economics*, edited by Peter Boettke and Todd Zywicki, 209–29. Cheltenham, UK: Edward Elgar, 2018.

"De Viti de Marco vs. Ricardo on Public Debt: Self Extinction or Default?" (with Giuseppe Eusepi). In *Debt Default and Democracy*, edited by Giuseppe Eusepi and Richard E. Wagner, 3–16. Cheltenham, UK: Edward Elgar, 2018.

"Debt Default and the Limits of the Contractual Imagination: Pareto and Mosca Meet Buchanan." In *Debt Default and Democracy*, edited by Giuseppe Eusepi and Richard E. Wagner, 51–62. Cheltenham, UK: Edward Elgar, 2018.

"Legal Disputes." In *Springer Encyclopedia of Law and Economics*, edited by A. Marciano and G. Battista Ramello. Berlin: Springer, 2019, 1265–9.

"Who Was James M. Buchanan and Why Is He Significant?" In *James M. Buchanan: A Theorist of Political Economy and Social Philosophy*, edited by Richard E. Wagner, 1–9. London: Palgrave Macmillan, 2019.

"Emergence, Equilibrium, and Agent-Based Modeling: Updating James Buchanan's Democratic Political Economy" (with Abigail Devereaux). In *James M. Buchanan: A Theorist of Political Economy and Social Philosophy*, edited by Richard E. Wagner, 109–29. London: Palgrave Macmillan, 2019.

"Samaritan's Dilemmas, Wealth Redistribution, and Polycentricity" (with Meg Tuszynski). In *James M. Buchanan: A Theorist of Political Economy and Social Philosophy*, edited by Richard E. Wagner, 291–311. London: Palgrave Macmillan, 2019.

"Administration vs. Politics in Theories of Democratic Budgeting." In *A Fiscal Cliff: New Perspectives on the U.S. Federal Debt Crisis*, edited by John Merrifield and Barry Poulson, 329–51. Washington, DC: Cato Institute, 2020.

"James Buchanan and George Stigler: Divergent Legacies from Frank Knight." In *George Stigler: Enigmatic Price Theorist of the Twentieth Century*, edited by Craig Freedman, 755–79. London: Palgrave Macmillan, 2020.

"Emergence and Entanglement in a Theory of Political Economy." In *Emergence, Entanglement, and Political Economy*, edited by David Hebert and Diana Thomas, 7–25. Cham, Switzerland: Springer, 2021.

"Frank Knight, James Buchanan, and Virginia Political Economy: The Long Shadow of Risk, Uncertainty, and Profit." *Research in the History of Economic Thought and Methodology* 39 (2022): 39–53.

"Fiscal Policy." In *Routledge Handbook on Classical Liberalism*, edited by Richard Epstein, Mario Rizzo, and Liya Palagashvili. London: Routledge, forthcoming.

"Public Finance and the Methodology of Scientific Research Programs." In *Psychological and Sociological Aspects of Taxation*, edited by Rana Dayioglu Eruj. Ankara: Gazi, forthcoming.

"My Non-ideological Path to Becoming a Libertarian Thinker." In *Encyclopedia of Autobiographical Sketches by Libertarians*, edited by Walter Block and Jo Ann Cavallo. London: Routledge, forthcoming.

"James M. Buchanan and the Corrupting Quality of Public Debt." In *A Companion to James Buchanan*, edited by A. Marroquin and C. Rodriquez. Citidad de Guatemala: Universidad Francisco Marroquin, forthcoming.

"Individualism vs. Holism in Economic Theory: Deconstructing an Incoherent Dichotomy" (with Sarah Moore). In *Palgrave Handbook on Methodological Individualism*, edited by Francesco Di Iorio. London: Palgrave Macmillan, forthcoming.

BOOK REVIEWS

Inside Bureaucracy, by Anthony Downs. *Public Choice* 4 (Spring 1968): 85–86.

The Economics of State and Local Government, by Werner Z. Hirsch. *Public Choice* 11 (Fall 1971): 119–21.

Fiscal Federalism, by Wallace E. Oates. *Public Finance Quarterly* 1 (April 1973): 231–35.

Redistribution through Public Choice, edited by Harold M. Hochman and George E. Peterson. *Journal of Business* 49 (January 1976): 109–11.

Public Finance, Planning, and Economic Development: Essays in Honor of Ursula Hicks, edited by Wilfred L. David. *Economic Development and Cultural Change* 24 (January 1976): 476–80.

Economics as a Coordination Problem: The Contributions of Friedrich A. Hayek, by Gerald P. O'Driscoll. *Kyklos* 31, no. 3 (1978): 538–40.

Government Spending: Trends and Issues, by Morris Beck. *Southern Economic Journal* 49 (October 1982): 596–98.

The Structure and Reform of the U.S. Tax System, by Albert Ando, Marshall E. Blume, and Irwin Friend. *Journal of Political Economy* 94 (December 1986): 1338–41.

Public Choice II, by Dennis C. Mueller. *Constitutional Political Economy* 1, no. 3 (1990): 113–15.

The Theory of Market Failure, ed. by Tyler Cowen. *Public Choice* 68 (1991): 295–97.

The Deficit and the Public Interest: The Search for Responsible Budgeting in the 1980s, by Joseph White and Aaron Wildavsky. *Journal of Economic Literature* 29 (September 1991): 1197–98.

Moral Foundations of Constitutional Thought: Current Problems, Augustinian Prospects, by Graham Walker. *Constitutional Political Economy* 2 (Fall 1991): 395–97.

Economics of Food Safety, edited by Julie A. Caswell. *Journal of Economic Literature* 31 (March 1993): 235–37.

Public Choice Analysis in Historical Perspective, by Alan Peacock. *Constitutional Political Economy* 4 (Winter 1993): 153–55.

Welfare Economics and Externalities in an Open-Ended Universe: A Modern Austrian Perspective, by Roy E. Cordato. *Constitutional Political Economy* 4 (Summer 1993): 287–89.

Öffentliche Finanzen in der Demokratie, by Charles B. Blankart. *Constitutional Political Economy* 4 (Fall 1993): 455–58.

Universal Economics: Assessing the Achievements of the Economic Approach, edited by Gerard Radnitzky *Cato Journal* 12 (Winter 1993): 737–39.

Private Choices and Public Health: The AIDS Epidemic in an Economic Perspective, by Tomas J. Philipson and Richard A. Posner. *Journal of Economic Literature* 33 (September 1995): 1365–67.

Public Entrepreneurs: Agents for Change in American Government, by Mark Schneider and Paul Teske. *Constitutional Political Economy* 6 (Summer 1995): 203–4.

The Myth of Democratic Failure, by Donald A. Wittman. *Constitutional Political Economy* 7, no. 2 (1996): 153–56.

The Austrian School and Modern Economics: Essays in Reassessment, by Nicolai J. Foss. *Constitutional Political Economy* 7, no. 3 (1996): 239–41.

Political Cycles and the Macroeconomy, by Alberto Alesina and Nouriel Roubini. *Public Choice* 100 (1999): 137–40.

Social Welfare and Individual Responsibility, by David Schmidtz and Robert E. Goodin. *Review of Austrian Economics* 13, no. 1 (2000): 97–100.

Democratic Choice and Taxation: A Theoretical and Empirical Analysis, by Walter Hettich and Stanley L. Winer. *Journal of Economics/Zeitschrift für Nationalökonomie* 72, no. 9 (2000): 122–23.

Controlling the State: Constitutionalism from Ancient Athens to Today, by Scott Gordon. *Independent Review* 6 (Winter 2002): 457–61.

A Theory of Employment in Firms: Macroeconomic Equilibrium and Internal Organization of Work, by Joseph Falkinger. *Kyklos* 56 (2003): 580–82.

Autocratic, Democratic, and Optimal Government, by William A. Niskanen. *Cato Journal* 24 (Spring/Summer 2004): 181–84.

The Philosophy of Taxation and Public Finance, by Robert W. McGee. *Journal of Public Finance and Public Choice* 22 (2004): 200–203.

The National Element in the Development of Fiscal Theory, by Orhan Kayaalp. *Journal of the History of Economic Thought* 27 (2005): 223–26.

Understanding Institutional Diversity, by Elinor Ostrom. *Journal of Economic Behavior and Organization* 65 (2008): 178–80.

Civilization and Self Government: The Political Thought of Carlo Cattaneo, by Filippo Sabetti. *Journal of Public Finance and Public Choice* 27 (2009): 91–94.

Jimmy Stewart Is Dead: Ending the World's Ongoing Financial Plague with Limited Purpose Banking, by Laurence J. Kotklikoff. *Review of Austrian Economics* 24 (2011): 319–22.

Living Economics, by Peter Boettke. *Public Choice* 153 (2012): 257–59.

Meeting at Grand Central: Understanding the Social and Evolutionary Roots of Cooperation, by Lee Cronk and Beth L. Leech. *Review of Austrian Economics* 27 (2014): 115–17.

Public Budgeting and Finance Primer: Key Concepts in Fiscal Choice, by Jay Eungha Ryu. *Public Finance and Management* 14 (2014): 106–9.

Austrian and German Economic Thought: From Subjectivism to Social Evolution, by Kichiro Yagi. *Journal of the History of Economic Thought* 36 (2014): 391–94.

Subjectivism and Objectivism in the History of Economic Thought, edited by Yukihiro Ikeda and Kiichiro Yagi. *Journal of the History of Economic Thought* 36 (2014): 394–96.

Boom Towns: Restoring the Urban American Dream, by Steven J. K. Walters. *Cato Journal* 35 (2015): 174–78.

Antonio de Viti de Marco: A Story Worth Remembering, by Manuela Mosca. *EH.net*, September 2016.

Termites of the State, by Vito Tanzi. *Independent Review* 23 (2019): 632–36.

Review of Public Debt and the Common Good, by James Odom. *Public Finance and Management*, forthcoming.

About the Contributors

Paul Dragos Aligica, senior fellow, F. A. Hayek Program for Advanced Study in Philosophy, Politics, and Economics, Mercatus Center at George Mason University

Chris Berg, associate professor, RMIT University, and principal research fellow and codirector, Blockchain Innovation Hub, RMIT University

Peter J. Boettke, university professor of economics and philosophy, George Mason University, and director, F. A. Hayek Program for Advanced Study in Philosophy, Politics, and Economics, Mercatus Center at George Mason University

James Caton, assistant professor of economics, North Dakota State University, and scholar, Challey Institute for Global Innovation and Growth with the Center for the Study of Public Choice and Private Enterprise, North Dakota State University

Christopher J. Coyne, professor of economics, George Mason University, and associate director, F. A. Hayek Program for Advanced Study in Philosophy, Politics, and Economics, Mercatus Center at George Mason University

Sinclair Davidson, professor of institutional economics, RMIT University

Abigail N. Devereaux, assistant professor, Wichita State University, and research fellow, Institute for the Study of Economic Growth, Wichita State University

Santiago J. Gangotena, professor of economics and dean of liberal arts, Universidad San Francisco de Quito

Cameron Harwick, assistant professor of economics, SUNY Brockport

Randall G. Holcombe, DeVoe Moore Professor of Economics, Florida State University

Adam Martin, associate professor of agricultural and applied economics, Gordon W. Davis College of Agricultural Sciences & Natural Resources, Texas Tech University, and political economy research fellow, Free Market Institute, Texas Tech University

Vincent Miozzi, PhD student in agricultural and applied economics, Texas Tech University, and research assistant, Free Market Institute, Texas Tech University

Mikayla Novak, senior fellow, F. A. Hayek Program for Advanced Study in Philosophy, Politics, and Economics, Mercatus Center at George Mason University, and associate director, Entangled Political Economy Research Network

Marta Podemska-Mikluch, associate professor of economics, Gustavus Adolphus College, and director, Entangled Political Economy Research Network

Jason Potts, distinguished professor of economics, RMIT University, and codirector, Blockchain Innovation Hub, RMIT University

Diana W. Thomas, professor of economics, Creighton University, and director, Institute for Economic Inquiry, Creighton University

Michael D. Thomas, associate professor of economics, Creighton University, and student programs director, Institute for Economic Inquiry, Creighton University

Meg Tuszynski, research assistant professor, Cox School of Business, Southern Methodist University, and assistant director, Bridwell Institute for Economic Freedom, Southern Methodist University

Viktor J. Vanberg, senior research fellow, Walter Eucken Institut

Index

Note: the letter n signifies a footnote.